THE
EDUCATIONAL
IMAGINATION

THE
EDUCATIONAL IMAGINATION

On the Design and Evaluation of School Programs

SECOND EDITION

ELLIOT W. EISNER

Stanford University

MACMILLAN PUBLISHING COMPANY
New York

COLLIER MACMILLAN PUBLISHERS
London

Acknowledgments

From "you shall above all" by E.E. Cummings. Reprinted by permission of Harcourt Brace Jovanovich, Inc. "you shall above all things be glad and young," in COMPLETE POEMS 1913–1962 by E.E. Cummings, copyright 1938 by E.E. Cummings; copyright renewed 1966 by Marion Morehouse Cummings. Reprinted from COMPLETE POEMS 1913–1962 by E.E. Cummings by permission of Harcourt Brace Jovanovich, Inc.

From "Little Gidding" in FOUR QUARTETS by T.S. Eliot, copyright 1943 by T.S. Eliot; copyright renewed 1971 by Esme Valerie Eliot. Reprinted by permission of Harcourt Brace Jovanovich, Inc.

Macmillan Publishing Company
866 Third Avenue, New York, New York 10022

Collier Macmillan Canada, Inc.

Library of Congress Cataloging in Publication Data

Eisner, Elliot W.
  The educational imagination.

  Includes index.
  1. Curriculum planning—United States. 2. Education
—United States—Aims and objectives. 3. Curriculum
evaluation. 4. Curriculum change—United States.
I. Title.
LB1570.E4254   1985   375'.001   83-26754
ISBN 0-02-332110-5

Printing   11   Year: 1 2 3

ISBN 0-02-332110-5

PREFACE

The nation, we are told, is at risk. The source of the risk is the quality of our schools. The challenge is to create an educational change that will once again make us competitive in the economic marketplace.

The most widely read policy paper on education has initiated a new national interest in education.[1] And interest is a necessary condition for improving anything. Yet interest alone is seldom enough. What is needed is a vision of what counts as desirable as well as the means appropriate for achieving what counts. Alas, the road to hell, someone said, is paved with good intentions. The basic message of the first edition of *The Educational Imagination* still needs to be heard, at least as I reflect upon the solutions those in high places believe will cure the perceived educational ills that have been discovered.

More homework, harder courses, longer school days, and an extended school year are important recommendations in the national study that has been disseminated so widely to Americans. The justification for concern about the quality of our schools is largely economic, despite the polite needs given to more lofty educational aspirations. I worry about such justifications and I worry even more about the prescriptions provided to remedy what those who write such reports believe need to be remedied. Why, if schools are so generally poor, would it be better for students to spend even more time in them? Such reasoning escapes the logic I am able to employ. Why more homework is better, why harder courses are good (it's not made clear what "harder" means) is not explained. I am reminded of a comment made by an educator at the turn of the century who believed in the "mental discipline rationale" for the curriculum. Believing as he did that the mind consisted of a set of muscles that were strengthened by hard work, he observed that "It really didn't matter much what students studied in school—as long as they didn't like it!" Requests—even demands—for harder subjects remind me of his comment.

The revised edition of *The Educational Imagination* develops and reaf-

---

[1] *U.S. National Commission on Excellence in Education, A Nation at Risk: The Imperative for Educational Reform: A Report to the Nation and the Secretary of Education,* U.S. Department of Education, Washington, D. C. 1983.

firms the conviction that there is no single conception or aim for education that is suitable for everybody, in all places, forever. It reaffirms the importance of *context* in making educational decisions, particularly with respect to curriculum. And it reaffirms the view that teaching is at base a craft that can be influenced by educationally relevant research in the social sciences but that social science research cannot, in principle, prescribe to teachers how to teach.

The second edition provides more attention to the processes of curriculum implementation than did the first. There was a period in American education when curricula developed by educational laboratories and commercial publishing houses were to be "installed" in schools. One engaged in curriculum installation, often in the same way that one installed carpeting or a new air filter in one's car. Nothing could have been further from the truth. Teachers need to have a stake in what they teach. They are not merely passive tubes or mechanical conveyers of someone else's ambitions and interests. The new section in this edition on the process of curriculum implementation is intended to shed some light on this matter.

Perhaps no sections in the first edition of *The Educational Imagination* received as much attention in the field as those chapters devoted to educational connoisseurship and educational criticism. This approach to understanding educational practice is reinforced in the second edition. Five, rather than three, educational criticisms are now included, none of which appeared in the first edition. In addition, a meta-criticism of one of those educational criticisms is included. In this meta-criticism one of the new educational criticisms is analyzed on a paragraph-by-paragraph basis. My intention is to show how a competent educational critic goes about her task, how she uses language, how she supports her conclusions, how she structures her writing. I hope that the analysis will be useful to those who wish to help others increase their levels of educational connoisseurship and to write educational criticism.

Finally, numerous small changes were made in virtually all of the chapters, some of fact, others to clarify what was written. Yet what I have tried to maintain is the tone and intent of *The Educational Imagination*. The need, in my view, for educators to have an educational imagination is greater now than it was when the first edition was published in 1979.

I wish to express my gratitude to those graduate students in the School of Education at Stanford who worked with me in my course on Educational Connoisseurship and Educational Criticism. They are an intelligently tough lot. Dealing with their comments and questions has been an education for me.

I wish most of all to express my thanks to the five individuals who gave me permission to include their work in this volume. Lorna Catford, James Marshall, and Barbara Porro were graduate students who worked with me. Tom Barone, whose work also appeared in the first edition, is now an Associate Professor of Education at Northern Kentucky University. Stuart Cohen is Professor of Educational Psychology at Purdue University. I had the pleasure of responding to his paper at the annual meeting of the American Educational Research Association and he was gracious enough to allow me to include it in this volume. The work of all of these individuals has added much to the second edition of *The Eductional Imagination.* I am grateful to them.

I wish to thank Lloyd Chilton, my wise and patient editor at Macmillan. His concern and sensitivity to my needs were very important to me as I worked on this volume. Finally, to my wife Ellie goes my deep gratitude for continuing support and assistance.

Elliot W. Eisner
Stanford University

CONTENTS

THE
EDUCATIONAL
IMAGINATION

I

The Curriculum Field Today:
Where We Are, Where We Were,
and Where We Are Going

ah yes,
We shall not cease from exploration
And the end of all our exploring
Will be to arrive where we started
And know the place for the first time.
Through the unknown, remembered gate
When the last of earth left to discover
Is that which was the beginning;
At the source of the longest river
The voice of the hidden waterfall
And the children in the apple tree
Not known because not looked for
But heard, half-heard, in the stillness
Between the waves of the sea.
T. S. ELIOT, *Little Gidding*

Where We Are

The quality of school curricula and the quality of teaching are the two most important features of any educational enterprise. Yet just what constitutes a curriculum of high quality and excellent teaching is far from agreed upon—at least among those who have reflected deeply on education. To

1

those who constitute the American public, however, the meaning of high-quality curricula and excellence of teaching is rather clear. It is clear, for example, that in every national poll regarding the aims of elementary education the three R's are always placed at the top of the list. At the secondary level, high-quality curricula are typically defined by four years of English, three years of history, at least two years (but preferably three or four years) of math, and at least two years of science. In addition, two, but preferably three years of a foreign language are also regarded as desirable. Occasionally—but only occasionally—one finds the fine arts in that list.

Yet the public hardly ever discusses the kind of science, the type of English education, and the emphasis on social studies that it desires. *More* appears to be good enough. And as far as elementary school children are concerned, the basics are clearly better than what is not basic—even though a thorough analysis of just what is basic for children from five to thirteen is seldom the subject of discussion or debate. What, for example, do we mean by learning to read? Do we mean the ability to read literature or simply to read utility bills? Do we want children to read "between the lines," to grasp the meaning of metaphor and connotation, or are we simply interested in decoding? Is wanting to read as important as being able to read? Alas, the bandwagons that command so much attention seldom slow down for people to reflect on the directions in which they are heading. Even educators who are professionally responsible for the conduct of schooling too seldom provide the kind of interpretation that the public ought to have to choose intelligently. We educators too frequently lead the parade.

How This Book Is Organized

To provide a perspective that I hope will be useful to you for thinking about such problems, questions, and issues, I have organized this book into fourteen chapters that can be divided into several major sections.

Chapters 1 and 2 focus upon the historical and contemporary social forces that affect our schools. I believe that an understanding of where schools have been and of what social forces affect them at present is extraordinarily useful for interpreting our present state of affairs. Without an historical perspective, our analyses are likely to be naive and misguided.

Chapters 3 through 7 provide an array of distinctions concerning the meaning of curriculum and the orientations and perspectives brought to bear on curriculum decision making. These chapters provide distinctions between the kinds of curricula that schools inevitably teach, and they identify the dimensions or factors that can be considered in designing educational programs.

Chapter 8 illustrates the relationship between the concepts described in

Chapters 6 and 7 and the work of an actual curriculum development group.

Chapter 9 focuses upon the art of teaching and provides an analytic description of what it means to think of teaching as a craft or an art.

Chapters 10 through 13 move into the realm of educational evaluation and pay particular attention to an artistic approach to what is usually regarded as a scientific activity.

A "final" word is provided in Chapter 14—recognizing, of course, that in educational inquiry, no word can be final.

This book is designed to complicate your professional life. If you want simple answers to educational questions, it would be better to stop reading and to look elsewhere. Newspaper columnists and television commentators would be good people with whom to begin. They seem to know not only what ills plague the schools but also what prescriptions will remedy them. The ills are found in declining test scores. The remedy is a longer school year, more discipline, more homework, fewer electives, and more "basics." Test scores, we are told, have been falling for over a decade: witness the decline in the Scholastic Aptitude Test (SAT) scores, a test that is administered to one-and-a-half million high school seniors each year. Students seeking admission to colleges and universities are encouraged to take the SATs as a part of a dossier they submit. From 1968 to 1981, test scores on the SATs declined. This decline not only causes the public to have doubts about the quality of schools. It also leads people to develop prescriptions to remedy the problems they believe to exist. What is seldom understood or explained is what the SAT test and the decline in scores actually mean. It is seldom realized that the SAT is designed to measure *aptitudes for college work;* it was not designed to assess the quality of secondary school programs. In the psychological literature, aptitudes are typically regarded as personal traits that are not particularly influenced by school programs. Hence, to draw conclusions about the quality of secondary school programs from test data designed to measure aptitudes is, at the very least, logically questionable. But equally as misunderstood is the magnitude of the test-score decline. The Scholastic Aptitude Test has two major sections, one verbal and the other mathematical. Each section contains eighty multiple choice test items. The raw scores from these two sections of the test are scaled so that the lowest score a student can receive is 200, the highest is 800, and the mean is 500. What the public is told is that the decline in verbal scores from 1968 to 1980 is 42 points. For math scores, the decline for the same period is 26 points. But what the public is not told is that a 26-point drop is a result of the student's missing three more items in 1979 than the population as a whole missed in 1968. A 42-point decline is the result of a test-taker missing six more items in 1968 than were missed by the population in 1979. Remember that these are multiple choice questions—eighty for the verbal section and eighty for the math section. It is, I believe, quite different to believe that there is a 41-point drop in test scores than to believe that six more multiple choice items were missed on an eighty-item test over a twelve-year period. My point here is that this information is not provided to the public. Therefore it is not surprising that the public is often in a poor position to interpret intelligently the meaning of the information it is given. In these matters the newspapers and television are of little help. The mass media seldom provide bland copy and equivocation: the sharper the image and the more acute the alarm, the better.

The reason I have chosen to start my discussion of the curriculum field with some observations on the impact of the testing movement is that I believe tests have a profound influence on the ways in which schools function. This influence is particularly strong with respect to the kind of educational programs they offer. One may wax eloquent about the life of the mind and the grand purposes of education, but must face up to the fact that school programs are shaped by other factors, as well. Communities led to believe that the quality of education is represented by the reading and math scores students receive come to demand that those areas of curriculum be given highest priority. When this happens, teachers begin to define their own priorities in terms of test performance. Indeed, I do not believe it an exaggeration to say that test scores function as one of the most powerful controls on the character of educational practice.

Consider, for example, the concept of *minimum competencies.* Concerned about the meaninglessness of high school diplomas, people are demanding that minimal competencies be identified and that students graduating from high schools be tested to demonstrate that these competencies have been achieved. As of 1983, thirty-seven states required students to meet such competencies in order to graduate.

But if there are minimum competencies for high school graduation, should there not also be defined standards for promotion from one grade level to the next? And if there are such standards and all students meet them, is it not likely that some will claim that the standards are too low? If all students meet the standards, teachers might be accused of teaching to the test, of creating something akin to grade inflation. In short, implicit in having standards is the expectation that not everyone will meet them: standards provide one way to differentiate among students. And for those who fail to meet them, the solution is clear: such students will be expected to repeat the grade.

If this narrative sounds strangely familiar, it's because you have heard it before. It may have been a part of the philosophy of educational practice you experienced when you were a child. It was a characteristic practice during the early part of the century. It is an attractive conception to many people because it is deceptively simple. Education is conceived of as a product that schools deliver into the performance systems of children. If the school does not have standards for student performance, it should have. Once such standards are determined, one teaches and tests to determine whether they have been met. If the standards are met, the student is promoted. If they are not met, the student is retained. At the end of the period of schooling, the effective school will graduate virtually all students, because they will have met the standards laid down.

To operationalize a graded conception of educational practice it is important to have definite goals and definite tasks. Performances, or competencies, should be demonstrable to the teacher, and children should have such performances checked on a card or contract that they carry. In 1920 Carlton W. Washburn described the principles of such a plan that was then used in the Winnetka public schools:

> The most important of these principles is that the goals of a grade's work in a subject must be absolutely definite, must be known to pupils as well as the teachers, and must be attainable by the slowest, normal, diligent pupil. The big goals of the grade must be subdivided so that a child's progress is obvious to himself. Goals must be in terms of concrete facts to be known, habits to be acquired, or skills to be developed. This is in contrast to the usual outline or course of study in which nothing is set forth but pages to be covered or general aims to be achieved.
>
> In the second place, the plan requires the establishment of tests which are complete and diagnostic. These tests must show whether or not a pupil has attained all of the goals and must show his specific weaknesses. For under the individual system each pupil must achieve 100 per cent efficiency in the work he undertakes. Eighty per cent on a test does not mean passing; it means that there is 20 per cent of the work yet to be done before the pupil goes on. The results of the test must indicate exactly what the pupil has yet to accomplish.[1]

If we read such prose in light of our knowledge about individual differences and about the importance of context in educational planning, we might conclude that in the past fifty years we have come a long way from such a simplistic view. But just listen to what a former associate U.S. commissioner of education has to say about the importance of establishing standards in order to meet the requirements of educational accountability:

> In its most basic aspect, the concept of educational accountability is a process designed to insure that any individual can determine for himself if the schools are producing the results promised. The most public aspect of accountability would be independent accomplishment audits that report educational results in factual, understandable, and meaningful terms. These independent accomplishment audits might be undertaken by groups drawn from universities, private enterprise, and state departments of education employed by local school authorities in a manner similar to the process now employed to secure and utilize fiscal audits. Such audits would serve our educational managers by telling them which educational processes are productive and which are nonproductive and by suggesting alternatives which are likely to be better.

Like most processes which involve a balancing of input and ouput, educational accountability can be implemented successfully only if educational objectives are clearly stated before instruction starts. One mechanism for insuring clarity in objectives is the performance contract.

An educational performance contract, as its name implies, would prescribe anticipated learning outcomes in terms of student performance. Unlike contracts which simply describe the work or service to be provided by one party and the payments to be made by the other, the educational performance contract would specify the qualities and attributes of the end product of the service or work performed. In other words, it would establish the quantity and quality of student learning anticipated rather than focussing solely upon the quality and quantity of effort expended by those providing the work or service.

Performance contracts make greater initial demands on both the purchaser and supplier, but they mitigate most postdelivery haggling because basically simple performance tests can be used to determine whether or not the product performs as promised.

If an air conditioning contractor promises that his installation will reduce interior temperatures 20 degrees below outside temperatures, it takes only an accurate thermometer to determine if the promise has been met. Similarly, if an educational manager promises that all children attending his school will be able to read 200 words per minute with 90 percent comprehension on their twelfth birthday as measured by a special test, simply giving the test to all children on their twelfth birthday will readily reveal if the promise has been fulfilled.[2]

The publication from which I am quoting, one issued by the Educational Testing Service,[3] is not fifty years old, but nine years old. One cannot help asking why this old wine, which has long since turned, should be fed not only to the lay public, who might not know better, but also to professionals attending a national invitational conference on testing problems. I believe that there are some plausible answers to this. But for the moment I would like to return to the impact of testing on the curriculum that is provided by the schools.

The impact of testing on the curriculum takes two forms. First is the impact on what is considered important in school programs. Schools whose quality is judged in terms of the test performance of their pupils tend to emphasize what the tests test. This means that the fields not tested are considered less important than those that are, at least operationally. At the kindergarten level, the playhouse is being replaced by the bookshelf; reading is tested and play is not, hence play is considered intellectually unimportant in school. At the primary grade level, social studies are becoming a vanishing species, and the arts are rapidly becoming thought of as areas that extraschool agencies such as community centers should care for. In California, for example, the number of art consultants in school districts dropped from 435 in 1970 to 128 in 1974,[4] and those who remain, probably fewer than fifty, provide, as a major portion of their professional responsibility, services in areas for which they have not been prepared.

The second way in which testing influences the curriculum is through the priorities that students feel compelled to set for themselves. Consider, for example, the influence of the Scholastic Aptitude Test. Students believe, whether true or not, that more work in mathematics will lead to high scores on the mathematics section of the SAT. To get such scores, some relinquish the opportunity to enroll in courses that genuinely suit their interests and aptitudes and enroll instead in courses that have little intrinsic meaning to them.

The students, like school administrators and teachers, are not ignorant. Important consequences flow from the choices they make, and therefore they yield to the criteria that have maximum payoff within the educational system. Students recognize that they must pay their dues if options in the future are not to be closed to them.

But not only are students influenced. Unfortunately, how students do on the SATs is believed by educators to be a reflection of the quality of the educational program that has been provided. To increase the probability that students will score higher on the SATs, special courses, designed exclusively to enable high school students to increase their Scholastic Aptitude Test scores, have been established in high schools. What the school is saying to students is that regardless of the educational significance of the tests, it is important to forego educationally substantive courses in order to practice the skills that will lead to high SAT scores. If those skills were educationally important, why are they not developed in the standard college preparatory curriculum in the first place? If these skills are not educationally important, why should the school acquiesce to such crass instrumental values? The reasons are not difficult to discern.

Now where in all of this are the curricularists? Where are the people who have made the focus of their professional attention the character and quality of school programs? I do not believe that those of us who work in the curriculum field have had much impact on the conduct of school practice. We do not at present have much of a political base. We have not been among the groups in education to receive much of the federal funding. We do not enjoy the status of either educational psychology or educational sociology as a field of scholarly inquiry. We have been concerned in much of our work with what schools ought to be and with the complex problems of practice. But we have created no tests that can measure "educational output." Our field has been largely devoted to conceptual problems and to, the preparation of practitioners, and, as in other fields, we have had our share of strengths and weaknesses in each.

Those of us who are university professors often find ourselves in the interstices between the position of our colleagues in education whose reference group is "pure" scholars working in the mother discipline and the position of educational practitioners working in the schools. We often find it uncomfortable to refer to ourselves as scholars, but find the term *curriculum worker* awkward and out of date.

We find our graduate students entering a declining market and we hear from our colleagues that our field is moribund. Even we, from time to time, seem to take perverse pleasure in pronouncing ourselves on the verge of death.[5] But somehow the problems with which we are concerned will not go away. These problems continue to breathe life into our beings, and we find ourselves talking, arguing, and writing about questions of genuine educational importance.

Where We Were

Why are we in such a position? Why do the schools, so often, pursue simplistic, mechanical solutions to complex educational problems? Part of the answer, at least, rests with the assumptions of those who have shaped the thinking of the curriculum field and who have contributed so much to the way in which school administrators and teachers have been trained.

These assumptions have been rooted in the aspiration to develop a scientifically based technology of educational practice, something akin to agriculture, engineering, or medicine. When the field of education was developing, around the turn of the century, it was dominated intellectually by two men—Edward L. Thorndike and John Dewey—who both looked to science as the most reliable means for guiding educational practice. Thorndike's work was particularly influential not only in the development of educational psychology as the key theoretical field of education, but also in the professional socialization of tens of thousands of teachers and school administrators through the incorporation of his ideas and assumptions into textbooks.

The general aspiration that Thorndike held for schooling was the creation of a science of educational practice. Through experimentation it would be possible, he believed, to discover the laws of learning so that teachers could rely not on intuition, chance, artistry, or talent but rather on tested principles and procedures for managing the student's learning. Thorndike provided educational psychologists with a control-oriented conception of educational research that would eventually lead to a highly predictive educational science.

In 1910 when the first issue of the *Journal of Educational Psychology* appeared, the lead article titled "The Contribution of Psychology to Education" was written by Edward L. Thorndike. In this piece he states without ambiguity his conception of the role of psychology in the development of a science of education.

A complete science of psychology would tell every fact about everyone's intellect and character and behavior, would tell the cause of every change in human nature, would tell the result which every educational force—every act of every person that changed any other or the agent himself—would have. It would aid us to use human beings for the world's welfare with the same surety of the result that we now have when we use falling bodies or chemical elements. In proportion as we get such a science we shall become masters of our own souls as we now are masters of heat and light. Progress toward such a science is being made.

Thorndike wrote regarding the work needed to be done:

The first line of work concerns the discovery and improvement of means of measurement of intellectual functions. (The study of means of measuring moral functions such as prudence, readiness to sacrifice an immediate for a later good, sympathy, and the like, has only barely begun.) Beginning with easy cases such as the discrimination of sensory differences, psychology has progressed to measuring memory and accuracy of movement, fatigue, improvement with practice, power of observing small details, the quantity, rapidity and usefulness of associations, and even to measuring so complex a function as general intelligence and so subtle a one as suggestibility.[6]

For Thorndike, evidence of progress was in hand and the future looked bright.

Dewey, too, regarded science as the optimal model for inquiry. It was scientific methods that would yield "warranted assertions," as he called them. It was science that provided both a public method and public criteria against which claims could be verified. If education were to have a solid, dependable base of knowledge for guiding practice, it was science that was believed to be best able to provide it.

Although Dewey regarded "the scientific method" as the method best suited to knowledge production, he was not naive or mechanistic in his approach to scientific inquiry. Indeed, in his 1929 publication, *The Sources of the Science of Education,*[7] he recognized the dynamic and contingent character of educational practice and he appreciated the differences between what was possible in the laboratory and what was feasible in the classroom. Yet, during the first quarter of the century it was science, not art, to which Dewey would give his deepest bow. It was not until he was seventy-four years old that we find his attention fully devoted to the kinds of meaning and experience that the arts make possible. Even then, his *Art As Experience,*[8] in some ways his magnum opus, never really took hold as a source of thinking about teaching, curriculum, evaluation, and other mainstream educational processes. Within the field of education, *Art As Experience* went largely unread. Only two reviews of the book appeared in education journals from 1934 through 1937.

I mention the influence of Thorndike and Dewey because these men, I believe, set the intellectual tone and direction for inquiry into education that, in turn, shaped the assumptions and practices of the curriculum field. Thorndike and Dewey differed in their view of the means and ends of education, but they shared a belief in the potential of scientific inquiries as a means of informing and guiding educational practice. In this respect they helped establish and legitimize a tradition that others were to follow. For example, Franklin Bobbitt's early published work also focused on the problem of creating scientifically efficient schools, and his early written work in curriculum shared the same set of assumptions. He saw curriculum planning as a species of social engineering. The problems were essentially to *discover* the appropriate ends through a type of needs-assessment, to formulate those ends in specific terms, to order them over time in increasing levels of difficulty, and to help children learn at each level what is laid out. Bobbitt writes: "In this analysis, one will first divide his field into a few rather large units, and then break them up into smaller ones. This process of division will continue until he [the curriculum worker] has formed the quite specific activities that are to be performed."[9]

The students of curriculum who followed the tradition initiated by Thorndike and Dewey did not make any major revisions in the basic theoretical assumptions that were to be used in the design and evaluation of curiculum. W. W. Charters, for example, continued the tradition in his efforts to identify the goals and content of the curriculum by the scientific analysis of the tasks that were typically performed by adults.[10] For Charters, as for Bobbitt, educational programs were to prepare the student for a competent life as an adult, and this required knowledge of the particular activites of which that life consists. Through activity analysis, as he called it, complex skills could be divided into component parts and then organized into a curriculum. The belief was one that grew out of the professional world-view that Thorndike advocated: Learning was regarded as the accretion of specific units or connections; gradually, as in the building of a house, the parts were put together to constitute a complex unit of behavior. These units of behavior eventually formed the architecture of human action. The major problem for Bobbitt and Charters was to identify what skills were useful for a productive adult life, to break those complex skills into simpler ones, and to organize them into a curriculum so that they could be efficiently learned. The implicit image is that of an assembly line that eventaully produces a finished product in which all of the component parts work together.

By 1932 the curriculum field saw the publication of *The Technique of Curriculum Making* by Henry Harap.[11] This work, too, like Bobbitt's, has a technological flavor. Harap viewed the technique of curriculum making as a linear systematic activity. One first defines the aims of education and then the term *objective*. From these one identifies the major activities of life, consults subject matter specialists, analyzes the activites of children, determines the child's social needs, and eventually formulates those activities that are instrumental to the achievement of the objectives one has formulated at the outset.

What is clear from Harap's work, as well as from that of his predecessors in the curriculum field, is the desire to create a systematic technology of curriculum development. In 1932, when his book appeared, Harap was able to write, "The process of systematic curriculum making is still in its infancy—it is hardly ten years old."[12] What I think we see in the work of these early curricularists is the desire to continue in the scientific tradition advanced by men as prestigious as Thorndike and Dewey. I do not believe that they anticipated that the tradition they embraced and used in their work would set such an important precedent not only for those in the field of curriculum, but for those in psychology, as well. Indeed, B. F. Skinner himself has said that he regards his work as a footnote to what Thorndike started.[13]

One cannot give an account of where the curriculum field has been without attention to the work of Ralph Tyler. Tyler's *Basic Principles of Curriculum and Instruction*[14] was first published in 1949 and since that time has undergone over thirty printings. One would be hard pressed to identify a more influential piece of writing in the field. In 128 brief pages, Tyler lays out the basic questions he believes must be answered by anyone interested in creating a curriculum for any subject matter field or level of schooling. Tyler's work follows the lead first laid down by Thorndike and Dewey and articulated for the field of curriculum by Bobbitt and Harap. From Thorndike, Tyler's curriculum rationale draws on the need for observable behavior as evidence of learning. He also shares both Thorndike's and Judd's faith in the educational utility of the social sciences, particularly in psychology, as a source through which curriculum decisions can be "screened."

From Dewey's work Tyler extracts a belief in the importance of experience as the basic condition influencing what children learn. Tyler's curriculum work also shares a family resemblance to that of his predecessors in the curriculum field, notably to Bobbitt and Harap. Bobbitt's emphasis on the importance of objectives is echoed in Tyler's observation that objectives are the single most important consideration in curriculum planning because, in Tyler's words, "they are the most critical criterion for guiding all the other activities of the curriculum maker."[15] Tyler's attention to the various data sources for objectives we find described twenty years earlier by Harap; the style is different, but the intent is essentially the same.

What Tyler has given the field of curriculum through his monograph is a powerful, although in my view oversimplified, conception of what considerations curriculum planning entails. Once learned, Tyler's four questions are hard to forget. These questions are:

1. What educational purposes should the school seek to attain?
2. What educational experiences can be provided that are likely to attain these purposes?
3. How can these educational experiences be effectively organized?
4. How can we determine whether these purposes are being attained?

Once having learned about the need for objectives and the form they should take, one is hard pressed to neglect them, at least in theory. The Tyler monograph on curriculum is a model of a rational, systematic approach to curriculum planning. Although it embraces no particular view of education, the technical procedures it prescribes are bound to have consequences for what individuals trained to use this rationale will come to consider professionally adequate decision making in curriculum. Ends, for example, are always to precede means, objectives come before activities; not a hint is given in the monograph that in complex organizations ends can be constructed out of action and that only a textbook rendering of educational planning would provide such a pristine view of rational thinking. Nothing is said in the monograph about the student's role in curriculum planning or about the idea that different views of education conceive of curriculum planning in different ways. Although Tyler emphatically says that the monograph deals with the principles rather than with specific steps in curriculum building, the tone of the work, like the tone of so much work that preceded it in the field, is a no-nonsense, straightforward, systematic conception of what in practice is a complex, fluid, halting, adventitious task.

Tyler's work on curriculum planning was and is influential not only because of the straightforward character of his writing—particularly his monograph on curriculum—but also because of the people in the field of education who had the opportunity to work with him. Robert Anderson, Benjamin Bloom, Lee Cronbach, John Goodlad, Ole Sand, Hilda Taba, and others constituted a generation of influential educators who devoted much, if not all, of their attention to curriculum matters. Like Tyler, these authorities can be characterized as basically scientific in their assumptions, systematic in their procedures, and means-ends oriented in their view of educational planning.

Where Do We Go from Here?

The position that Tyler advocated regarding curriculum planning is in many ways a far more liberal and far less mechanistic position than the views espoused by those who made their curriculum mark during the 1960s. From the 1960s to the present, this nation has seen the emergence of individuals, who are trained not in the curriculum field but rather in psychology, developing both curriculum materials and ideas about curriculum planning that have had considerable impact in the field of education. I refer to such people as Carl Bereiter, Robert Gagne, Robert Glaser, Robert Mager, James Popham, Lauren Resnick, and Patrick Suppes. For each of these individuals, the essential characteristic of curriculum and instruction is that it be a planned, sequential series of steps that leads to ends that are known in advance and that are realized with a maximum of pedagogical efficiency. Mager's monograph on instructional objectives[16] is a classic example of how educational aims can be converted into observable forms of behavior. Mager's monograph succeeds in reducing educational aspirations into test items, even when they lose what might be educationally significant in the translation.

Popham follows this tradition; the thrust of his work is technical.[17] It focuses on how one should form objectives—and if one cannot or does not want to create them, one can purchase them from the Instructional Objective Exchange that Popham has established in Los Angeles. For Glaser, one of the central problems of teaching and curriculum planning is that of finding or creating the correct sequence of tasks for a student;[18] again, systematics that yields predictable forms of student behavior is the desired end in view.

Perhaps the ultimate position that this line of thinking has led to is found in Bereiter's argument that schools are misguided in their attempts to educate students.[19] The role of the school, according to Bereiter, is to train children in the basic skills and to provide child-care services that make no attempt to educate the young. What schools should do is provide training; they should not attempt to influence the values or visions that students hold. That, according to Bereiter, is for the family. Lest you think I overstate his position, I quote him here:

> The argument of this paper is that schools should drop their educational function in order to do a better job of child care and training, and that furthermore child care and training should be separately carried out by different people according to different styles. Let me try to clarify my use of the terms *education, child care* and *training* . . . Child care is distinguished from education by its relative neutrality. It consists of providing resources, services, activities, love, and attention for children, but no attempt to influence the course of their development. . . . Training is also directive in its intent. However, its objective is not to produce a certain kind of child, but merely to produce a certain kind of performance in the child. What the child does with his acquired skill, how it is integrated into his personality, is a concern that lies beyond training. It is an educational concern. Therefore, to say that schools

should abandon education but continue training children is to say that schools should narrow their teaching efforts to a simple concern with getting children to perform adequately in reading, writing, and arithmetic.[20]

I do not believe it necessary here to demonstrate the hopelessness of a value-free training program for the young. The problems with Bereiter's views in this regard are abundantly clear. What is perhaps not so clear are the consequences that views such as these have not only for the field of curriculum, but for education and educational research in the United States.

Consider the influence these views have had on educational research. To do research has come to mean to do scientific inquiry, and to do such scientific inquiry in education has meant to do inquiry in which variables are identified, measured, and analyzed statistically. The desired image of the educational researcher is that of a scientist who as far as possible emulates his colleagues in the natural sciences. To engage in other forms of inquiry, to do historical or critical analysis of existing educational or social problems, to engage in philosophic inquiry, is not to do research. To pursue such activities is to write, as they say, "think pieces," a phrase that is curiously pejorative. To count is somehow better, perhaps, because counting or measuring yields numbers that can be carried to the third or fourth decimal place and hence provides the illusion of precision. The belief that educational research is a form of inquiry whose conclusions can be couched only in numbers is so pervasive that, of the seventy-five articles published in the *American Educational Research Journal* from 1981 through 1983, only two were nonstatistical.

The consequences of the scientific view for education as a field and for curriculum as a part of that field emerge not only within the conception and conduct of educational research, but also within the methods that people believe appropriate for educational evaluation. Because evaluation methods are largely the offspring of the educational research community as it is presently defined, this is not surprising. But surprising or not, I believe that these practices have had deleterious consequences for the curricula that are provided to children in American schools. One of these consequences is to reduce the term *evaluation* to *measurement*. Although each term is entirely independent—that is, one can evaluate without measuring and one can measure without evaluating (one can, of course, do both)—the belief that one must measure in order to evaluate is widespread. When this occurs, the fields that are most amenable to measurement are measured and those that are difficult to measure are neglected. What is measured then is emphasized in school programs because measurement becomes the procedure through which educational quality is determined.

For the curriculum of the school this means that evaluation practices, determined largely with respect to what can be measured, influence to a very large degree the kinds of programs that will be offered to the young. Educational practices based on a scientific model too often become not a tool for improving the quality of teaching and learning but rather an impediment to such ends. Students and teachers alike gear up to take tests, even though none of them believes those tests to be intrinsically important or that the tests really assess much of what has been learned and taught in schools.

The consequences of scientifically based approaches to educational evaluation extend beyond the issue of what subject matters should be emphasized. In many schools they influence how curricula will be organized and how teaching will occur. If one conceives of the curriculum as a kind of assembly line that produces at predictable intervals a certain complex of behaviors, then it appears reasonable to specify those behaviors and to set up the mechanism through which they can be measured. This involves breaking up complex forms of learning into smaller units of behavior or performance and then using a monitoring system to determine if these microperformances have been achieved. When combined with a reward structure to care for problems of student motivation and a set of minimum standards to ensure the public of good quality education, we have a complete system—at least in theory—for the management and control of school programs. What happens is what Lewis Mumford described in the 1930s.[21] The technology we design to expand our freedom and flexibility becomes our constraint. The teacher who does not conceive of the educational process as a type of assembly line that processes the child in fields that are amenable to measurement has no alternative but to adapt to the demands placed on him or her by the school or school district, or to leave teaching, or to attempt to beat the system by providing the illusion of compliance.

The consequences I have described thus far have focused on the way in which evaluation is conceived: how scientific assumptions influence curricular priorities and how they affect the organization of curriculum and teaching. But the influence does not stop there.

As the current recapitulation of the efficiency movement grows, it widens the growing breach between teachers and administrators. If the school is to be judged in terms of measured student performance, then it also seems reasonable to evaluate teachers by their measured performance. The Stull bill in California is the natural offspring of an engineering view of the educational process. Now, if teachers are going to be judged by their performance, then the standards for teacher performance need to be specified and they need to be the same for all teachers. Furthermore, they need to be objectively applied. Teacher organizations make certain that administrators will not be cavalier in their evaluation of teachers, that they will use objective evidence in their assessments, and that there will be no room for vindictive administrators who want to take out their frustrations on teachers.

What occurs is that both administrators and teachers accept the assumptions implicit in this model of education and increasingly view themselves as managers on the one hand and as workers on the other. The workers protect themselves from managerial exploitation through unionization, and the administrators affirm their identity by creating organizations that bar teachers from membership. Each group hires negotiators to work out contractual arrangements under which relationships between labor and management are explicitly defined in thick, written documents. In the meantime, hundreds of thousands of dollars and years of man-hours are spent working out agreements between parties that increasingly see themselves as adversaries.

What is truly said is that those of us in the field of education—teachers, administrators, professors of education—have so seldom tried to help the public understand the complexities of education as a process. Why have we been so willing to accept assumptions about teaching, curriculum, and evaluation that have at least questionable validity? Why is it that we have so seldom pointed out the practical naïveté of promises to make schools more effective by setting up minimum standards and by measuring, as the former associate U.S. commissioner of education said, the equivalent of educational air-conditioning?

Perhaps one reason for our apparent inability to function as educational leaders is that we have been professionally socialized to accept simplistic assumptions about acceptable methods of educational inquiry, methods that leave no room for nonscientific forms of understanding. For those of us who are professors, it is relatively easy to be seduced by the status system within the field of education in the United States, a status system that regards conceptual and practical work in education as unscholarly and of low status. In our professional culture a pound of insight is not worth an ounce of data. Too many of us are too willing to hop aboard the train, regardless of whether we believe it is going somewhere. Professional success has demanded it.

For school administrators, the tendency to acquiesce to demands for the scientific management of schooling is, I believe, explained adequately by Callahan's vulnerability thesis.[22] School administrators were vulnerable to public pressure in 1915, and they are vulnerable today. To keep one's job in a complex system, one must do what will look good, what is considered up to date, and what will be regarded as acceptable. The maintenance model of educational administration that I believe most school administrators embrace has as its first principle personal survival in the job. For this, the most useful tool is a wet finger in the wind.

One might hope that schools of education that prepare school administrators would provide the kind of professional education that would enable them to think critically about the virtues toward which education aims. One might hope that such people would be encouraged to think deeply about the aims of education and to provide leadership and educational services to the community on whose support the schools depend. Unfortunately, as schools become more industrialized, the training programs for administrators focus more and more on the development of skills of labor negotiation and on courses offered in business schools, departments of economics, and the like. Such courses might have utility for some aspects of educational administration, but they are essentially technical studies. Embedded within technique are implicit visions of what is important, and these visions are seldom appraised by criteria emanating from a conception of education itself.

For teachers, the buy-in to the technical/business orientation to schooling is, I believe, another form of self-preservation. Although there are some teachers who find professional security in an approach to educational practice that does not expect professional ingenuity, most teachers, particularly at the elementary level, regard that accountability movement a gross oversimplification of their work. Yet, I believe, we have to face the fact that in their professional education teachers are not given the kind of conceptual tools that would enable them to become sophisticated students of one of the most complex and intellectually challenging fields of study in existence: education. Although teachers may often feel that a set of prescriptions or demands is wrongheaded, they frequently find it difficult to say just what the problem is. They, too, acquiesce, like almost everyone else, to demands and expectations about which they have deep reservations.

All in all, when one looks back on the consequences the behavioristic, positivistic, scientific tradition has had on education in general and on the curriculum field in particular, the following seem to me to be important.

First, the dominance of a scientific epistomology in education has all but excluded any other view of the way in which inquiry in education can legitimately be pursued. Scientific assumptions have not only set theoretical constraints on the field by prescribing the acceptable criteria for knowledge about educational problems, but they have also defined the parameters within which those problems can be posed. Problems that do not lend themselves to measurement or to scientific solutions have been considered intellectually ill-conceived.

Second, the kind of science that has dominated educational research has, in my opinion, been preoccupied with control. The goal of the educational scientist was not only to be able to understand and predict, but also to control the phenomena into which he or she inquired. The offshoot of this view has been to regard educational practice, including curriculum development, as a technology that uses knowledge provided by the social sciences as the primary basis for its management and control. The models to be emulated are medicine, agriculture, and engineering. What has been sought is a set of procedures derived from social science research that will prescribe methods that curriculum developers and teachers can follow. In the field of curriculum this has found its apotheosis in the aspiration to create teacherproof curriculum materials. In teaching it has manifested itself in the belief in the diagnostic-prescriptive model. In school evaluation it has shown up in an input-output model of productivity. Seldom have the basic assumptions underlying such beliefs been subject to the kind of critical scrutiny they deserve.

One astute observer of American education has had this to say about the use of an agricultural or medical model for improving the quality of educational practice:

> A prominent congressman, noted for his interest in education, not long ago asked a conference of educational pundits why colleges of education did not serve their clientele as do colleges of agriculutre or engineering. He noted that colleges of agriculture employed 1) scientists in chemistry, genetics, mathematics, and economics; 2) technologists who invented or perfected methods of planting, fertilizing, cultivating, harvesting, and marketing a wide variety of crops; of breeding, feeding, and marketing livestock; and 3) extension specialists who delivered help to the farmer in every phase of his operation, from planting to filling out income tax forms.
>
> Why, the legislator wanted to know, could not colleges of education, employing the same types of personnel, deliver remedial services to the classroom door? Why could they not revolutionize instruction as colleges of agriculture have revolutionized farming? Why, we may all ask, is an educational establishment that boasts of a giant research effort and a training program that has staffed the schools with nearly three million teachers and administrators so continuously criticized for its inefficiency? Why, indeed, are the problems so tediously the same, generation after generation? Why, in short, could the American citizen of 1776 find so much that is so familiar in the schools of 1976?
>
> . . .   . . .
>
> My own impression is that the congressman was really asking about a technology that would produce desired results efficiently. Whether it was science-based or not was incidental, although the success of science-based technology in agriculture and the existence of the educational research establishment naturally influenced him to pose the question in this form. These hopes, one must confess, are not likely to be fulfilled, not because educational researchers are incompetent or lazy, but rather because the desired results are not analogous to the ear of corn that meets certain specifications or the automobile that travels so many miles on a gallon of gasoline. "Growing corn" and "growing children" are not analogous expressions, one reason for not taking the teacher-gardener metaphor too seriously. The goals of education (as distinguished from a particular school activity) are not this or that behav-

ior, this or that habit or disposition, but a style of life for a whole person. None of the professions we have been holding up as models is responsible for such a totality of results. The structure of the good life may be constant, but the constellation of action, thought, and feeling consistent with this structure varies for each individual.[23]

Third, a consequence of these assumptions has been the preoccupation with standardized outcomes. The testing movement that has grown out of the field of educational psychology depends on assumptions that required a uniform set of test items and a uniform set of methods of test administration to measure educational achievement. Indeed, until quite recently, the major function of tests was to differentiate student from student on a common scale. The statistics used to determine test reliability and test validity required that all students be given the identical tasks so that differentiation among students could be made, variances computed, and reliability determined. Test items that all or nearly all students answered correctly or incorrectly were dropped from the test; such items do not contribute to the test's reliability. However, such items may be extremely relevant to course aims or to the material that the students study. It is ironic, but a teacher who has taught extremely well and whose students learned what the test happened to test would produce a distribution of test scores that would be regarded as unreliable. The items that all or most of the students answered correctly would be eliminated from the test if the test were in the process of being developed. What we have in such cases are statistical criteria superseding educational criteria. As long as the major function of tests is to sort students into high, medium, and low achievers, lack of variability in test performance will be regarded by test constructors as a problem to be overcome.

Fortunately, the advent of criterion-referenced tests to replace norm-referenced tests ameliorates this problem. The criterion-referenced test is referenced to course objectives. Its function is to assess the extent to which course aims have been achieved; it is not designed to sort students into categories or to produce a normal distribution among scores. But the development of criterion-referenced tests is relatively new. Most nationally used standardized achievement tests are norm-referenced rather than criterion-referenced. The use of such practices, built into the technology of test construction, has undermined any educational inclination to cultivate the student's positive idiosyncrasies or to use forms of assessment that are different for different students. Under the press of such instruments, a truly individualized form of teaching could hardly take place.

Fourth, under such assumptions, little or no role can be given to the pupil for participating in the creation of his or her educational program because the provision of such opportunities would make the system difficult to control, hard for educators to manage, and complex to evaluate. It would be like giving workers on an automobile assembly line the option of making choices about the upholstery or paint to be used on the cars that come along; such options would, in a technological view, create chaos. The result of such assumptions in educational practice is to regard the pupil as an essentially passive material to be molded by the impact of the treatment. Indeed, the language of research is revealing in this regard. One applies treatments to subjects in order to secure responses that yield statistically signficiant main effects.

Fifth, the consequences for curriculum of the interest in control and measurement have been to break up complex tasks into small, almost microunits of behavior and in the process to render much of the curriculum meaningless to children. If one is primarily interested in control and measured outcome, the best way to do it is to disallow the adventitious, to focus attention on highly discrete and highly defined tasks, and to assess after each task in order to determine whether the objectives of the tasks have been achieved. One model of such an approach is the Distar Reading Program, which not only prescribes what students are to do and say, but also prescribes exactly what teachers are to do and say. The prescriptions in that program are to be followed scrupulously. A second model is the programs used in computer-assisted instruction. In such instruction, each frame must be defined and focal attention ensured. This is done by blocking the student's peripheral vision, by having the student wear earphones, and by keeping the student 12 to 18 inches away from the cathode-ray tube. The aspiration is for an errorless program. These models serve well as examples of connectionist psychology, and although they are extreme in form the tendency in curriculum and other areas shares many of their features. The tacit image is that of an assembly line.

Finally, one is struck by the sober, humorless quality of so much of the writing in the field of curriculum and in educational research. The tendency toward what is believed to be scientific language has resulted in an emotionally eviscerated form of expression; any sense of the poetic or the passionate must be excised. Instead, the aspiration is to be value-neutral and technical. It's better to talk about subjects than students, better to refer to treatment than to teaching, better to measure than to judge, better to deal with output than with results. And if one is to do research, it is much more objective to speak in the third person singular or the first person plural than in the first person singular. Cool, dispassionate objectivity has resulted in sterile, mechanistic language devoid of the playfulness and artistry that are so essential to teaching and learning.

Now the reason for the paucity of scientifically based educational practice is not that teachers are ignorant or recalcitrant or unwilling to use what's new and effective, but that there is little that conventional forms of educational research have to offer educational practitioners. At the very minimum, as Dewey himself said, scientific conclusions have to be artfully interpreted and applied to particular educational situations, even if we grant that there is something to apply. What I think is beginning to occur is that more and more of the really bright, courageous students of education are beginning to look elsewhere to find ways of dealing with the problems of practice. The line of former educational scientists that are engaged in this search is growing longer. Donald Campbell, Lee Cronbach, Gene Glass, Philip Jackskon, Lou Smith, and Robert Stake are a few of those whose more recent work raises serious questions about the utility and limits of science in the study of education. There are others within the curriculum field itself who have long held this view: Mike Apple, Mike Atkin, Herbert Kleibard, Steve Mann, Gail McCutcheon, Jim McDonald, Vincent Rogers, Joseph Schwab, Decker Walker, and myself. In Europe people like Torstein Harbo in Norway, Ulf Lundgren in Sweden, Lawrence Stenhouse and Barry Moore in England, and Hartmut von Hentig in Germany, represent individuals whose views of curriculum, teaching, and evaluation are considerably more complex than can be encompassed by a simple means-ends model of educational practice.

Now the significance of this discontent is the promise it provides for the development of new ways of conceptualizing educational problems, formulating educational questions, and pursuing educational aims. What we badly need are models that are heuristic and useful, ways of talking about educational problems that are clear but not stilted. We need to avoid the pitfall that so many progressives fell into, both in the 1930s and in the 1960s: namely, the tendency toward romantic obscurantism, the infatuation with vague rhetoric that has little intellectual rigor. In a certain sense, we need to become hard-nosed about what has often been regarded as soft-nosed thinking. What I believe we need are approaches to the study of educational problems that give full range to the varieties of rationality of which humans are capable, that are not limited to one set of assumptions about how we come to know, that use methods outside of *as well as* inside the social sciences to describe, to interpret, and to evaluate what occurs in schools. Orthodoxy often creates blinders to new possibilities, and I believe the field of education has worn such blinders for too long.

I believe that we need evaluation methods that exploit the variety of expressive forms through which we understand and make public what we know. So much of the current evaluation methods emphasizes written language and ability in mathematics; yet, these forms of expression in no way exhaust the ways in which conception and expression occur in the culture at large. We need evaluation methods that give students the opportunity to use, for example, artistic forms of expression that are intellectually legitimate and that cease penalizing students whose aptitudes and interests motivate them to work in such areas. Evaluation methods should be instrumental to the ends we seek; they should not, as so many of them do now, impede the realization of such ends.

I believe we need theory that unapologetically recognizes the artistry of teaching and that is useful in helping teachers develop those arts. The model of the teacher as a scientist who first hypothesizes before he or she acts may fit some aspects of teaching but certainly does not fit all of teaching. In what sense is teaching an art? How do teachers and school administrators use qualities of expression, timing, and the perception of expressive forms as a basis for action? What aspects of teaching can be routinized and what aspects require ingenuity and inventiveness? Questions such as these need to be dealt with in any adequate theory of teaching or school administration. The study of the arts of teaching might help us elucidate the basis for such theory.

I believe we need to be willing to recognize the interaction between the character of the curriculum and the kind of teaching that occurs, and the ways in which the school is organized and how the reward structure of the school is employed. For too long we have operated as though decisions about school organization were one thing and decisions about curriculum were something else. All of us who work in schools, whether elementary schools or universities, work and live within a culture. This culture functions as an organic entity that seeks stability yet reacts to changes in one part from changes made in others. We need to try to understand these interactions if we seek intelligently to bring about significant change in schools. The study of curriculum in isolation from the rest of schooling is not likely to reveal the ecology of the school.

Finally, I believe we need to develop methods that will help us understand the kinds of experience children have in school and not only the kind of behavior they display. The behavioristic-positivistic tradition in American educational research tended to regard experience as unknowable and focused therefore on what children did. Although such an approach has its virtues operationally, behavior does not tell the whole story. As students of the hidden curriculum have told us, students learn more than they are taught and teachers teach more than they know. Attention only to what the school explicitly teaches or to what students do may be misinformative with respect to what they are learning and experiencing.

To deal with the new-found appreciation for experience will require approaches to inquiry that differ markedly from those prescribed by behavioristic psychology and a positivistic philosophy of science. These new approaches are being developed. Although they have long been present in the humanities and the arts, until recently the humanities and the arts were not regarded as appropriate providers of tools for studying educational practice or for doing educational research. The aspiration to create a science of education that would be as sure-footed as the sciences that are used to study nature, notably physics and chemistry, have remained the methodological ideal for eighty years. It is only since the early 1970s that forays have been made into other domains. The exploration of anthropological methods is one of the exemplary cases. Anthropology, compared to the kind of experimental psychology that both Thorndike and Skinner have so admirably explored, is a "soft" science. But it is still within the family of the social sciences. We should applaud its exploration as a way of understanding the culture of schooling. We indeed do need to know more about what actually occurs in schools. At present we know very little.

The major expansion of method, however, is not to a "soft" social science but to modes of inquiry in the humanities and the arts. I speak here of the fertile but relatively unplowed field of criticism. Art criticism has much to offer to help us understand the arts of teaching and the qualities of the particular situations in which curriculum decisions must ultimately be made and applied. It is ironic that although most people regard both teaching and educational administration as arts, the conceptual tools for studying the arts and criticizing them have seldom been used to assess them in education.

What I believe we are seeing is the emergence of new models, new paradigms, and new sets of assumptions that are finding increasing acceptance in the professional educational community. Whether the salient model will turn out to be a literary form of ethnography, the legal adversary model of evidence, or the model of art criticism is not yet clear. I believe the field has more than ample room for these three models and for scientific models, as well. For what I believe the study of education needs is not a new orthodoxy but rather a variety of new assumptions and methods that will help us appreciate the richness of educational practice, that will be useful for revealing the subtleties of its consequences for all to see. It is the function of this book to contribute to the work that has been going on.

References

1. Carlton Washburne, "The Individual System and Curriculum," *The Elementary School Journal* (75th Anniversary Issue), Vol. 75, 1975, pp. 43–44.
2. Leon M. Lessinger, "Accountability in Public Education," in *Proceedings of the 1969 Invitational Conference on Testing Problems,* Educational Testing Service, Princeton, N.J., 1969, p. 110.
3. Ibid.
4. Lou Nash, "The Politics of Education in California," in *The Arts, Human Development and Education,* McCutchan Publishing Co., Berkeley, Calif., 1976.
5. See, for example, Joseph Schwab, "The Practical: A Language for Curriculum," *School Review,* Vol. 78, November 1969.
6. Edward L. Thorndike, "The Contribution of Psychology to Education," *Journal of Educational Psychology,* Vol. I, 1910, pp. 6, 8.
7. John Dewey, *The Sources of a Science of Education,* H. Liverwright, New York, 1929.

8. John Dewey, *Art As Experience,* Minton, Balch and Co., New York, 1934.
9. Franklin Bobbitt, *How to Make a Curriculum,* Houghton Mifflin, Boston, 1924.
10. W. W. Charters, *Curriculum Construction,* Macmillan Co., New York, 1923.
11. Henry Harap, *The Technique of Curriculum Making,* Macmillan Co., New York, 1928.
12. Ibid.
13. See Geraldine Joncich, *The Sane Positivist: The Biography of Edward L. Thorndike,* Wesleyan University Press, Middletown, Conn., 1968.
14. Ralph Tyler, *Basic Principles of Curriculum and Instruction,* University of Chicago Press, Chicago, 1950.
15. Ibid., p. 40.
16. Robert Mager, *Preparing Instructional Objectives,* Fearon Publishers, Palo Alto, Calif., 1962.
17. James Popham, *Instructional Objectives,* Rand McNally, Chicago, 1969.
18. Robert Glaser, "Instructional Technology and the Measurement of Learning Outcomes," *American Psychologist,* Vol. 18, 1963, pp. 519–521.
19. Carl Bereiter, "Schools Without Education," *Harvard Educational Review,* Vol. 42, No. 3, August 1972.
20. Ibid.
21. Lewis Mumford, *Technics and Civilization,* Harcourt, Brace and Co., New York, 1938.
22. Raymond Callahan, *Education and the Cult of Efficiency,* University of Chicago Press, Chicago, 1962.
23. Harry Broudy, "The Search for Science of Education," *Phi Delta Kappan,* Vol. 58, September, 1976/77, pp. 104–105.

2

Social Forces Influencing
the Curriculum

*For those who have eaten of the tree of knowledge, paradise is
lost.*

K. R. POPPER

The aim of the previous chapter was to provide an overview of the development of the field of curriculum since the turn of the century. From that overview it is clear that the field of curriculum has been shaped in significant measure by certain intellectual paradigms. The desire to develop a science of education and the aspiration to provide efficient and effective schools that would yield measurable outcomes are two factors that have influenced how students of curriculum regard their tasks. But it would be a serious error to assume that the contours of curriculum and educational practice have been shaped only by the ideological commitments of educational theorists.

The curriculum is also shaped by an array of social forces over which curriculum planners have no control. Like a giant gyroscope that strives to maintain its upright position in a wind-blown sea, the school and the programs it offers attempt to withstand or adapt to outside forces. This shifting set of conditions is one of the factors that makes educational planning so challenging. It is what differentiates educational planning from the kind of planning that is possible when one works with materials that are unresponsive to social forces or that respond identically to identical stimuli. What educational planners have to cope with is a kind of organism whose contours are influenced by and which in turn influence the context in which the organism functions.

Six Forces Influencing the Curriculum

What forces operate at present? Which of these affect educational practice? How powerful are these forces, and what influence, if any, do educators have over them? There are many social forces that in one way or another influence schools, but the following six seem to me to be especially important for influencing educational priorities, curriculum content, and the general climate of schooling.

1. The decline in school enrollment.
2. Faith in scientism as applied to education.
3. The unionization of teachers.
4. Growth of educational consumerism.
5. The influence of textbooks.
6. Federal legislation and court decisions.

The Decline in School Enrollment

These six factors do not operate independently; they influence one another. Nevertheless, each is sufficiently important to warrant special attention as an identifiable factor affecting our schools. Consider the decline in student enrollment during the period from 1970 to 1980. In about 1970, 30,000,000 students were enrolled in grades one through eight in public elementary schools in the United States.[1] By 1980, enrollment had dropped to 25,209,000, a reduction of 16 per cent. At the secondary level, in grades nine through twelve in 1970 the number of students enrolled in American public schools was 13,000,000. By 1980, it was 13,700,000, a slight increase. At first sight the overall decrease in school population might seem to have no relationship to curriculum, to educational aims, or to the quality of teaching that students receive. This is not the case. With decreased enrollment in the schools come decreased funds for operating the schools. In most of the nation's 16,000 school districts, the amount of funds received is directly related to the number of students the district serves. Reduction of funds means, in educational terms, less money for salaries because about 90 per cent of the funds a district spends go to the salaries of its employees. While there is some drop in the number of employees in school districts, that drop is seldom commensurate with the decline in enrollment. In addition, the cost for lighting, heating, and maintenance does not decrease. The economies of volume are compromised when a district serves 10 per cent fewer students than it once did.

To cope with declining fiscal resources, school districts must either reduce expenditures—which usually means reducing the number of people employed and hence reducing the scope of the curriculum offered— or they must secure additional funds. One source of funds is school bond issues. The public is asked to tax themselves to pay for the same level of programming in schools that it has received in the past. When the public believes that schools are not particularly effective, it becomes especially difficult to secure public approval for such bond issues. In the decade between 1967 and 1977, it is estimated that 44 per cent of all school bond issues failed.

More recently, another tactic has been taken by some communities to secure funds that they believe schools need to have in order to offer the range of curricula their students ought to have. Citizens in these districts have created not-for-profit foundations to which contributions from members of the community can be made for the funding of programs that would not otherwise be available. In California alone approximately forty-five of such not-for-profit foundations have been created.[2]

It should be clear that the use of such a device, while making programs available that otherwise could not be offered, compromises the public tax based character of public schools. While the size of such funding compared to the total expnditures is small, it represents private support for what had been originally regarded as a public responsibility. In any case, the decline of students and concomitant decline of fiscal resources has an important effect on the school curriculum and on the quality of teaching that is provided. Curricula suffer because when educational priorities need to be defined within the constraints of a tight budget, the subjects that are regarded desirable, but not essential, suffer.[3] The quality of teaching declines because when the seniority system determines which teachers shall be retained and which shall be terminated, those having seniority are retained, even if it means that they will teach subjects for which they have not been prepared.[4]

Faith in Scientism as Applied to Education

A second force affecting American schooling is the offshoot of the faith in science and of the aspiration to create a science of education (described in Chapter One). It must be noted that I regard this force as *scientism* rather than as science. Science is aware of its subject matter, and it employs methods and assumptions that are appropriate to it. Scientism is the belief that everything that exists can be understood through the same methods, that there is only one legitimate way to verify knowledge of the world, and that unless something can be quantified it cannot be truly understood or known. In education these assumptions, or assumptions related to them, emerge in the belief that *measurement* of "educational payoff" is the only kind of educational effect that has any significance. It manifests itself in an evaluation system that appraises teachers simply on the basis of their students' measured achievement. It shows up in research practices that liken classrooms to laboratories and that assume the controls that are possible in the laboratory setting are also possible and desirable in the classroom. It appears in teacher-training programs that assume a curriculum can be dissected into a series of discrete parts, taught and learned piecemeal. Supporters of these programs believe that in the end the whole is no more and no less than the sum of those discrete parts. Scientism embraces the belief that the only thing that counts in education is how students behave, not what they believe, feel, or experience.

Scientism provides several types of comforts. First, by emphasizing measurement as the primary means for assessing the outcomes of schooling, it makes human judgments unnecessary. The impersonal instrument of a so-called objective test gives us so-called objective results. Risking one's beliefs about what has occurred is not necessary—one can point elsewhere, namely to the measuring instrument. Second, scientism focuses on the manifest behavior of the student. It is not necessary to be empathetic or to look beyond what a student does to what a student might feel. Complexity is thus simplified and the need for inference reduced. For those who seek such comforts and for those who, because of their socialization, take them as givens, scientism is an ally. But for those who have a wider educational vision, such assumptions interfere rather than aid because they too often neglect what is genuinely central in education. When the public is anxious about the quality of schooling, the quality of teachers, and the quality of teaching, it often embraces scientism as a way of objectifying, assessing, and improving the quality of schooling. This may be a supreme irony.

The Unionization of Teachers

The unionization of teachers is a third force that affects schooling. Unionization among teachers is growing in the United States. In 1950 a total of 41,000 teachers belonged to unions.[5] In 1962 there were 71,000.[6] By 1970 there were 1,735,951 teachers who belonged.[7] In 1980 2,235,000 teachers belonged to the NEA and AFT. This trend, as far as I can see, is not going to stop. Twenty years ago there was little a teacher could do to protect himself or herself against having classes that were too large or a teaching schedule that did not provide adequate time for preparation. One could, if one had the courage, complain to the principal, but if the principal chose to do nothing, that usually was the end of it. Today classes beyond a certain size consitute a violation of a contract. Administrators and school boards know this, and are often reluctant to deal with the grievance that would surely follow if the contract were violated. In this respect, there is truth in the assertion that better working conditions for teachers tend to improve the educational conditions for students. The problems emerge when union demands are so one-sided that meeting them in fact diminishes the quality of education children receive. For example, in some schools, even teachers who elect to teach an extra class or who choose to stay late to work on materials or projects they need for a class will have a grievance filed by the union representative in that school. In addition, the union members may make it difficult for such teachers to put in the extra effort, even if they want to. To provide "extra" service without extra pay is regarded as poor professional judgment: a form of economic liability for other teachers who are not so inclined.

Thus we do not have a black or white, clear-cut position regarding the virtues and liabilities of unionization but rather a picture filled with subtle complexities. Unions can ensure teachers that their rights as professionals will be safeguarded, that they will not longer need to occupy the role of a servant whose position in the community is low and whose prerogatives are few. Teachers need no longer agree to "carry the coal pail and be off the street by 9 P.M." as they were once expected to do. Professional affiliation, whether in formal unions such as the American Federation of Teachers (AFT) or in unionlike professonal organizations such as the National Education Assocation (NEA), provides a professional solidarity that can protect decent educational conditions for students as well as for teachers.

At the same time, unions and unionlike organizations can become so preoccupied with the financial well-being of their members that in their efforts to achieve greater economic benefits the educational well-being of students suffers.

Similar complexities pervade the situation with respect to declining enrollment. There was a time, not so long ago, when school districts such as Los Angeles had such a growth in student population that they had to open the equivalent of a new elementary school every four weeks. In such situations, attention to substantive educational improvement is likely to be marginal because teachers as well as school administrators are simply trying to keep their heads above water by finding places for new students who are entering each day. New buildings must be built, movable classrooms must be set up, new teachers must be hired, and in some cases split shifts must be instituted to cope with the increasing numbers of students. The major efforts and energies of the professional staff are devoted to organizational maintenance.

Now, for the first time in many years, school districts do not have these pressures bearing on them. Now there is time—at least theoretically—for reflection, for attention to substantive educational matters: what shall be taught, what ends shall be pursued, what kinds of programs shall be offered? For the first time, there is space available in schools to offer students opportunities to work in areas that previously were unavailable: art studios, science laboratories, teacher curriculum materials centers, photography workshops, and the like. Now there is time to engage in a professional dialogue on what is genuinely educational for students—and for the professional staff as well. Yet paradoxically, now that the time is available, the climate is not right. There are few school administrators who at present are inclined to be "innovative," a word overused in the past. Today the risks for serious innovation are too great for many school administrators. The climate is a conservative one; major concerns are expressed in demands for the so-called basic education. Thus, the educational opportunities that more space and fewer students provide are foregone in an educational climate that has little desire for experimentation.

Educational Consumerism

What is fascinating when one looks at the social forces affecting schooling is the fact the these forces do not operate independently. As in a living organism, they interact with each other as various groups and beliefs come into contact and into conflict. Educational consumerism—the public's demand to participate in educational policy formation and its demand that teachers and school administrators be held accountable—finds expression in legislation requiring that pseudoscientific methods be used to appraise teaching and learning. Teachers and administrators, although often skeptical about the appropriateness of such methods, believe that scientific objectivity is preferable to the tyranny of personal subjectivity. Meanwhile, teachers defend themselves through new forms of professional solidarity represented by unionization. The triangle is formed: school boards represent one apex, administrators a second, and teachers a third. In some communities, parents are forming "learners' associations" because they believe that school boards are too political, too responsive to a handful of vocal parents, too weak before powerful teacher groups, and therefore not sufficiently independent to protect the educational interest of their children. The plot thickens. The population decline exacerbates the situation further by reducing opportunities for mid-career teachers who once hoped for professional mobility through opportunities to become supervisors or administrators. At present those opportunities are vanishing. Finding increasing pressures in the environment and publicity from the press, teachers often look foward to sabbaticals, but, of course, these too are less available than they once were.

The logic of these interactions is clear, and from the standpoint of each group of players understandable. Groups who feel under attack are well advised to unify to protect their interests. Adults who are led to believe that there are clear-cut answers to complex questions (consider presidential debates and other political analyses provided by aspiring politicians) extend these expectations to the realm of schooling. When there are more teachers than needed and less funds than were once available, expectations for performance rise and the real educational priorities emerge.

The forces—the decline in student population, unionism, scientism, and educational consumerism—do not exhaust the major social forces affecting schooling. Two other forces must also be considered.

Influence of Textbooks

The enormous influence of the textbook cannot be left out when the forces influencing education are being identified. Regardless of what one might want to create with respect to curriculum materials, at present the textbook holds a place of unparalleled importance in influencing what shall be taught in the schools. The reasons for its importance are not difficult to determine. Consider the range of subject matters and tasks with which elementary school teachers must deal. The typical teacher teaching, say, the fourth grade in a self-contained classroom is responsible for the following: reading, language arts, arithmetic, social studies, science, music, art, and physical education. In addition to these areas, many elementary school teachers are responsible for health education, career awareness education, human relations education, and environmental education. Within language arts education they are responsible for penmanship, grammar, punctuation, spelling, and creative writing, as well as library skills. Given the variety of these demands, is it any wonder that many teachers— perhaps most—would welcome textbooks and other kinds of workbooks that in effect decide for them what children shall study, in what order, for what ends? Combine these demands with the expectation that teachers individualize instruction and there is even less wonder that prepackaged delivery systems should be regarded as time-savers; besides, it is consistent with our culture's proclivity for fast-food service and TV dinners. I say this not to be snide, but because it is reasonable to expect that the values that pervade the culture at large should manifest themselves in our schools. In fact, to expect otherwise would be unreasonable.

The textbook and its partner, the workbook, provide the curricular hub around which much of what is taught revolves. Their utility is straightforward. First, they provide a level of content expertise that few teachers possess. Second, they organize that content around topics that usually have some logic; in other words, the task of sequencing material for educational purposes is largely done—or at least believed to have been done. Third, the textbook provides both teachers and pupils with a kind of security: it lays out the journey that students and teachers will take; one knows what follows what and where it all ends. The coverage of this content becomes important because implicit in the textbook is the idea that if the children do not cover all of the material they are being cheated. Fourth, the textbook, which usually has a teacher's version, gives teachers the questions they should ask students, provides test items they can use, suggests activities students can engage in, and provides teachers with the correct answers. The workbook that frequently accompanies the textbook provides a simple way to keep children engaged, and if the culture of the classroom is such that using a workbook is an expected aspect of the school day, it is not likely that the teacher will meet with much resistance. In addition, individualization can be achieved by allowing all the students to work toward the same ends, using the same means at different grades. Individualization is thus converted into a form of depersonalized isolation for many students.

The importance of textbooks in defining content for students and teachers should not be underestimated. The inclusion of, say, the Westward movement means the exclusion of other topics, issues, or themes that might otherwise have been included. In addition, inclusion of a body of content in a textbook means, at the least, that students will have the opportunity to encounter it, and it is this opportunity that has the greatest impact on what is learned as a part of a formal curriculum. The absence of a content area increases the probability enormously that students will not learn "x," assuming that "x" is not likely to be learned in the culture outside of school.

Content-inclusion and content-exclusion policies—as they affect what students have an opportunity to learn—are related to the recent research on academic engaged time (or, as it is more often called, "time on task"). These decisions define the parameters of what students will encounter in a formal way as a matter of curriculum content. If secondary students of U.S. history do not study the First World War, there is little reason to expect them to know what it was, when it occurred, who was involved, and what relationship it had to the wars that have followed. But once a decision is made to include such material as a part of the curriculum, the extent to which students are actually engaged in studying such material—their academic engaged time—defines for some researchers what the students are likely to learn. Hence, textbook content and the definition of content areas within the curriculum are shaped by financial considerations that affect the learning opportunities students will have. Textbooks have other consequences as well, and these emerge in much more subtle ways.

Textbooks not only define a substantial proportion of the content, sequence, and aims of the curriculum. They also influence the way in which certain topics will be regarded. The most obvious illustration of this is found in the ways in which textbooks have treated women's and minorities' rights and other controversial issues. The kinds of biases subtly conveyed to young children about sex roles and minority groups have been so egregious that some states require that all state-provided texts be specifically screened for biases with regard to sex, race, ethnic group, religious orientation, and the like. Awareness of sex stereotyping and racial bias as far as white middle-class Americans is concerned is relatively recent. Thirty years ago one did not hear much about the covert messages in *Dick and Jane*. We have to thank the courage of vocal men and women who raised our consciousness regarding these matters. The initiation of change did not emanate from publishers, but from the kind of social pressure that groups supporting human rights brought to bear on the consciousness of America.

Yet, even today, sensitive issues are frequently defused or avoided altogether by textbook publishers seeking a wide market. Stockholders' investments are not to be jeopardized in the service of education. Darwin's theory of evolution is still approached with great caution among many publishing houses that seek to sell their books in communities whose religious beliefs are fundamentalist. Perhaps this is the way it ought to be. Perhaps there should be a compliant attitude toward the educational marketplace on the part of those in the education business. Yet I believe that a nation's capacity for growth is determined, at least in part, by the scope of intellectual tolerance it provides those whose beliefs deviate from the mainstream. The society that seeks stasis also seeks conformity. More, it seems to me, should be expected, even from those whose major motives are profit.

If reliance on the textbook and the workbook cultivates a form of pedagogical dependency on the part of teachers, if it inadvertently fosters stock curricular responses, and if at the same time the textbook meets real needs growing out of a situation that perhaps demands too much from teachers, what can be done about it? Perhaps under present-day conditions very little. If the expectations of educational ingenuity for a teacher teaching eight or nine subject areas in a self-contained classroom or for a high school teacher teaching five or six classes of 180 students are unrealistic, then what kinds of changes need to be made if teachers are to be pedagogically ingenious? It seems obvious that piecemeal, ad hoc changes are not likely to redefine or restructure the conditions that make the textbook a necessity. What is needed is a large, comprehensive view, one that appreciates the organic relationship between the schools and those who work in them plus those who provide the resources and support to make schooling possible in the first place. Furthermore, I believe that individual teachers and school administrators can make important differences in the educational lives that students lead. I do not believe that either teachers or school administrators must take to the streets to bring about improvement in the conditions of schooling. However, this is not to say that teachers should not be political; education itself is a political undertaking. It is to say that the larger picture should be appreciated and that incremental change can be brought about within the context of the larger views that one holds. In a society such as ours, there will always be a variety of images of the good educational life. The task is to understand the range of factors that influence their particular realization.

Federal Legislation and Court Decisions

The sixth major social force influencing the curriculum and schooling are those influences emanating from court decisions and state and federal legislation. Undoubtedly, the most significant of these occurred in 1954 with *Brown v. the Topeka Board of Education*. The importance of the court's judgment that separate schools, defined in terms of legal segregation, could not provide equal education to children was a landmark in social influence, but not because it rapidly desegregated schools; for it didn't. It was a landmark because it initiated the era in which the legal segregation of school children was considered a violation of constitutional rights by the highest court in the land. From this judgment, a host of other legal decisions was rendered that has served to generate other forces affecting schools and, hence, the programs that they provide. For instance, the busing of school children for purposes of racial desegregation could not have occurred without the Supreme Court's 1954 decision. The decision of the Los Angeles City Schools to assign teachers to schools on the basis of racial mix stems from the judgments made first in 1954.

There is little question that the desegregation of schools through busing, supported by legal decisions of the courts, has increased white flight from the cities to the suburbs. In 1950 the proportion of whites living in the ten largest cities in the United States was 86.5 per cent.[8] By 1970 it was 56.9 per cent.[9] It is as though the effect of the 1954 decision in practice was contrary to what the court intended. Because of the segregated character of housing in urban areas, schools have become increasingly segregated. Busing for purposes of desegregation.is seen by the court as a way to remedy the school segregation created by such housing patterns.

For blacks and for other racial minorities, the creation of all-black schools in all-black communities in urban areas has meant the opportunity to take hold of policies determining what such schools teach. In many black communities, the call for curricular change has been twofold. First, blacks want programs that help children recognize and appreciate the high achievements of members of their race; they want their children to know something about their cultural heritage both in this country and in Africa. The commercial achievements of the Ibo, the art of Benin and Ife, the high cultural achievements of ninth-century Africa, as well as the works of Marcus Garvey, Booker T. Washington, Ida Wells Barnett, Fannie Barrier Williams, W. E. B. Du Bois, and Martin Luther King, Jr., must have a place in the school curriculum. Second, many blacks want their children to have what they regard as a solid academic education. They do not want the school to provide a watered-down or condescending curriculum. They do not want second-class programs that lead to educational dead ends.

I will not attempt to discuss the distinctive aspirations and consequences of the legal decisions for each racial and ethnic group. I use the preceding example simply to illustrate how one kind of legal decision, a decision aimed at the desegregation of schools, had consequences for what schools teach and how they are staffed. Legal decisions about desegregation are by no means the only kinds of legal and legislative decisions affecting minorities and the schools.

Recent legislation that also pertains to minorities deals with the school districts' distinctive legal obligation to offer bilingual forms of intruction. Describing AB 1329, the *Legislative Counsels Digest* says:

> This bill would require each limited-English-speaking pupil, as defined, enrolled in the California public school system in kindergarten through 12 to receive instruction in a language understandable to the pupil which recognizes the pupil's primary language and teaches the pupil English. The specific type of instruction or program a school district is required to provide would depend on the presence of a specified number of non-English-speaking or limited-English-speaking pupils, as defined, in a school with the same primary language in the same grade level or with the same primary language, in the same age group, in a multigrade or ungraded instructional environment. The pupil's parent, parents, or guardian would have the right not to have their child or ward enrolled in such an educational program. Limited-English-speaking pupils in kindergarten through grade 12, who are not enrolled in one of these specified programs would be required to be individually evaluated and receive instructional services in an individual learning program.[10]

Obviously such legislation has important consequences in terms of who shall be hired as teachers, what types of materials shall be provided, and how the effectiveness of the school shall be determined. What schools provide and the mode of instruction teachers use must now take into account the linguistic and cultural backgrounds of the students the schools serve. To do less is to deny children and their parents the equal protection provided by the Constitution.

A decision rendered by the Court, one that will have profound consequences in California and elsewhere, is the Serrano-Priest decision. This decision holds that the range of financial resources among school districts in the state of California is so great as to deny children living in poor districts an opportunity to secure an education commensurate with that obtained by their peers living in districts whose tax base is strong. The court said the following:

> It is an inescapable fact that under SB 90 and AB 1267, the high-wealth school districts, with far greater funds available per pupil than are available to the low-wealth districts, have the distinct advantages of being able to pay

for, and select, the better-trained, better-educated and more experienced teachers, the ability to maintain smaller class sizes by employing more teachers, the ability to offer a wider selection of courses per day, the ability to provide better and a greater variety of supportive services such as more counselors and teacher aides, the ability to obtain the latest and best educational materials and equipment, and the ability to keep the educational plants in tip-top shape. These are the kinds of items that go into the making of a high-quality educational program that benefits the children of a school district that has a relatively high level of expenditures flowing from high assessed valuation of property.

Therefore, the court held that California's financing system for public elementary and secondary schools, including the changes made by SB 90 and AB 1267,

constitutes a violation of the California Constitution's equal-protection-of-the-laws provision. This violation results from the fact that, even though SB 90 and AB 1267 have made significant improvements in the foundation-program system of financing public schools, including the narrowing of expenditure differentials between school districts, there remain substantial disparities in per pupil revenues and expenditures between school districts because of the substantial variations in assessed valuations of taxable property between school districts. Under these circumstances, such per pupil expenditure differentials between school districts constitute a denial of equality of education and uniformity of treatment to the children of the low-wealth school districts and does not comply with the *Serrano* court's demand for statewide educational equality and uniformity of treatment for *all* the school children of California.[11]

The range in pupil expenditure among the one thousand school districts in California is from $1,030 to $2,874.[12] To rectify what the courts regard as an educational inequity, they have decreed that, after 1977, school districts in California that spent more than 150 per cent of the state-guaranteed foundation per child must share their locally voted tax increases with lower-wealth school districts. Equalization of educational opportunity will occur by diminishing the range and by raising the median levels for each child attending the public schools.

One consequence of this decision is to motivate parents who can afford to send their children to private schools to do so. No fiscal limit is prescribed for such schools. Thus, parents who have the resources may very well elect to have their children go to schools that can afford to offer the class size, the curricular scope, and the personal attention that the public schools cannot afford. Should large numbers of children from affluent families leave the public schools for the anticipated benefits provided by private schools, important curricular consequences are likely to occur. The public school will serve the lower, the upper lower, and the lower middle classes, and the upper middle and upper classes will be elsewhere. Another form of segregation will have been inadvertently created.

My task here is not to provide a substantive analysis of legal decisions bearing on education; that would require both another book and a set of skills I do not possess. I identify these legal decisions for illustrative purposes. The courts have always influenced educational practice: the laws of 1642 and 1647 in the Massachusetts Bay Colonies mandated reading instruction; the Morrill Act established land grant colleges; *Plessy v. Ferguson* established equal but separate schools; the child labor laws increased enormously the number of children attending the public schools. But during the last two decades, the number of significant decisions has increased. As the attitude of the nation has moved toward a greater concern, at least judicially, for the rights of individuals and minorities, court decisions supporting those rights have been rendered. These decisions, in turn, affect the schools. They influence where people choose to live, what monies will be made available, what schools are obliged to teach, how schools will be populated, and where teachers will be asked to work. Clearly, no one concerned with the planning of school programs or interested in the study of curriculum decision making can afford to neglect the parameters that court decisions establish. Combined with state legislation, such decisions constitute the sixth major social force influencing the character of school programs today.

I have thus far attempted to identify and describe some of the influences these six social forces have on what schools teach and what priorities and aims they hold. At present these six forces—decreasing enrollment, scientism, unionization, educational consumerism, textbooks, and court decisions—are the salient forces. But this does not mean that they are the forces that will always have a major impact on the content and direction of schooling. If the Russians land a person on Mars, we might very well have, as we did in 1957, a deluge of funds and a congressional mandate for more work in the sciences and mathematics. If drug abuse gets out of control, we may very well see a new emphasis in school programs dealing with the effects of drugs on individuals and on society. As an organ within a larger system, schools can isolate themselves from that system about as much as the liver can isolate itself from the heart and lungs. We cannot easily or accurately predict what new developments, crises, and the like will occur, either within our nation or outside of it; thus there will always be a need for those planning educational policies and programs to make judgments in context and to exercise practical wisdom. Such wisdom consists in part in being able to distinguish between the kind of data and information that one can get and reasonably depend on and the kind that one is not likely to be able to secure. The hunt for recipes, rules, formulas, and other nostrums to solve educational problems is a hopeless one. Contexts change and the configurations of schooling within those contexts also change. Sophisticated educational planning needs to consider both and to anticipate that "final" solutions will always be temporary at best. To say this is not to argue for slipshod thinking, bootstrap judgments, or seat-of-the-pants analyses. I am not arguing for innocence on the part of educational scholars or professionals. I am arguing against unrealistic aspirations, pseudoscience, and the host of other bandwagons, bad analogies,and panaceas that emerge in the field each year. We need, I believe, to recognize the contingent character of educational practice, to savor its complexity, and to be not afraid to use whatever artistry we can muster to deal with its problems. For the curriculum planner this means a life of continual uncertainty: the contingent is inherent in educational planning; yet these emerging contingencies need not provide a sense of discomfort but an array of opportunities to exercise one's imagination, to cope with new problems, to make qualitative judgments as well as theoretical ones. What one uses to deal with these contingencies are not pat procedures, but ideas, concepts, frames of reference. One must work with such tools as means guided by a flexible form of intelligence. In the next chapter some of those tools are presented, first by asking what *curriculum* means and then by examining some of the assumptions on which this book is based.

References

1. *Statistical Abstract of the United States,* U.S. Department of Commerce, Bureau of the Census, U.S. Govt. Printing Office, Washington, D. C., 1981.
2. Ibid.
3. Ibid.
4. *Time* Magazine, October 4, 1976.
5. T. M. Stinnet, *Turmoil in Teaching: A History of Organizational Struggle for America's Teacher,* Macmillan Publishing Co., Inc., New York, 1968.
6. Ibid.
7. Lorraine McDonnell, "Teacher Collective Bargaining and School Governance," working paper for the Rand Corporation, June 1976.
8. Joel S. Berk and Michael Kirst, *Federal Aid to Education,* Lexington Books, Toronto, 1972.
9. Ibid.
10. Assembly Bill No. 1329, California, 1976.
11. Thomas A. Shannon, "The Second *Serrano* Case—Important Implications for California School Finance," *Special Report,* Association of California School Administrators, Vol. 3, No. 15, n.d., p. 9.
12. Bureau of School Appointments and Reports, California State Board of Education, n.d.

3

Some Concepts, Distinctions, and Definitions

It is the creative image, vital and burgeoning, that we see before us in the work of these artists, and the new reality that takes shape is not the inhuman world of the machine but the passionate world of the imagination.

HERBERT READ

In the previous two chapters I have described the ways in which the field of curriculum has developed over the past eighty years. I have identified six of the several forces that are currently important in shaping curriculum priorities and forms of teaching that operate in our schools. But what I have not done is to provide an analysis of the term *curriculum*. It is to that task that we now turn.

The Meanings of Curriculum

Curriculum as "The Course to be Run"

As a term in educational discourse, *curriculum* is used in a wide variety of ways. It has a common-sense meaning as broad as "what schools teach" to as narrow as "a specific educational activity planned for a particular student at a particular point in time." Yet, the term itself warrants analysis. Initially, the word derives from the Latin word *currere*, meaning "the course to be run." This notion implies a track, a set of obstacles or tasks that an individual is to overcome, something that has a beginning and an end, something that one aims at completing. This metaphor of a racetrack is not altogether inappropriate. Schools have historically established "courses" of study through which a student is to pass. Successful completion of the course warrants a diploma or degree certifying competence. In other ways, too, the idea of a curriculum as a course filled with increasingly difficult obstacles is an appropriate metaphor. Schools have functioned historically as institutions that serve as a type of educational sieve, selecting the more from the less able at each higher level of schooling. Thus at the various levels of schooling there were—and are—increasingly difficult examinations to pass that open or close the doors to further schooling. The concept of the curriculum as the course to be run is one that fits one of the school's historical functions.

Curriculum as School Experiences

Curriculum has also been conceived of and defined as "all of the experiences the child has under the aegis of the school." This conception of curriculum was created by progressive educators during the 1920s to emphasize several beliefs that they consideed central to any adequate conception of education. First, they wished to remind other educators that the reality of a curriculum for a child was determined by the quality of the experience that the child had in the school and was not simply a piece of paper on which lesson plans were prepared. Although some degree of planning was considered appropriate and important, the real curriculum for the child, the one that made a difference in his or her life, was the curriculum that he or she experienced. Second, because children differ from one another in background, aptitudes, interests, and the like, the curriculum was never identical for different children. In a sense, one could have a curriculum only *after* it was experienced by a child. The curriculum was, one might say, to be discovered by looking backward. To their credit, these same progressive educators recognized that what children learn in school is wider than what goes on in classrooms and more varied than what teachers intend to teach. The experiences secured in the hallways and the playgrounds of the school were also influential aspects of educational life and should not, in their view, be separated from the responsibility educators should assume for guiding the child's experience in other aspects of school life. It was educational folly to care about the child's experience in the classroom but to disregard it in the playing fields. Indeed, progressive educators felt so strongly about the need to focus on the kind of experience the child had under the aegis of the school that they made a formal distinction between the curriculum, which was that experience (and hence each child had a different curriculum because his or her experience was never the same as another's), and the course of study, which was a written document that outlined the content, topics, and goals that a teacher was to use in planning the curriculum for a class or a child.

Whatever the conception of *curriculum*—and each of the two conceptions described has important consequences for the way in which one thinks about educational planning—it is clear that a school cannot function without some kind of program that it offers to its students. Whether that program is conceived as a preplanned series of educational hurdles over which the students must jump or the entire range of experiences a child has within the school, the school as an institution has some mission, some set of general aims or direction, and must provide some activities, programs, or means that engage those who work and study there. The design and evaluation of these activities and programs are what we are attempting to understand.

In considering such a plan or program, there are some distinctions we can make regarding the scale or scope of our attention and the location of our planning over time. In Figure 1 two continua are outlined, one dealing with *scale* and *scope*, the other dealing with *time*.

Levels of Curriculum Decision Making

The design of an educational program is influenced by a wide variety of decisions that range from the broadest types of educational policy bearing on the aims or content of educational programs to those decisions that

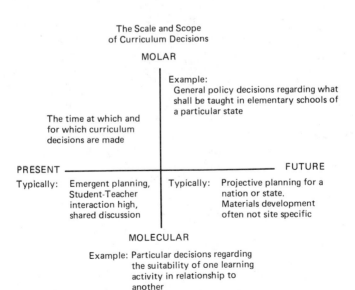

Figure 1

have to do with very specific, highly focused aspects of a particular program. Take, as an example, decisions about what the schools of a state should be required to teach. Virtually all states have in their education code a section that presecribes the content of instruction. In California, for example, it is required that schools teach reading, writing, arithmetic, social studies, art, music, physical education, and science at various grade levels.[1] The decisions that led to these policies were curriculum decisions. Some group (in this case the state board of education) decided that schools should devote their attention, energy, time, and resources to a particular array of subject matters. And in New York, books or the resources to purchase books to ensure adequate attention to these fields are also provided. This type of decision, like other large-scale decisions bearing directly on the program that the schools provide, exemplifies large-scale, molar curriculum decisions. The creation of a Computer Education Program, the decision to emphasize the so-called basic skills, and the formulation of policy bearing on the development of new approaches to the teaching of science all represent molar types of curriculum decision making. The point here is that when one talks about curriculum planning or about the design of educational programs, one might be referring to planning at this level: the planning of curriculum policy or curriculum priorities. Obviously, such policies do not exhaust the decisions that need to be made, nor are they adequate for operating programs within schools, but they do establish the directions and boundaries for other decisions.

At the other end of the continuum are highly specific molecular decisions bearing on a particular educational situation or a specific set of curriculum materials. Does *this* particular curriculum activity build on what has preceded it? Are *these* examples likely to be meaningful to *this* group of students? Does *this* content adequately exemplify the generalization the students are expected to learn? Does the visual quality of the material stimulate interest or is it dull and unimaginative? Questions such as these are asked by anyone or any group concerned with the creation of curriculum materials. Obviously, such decisions are almost always made after more general, molar curriculum decisions have been made, after one decides, for example, that a social studies program dealing with sex-role socialization is to be created.

The point here is that when one asks what kinds of problems curriculum decision makers encounter or curriculum scholars study, one can point to a range dealing with the most broadly based molar types of policy that bear on the shape and character of educational programs to the specific, molecular decisions that must inevitably be made within particular educational contexts.

In some countries, there is a formal separation between those who make the large-scale molar decisions about the content and aims of the curriculum and those who work within the parameters set by those decisions to create specific learning activities and teaching materials. In Norway, for example, a national board will appoint a national educational committee made up of prominent lay persons and scholars from various disciplines to outline the basic topics, content, and aims of the curriculum for children in primary and secondary schools. This committee, representing the views of the polity and the specialized scholarly competence of the school-related subject-matter disciplines, is responsible for formulating directions and priorities in school programs. By using lay people, the broad interests of the public are believed to be served, and by utilizing scholars from school-related subject fields the most up-to-date and important ideas within the subject-matter fields are likely to be identified. Once these molar decisions have been made, it is up to others to translate them into specific programs suitable for the interests and abilities of, say, ten-year-olds. The curriculum work here is to translate "new subject matter" into materials that will become useful for creating educational events in the classroom, something for which neither a university scholar, nor a lay person has any particular preparation.

What we see here is not only a division of labor but also a political separation based on perceived areas of competence. Educators responsible for curriculum development perform an essentially technical role in attempting to actualize the collective decisions of selected lay people and scholars. Educational expertise in such an arrangement is aimed at the translation and implementation of educational policy.

The horizontal axis in Figure 1 extends from decisions made in the present for the present to those that are made to serve as a kind of blueprint or guideline to be followed in the future. Some examples will be useful. Much curriculum work consists of the creation of curriculum materials that are intended to be used by teachers to help students acquire more sophisticated skills or ideas. Typically, such materials are developed for use over one or more academic years. *Man: A Course of Study,* the Physical Science Study Committee's materials, and *Science: A Process Approach* are curriculum materials designed to improve the quality of teaching and learning in elementary and secondary schools. These materials have been developed largely through federal funds by curriculum development groups and are intended for students and schools throughout the country. The general assumption underlying the work of these groups is that teachers would welcome such materials, that national groups having funds and access to nationally known scholars would be able to provide teachers with a higher quality of materials than teachers could create on their own, and that use of such materials over extended periods would result in a higher quality of learning in the fields represented by those materials.

The creation of such materials represents an effort to influence the educational futures of students and teachers for a substantial period of time. Content and sequence are determined; the roles of the teacher and students are defined well in advance of the particular context in which the materials are to be used. Like the minister of education in France who was said once to have boasted that at 11:00 on any morning he knew what all the children in French schools were studying, nationally developed materials often tend to formulate long-term educational plans that are intended to become the course to be run.

At the other end of the continuum is another image of curriculum planning, one that is not so well defined or so long-term in character. That model is perhaps best exemplified by the kind of curriculum planning that goes on in some progressive schools. This model conceives of planning as a joint effort between teacher and student, one that cultivates shared responsibility and that exploits emerging educational opportunities when they occur. At this end of the continuum, the teacher is likely to see his or her role as providing the kind of environment where new, unexpected interests can emerge and where "flexible purposing," to use Dewey's phrase, is both possible and desirable.[2]

The point here is simply that curriculum planning does not need to be long-term and preplanned weeks or months before engagement with students is to occur. The teacher who decides that in the next hour his or her class might find a discussion about the effects of robotics or space stations on our lives is engaged in curriculum planning, even though such decisions do not result in the creation of written plans, elaborate visual illustrations, or well-designed boxes of self-instructional materials.

In making this observation I am not writing a brief either for no planning or for elaborate materials. I am attempting to point out that the planning of curricula is something that everyone does who provides an educational program for students. Such planning may be short term or long term, shoddy or careful, tasteful or ugly, appropriate for students or inappropriate. Whatever the quality of the planning, we all decide what we will do or allow to occur. The extent and scope of such planning depend on the context in which one works and on the view of curriculum and teaching that one holds.

Let me review the major points I have tried to make thus far. First, I have tried to show how curriculum planning spans a range that extends from the broadest types of decision about the content, scope, and aims of programs serving millions of students to highly specific, molecular decisions made by curriculum development specialists wrestling with problems of sequence in a particular mathematics curriculum or by a teacher deciding on a particular project for a class or a student. Curriculum planning is not limited to a single level of specificity along the continuum.

Second, I have tried to show that the planning of curriculum is an inevitable aspect of schooling; it *must* occur. The significant question is how well it is done. One need not have long-range plans or printed materials to have an educational program. Teachers can use the present situation to develop short-term plans with or for their students. Time is a variable that will vary in relation to the context or the view one holds about what constitutes an appropriate teaching role.

Thus, if someone asks what curriculum specialists do, given these distinctions, it is possible to respond by saying that their responsibilities extend from the shaping of educational policy bearing on the aims and content of educational programs to work dealing with the design of specific elements within particular educational programs. Where and when are such decisions made? They are made by groups developing materials or creating educational policy intended to serve a large educational constituency as well as by teachers deciding on the value and appropriateness of a specific project or task for a particular group of students.

A Definition of Curriculum

Let's return for the moment to the concept *curriculum* and redefine it. *The curriculum of a school, or a course, or a classroom can be conceived of as a series of planned events that are intended to have educational consequences for one or more students.* In formulating this conception, or definition, of curriculum, I am not claiming to formulate a "real" definition. Curricula are not natural entities whose necessary and sufficient properties are capable of being discovered once and for all. What I am doing is formulating a concept of curriculum that I believe to be useful. Let's examine this concept more closely. A curriculum is a series of planned events. This implies that there will be more than one event planned, and this is typically the case, although theoretically one could have a single event constituting curriculum (but that likelihood is small). A second feature of the conception is that curricula are planned; someone must do something that has some aim, some purpose, some goal or objective, even though it might be highly diffuse or general. A third feature is that the intention be educational in character. Now this qualification, I readily admit, need not be a part of the definition of curriculum; one could formulate a curriculum designed to train bigots, burglars, or murderers, but within the context of this book and my purposes the qualification that the consequences are intended to be educational is important, if for no other reason than to highlight the fact that schools are supposed to be educational institutions. A fourth feature of this concept deals with the term *consequences*. Educational events or activities do much more than what is intended; they influence people in a wide variety of ways. Furthermore, I want to leave room for the teacher or curriculum developer to plan activities or events that do not have specific, highly predictable goals or objectives. I want to leave room for planning if events that appear to be educationally fruitful but whose specific consequences for different students might not be known in advance. The term *consequences* is sufficiently wide to allow for such planning. In other words, a curriculum is a program that is intentionally designed to engage students in activities or events that will have educational benefits for them. Some of these benefits might be delineated or specified in advance in operational terms; others will be general, broad, and diffuse, but in part capable of being recognized subsequent to the activity. Like other issues in this book, this issue—the character of educational goals—will be discussed in greater detail later.

When one is engaged in long-term planning and has formulated an array of goals or objectives, designed materials of various sorts, created learning activities to be used in the classroom, and prepared visual and auditory resources, it is possible to inspect the curriculum to see what its contents are and how they have been related. The curriculum in this context has a physical existence; it is embodied in a set of materials. These materials can be the subject of analysis and criticism in a measure similar to the criticism applied to books, paintings, symphonies, architecture, and the like. To be sure, the criteria will differ, but the principle of being able to criticize what has been created is the same.

The physical existence of such materials also means that they can be transported; the same curriculum can be used in different classrooms and in different schools. School administrators can discuss the strengths and weaknesses of the curriculum. Parents can inspect it and students can use it.

But curriculum planning need not result in the creation of physical materials. The teacher whose plans are in his or her mind alone might have planned a curriculum of an excellent sort, but because the plans are not public, they can neither be shifted about, inspected, nor shared with others. The only way to appraise the quality of the curriculum is to watch the teacher and the students in the class. One must attend to the attributes as they unfold, make judgments about the significance of the content as it is revealed, and appraise the quality of the resources as they are used. One must make one's judgment by observing the curriculum in use. For the teacher who does not make extensive or long-term plans, even of a mental sort, the curriculum may in fact be planned in process. In this situation, it is not simply that plans have been made but have not been written down; in this situation, the teacher plans in process. What the teacher uses are initiating activities, but such activities are employed simply to get the ball rolling, to begin a process whose course is shaped in the conduct of teaching.

The Intended and Operational Curriculum

The differences between what is planned in the way of aims, content, activities, and sequence and what actually transpires in the classroom can be formalized into a distinction between *the intended* and *the operational* curriculum. The intended curriculum is like the course of study: it is that which is planned. Such plans can, as I have already indicated, be inspected, critiqued, revised, and transported to a multitude of locations. The operational curriculum is the unique set of events that transpire within a classroom. It is what occurs between teachers and students and between students and students. To critique or appraise the operational curriculum requires one to be in a position to observe what classroom activities actually unfold. Inspection of plans or of the intended curriculum is no assurance that those plans are actualized.

In a variety of ways, it is useful to distinguish between the intended and the operational curriculum. If in a school or classroom there is an educational problem concerning what students are or are not learning, one can ask whether the source of the problem resides in the curriculum as it is intended or as it is operationalized. It might be the case that the intended curriculum is so rigidly structured that it negatively influences the teacher's operational curriculum. Alternatively, though the intended curriculum might be judged excellent on relevant criteria the operational curriculum may not resemble what was intended. Because the examinations that a school district employs purportedly reflect the intended, rather than the operational curriculum, the students do poorly. What one does, therefore, is either reduce the discrepancy between what was intended and what was operationalized or one creates an examination system that more adequately reflects what was actually taught.

It is interesting to note that in efforts to upgrade the educational quality of the schools, "solutions" are often provided that take the form of "new courses in subject X or Y," or more instructional time in courses already being taught. Yet it is clear that more of something that is badly handled will be educationally counterproductive. If both the intended and operational curriculum are poor in quality, more of such quality will cause impoverishment rather than enrichment of education. Although one wants to know about the quality and character of what is intended, one also wants to know—and this is extremely important—what the operational curriculum is in the classroom. This is a complex, arduous, and demanding task that requires one to be in a position to see and understand what actually goes on in classrooms. Yet this method is of extreme importance for improving the quality of education. I will have more to say about how such observations might be made in Chapter 13. At this point it is important to understand the distinction between the intended and the operational curriculum and to appreciate the implications of this distinction for improving curriculum and teaching.

Although curriculum and teaching are regarded as separate aspects of educational practice, the distinctions between them are often difficult to make when one examines each carefully. Nevertheless, the general distinction between curriculum and teaching is useful, as I will discuss later in this book, even though there are cases in which the distinction between the two is not clear.

It might be noted that the planning of a curriculum on a long-term basis with clear specifications regarding its use can be compared to the creation of a score written by a composer or the plans prepared by an architect. Although these two examples are much more specific and detailed than what most curricula provide, the relationship between the composer and the pianist or the architect and the builder has similarities to that between the curriculum planner and the teacher. In each case the planner designs, and the performance is executed within the constraints of the design. And in each case the performers have degrees of freedom with which to interpret the plans that have been made. One can inspect the score, the architectural specifications, and the curriculum as planned and assess the ways in which those plans have been executed.

For those using a more emergent model of curriculum planning—the model in which plans are created in process—activities are much closer to the work of the painter or poet. In this model, decisions to do one thing rather than another are decisions that can be made only by considering options as they develop, by "reading" the situation, by exploiting the adventitious, and by allowing intentions to grow out of action rather than requiring them to precede it. This is the way a great many artists as well as teachers work. To work this way is not necessarily a mark of incompetence but could be the result of a preference for a particular way of working, the result of a considered view of one's professional role, or a sign of commitment to a particular image of education. In such a model of curriculum planning one must place a good deal of faith in the ability of the teacher. To work this way requires, I believe, a great deal of experience, competence, and confidence as a teacher. While the availability of a curriculum that has been well planned and accompanied by interesting and attractive resources for in-classroom use breeds confidence that what will be offered will be worth the student's time and effort, curriculum materials and particularly that species of materials called curriculum guides are often disregarded by teachers. The existence of a well-planned body of curriculum material is no guarantee that they will be used effectively or with enthusiasm in the classroom. To know that, there is no substitute for direct observation in the classroom.

Thus, when we talk about "the curriculum," we can mean that body of material that is planned in advance of classroom use and that is designed to help students learn some content, acquire some skills, develop some beliefs, or have some valued type of experience. We call this curriculum the *intended curriculum*. We also mean by the term *curriculum* those activities that occur in the classroom, taking into consideration the materials, content, and events in which students are engaged. We refer to this curriculum as the *operational curriculum*. Approaches to the former can be made by inspecting the materials and plans that have been formulated. Approaches to the latter can be made only by directly observing the classroom itself.

Normative and Descriptive Curriculum Theory

When we speak of theory we can distinguish between two types. Normative theory is concerned with the articulation and justification of a set of values. Its aim is to provide a persuasive case for the value of a particular end or state of being. In education, normative theory argues the case for certain educational goals on the basis that the goals themselves are intrinsically valuable. Thus, a theory of education that argues that education should aim at fostering the growth of the individual and that defines growth as the development of those modes of intelligence that enable individuals to secure meaning from experience is normative in character. Such a statement or position becomes theoretical as it presents to the world a coherent set of reasons and concepts that justifies its claims. Although one could ask for further justifications for the claim that education should be conceived of as a process concerned with fostering growth, once having received such justification, further justification leads either to an infinite regress or to a circular argument. Eventually, one arrives at value assumptions that are made rather than justified.

Normative Theory in Education

In educational theory in general, and in curriculum theory in particular, normative ideas are central. Education itself is a normative enterprise— that is, it is concerned with the realization of aims that are considered worthwhile. Thus, educational activities are not simply concerned with learning, because what a person learns might have negative consequences for his or her development. What makes experience educational is its participation in a set of values. To the extent to which those experiences participate in those values, they are educational. To the extent to which they contradict those values, they are miseducational.

For the planning of curricula, normative commitments are also crucial. Such commitments, or images of educational virtue, influence what is regarded as relevant in planning and what data are considered important in making curriculum decisions. Without such values, neither education nor curriculum has a rudder. Now it should be noted that "theoretical" in the context of normative theory is not the same as a bald statement of values or belief: it is the coherent articulation of a view and a presentation of the grounds for holding it. Such theory is not necessarily predictive and need not employ scientifically verified facts to sustain it. What one looks for is coherence. The value orientations to curriculum that will be presented in the next chapter are examples of such theoretical views.

In saying that normative theory is not simply a bald statement of what someone values, I am not implying that there are necessary and sufficient conditions that can be used as criteria for determining whether a statement is theoretical. Normative theory extends from general statements and beliefs to highly elaborate efforts to justify a view of what is good or beautiful. Thus, the roots of such theory begin as humans speculate on what is good in life and worth achieving. Commonsensically, we call such speculation philosophies of life, and although few philosophers would consider such commonsense speculation philosophical in the technical or professional sense, the difference is one of degree rather than kind.

To say this is not to equate the commonsense theorizing that all of us do with the heady work of a Paul Tillich, Plato, Boyde Bode, or John Dewey. It is to recognize that the theoretical construction of value is not the sole province of those who are professional philosophers but is a part of the intellectual activity of ordinary men and women. The differences between the two reside in consistency, subtlety, scope, and coherence. These are differences that distinguish levels of quality rather than differences in kind.

Education Not the Same as Schooling

I said earlier that normative theory is critical for education, and this point is worth emphasizing. Education is not the same as schooling, nor is it the same as learning. One can learn many things that are personally and socially dysfunctional: to become neurotic, fearful of people, a torturer, a racist, and the like. In each case, learning has taken place, but whether one considers such learning an instance of education depends on a normative theory of education. The claim that some groups or individuals do or would regard such learning as educational is not in dispute. This might be true, but to make such a claim is not to make a value statement but to describe a social fact. The question is whether one ought to regard such forms of learning as educational. Would you, given your normative theory of education, regard becoming neurotic or becoming a torturer an instance of education? I would not.

Without some view of what counts as education, one is in no position whatsoever to make judgments about the educational quality of the processes of schooling or their consequences. One cannot know whether research conclusions have any relevance to educational practice. One has no basis for appraising the educational merits of teaching. John Dewey makes this point very well, when he says the following:

> That a man may grow in efficiency as a burglar, as a gangster, or as a corrupt politician, cannot be doubted. But from the standpoint of growth as education and education as growth, the question is whether growth in this direction promotes or retards growth in general. Does this form of growth create conditions for further growth, or does it set up conditions that shut off the person who has grown in this particular direction from the occasions, stimuli, and opportunities for continuing growth in new directions? What is the effect of growth in a special direction upon the attitudes and habits which alone open up avenues for development in other lines? I shall leave you to answer these questions, saying simply that when and only when development in a particular line conduces to continuing growth does it answer to the criterion of education as growing. For the conception is one that must find universal and not specialized limited application.[3]

Education, Noneducation, and Miseducation

Dewey goes on to distinguish between three types of experience: those that are *educational, noneducational,* and *miseducational.*[4] Education experiences are those, as I have suggested earlier, that contribute to the individual's growth. Growth, for Dewey, represents the extension of human intelligence, the increase in the organism's ability to secure meaning from experience and to act in ways that are instrumental to the achievement of inherently worthwhile ends. Noneducational experiences are those that are simply undergone and have no siginificant effect on the individual one way or the other. There are many such experiences undergone each day— the activities of habit—that punctuate our lives. Such experiences are had but without significant effect one way or another on our growth. We tie our shoes, walk across the room, drive our car, without contributing to or detracting from our growth.

Miseducational experiences are those that thwart or hamper our ability to have further experiences or to cope intelligently with problems in a particular arena of activity. In schooling, many students develop disinclinations to encounter certain fields of study. Their experience, say in mathematics, has been so unfortunate and uncomfortable that they avoid that field of study whenever it is their option to do so. For such students, mathematics was miseducational. It closed rather than opened them up to the intellectual and aesthetic possibilities of the field.

More radical examples of miseducational experience are found in the acquisition of phobias that children are prone to because of the anxieties of their parents. Such phobias might deal with animals, airplanes, failure, and sex. Children learn to become fearful and become incompetent in the areas in which these phobias function. Their experience constrains rather than expands the possibilities that life makes available. In these areas, miseducational experience results in a deep sense of personal discomfort.

Dewey's writings are a prime example of normative theory. He conceptualizes a value, namely growth, and then justifies its significance in argument. He locates the sources of growth in experience and then indicates the relevance of different types of experience for education. The position is thought through, well argued, and has practical consequences for teaching and curriculum planning. Such theory, rooted as it is in a metaphor of a growing organism, shapes our view of what is appropriate and inappropriate in educational practice. The appeal of Dewey's theory has been extraordinary for educators throughout the world, but it is not only the normative theory that appeals, and in the following chapter other conceptions of educational value will be presented.

Descriptive Theory

Thus far, I have spoken of normative theory in education and curriculum, but what of descriptive theory, those statements or concepts that attempt to explain, usually through their power to predict, the events of the world? Descriptive theory with respect to the sciences is perhaps best exemplified in the natural sciences: They have provided the model that the social scientists have attempted to emulate. In the natural sciences, the task has been both to give an account of and to account for a set of phenomena. "What has occurred and how?" are major questions theorists ask. With a theory that is useful, one can anticipate the future; one knows what to expect given some set of conditions or circumstances. In some cases, such theory has made it possible not only to predict, but to control—although this is not always achieved. While scientists are able to land a spacecraft on Mars, astronomical theory is not yet able to control the path of stars. In the field of curriculum, theory in no way approaches that level of power, and for good reasons. Educational matters are value laden in ways that physics is not. In education, what one seeks is not the explanation of what is, but the achievement of what ought to be. Nucleii, as far as anyone knows, do not form purposes or have intentions: people do. Increasingly, social scientists are coming to appreciate the distinctive characteristics of theory in dealing with the human as a social creature and the institutions humans create. Lee Cronbach, a social scientist who recognizes this difference, writes the following:

> Social scientists are rightly proud of the discipline we draw from the natural science side of our ancestry. Scientific discipline is what we uniquely add to the time-honored ways of studying man. Too narrow an identification with

science, however, has fixed our eyes upon an inappropriate goal. The goal of our work, I have argued here, is not to amass generalizations atop which a theoretical tower can someday be erected (cf. Scriven, 1959b, p. 471). The special task of the social scientist in each generation is to pin down the contemporary facts. Beyond that, he shares with the humanistic scholar and the artist in the effort to gain insight into contemporary relationships and to realign the culture's view of man with present realities. To know man as he is is no mean aspiration.[5]

What I believe descriptive theory in curriculum has to provide primarily are concepts that enable us to make more subtle and powerful distinctions. At times, such theory might lead to empirical generalizations that can be considered in making particular decisions for specific circumstances, but such generalizations always need to be applied and interpreted with caution, not as rules but as considerations. No set of generalizations will adequately treat the particular characteristics of specific situations.

In the field of curriculum, descriptive theory has largely been borrowed from psychology. Theories of reinforcement, cognition, perception, learning, sequence, problem solving, and the like have influenced the ways in which curriculum theorists have conceptualized curriculum. Indeed, Dewey himself was greatly influenced by the descriptive theoretical work of Darwin. Dewey's conception of man is biological, as is Piaget's, whereas Bobbitt, particularly in his early work, attempted to apply the theories of scientific management to curriculum and teaching in order to increase the efficiency of schools. What we see both in Dewey and in Bobbitt is the influence descriptive theory has had on their normative theory of education. Once norms are formed, these norms in turn influence the kinds of descriptive data one uses to support one's norms. In short, a dialectic between the normative and the descriptive occurs.

To talk about the differences between normative and descriptive theory implies that the two are wholly distinctive. This is not the case. Normative theory is buttressed by descriptive claims emanating from descriptive theory: Dewey's theory of education is a case in point, as I have indicated. The way in which we understand the world to be influences our conception of its possibilities and therefore shapes our aspirations.

Descriptive theory is in a subtle but important sense pervaded by normative theory because the methods of inquiry we choose and the criteria we choose to apply to test truth-claims reflect beliefs about the nature of knowledge. These beliefs are basically value judgments. Those embracing a different conception of knowledge will employ different methods of inquiry and may therefore come to different conclusions about the world. In short, epistemological commitments reflect a set of values. Theory in curriculum is therefore of two types, each of which penetrates the other: normative and descriptive. Normative theory articulates the values to which the educational program is directed. Descriptive theory provides the concepts and generalizations that are taken into account in planning the school program.

Theory, however, is ideational and problems of curriculum development practical. It is important to distinguish between the ideas one works with and the practical act of constructing an educational program. Curriculum development is the process through which those ideas are transformed by an act of educational imagination. I say imagination because no theory—either normative or descriptive—prescribes what is appropriate for different students. Ideas are guides; they are not recipes. One works with them; one does not follow them. To engage in curriculum development, one must put together much more than any of the theories can provide either individually or collectively. Schwab makes this point well when he writes:

> A curriculum grounded in but one or a few subsubjects of the social sciences is indefensible; contributions from all are required. There is no forseeable hope of a unified theory in the immediate or middle future, nor of a meta-theory which will tell us how to put those subsubjects together or order them in a fixed hierarchy of importance to the problems of curriculum.[6]

It should also be noted that the competencies needed to design curricula are not identical with those needed to create sophisticated and useful curriculum theory. Aptitude differences exist among individuals, and the kind of experience one needs in each realm of activity differs. Theoretical training requires intensive study of relevant disciplines within philosophy and the social sciences and the critical analysis of one's written work by competent critics. The skills of curriculum development are acquired in the act of designing curricula and in experiencing firsthand the problems of transforming ideas into educational materials and events. Those skills include the ability to work with others, the ability to deal with the complexities of practical deliberation, the ability to establish distance between one's work and oneself in order to see it more clearly, and the ability to envisage the way in which activities might function within a classroom. It requires the ability to appreciate the demands that a task makes on teachers and students and to be able to judge how much guidance they might need to engage in that task. Such skills are not trivial, nor are they non-intellectual. They are demanding, requiring a sense of taste and style and the ability to deal with frustration.

What would a comprehensive, scientifically descriptive theory of curriculum look like if we had one? Such a theory would identify relevant phenomena in the planning of a curriculum. It would provide guidelines for relating these phenomena to each other so that they were maximally effective with a group of students, given a description of the student's characteristics. And it would provide a credible explanation of why the relationships between the curriculum and the student were effective for realizing particular ends. Such a theory would, in short, enable the curriculum developer to design curricula that were optimally suited to particular students, given some view of what was educationally desirable. In addition, such theory, if it were necessary for its efficacy, would specify the context conditions that would need to be obtained if the theory were to operate. If the theory were entirely comprehensive, it would provide such guidance for different subject matters, disciplines, or fields of study, and it would be able to accommodate the developmental levels and other relevant personal characteristics of students.

One does not have to exhaust the literature in curriculum to recognize that such theory is nowhere to be found. Instead, we have concepts, rules of thumb, perspectives, and frames of reference. We have theoretical ideas that are to be used flexibly rather than the equivalent of Boyle's Law or Bohr's atom. I believe man's ingenuity and need for forming his own purposes, his curiosity, and his irascibility foreclose on the possiblity of developing a theory of curriculum comparable to that of atomic particles. We are "condemned" to a life of exciting uncertainty in which the flexible use of intelligence is our most potent tool.

Curriculum Diffusion

The task of developing curriculum materials and disseminating them to schools does not insure that such materials will be used. The problem of creating ways in which such resources will be used is a problem concerned with curriculum diffusion. The concept of diffusion suggests that ideas and materials affecting school programs need in some way enter the mainstream of schooling, that the process has something of an organic character to it, and that it is not likely to occur if it is treated as a mechanical or bureaucratic task or something that will occur automatically simply because good materials are available. I mention the connotative implication of the term *diffusion* because for many years the term that was employed to describe this process was *curriculum installation. Installation* suggests something akin to changing a muffler or air cleaner on an automobile: one first designs and produces some artifact and one then installs it onto some ongoing enterprise. Curriculum change does not occur in such ways. Teachers have their own priorities, the school posseses its own equilibrium, and the organization has numerous ways of providing superficial accommodations to foreign intruders without making any significant alteration in what it has been doing. To regard educational change—and particularly curriculum change—as something analogous to installing a mechanical device onto another mechanical device is to reveal a profound naivete about how schools operate. Hence, *diffusion,* a softer word, is much more appropriate than *installation.* But it is not simply the word that is at issue, but rather the idea behind the word: the improvement of educational practice is a process that is adaptive in character. In this adaptive process, both the classrooms *and* the materials undergo change. To appreciate the mutually adaptive character of curriculum change is also to recognize that the one widely held aspiration of psychologists and curriculum developers to produce what was called "teacher proof" curriculum is, like the concept of installation, similarly faulty. The idea that it is both possible and desirable to develop curriculum materials that will withstand the most incompetent teachers, or that it is desirable to develop methods that do not require the use of the teacher's judgment, is to demean teachers and to expect them to function as automatons rather than as professionals who have a stake in what they are doing in classrooms.

In Chapter 2, I identify a continuum describing the scope and scale of curriculum decision-making. I point out that at one end of the continuum curriculum decisions are made at very general levels of abstraction that are intended to shape educational policies. At the other end of the continuum, decisions are made about specific curriculum tasks such as the suitability of a particular idea or skill within a sequence of other ideas or skills that are being defined within a body of curriculum materials. Curriculum diffusion can take place at virtually every level, from the most general to the most specific, at which curriculum decision-making occurs. For example, assume that the state of New York wanted to encourage school districts to develop programs that teach students to use microcomputers There is much in the way of curriculum diffusion that the state could do to increase the probability that school districts would consider this area. First, high-ranking officials could use the mass media to announce publicly the importance of microcomputers to the school curriculum. Second, the state could sponsor conferences and workshops to discuss the uses of the computer in the schools and to sensitize educators further to its importance. Third, it could encourage local computer industries to provide computers to schools, to offer workshops to teachers, and to provide funds for summer study. Incentives and stimulation would be generated within the state as a result of a general policy position on an important curriculum issue. Such activities heighten consciousness, they stimulate the public, and, in the process, they diffuse the idea that in this electronic age students who will spend most of their future in the twenty-first century should become literate in the tools that will be used.

The Use of State Curriculum Frameworks

There are other ways in which curricula are diffused in the schools. One of these is through state curriculum frameworks within each of the subject areas of the school curriculum. In California, a new state framework for curriculum development within a particular field is produced every five years. This framework is generally the product of a committee appointed by the state superintendent of public instruction. The committee usually includes school administrators, teachers, university professors, and subject specialists from the schools. It meets on a regular basis over three or four years to develop a framework designed to encourage local school administrators and teacher-training institutions to revise the program currently in effect so that it is consistent with the ideas and general philosophy of the new framework. For example, the 1982 social studies framework for the schools in California places emphasis on using the humanities as both a means and as a content for teaching the social studies. The framework provides a theoretical rationale for this new approach to social studies education. It identifies leading concepts and generalizations from fields in the humanities that are relevant to social studies education. It also provides examples that illustrate how these ideas can be used in classrooms. It does not—and frameworks typically do not—constitute a curriculum that school districts can adopt. It provides a structure, a rationale, a set of examples and, perhaps most of all, an orientation to the teaching of a particular field or collection of fields. It is intended to infuse new ideas within existing curricula. It does this by serving as a centerpiece for conferences sponsored by the state, by the fact that it enjoys the endorsement of the state board of education and the superintendent of public instruction, and because school administrators often wish to comply with the expectations of their superordinates.

Use of Textbooks and Curricular Materials

Still another way in which new ideas enter the curriculum of schools is when states adopt or endorse textbooks and other educational materials.

About every five years, many states review for the purposes of adoption or endorsement the textbooks that it provides to local school districts. The state reviews, for example, such texts to identify and proscribe bias in race, sex, ethnicity, and religion. It also reviews such texts to insure that their content in other ways is not objectionable, that reading levels are appropriate, and that the content includes a balanced political point of view. The adoption or endorsement of a book is an extremely important decision for textbook publishers. The amount spent on textbooks for elementary and secondary schools and for colleges in the United States in 1980 was estimated at 2 billion dollars. Even a small share of the market is significant. But it is also significant for teachers and students. Because textbooks are frequently the hub around which school programs revolve, the choice of a textbook and the endorsement of the state in facilitating its use is a significant factor in the diffusion of new ideas in the curriculum.

School districts also diffuse ideas into school programs by adopting existing commercial curriculum materials. Such decisions influence rather directly the ideas students encounter at school. The adoption of a reading series by the Los Angeles School District can have an impact upon 300,000 students. In New York, it can influence 500,000 students. Thus, to choose a new program to be used in mathematics, reading, or even in the arts is to influence what teachers are likely to do and to define to some degree what students will study. When the new math was adopted by school districts across the country, elementary and secondary school students had access to mathematics curricula that stressed understanding of mathematical principles more than they stressed skill in computation. What became educationally important was not so much whether students got the right answer to mathematical problems. but rather whether they understood the operations and the assumptions upon which those operations were built. Grasping the meaning of set theory was more significant than knowing the number facts. Yet, the power of such programs is mediated by a teacher. The teacher's comprehension of the materials, the teacher's commitment to the program, and the teacher's sensitivity and support of the spirit of the curriculum is extremely important in affecting the extent to which materials will have educational efficacy.

Because commercial publishers recognize that the teacher is such an important agent in mediating their programs, many of the large publishing houses employ former teachers to "in-service" classroom teachers in those school districts that adopt their materials. These commercial publishers employ dozens of such people to travel across the nation to conduct workshops for teachers and to maintain rapport with school administrators. Their general aim is to maintain their psychological presence within the schools and to provide the kind of guidance regarding their materials that many school districts could not otherwise provide. In the end both education and profits are to be enhanced.

Another means for curriculum diffusion emanates from the district itself. A school district may engage teachers in developing its own materials and in designing its own curricula for purposes that are especially relevant to the educational values of the district. For example, in a district that serves an educationally diverse population, teachers were employed to develop a body of curriculum materials that presented to students the history of ethnic immigration in that particular community. Oral histories from the eldest of community residents were taken; old photograph albums, newspapers, and magazines were secured and reproduced; and letters and other paraphernalia that would enhance children's understanding of the history of the area were secured. The materials were then used as resources that students could study. Students were encouraged to take their own oral histories of their own family, and to put together reports describing the immigration of people from other areas to the area in which they now live. In short, the district, largely motivated by the work of its multicultural committee, made the resources available to teachers to prepare curricula that had special relevance for the district. In most large school districts some curriculum development is currently underway.

There are other factors as well that serve to diffuse curriculum to the schools. One of these is the policy that some districts have of sending teachers, and particularly curriculum consultants, to conventions and conferences to find out what is current within their particular specialty. In all of the large state and national conferences, publishers display their wares: new curricula, new textbooks, new instructional devices. Symposia are presented on new approaches to teaching X, Y, or Z. Speeches are given advocating the virtues of a new approach to science, or to the fine arts. Workshops are held that introduce teachers to new teaching techniques. Historically school boards and school administrators have recognized the importance of such conferences for motivating their staff and for keeping in touch with what is educationally current.

Curriculum diffusion, or more broadly curriculum change, occurs in still other ways. When the state university system alters entrance requirements, curriculum change at the local high school is likely to occur. This in turn brings about change at the middle school level and at the elementary school level as well. School districts are particularly sensitive to the requirements set by universities and colleges. Hence, when the state university says that three rather than two years of mathematics are required for admission, in most states the school district has a legal obligation to offer programs that allow students to meet the entrance requirements of the state university. But even if the requirement were not a legal one, the fact that it is a requirement would be reason enough for most districts to provide such courses within their programs. Furthermore, such new university entrance requirements would, de facto, be required courses of study for college-bound students.

Another source of curriculum change in the schools is related to the timetable. Because of fiscal constraints, some school districts are reducing the number of periods per day that they can offer to students. The reduction may be from a seven-period day to a six-period day. What this reduction does is effectively to eliminate courses in the fine arts and in other areas that are regarded as desirable but not essential. The effect is, of course, to reduce the student's access to educational opportunity, a loss that is particularly severe for those students whose aptitudes and interests are in the areas that are cut from the program. When such areas are eliminated, the need for teachers in these areas is similarly diminished, as is the need for curriculum consultants or supervisors in those areas. In very little time, the presence of the area within the district is virtually eliminated: the so-called nonessential curricula gradually come to be regarded as being the responsibility of other agencies.

In the last analysis, it is what teachers do in classrooms and what students experience that define the educational process. The character of this process might initiate with a vague image of a new way of teaching biology or art or the study of American political behavior. That image might eventually get transformed into a body of handsome resources, well-written prose, and imaginatively conceived opportunities for learning. But such materials, like a brilliantly composed musical score, need skillful and sensitive interpretation and a group of people who can interact meaningfully with what has been created. If any of these components is missing, the process fails. If the score is poor, it is not worth playing. If the performance is poor, it will be poorly received. If the audience is ill-prepared to deal with it, it will fall on deaf ears. Composers need competent performers and performers need an appreciative audience. In education, similar relationships hold. The teacher might be, in some models of education, his or her own composer, but the need for competent performance, if not an artistic one, still exists. And the fit between the teacher's "score" and the students remains as critical in the classroom as it is in the concert hall—probably even more so.

References

1. California Education Code: Statutes (1976), Sacramento: Department of General Services, Documents Section, 1967.
2. John Dewey, *Experience and Education,* Macmillan Publishing Co., Inc., New York, 1938.
3. Ibid, pp. 28–29.
4. Ibid, passim.
5. Lee Cronbach, "Beyond the Two Disciplines of Scientific Psychology," *The American Psychologist,* Vol. 30, No. 2, February 1975, p. 126.
6. Joseph Schwab, "The Practical: A Language for Curriculum," *School Review,* Vol. 78, No. V, November 1969, p. 10.

4

Five Basic Orientations
to the Curriculum

*The subject which involves all other subjects, and therefore the
subject in which education should culminate, is the Theory and
Practice of Education.*

HERBERT SPENCER

The content and aims of school programs have long been the subject of
debate. In these debates, differences seldom emerge in the form of
abstract issues or bald-faced confrontations of competing ideologies.Most
often they emerge in the form of differences about specific practical matters: Should children be given letter grades? Should children be assigned
to tracks according to their ability in school subjects? Should corporal punishment be used or threatened in school? Should the three R's be emphasized, and should children be kept back if they do not achieve grade-level
standards?

Although the arguments that these questions elicit seldom broaden into
an examination of principles, it is important for those concerned with
designing educational programs to see behind the issues, to go beyond the
immediate controversy, to penetrate the current debate in order to locate
the values and premises behind the questions.

It is my contention that through such analysis the contending parties
will have a clearer and more adequate basis for dealing with what is at
issue. Furthermore, an awareness of the various orientations to schooling
expands one's options in curriculum planning and thus contributes to

one's degree of professional freedom. In this chapter, a framework is presented for the description of five important curriculum orientations. In addition, it provides examples to indicate how these orientations manifest themselves in the classroom.

The function of these descriptions is to make vivid the major ways in which individuals think about the aims and content of the curriculum, the role that teachers should play in schools, and the criteria that should be applied to assess the quality of schooling. Each of these five major orientations is described more pointedly than one is likely to find in any school; most schools and most debates about the aims or forms of education are not nearly as clearly defined as these descriptions suggest. I have elected to make them vivid (and in this regard somewhat oversimplified) so that their very important features can be grasped more easily than if their details were either extremely subtle or overly complex. Once one understands the values within each position, appropriate modifications and complexities can be provided for.

Development of Cognitive Processes

One major orientation to schooling emphasizes the belief that the curriculum provided and the teaching strategies used should foster the development of the student's cognitive processes. In this view, the major functions of the school are (1) to help children learn how to learn and (2) to provide them with the opportunities to use and strengthen the variety of intellectual faculties that they possess.

In this view, the mind is conceived of as a collection of relatively independent faculties or aptitudes: the ability to infer, to speculate, to locate and solve problems, to remember, to visualize, to extrapolate, and so on. It is these faculties that must come into play in order to deal adequately with the problems that individuals inevitably have to cope with during the course of a lifetime. For the school to emphasize the mere acquisition of information, the accumulation of fact, or even the dissemination of theory is not in the long run useful, for surely both facts and theories change, and at an alarming rate. If what is already known is emphasized, the student is in a poor position to deal with problems and issues that will inevitably arise in the future, many of which cannot at present even be envisioned. The most effective way to deal with such problems is not by storing bodies of knowledge in one's memory but rather by strengthening those cognitive processes that can be used later to deal with them. For this to occur, the curriculum used in the school and the forms of teaching employed are crucial. The curriculum is not to emphasize content, but process. Teaching is not to impart, but to help students learn to inquire.

The roots of this orientation to curriculum go back to the work of the phrenologists and faculty psychologists of the nineteenth century and to the progressive era in American education, particularly during the 1920s. For the phrenologists, the mind consisted of a collection of thirty-seven muscles that were located in different parts of the brain. Each section of the skull showed the location of these intellectual muscles. Following the phrenologists' lead, the faculty psychologists emphasized the importance of strengthening these mental faculties through practice, especially practice that was tough and demanding. Their slogan might be said to have been, "It doesn't matter much what a student studies in school, as long as he doesn't like it." In short, what was important was that the tasks encountered exercise the relevant faculties so that through exercise these faculties became "strong."

Although it was believed that content, per se, was not the crucial issue in building a curriculum, it was believed that some subject matters were particularly useful for the development of specific faculties. Mathematics, for example—subjects such as algebra, geometry, trigonometry, and calculus—was justified not because it imparted content but rather because it fostered mental discipline and strengthened the student's ability to reason. Mathematics was justified because of its contributions to the development of a rigorous mind rather than because students need to know the meaning of Euclid's first theorem.

It should be noted that in this view the criteria for the selection of curriculum content have an elegance and economy. If tasks or subject matters could be identified that strengthen the muscles of the mind, then it would be possible to accomplish a great deal with relatively little effort. For example, if the ability to deduce were a product of processes strengthened through exercise on particular tasks, then one's deductive ability could be strengthened with the expectation that those processes would be useful for tasks unlike those used to strengthen them. This view assumes, in short, general transfer. What transfers is not content, but process: the ability to use the variety of processes that the curriculum strengthened through exercise.

It was this belief that the work of Thorndike and Woodworth in 1901 undermined.[1] Testing for the transferability of learning, Thorndike and Woodworth demonstrated that transfer was not general but specific. What one learned transferred only insofar as the elements constituting the second task were identical with those of the first. Thorndike's theory of "identical elements," and the psychology of learning that he promulgated, had a great impact on beliefs about how the curriculum was to be built.

One such impact was that it could no longer be assumed that the student would automatically learn to perform tasks not taught specifically, or at least taught in a way that encouraged the transfer of training. Thus, in preparing a curriculum in arithmetic, it was not assumed that if a student learned that three times four equaled twelve he or she would also know that four times three equaled twelve, or that two times six equaled twelve. One could not safely assume general transfer or the use of "reason" as a way of coping with new tasks. As a result, arithmetic textbooks placed heavy stress on the catch phrase of connectionist psychology—"practice makes perfect"—and "recency," "frequency," and "intensity" became the guiding principles of effective pedagogy.

The modern-day resurrection of process-oriented psychology emerged in part in the work of J. P. Guilford,[2] a psychologist whose major efforts have been devoted to the empirical articulation and assessment of a model of the structure of the intellect. The model that Guilford conceptualized— a complex structure that distinguishes over one hundred independent intellectual operations—could, in principle, be used to define the variety of tasks that could constitute a process-oriented curriculum. For example, if ideational fluency and ideational flexibility using figural material were considered important educationally, programs in schools could be designed to give children opportunities to use such processes on tasks that were intentionally designed to elicit them. What is important here is that specific mental operations are thought to be strengthened through activities especially designed to require their use. It is on the ability to use such processes that the individual must eventually depend. The major mission of schooling, in this view, is to increase the probability that maximum realization of those processes occurs.

Related to this conception of mind are the various levels of cognitive operation in the *Taxonomy of Educational Objectives: Cognitive Domain.*[3] The six levels that are identified—possession of information, comprehension, application, analysis, synthesis, and evaluation—represent increasingly complex forms of thinking. The tacit value position embedded in the taxonomy is that educational objectives should be developed so that they traverse the entire range of cognitive processes and not simply remain at the lower level of cognitive functioning. Implicit in this view is the belief that cognitive processes can be cultivated, that educational objectives should be derived from levels of cognitive functioning, and that test items should be designed to assess the levels of cognitive achievement that students have reached.

Within the curriculum field, a variety of programs have been designed that are directly related to the belief in the primacy of cognitive development as an aim of education. One such program, *Science: A Process Approach,*[4] emphasizes the use of those operations that are central to scientific inquiry but are also justifiable in their own right. *Elementary School Science*[5] is another program that places heavy emphasis on the cultivation of those intellectual abilities that are consistent with the spirit of scientific modes of thought. Jerome Bruner's seminal work *The Process of Education*[6] is an example of a hybrid orientation that marries forms of inquiry used in the natural and social sciences with the central concepts and generalizations within specific academic disciplines. What these curriculum orientations have in common is their emphasis on using curriculum tasks as a means of fostering processes that presumably will outlive the problems or concepts they were developed from. The major aim of these programs is the development of intellectual power rather than the simple dissemination of a body of ideas or information.

Given this orientation to the aims of educational programs, what might be expected of a teacher working within this framework? What might we expect to see in the way of teaching, curriculum content, and evaluation procedures? How might the values embedded in a cognitive process orientation to the curriculum manifest themselves in the conduct of schooling?

First, the curriculum used in the school would generally be problem-centered; that is, students would be encouraged to define problems they wish to pursue, and with the teacher's help the appropriate materials and guidance would be provided. Some of these problems would be those defined by individual students, whereas others would be the result of deliberations by the class or of small groups of students. The reason a problem-centered curriculum is attractive to those emphasizing the development of cognitive processses is that the opportunities to define and solve problems are among the most critical intellectual abilities the school can foster. Without the opportunity to conceptualize, to analyze, to deal with ambiguity, to locate relevant resources, to evaluate the results of one's efforts, the child is unlikely to use his or her most sophisticated abilities. What matters most is not the particular content on which these processes are employed—the repair of a carburetor can be treated imaginatively, while the reading of *Othello* can be done mindlessly—but the exercise of the intellectual faculties. And for this to occur, content that is meaningful to the student and problems that are intellectually challenging are critical.

Teaching in this orientation requires not only the ability to generate problematic situations for students, but also the ability to raise the kinds of questions with students that direct their attention to levels of analysis they would not be likely to use without the teacher's aid. The teacher has a positive role to play in cultivating "the higher mental abilities" by virtue of the tasks provided in the curriculum, the materials that are used, and the kinds of questions he or she raises while teaching.

A classification of the kinds of questions teachers and students raise in class ideally reveals a wide range of types and levels. Similarly, the kinds of problems and materials with which students work would include not only the verbal and mathematical but also visual and auditory modes of conception and expression. Students might be asked, for example, to transform ideas held in one conceptual modality, say a visual mode, into their verbal or mathematical "equivalents." The contrary would also occur. Concepts framed in linguistic or mathematical terms would be transformed into visual or auditory "equivalents." The point here is that the focus of curriculum content is derived from a conception of mental operations; the curriculum is essentially an invention to bring those processes into play and to strengthen them.

Academic Rationalism

One of the oldest and most basic orientations to curriculum goals and content may be called academic rationalism. This orientation argues that the major function of the school is to foster the intellectual growth of the student in those subject matters most worthy of study.

Schools that devote their time to subjects that while important are also capable of being taught by agencies other than the school—driver training, home economics, parenting, and so forth—are diverting the schools' most precious resource, namely time, away from the schools' proper aims. Thus, the expansion of the curriculum to include virtually everything that any special-interest group believes important actually weakens rather than strengthens the quality of education. What the school should provide is attention to the major concepts, issues, and problems that humans face in the course of their lifetime. The school's curriculum should help students acquire the techniques necessary for reading what able thinkers have said about such concepts, issues, and problems. And the school should develop the students' abilities to discuss critically the meaning of these works. The good schoolmaster is known by the important subjects he or she *refuses* to teach.

The most recent expression of this view is to be found in Mortimer Adler's *Paideia Proposal,* a manifesto on education that prescribes a secondary school curriculum that allows no room for electives. For many, the clarity of Adler's manifesto, its certainty and inflexibility, is a desirable remedy to a curriculum that has grown like Topsy, without direction or rationale, and which has resulted in a gross lack of curricular coherence.[7]

But who is to determine which subjects are best? Are there intrinsic differences in the value of various academic disciplines? The answers to these questions for those holding an academic rationalistic position are clear: not all disciplines are created equal. Some disciplines—biology, for example—deal with processes that inform one about the nature of life, a topic so important that the achievements in biological inquiry should be a part of the intellectual repertoire of all educated people. Furthermore, if biology or the sciences more generally are not taught in school, it is not likely that their ideas will be learned. Unlike driver training or home economics, education in the sciences is the special province of the school.

This position is argued in several ways. First, it is argued that biology (I use biology only as an example) as a branch of science not only represents a particular discipline having its own content, concepts, and patterns of inquiry, but it also represents a special mode of thought—science. Science is a fundamental form of human understanding and as such should be made available to students. In this argument, biology is a special case of a more general and powerful paradigm of human understanding that the school should foster, especially because an understanding of its concepts and procedures requires specialized forms of instruction. If it is not fostered by the curriculum, it is not likely to be learned.

The second ground on which academic rationalists argue is that all children should be introduced to basic fields of study because it is only in this way that they can discover if they have any interest in or aptitude for an area. It is through contact with the various disciplines that interests and aptitudes are stimulated. Part of the task of the school is to enable students to discover these interests and aptitudes.

It is clear that the latter argument is not as strong as the former. The number of subjects within the various modes through which humans come to know are extremely large. If biology should be taught, why not paleontology or meteorology? Interests and aptitudes could be revealed by those areas of study, as well. The school must make certain choices; it cannot teach everything. But if that is true—and it certainly seems true—what is the basis on which choices are to be made? The academic rationalist believes that the basic fields in the arts and sciences are important because they best exemplify and exercise the human's rational abilities. Their study is what education is basically about. Furthermore, within the various fields to be taught, the very best content, and the most intellectually significant ideas, should be what students encounter. The greatest ideas created by the greatest writers, exemplified by the greatest works humans have produced, are the proper objects of educational attention.

An academic rationalist view of the curriculum has been admirably argued by one of its chief proponents, Robert Maynard Hutchins. When he was chancellor of the University of Chicago he established an undergraduate program that emphasized the study of the great books, the use of primary source materials, and the tradition of teaching in the context of small-group discussion. Hutchins was interested in helping students secure what he regarded as a basic liberal education, a form of education that enables students to ask basic questions about life, truth, justice, and knowledge and to read the works of individuals who have provided powerful and lasting answers to such questions. Of this form of education, Hutchins writes:

> Liberal education consists of training in the liberal arts and of understanding the leading ideas that have animated mankind. It aims to help the human being learn to think for himself, to develop his highest human powers. As I have said, it has never been denied that this education was the best for the best. It must still be the best for the best unless modern times, industry, sci-

ence, and democracy have made it irrelevant. The social, political, and economic changes that have occurred have not required that liberal education be abandoned. How could they? It is still necessary to try to be human; in fact it is more necessary, as well as more difficult, than ever.

Liberal education was the education of rulers. It was the education of those who had leisure. Democracy and industry, far from making liberal education irrelevant, make it indispensable and possible for all the people. Democracy makes every man a ruler, for the heart of democracy is universal suffrage. If liberal education is the education that rulers ought to have, and this I say has never been denied, then every ruler, that is every citizen, should have a liberal education. If industry is to give everybody leisure, and if leisure, as history suggests, tends to be degrading and dangerous unless it is intelligently used, then everybody should have the education that fits him to use his leisure intelligently, that is, liberal education. If leisure makes liberal education possible, and if industry is to give everybody leisure, then industry makes liberal education possible for everybody.[8]

What Hutchins and other academic rationalists argue is that schools should develop man's reason so that life can be critically examined and led intelligently. For reason to be optimized, the most appropriate pedagogical mode is dialectic discussion. Reason develops best when it is used, and if it is to be used, it should be used on the problems that are most fundamental to human existence. Because such problems have been addressed by humans of every generation and because the products of their work vary in quality, only the very best should be studied by students today. For practical purposes, this means that the curriculum should consist of not just the major academic disciplines in the arts and the sciences, but the very best, the most powerful, the most profound, the grandest of man's intellectual works within those disciplines. For the period of the past 150 years, the works of Darwin, Marx, Freud, Einstein, Ghandi, Stravinsky, Picasso, Louis Sullivan, Corbusier, Joseph Conrad, Camus, Paul Tillich, and Max Weber would receive attention. And they would receive attention in a dialectical mode: through discussion, analysis, and comparison. The central aim is to develop man's rational abilities by introducing his rationality to ideas and objects that represent reason's highest achievements.

Some might argue that such an education is fit only for a few, perhaps the "top" 10 or 15 per cent of the student population. Academic rationalists—at least those like Hutchins and Mortimer Adler—believe that all men are concerned with essentially the same fundamental questions, questions that deal with what is true, what is good, what is beautiful, how life might be examined, and the like. Although there will certainly be individual differences among students with respect to the rate at which they deal with such material and the depth to which it is penetrated, such an education, once reserved for rulers, is the right of every free person. The substitution of skimmed milk for rich educational cream is not the way to deal with individual differences when it comes to the content and aims of education.

Furthermore, the differentiation of content for students of different intellectual abilities ultimately leads to a kind of social stratification that makes it increasingly difficult for people to communicate with each other. Because no common educational grounding has been provided in the schools, the ideas people can discuss are those provided through the experiences they share. Increasingly, such experiences are provided by the mass media, and the mass media, the academic rationalists argue, have very little intellectual substance. Thus, the absence of a common educational program in the long run undermines the very foundations of a social democracy. It undercuts the common intellectual base that a nation needs. But perhaps most importantly, differentiation of programs for individuals of different ability creates a self-fulfilling prophecy that sets limits to aspiration, forecloses one's options in life, and provides only a small portion of the total population with the kind of intellectual repertoire that optimally fosters the development of rationality.

Personal Relevance

A third orientation to curriculum is one that emphasizes the primacy of personal meaning and the school's responsibility to develop programs that make such meaning possible. In operational terms, this requires that teachers develop educational programs in concert with students rather than from a mandate handed down from the staff of a central office who don't know the child. The curriculum is to emerge out of the sympathetic interaction of teachers and students within a process called teacher-pupil planning.

A major argument supporting this orientation to curriculum is that for experience to be educational students must have some investment in it— must have some hand in its development—and that without actual participation or the availability of real choices within the curriculum schooling is likely to be little more than a series of meaningless routines, tasks undertaken to please someone else's conception of what is important.

For a meaningful form of educational experience to occur it is critical that teachers regard children as individuals and not as mere members of a class or a group. Furthermore, the teacher must be able to establish rapport with students; he or she must understand how the child actually feels when engaged in activities in school. Without rapport it is not likely that the teacher will be in a position to understand the character of the child's experience, and unless this occurs both student and teacher are likely to deal with each other as role incumbents rather than as living creatures attempting to broaden and deepen the quality of their experience.

Another major argument underlying this view of the curriculum is that human beings from birth on are stimulus-seeking organisms, not stimulus-reducing organisms. The task of the school is to provide a resource-rich environment so that the child will, without coercion, find what he or she needs in order to grow. The metaphor is biological: growth is the aim of life.

In developing this view further, it is argued that organisms develop not so much from the outside in as they do from the inside out. Education is regarded as a process of leading forth from the native ability that the child possesses; thus, the image of the teacher is not so much that of a sculptor, someone who gives shape to formless clay, but rather that of a good gardener who cannot change the basic endowment children possess but who can provide the kind of environment that can nurture whatever aptitudes they bring with them into the world. Out of the interaction of aptitudes and environment, interests and intelligence develop. Once having discovered such interests, the teacher is to foster them by the artful construction of educational situations in which those interests can deepen and expand. Another way of identifying interests is to talk to children about their interests and thus to be in a position to provide for their development through the curriculum.

The admonition to build on the child's interest is often made as a corrective for educational programs that neglect them as sources of curriculum aims and content. Traditional educational programs are developed out of principles that identify educational value within particular subject matters or disciplines. Becoming educated means learning how to use the ideas within these disciplines. This approach, it is argued, has two educationally devastating consequences. First, it is often irrelevant to the child. Second, it fails to cultivate the child's idiosyncrasy by providing few opportunities that are of particular importance to the individual child.

One of those who has supported a child-centered approach to education is A. S. Neil.[9] He believed that the child should play a major role in determining what he or she shall study. In the United States, the emergence of "free schools" in the 1960s represented a similar orientation; the child is to be given the "freedom" to choose. The teacher's responsbiility is not to coerce but to facilitate. John Holt, a leading and articulate spokesman for this view of curriculum makes the case this way:

> As a friend of mine put it, we teachers can see ourselves as travel agents. When we go to a travel agent, he does not tell us where to go. He finds out first what we are looking for. Do we care most about climate or scenery, or about museums and entertainment? Do we want to travel alone or with oth-

ers? Do we like crowds or want to stay away from them? How much time and money do we want to spend? And so on. Given some idea of what we are looking for, he makes some suggestions. Here is this trip, which will take so long and cost so much; here is this one, here is that. Eventually, we choose, not he. Then, he helps us with our travel and hotel arrangements, gets us what tickets and information we need, and we are ready to start. His job is done. He does not have to take the trip with us. Least of all does he have to give us a little quiz when we get back to make sure we went where we said we would go or got out of the trip what we hoped to get. If anything went wrong he will want to hear about it, to help us and other clients plan better in the future. Otherwise, what we got out of the trip and how much we enjoyed it is our business.[10]

What one senses from the metaphor of teacher as travel agent is a conception of the teacher's role and of curriculum that values above all else the child's freedom to choose, and thus the opportunity to learn how to choose as a central aim of educational programs. Holt and others who share this view believe that in the process the child's talents will be cultivated; such a school allows the child to become his or her own person.

Related to the view that the child should play a significant role in choosing what he or she shall study is the more recent view of some reconceptualists, such as Max Von Mannen, Madeline Grumet, and William Pinar, who emphasize the importance of authentic personal experience and who claim that much of schooling remains external or superficial to the deep private life that all humans possess. Education, they claim, occurs when those engaged in events or activities do so out of choice and with a deep personal commitment.

One can, of course, question the premise that the greatest of all educational goals resides in allowing children to choose what they think best. For one, choice is possible only when one has options *and* knows of their existence. Do children have the experience that will enable them to consider alternatives? If experience is limited, won't choice be limited? How can children follow their interests if they haven't had an opportunity to learn about possibilities, ideas, skills, and materials they have never dreamed of? Do children of eight, ten, twelve, or fifteen really know what is in their best interest in the long run?

What is it that children need? And who should decide? It can be and has been argued that "needs" are products of adult judgments of the gap existing between the ideals that adults hold and the state at which children are during their schooling. Schooling as an institutionalized form of education is intended to eliminate or at least reduce that gap. Furthermore, the belief that each child is so different that there can be no common educational program suitable for the vast majority is wrong to begin with. And so the counterarguments proceed. Boyd Bode, an influential American philosopher of education during the 1930s and honorary vice-president of the Progressive Education Association, underscored this point when he chastised his fellow progressive educators for overemphasizing the "needs" of children:

> The point is far more than the verbal question of how the term "need" is to be employed. It concerns the question of what education should be primarily concerned to achieve. The failure to emancipate ourselves completely from Rousseauism and the instinct psychology is responsible for most, if not all, the weaknesses of the Progressive movement in education. The attitude of superstitious reverence for childhood is still with us. The insistence that we must stick like a leech at all times to the "needs" of childhood has bred a spirit of anti-intellectualism, which is reflected in the reliance on improvising instead of long-range organization, in the over-emphasis of the here and now, in the indiscriminate tirades against "subjects," in the absurdities of project planning, and in the lack of continuity in the educational program. It has frequently resulted in an unhealthy attitude towards children, an attitude which suggests that there is no such thing as a normal child, and that we must be everlastingly exploring his insides, like a Calvinist taking himself apart day after day to discover evidence of sin.[11]

Even some of the most ardent progressives began to recognize limits of self-determined "needs" as a basis for the design of educational programs. Alas, we have yet to learn their lessons a generation later, as we search for needs not in the child but in the community through a process called needs assessment, a process often described as though the needs of a community somehow existed independently from someone's judgment. Needs can be regarded as the gap between what is and what ought to be.

It is partly because the students' orientation to schooling is regarded as largely governed by extrinsic souces of motivation that those emphasizing personal relevance believe it to be so important. Schooling, they believe, is not likely to provide intellectual experience that becomes internalized unless students participate in the formulation of their goals. The elective system that most secondary schools offer is largely a hoax. In the first place, much too much of the student's program is determined by the timetable rather than by his or her choices. In the second place, institutions of higher education usually prescribe such a large number of required courses that few real choices are left for students. Students, therefore, too often find themselves waiting for the last half of their senior year when all of the required courses are out of the way to take the courses in which they have genuine interest. Their dues are paid beforehand so that they will have the freedom to pursue their education just before they are about to graduate.

What would we expect to find in a school that emphasized a personal relevance orientation to curriculum? How would time be used? How would students be evaluated? What modes of teaching would be employed? What kinds of content would be studied?

In the first place, we would probably find schools that are considerably smaller than the ones we have at present, at least smaller than those in urban areas. Size, especially when schools exceed seven or eight hundred students, often becomes an obstacle to flexibility. When one is dealing with hundreds of faculty members and thousands of students, the differentiation of programs for individuals becomes difficult. The machinery of organization takes over, despite the claim that large schools can better provide a wide array of options for students with special needs or interests.

What we would find in schools that were genuinely concerned with personal relevance is a place where interests and the demands of the tasks define the amount of time students spend in a course. We would also find small classes—perhaps with fifteen students—that were organized around a common set of interests and included students of different ages who shared that interest. Thus, for example, students of ages eleven through fourteen interested in astronomy, in weaving, in geology, or in the care and feeding of animals might work together in the same situation. It would not be assumed that all children of the same age would have to study the same content at the same rate, for the same aims, for a uniform period of time.

The role of the teacher would be one of providing sufficient structure and guidance for the child's experience to be educationally productive, but it would not be prescriptive or coercive. The teacher would be expected to stimulate and guide, to introduce the child to new materials and ideas, but the specific tasks and aims would be developed in a shared relationship. It would not be the kind of bureaucratized relationship that often occurs in forms of contract learning. Neither the student nor the student's parents would need to sign pseudolegal documents in order for commitments to be honored. Indeed, the use of such procedures would be anathema, because they exemplify many of the features in our society that those advocating truly personalized forms of education seek to ameliorate.

Evaluation would pay great attention to the processes in which students were engaged. How meaningful was the task to the child? What did he learn from it? How well, given where the child is, has the task been accomplished? What does the student believe she has learned from what she has done? How does he think the work could have been improved? What ideas did she formulate that might be pursued in forthcoming projects?

These are some of the questions that might guide an evaluation process within a personal-relevance orientation to curriculum. The major focus is on the educational development of the individual child, because it is believed that it is his or her development by means of a personal relevant curriculum within a noncoercive environment that really promotes the realization of psychological freedom.

Social Adaptation and Social Reconstruction

A fourth orientation to curriculum is one that derives its aims and content from an analysis of the society the school is designed to serve. In this orientation it is argued that schools are essentially institutions created to serve the interests of the society. As such their mission is to locate social needs, or at least to be sensitive to those needs, and to provide the kinds of programs that are relevant for meeting the needs that have been identified.

Social Adaptation

It is precisely in the identification of social needs that differences among various groups become most acute. One segment of the society regards the manpower needs of society as most salient, another segment the need for conformity to existing values, still another the need for children to take their place in the social order. The conception of needs among all such groups is essentially conservative; the role of the school is to maintain the status quo. If the society needs more engineers, doctors, physicists, skilled blue-collar workers, the school is regarded as the agency through which they will be provided.

Perhaps the classic case of using schools to meet social needs was the response made by Americans to Sputnik I. When on October 4, 1957 the Russians sent an unmanned satellite circling the earth, critics lambasted American schools for being lax, for failing to provide rigorous programs in mathematics and science, and even for being the prime cause of our second place in space technology. The schools were urged to remedy these deficiencies by emphasizing the teaching of mathematics and the sciences in the curriculum. The National Science Foundation, whose attention to education had preceded the rise of Sputnik I, embarked on a major funding program to support curriculum development in these areas. It was clear to many that the Russian success in space was ample evidence of our failure to offer the kind of educational program that the nation needed. From 1958 to 1968 over one hundred million dollars of federal funds was spent to sponsor curriculum development projects and to establish summer institutes for teachers of science and mathematics.

During the past decade, people have become alarmed that many students are leaving school at age eighteen without a clear conception of the kind of vocation they wish to pursue. Children should be helped—some people believe—from the beginning of schooling at age five or six to the point at which they graduate to reflect about the world of work and to develop gradually the skills and attitudes that will increase their employability. Partly as a result of this concern, career education programs were developed. Funded by the National Institute of Education, career education curricula have been promulgated in schools in every state of the nation.

Or consider what has come to be called the computer revolution. It is often argued that to insure our economic position in the world we need individuals who are "computer literate." In California, computer literacy, calculation, and communication have been decreed the new three C's of education. Industry is interested in students who can use the microcomputer, and because the future of high technology is said to require people who understand its use, it follows in the eyes of some that schools should offer, even require, programs of study in the computer.

What we see is a general example of the forces of social adaptation shaping the priorities of the curriculum. Seldom is there discussion of what the time and resources required for effective computer education will mean for the time available for teaching other fields. Rarely is it questioned that it is the schools' responsibility to take on this task. The message seems to be "our economic well-being will depend upon it, and therefore it becomes, de facto, the schools' responsibility."

The point here is not simply to emphasize curriculum development projects in mathematics, the sciences, in career education, or in computer literacy, but rather to illustrate the historical use that society has made of the schools, namely, as mechanisms for meeting what are regarded as critical needs within society.

The conception of these needs often emanates from what are regarded as particularly pressing social ills. Drug abuse, sex education, parenting programs, and ecological studies represent areas of concern for some groups, whereas black studies, sexism studies, and Chicano and Native American programs represent efforts to provide attention to what other groups believe to be important. What we see in these programs are the results of problems or deprivations that influential individuals or groups believe to exist. The curriculum becomes the vehicle for remedying such situations.

For a substantial proportion of those concerned, the needs that are perceived are not radical in nature; that is, they seek no fundamental change in the basic structure of the society. The development of a career education program, for example, seeks largely to raise the consciousness level of students to the world of work as it exists. Career education programs are not intended to encourage children or youth to consider alternatives to work as it is now generally defined or to question seriously the premises and values that give work such a central place in our lives.

Social Reconstructionism

A radical social perspective leads to the social reconstructionist orientation to the curriculum. This orientation is basically aimed at developing levels of critical consciousness among children and youth so that they become aware of the kinds of ills that the society has and become motivated to learn how to alleviate them. Programs having this orientation will frequently focus on controversial issues, what some writers in the social studies have called the closed areas of society: religious values, sexual preferences, political corruption, race prejudice, and the like. The aim of such programs is not primarily to help students adapt to a society that is in need of fundamental change but rather to help them to recognize the real problems and do something about them.

During the Vietnam war students in many high schools became politically involved for the first time. They felt strongly about what they believed to be moral inequities within the society—the drafting of high school dropouts while their college-going peers were exempted—and protested what they regarded as an unjustifiable war. Many of those students demanded and received in their school programs attention to the politics of the day. They demanded and received opportunities to design courses of study that they believed to be socially significant and to invite speakers to the campus who had messages that were unpopular in the general society.

At the college level, the revolt against courses that were prescribed and believed to be irrelevant to acute social needs was even stronger. The major theme in both cases—at least for some of the protesting students—was that a different view of what the school or the university should be was needed. In particular, such students argued the need to redefine their role and responsibility within the academic community. Their conception of relevance was derived not from the desire to adapt to what many of them regarded as a sick society but rather to build a new, healthier, and more just social order. The program of the school, in principle, was to support the achievement of such an end. Describing the situation during the late 1960s, Stephen Mann writes:

> A fundamental difference in world view is reflected here, and it is by virtue of this difference that the various protests blend into one. But this blending ought not to obscure what I believe is a matter of fact: that the center of gravity of student protest is nausea and rage over the way they are treated in school in the name of education. Nor is this fact mitigated by another equally apparent fact: that what passes for education is a consequence of very much the same forces as what passes for foreign policy. Protesting students are engaged in a struggle against many forms of oppression, but they are willing to put a good deal of their considerable energy and talent to work in the struggle against the oppression most immediate to their own experience, and that is the oppression of schooling.[12]

What we see here is an attack on schools and, hence, on curriculum, because of the roles students are forced to occupy. For some, who take their cues from the society, the relationship of the school to the society is essentially one of accommodation. The society orders and the school obeys. For others, educators such as Mann, the school should cultivate those attitudes and skills that will enable the young to build a better nation—indeed a better world—than the one in which they live. This means, at least for some arguing this view, that the school will have to change its structure so that it becomes *in form* what it hopes its students will learn. Thus, if bureaucratized, hierarchical social structures foster social inequities and if the school is organized on such a model, it must alter its structure in order to be effective. If it cannot change within the existing structure of state-funded schooling, alternative private schools must be established. Indeed, some individuals holding the social reconstructionist view of the curriculum are not at all sanguine about the likelihood that public schools can actually convey to students the kind of social message that they believe students need to hear. They fear that rather than the message changing the school, the school will change the message. The only viable route to the kind of curriculum that they believe significant is the establishment of alternative schools beyond the control of the existing power structure. John Galtung, a leading advocate of peace education, an orientation that is social reconstructionist in its aims, says:

> First a few general remarks about the form of peace education. It has to be compatible with the idea of peace, i.e., it has in itself to exclude not only direct violence, but also structural violence. Only rarely is education nowadays sold with direct violence; the days of colonialism and corporal punishment are more or less gone. But the structural violence is there, and it takes the usual forms: a highly vertical division of labor which in this case expresses itself in one-way communication; fragmentation of the receivers of that communication so that they cannot develop horizontal interaction and organize and eventually turn the communication flow the other way; absence of true multilaterality in the education endeavor. All this relates to form; and if in addition the content of education is included, the structural violence becomes even more apparent.[13]

Galtung is a Norwegian who writes out of the European tradition. Closer to home we find Americans, such as Michael Apple, sharing similar concerns. Apple, a curriculum theorist, believes, with Mann and Galtung, that much of schooling exploits students, that the form of the curriculum defines content of what students actually learn. He writes:

> An examination of these curricular 'systems' illuminates the extent to which this kind of ideological movement is occurring in increasingly dominant curricular forms. Here, the *rate* at which a student proceeds is individualized; however, the actual product as well as the process to be accomplished are specified by the material itself. Thus, it is not 'just' the teacher who faces

the encroachment of technical control and deskilling. The students' responses are largely prespecified as well. Much of this growing arsenal of material attempts as precisely as possible to specify appropriate student language and action as well, often reducing it to the mastery of sets of competencies or skills.[14]

The curricular implications of social reconstruction for specific subject fields are profound. Content for the social studies, for example, is to be drawn from pervasive and critical social problems and from the hubs of social controversy. One does not learn how to cope with problems or controversy by systematically avoiding them in school. Content in the science curriculum is not exclusively to be drawn from the problems with which scientists work, but from the individual and social problems for which scientific inquiry has some relevance: the causes and consequences of stress, community mental health, the implications of the right to die, eugenics, environmental pollution, the location of nuclear energy plants. In the arts, curriculum content might focus on the hidden forms of persuasion in advertising, the impact of new technology on the character of art forms, the ideals conveyed to the young by the mass media. What we see here is an emphasis on the questions that citizens have to deal with or that in some significant way affect their lives. One does not avoid dealing with such questions by retreating to the abstractions of the academic disciplines; one uses the knowledge provided by the academic disciplines as a tool for dealing with what is socially significant.

The other side of the social reconstruction–social adaptation orientation is aimed not primarily at preparing students to improve the social order by focusing on its problems, but rather at helping students acquire the skills needed to fit into the society, largely as it is. Thus, social reconstructionism and social relevance are at opposite poles, but what they have in common is that both look to the society to decide what the aims of the school's program should be. The social reconstructionist looks at the society to locate its difficulties. Once they have been found, the program of the school is designed to help children understand these difficulties and to be able to cope with them. The person concerned with social relevance looks to society to find out what students need in order to get ahead and builds a curriculum that aims to achieve that goal.

The analysis of society as a basis for the formulation of curriculum content and goals is not as modern as one might believe. Its first formal use in American education was in the school survey movement initiated in around 1910. The major effort here was to use scientific methods to identify the strengths and weaknesses of school programs. The field of education during that time was in the process of establishing and testing its newfound scientific approach to education. University professors such as Elwood Cubberley and Jesse B. Sears were called on to provide services to schools while refining the methodology used in such work. Sears' book *The*

School Survey[15] described the theory and methods of such work and appeared in 1928.

But in the field of curriculum the seminal work was done by Franklin Bobbitt, who argued that education should prepare for the fifty years of adult life the child eventually would lead and not merely be concerned with chilhood, per se. To prepare for this life, "the curriculum discoverer," to use Bobbitt's term, was to identify the various areas of life for which schools should prepare the young. Bobbitt identified ten such areas. The next step, according to Bobbitt, was to identify those people in the community who displayed excellence in each of the ten areas. Their behavior, their understanding, and their attitudes, once analyzed by curriculum specialists, would constitute the goals of curriculum:

> The central theory is simple. Human life, however varied, consists in its performance of specific activities. Education that prepares for life is one that prepares definitely and adequately for these specific activities. However numerous and diverse they may be for any social class, they can be discovered. This requires that one go out into the world of affairs and discover the particulars of which these affairs consist. These will show the abilities, habits, appreciations, and forms of knowledge that men need. These will be the objectives of the curriculum. They will be numerous, definite and particularized. The curriculum will then be that series of experiences which childhood and youth must have by way of attaining those objectives.[16]

Bobbitt's view was a conservative one. But the point of his work was neither the virtue nor the vice of being conservative; it was his assumption that goals for education reside in the society and that the analysis of that society (in his case, successful adults) would provide the basis for the curriculum. Those who aim at social relevance of an adaptive variety as well as those seeking to reconstruct the social order share with Bobbitt the inclination to look to the world to find out what schools should teach. This aim they share; the images of the world that they see and the aims that they espouse, however, could not be farther apart.

Curriculum as Technology

A fifth orientation to curriculum is normative in a way that the preceding orientations are not. It conceives of curriculum planning as being essentially a technical undertaking, a question of relating means to ends once the ends have been formulated. The central problem of the technological orientation to curriculum is not to question ends but rather to operationalize them through statements that are referenced to observable behavior. Once this task has been performed adequately, the problem is essentially one of designing appropriate means. This means-ends model of curriculum planning has the virtue of systematizing educational planning; it reminds educators to formulate purposes and to use those purposes as criteria for evaluating the efficiency and effectiveness of the plans that were made. It is argued that schools should be purposive; they should have meaningful goals, and it should be possible to determine—indeed measure—the extent to which they have been achieved. The curriculum is the course to be run; the obstacles or hurdles are the learning tasks that have been formulated. If they are well formulated, if they provide appropriate challenges and are neither too difficult nor too easy, the lessons to be learned will be learned and the objectives will be attained.

This orientation to curriculum planning, as I have already indicated, has a long history in education. Benjamin Bloom, Franklin Bobbitt, John Dewey, Virgil Herrick, Hilda Taba, Ralph Tyler, and other important educational planners and theorists have used such a planning model or have advocated its use. In addition, the means-ends orientation to planning is consonant with the Western world's efforts to control human activity. By conceiving of curriculum planning and teaching as technological problems, the power and precision of "applied science" could be employed in the schools, the vagaries of romanticism could be excised, and the uncertainties of art could be replaced by the replicability of the science of curriculum development and instruction.

The offshoots of this way of conceiving of proper curriculum planning are apparent in several of the major educational movements in the United States. One of these is called the accountability movement and is often associated with program-planning-budgeting systems. Although accountability can be conceived of in many ways in educational practice, it is often regarded by school administrators and members of school boards as essentially a problem of demonstrating that educational investments yield educational payoffs. The curriculum of the school is to be so designed and evaluated that teachers will be able to provide evidence of educational effectiveness. Expectations that operate in industry are transferred to the school. Because schools are intended to have a product—learning—there is no reason why the procedures used to increase the efficiency and effectiveness of factories should not also be applied to schools. Furthermore, the application of such criteria and the use of industrial management techniques give school administrators greater control over the system. Within such a rationale for curriculum, quality-control procedures are conceived of not just as a possibility but as an educational necessity.

Other spinoffs of the technological orientation to curriculum include contract teaching, programmed instruction, precision teaching, and laws such as California's Stull Bill, which was designed initially to identify incompetent teachers through mandated evaluation.

What is often neglected or underestimated by those who regard the tasks of curriculum development as essentially technical ones is the way in which a technical orientation influences the values the curriculum emphasizes. Technique is never value-neutral. And techniques patterned after scientific models are particularly likely to produce specific consequences for the form, content, and aims of schooling. For example, the position that curriculum development is at base a technical undertaking and that curriculum has no value position to offer regarding educational ends deprives the people with whom the specialist works of judgments about the ends to which he or she has a professional commitment. In fact, to take no position regarding ends *is* to take a value position, but it is one of absence rather than of presence, as far as educational goals are concerned.

A second consequence is the impact that a scientific technology has on the form of schooling. Scientifically based technologies place high priority on the specification of objectives, the development of units of performance that can be evaluated after relatively short time intervals, and the standardization of those features that lead to the ends that have been specified. The general tendency is to try to increase efficiency and effectiveness by the creation of routines that are common across the enterprise. In many situations, such efficiencies do emerge.

The cost of such routines, however, is not trivial if one embraces a view of education that regards the cultivation of productive idiosyncrasy a virtue. The personal relevance orientation described earlier, for example, would offer serious objections to the putative virtues of standardization within a technological orientation to curriculum.

What happens when method becomes a salient consideration is that method, or technique, becomes the criterion that defines what is acceptable. It is not at all unusual for those in school districts who review the behavioral objectives that teachers formulate to pay no attention to the substance of the objective; the concern is whether it has been stated properly—i.e., in conformance with the criteria for stating behavioral objectives. Those aims that cannot be so stated fall by the wayside. Form sets the boundaries within which the substantive goals of education can be articulated.

What would we expect to see in schools and classrooms in which the orientation to the curriculum were technological? How would teaching occur? How would students be evaluated? How would the aims of the curriculum be expressed?

One thing we could expect to see is that each teacher would have specific measurable goals for each subject area being taught. They would be, as Franklin Bobbitt said, "numerous, definite, and particularized." Furthermore, each objective would have some quantitatively defined test or test item that would be used to determine whether the student had achieved the objective. The students might be given a list of these objectives at the outset of each project or curriculum activity in order that they would fully understand what they were expected to accomplish. As far as possible all ambiguity with respect to goals would be eliminated.

At the beginning of the school year or at the beginning of a section of the curriculum, students would be pretested to determine their level of entry behavior. The measurement of these behaviors would be considered important because it would define the educational development the student had attained and would be used to prescribe the content and tasks he or she needed in order to move toward the achievement of curriculum objectives.

After this had been done, units of work would be laid out for each student or for groups of students, and tests would be administered after each unit of work to monitor the achievement of students over time. When a treatment was ineffective, the student would be recycled into another set of tasks, or the tasks would be revised by the teacher so that they were pedagogically more effective.

This approach is specificially employed in the teaching of reading in the city of Chicago. In an effort to increase the reading skills of its students, the Chicago Public Schools use an approach that specifies in detail what teachers are to say to students in the teaching of reading and how students are to respond. This program begins in kindergarten and proceeds through the eighth grade.

A curriculum having these features would be very sequential. Each task would build on what preceded and would prepare for what was to come. The implicit image of the curriculum is that of a staircase with few landings and no hallways feeding into it. The aim of the staircase is to increase the efficiency with which one arrives at the top floor. In a technologically oriented classroom, curriculum activities would often be available in workbooks or in boxes of sequential instructional materials. Students would come to regard it as their responsibility to proceed through the workbook or curriculum materials box on their own, although when they needed the teacher's assistance they could ask for and get it. More often than not, the materials would be color-coded, so the students could know visually where they were in the program. Students would also be able to compare their location in the work to be done by comparing their colors.

Students as well as teachers would record the progress they had made by maintaining charts or records of the scores derived from their tests. In some classrooms these records would be publicly posted, particularly in the elementary grades. At the high school level, each student would record his or her score in a notebook and would be responsible for determining the final grade by calculating the average of the test scores. Specific scores would be assigned a specific meaning so that the students would know what scores they needed to achieve A, B, C, D, or F. Deviation from these standards by the teacher would be regarded as a social inequity by the students.

The point in having such standards is to objectify the assessment of performance and the rewards that are provided. The tacit image of such a classroom is the efficient and effective machine.

The Import of the Five Conceptions

Again, what we find is that the dominant framework for viewing curriculum has consequences for the practical operation of schools; each orientation harbors an implicit conception of educational virtue. Furthermore, each orientation serves both to legitimize certain educational practices and to sanction others negatively. It also functions as an ideological center around which political support can be gathered.

It is difficult to overemphasize the importance of the various orientations to curriculum that have been described. Rather than being "mere abstract" philosophies that have little bearing on the conduct of educational practice, these orientations are permeated through and through with values that shape one's conception of major aspects of practice. What the teacher's role is to be is not separable from what one believes the content of the curriculum to be. If one views optimal educational practice as the form that yields predictable and measurable consequences, the teacher's role and the character of the curriculum are partly defined. It's no good talking about nonempirical outcomes to be realized long after a course is completed if results are to be demonstrated in June. If one believes that the problems of the society should be the focus for identifying the contents of the curriculum, the likelihood of classical studies being important is remote. If one believes that the major function of the school is to ensure acquisition of the three R's, it is not likely that inductive or discovery learning will be given high priority as techniques for instruction.

Furthermore, each of the five basic orientations has specific implications for the goals and content of specific subject matter curricula. For example, *Science: A Process Approach,* a science curriculum for elementary-age children, was developed to foster certain cognitive process skills. Each unit of this curriculum is designed to sharpen children's ability to classify, to observe, to measure, and so forth. Cognitive processes play a critical role in determining what counts in scientific learning. The evaluation of the units that are taught is intended to determine whether children can employ these processes.

The significance of each of the five orientations to curriculum also becomes apparent if one considers the importance of content inclusion–content exclusion as an influence on what students learn in school. Each of the orientations emphasizes a particular conception of educational priorities. Each set of priorities defines the content and influences the climate within which students and teachers work. Thus the formulation of these priorities has a direct bearing on the kinds of opportunities for learning that students are provided. If one believes that students should learn to form their own purposes, to seek the resources with which they will work, to speculate on and consider alternative routes to an end-in-view, the ability to perform these functions and to use the modes of thought that they require is enhanced if the curriculum provides students with a climate and content to practice such skills and attitudes. A process-oriented curriculum establishes the boundaries within which such learning opportunities will be made available to students.

If one believes that students need to learn how to cope with the political system used in the community and that the best way to learn how to cope with it is to focus on real social problems, then it becomes important for the curriculum to provide those opportunities to students. A social reconstructionist view of the curriculum influences what shall be made available to students and what shall be regarded as of marginal educational worth.

The same ramifications exist for each of the other orientations to curriculum. Each has a consequential effect on what is included in and what is excluded from school programs as those programs operate both informally and formally. The general environment and educational climate as well as the specific content as such are influenced by the orientation to curriculum that one embraces. Because the provision of learning opportunities is probably the single most important factor influencing the content of learning in school, the importance of an orientation to curriculum can hardly be underestimated. We make a major decision about what shall be taught when we decide what image of education is most appealing.

What stance with respect to these orientations should the student of education take? Is one orientation better than the other? Are some orientations unjustifiable? There are two caveats that must be entered with respect to each of the orientations. One is the fact that they have been described independently of the context in which they are to function. They have been described as models or paradigms of educational virtue. In practice they are seldom encountered in their pure form, although in many forms of educational practice one of the five views dominates. Furthermore, because they have been described without reference to context, it is extremely difficult to determine which view is most appropriate to a particular population of children. Thus, although in general one might find one orientation closer to one's educational values than another, one might be willing to employ another view under particular circumstances.

The second caveat has to do with the problem of justification. It is my position that what distinguishes lay opinion from professional judgment with respect to the values guiding curriculum decisions is the extent to which the assets and liabilities of particular positions are recognized, as well as those of competing positions. Thus, what is reasonable to expect from a student of education are good grounds for the position or orientation embraced. This includes not only knowing what has been accepted for practice, but what has been rejected as well.

To provide such grounds in the course of argument requires a fine conceptual analysis of the problems or decisions that one encounters. It means learning how to look at a problem or decision from different perspectives and being satisfied with partial data and incomplete answers. It means knowing what research has to say, if anything, about different forms of practice. The ability to be content with inadequate data for making educational decisions is a condition of educational life. The data are never adequate to justify completely a practical decision, especially if the proposal for educational change is "innovative." In such cases, there is virtually no possibility that data will already have been provided to justify scientifically the use of a particular technique or program.

I have attempted in the preceding pages to characterize five major orientations for dealing with problems of content, aims, organization, teaching roles, and the like in designing educational programs because I believe that much of the controversy over what schools should be, how they should function, and what teachers should teach arises from conflicting assumptions and images of schooling. What we encounter at the point of controversy and contention are often the symptoms of more deep-seated differences.

I am not taking the position that one of the five orientations is better than another. Indeed, one thesis of this book is that educational decisions always must be made with an eye to the context in which the decisions are to operate. Different contexts may justify emphasis on different orientations. Furthermore, it is unlikely that any school will have only one orientation; one may dominate, but it is far more likely that schools will be somewhat eclectic in what they do. The five orientations I have described are intended to function as tools for the analysis of existing school programs and as foundations for a sharpening of discourse about the planning of new programs.

References

1. Edward L. Thorndike and Robert S. Woodward, "The Influence of Improvement in One Mental Function Upon the Efficiency of Other Functions," *Psychological Review*, Vol. 8, 1901.
2. J. P. Guilford, *The Nature of Human Intelligence*, McGraw-Hill, New York, 1967.
3. *Taxonomy of Educational Objectives: The Cognitive Domain* (Benjamin Bloom, ed.), Longmans, Green and Co., New York, 1956.
4. *Science: A Process Approach*, Commisssion on Science Education, American Association for the Advancement of Science, Washington, D.C., 1965.

5. *Elementary School Science Project,* University of California Printing Department, Berkeley, Calif., 1966.
6. Jerome Bruner, *The Process of Education,* Harvard University Press, Cambridge, Mass., 1961.
7. Mortimer Adler, *Paideia Proposal,* Macmillan and Co., New York, 1983.
8. Robert Maynard Hutchins, *The Conflicts in Education in a Democratic Society,* Harper, New York, 1953.
9. A. S. Neill, *Summerhill,* Hart Publishing Co., New York, 1960.
10. John Holt, *What Do I Do Monday?* Dell Publishing Co., New York, 1970, pp. 70–71.
11. Boyd H. Bode, "The Concept of Needs in Education," *Progressive Education,* Vol. 15, No. 1, 1938, p. 9.
12. Stephen Mann, "Political Power and the High School Curriculum," in *Conflicting Conceptions of Curriculum* (Elliot W. Eisner and Elizabeth Vallance, eds.), McCutchan Publishing Co., Berkeley, Calif., 1974, pp. 148–149.
13. John Galtung, "On Peace Education," *Handbook on Peace Education* (Christoph Wulf, ed.), International Peace Research Association, Frankfurt-Main, 1974, p. 155.
14. Michael W. Apple, *Education and Power,* Routledge and Kegan Paul, Boston, 1982.
15. Jesse B. Sears, *The School Survey,* Houghton Mifflin, New York, 1925.
16. Franklin Bobbitt, *The Curriculum,* Houghton Mifflin, Boston, 1918, p. 42.

5

The Three Curricula That All Schools Teach

Perhaps the greatest of all pedagogical fallacies is the notion that a person learns only the particular thing he is studying at the time.

JOHN DEWEY

The Explicit and Implicit Curricula

In the preceding chapter five basic ways were described in which the goals, content, and methods of curriculum have been conceived. These five orientations provide a way of rationalizing what schools teach. But schools teach much more—and much less—than they intend to teach. Although much of what is taught is explicit and public, a great deal is not. Indeed, it is my claim that schools provide not one curriculum to students, but three, regardless of which of the five curriculum orientations a school follows. The aim in this chapter is to examine those three curriculums in order to find out how they function.

One of the most important facts about schooling is that children spend a major portion of their childhood in school. By the time the student has graduated from secondary school, he or she has spent approximately 480 weeks, or 12,000 hours, in school. During this time the student has been immersed in a culture that is so natural a part of our way of life that it is almost taken for granted. In that culture called schooling there are certain publicly explicit goals: teaching children to read and write, to figure, and to learn something about the history of the country, among them. There are, of course, other aims, many of which are associated with the explicit curriculum that the school offers to the students. There are goals and objectives for the sciences, the arts, physical education, social studies, and foreign language instruction. Not only do these goals appear in school district curriculum guides and the course-planning materials that teachers are asked to prepare; the public also knows that these courses are offered and that students in the district will have the opportunity to achieve these aims, at least to some degree, should they want to do so. In short, the school offers to the community an educational menu of sorts; it advertises what it is prepared to provide. From this advertised list, students have, at least in principle, an array of options from which to choose.

But is this all that schools offer? Does this advertised menu exhaust what schools teach? The answer to these questions is clear: no. Work by Dreeben,[1] Jackson,[2] Sarason,[3] Vallance,[4] Apple[5] and others have illuminated the ways in which the culture of both the classroom and the school socializes children to values that are a part of the structure of those places. Dreeben attends primarily to the sociological aspects of school learning, relating and contrasting school learning to the type of learning that takes place in the family. Jackson has discussed with great perceptivity how the structure of the classroom and the demands that it makes upon teachers, in turn, affect the expectations of students and therefore shape the content of what they learn. For example, the fact that classrooms are crowded places and because teachers need the attention of students whom they teach, children, Jackson argues, must learn how to delay their gratification because teachers cannot satisfy all of the wants and needs of a child when he or she is in a group of thirty or more other children. The child who knows the right answer to a question raised by the teacher does not always—even usually—get an opportunity to provide it. Other children compete for a place in the sun. Hence, a child learns quickly that gratifications and successes need to be shared with other members of the class.

Vallance's research has focused on the covert manner in which text material persuades. Materials as well as the structure of the classroom influence the values that are not recognized by students or teachers. These values are expressed in the kinds of illustrations that textbooks contain, in the language that is employed, and in the emphasis that is given to the characters that constitute the stories that are read. These messages are often numerous, subtle, and consistent. It requires a subtle critical analysis of text materials to discern the kinds of social values that are being promulgated within the materials that students and teachers employ. These investigators have helped us understand how schools socialize children to a set of expectations that some argue are profoundly more powerful and longer-lasting than what is intentionally taught or what the explicit curriculum of the school publicly provides. Take, for example, that form of human behavior called initiative. It is possible to create a school environment in which the taking of initiative becomes an increasingly important expectation as children mature. In such an environment, as children get older they would be expected to assume greater responsibility for their planning; they would be expected increasingly to define their goals and determine the kinds of resources that they would need to pursue the ends they have formulated. One general goal of such an institution would be to enable children to become the mappers of their educational journey, so that when they leave school they are in a position to pursue goals and interests that are important to them. If this were an important aspiration of schools, schools would make it possible in dozens of ways for initiative to be developed; it would be a part of the culture of schooling.

Critics of schooling point out however, that rather than cultivate initiative, schools foster compliant behavior. One of the first things a student learns—and the lesson is taught throughout his or her school career—is to provide the teacher with what the teacher wants or expects. The most important means for doing this is for the student to study the teacher, to learn just how much effort must be expended for an A, a B, or a C grade. How long should the term paper be is a question heard not only in secondary school; it is heard in graduate school, as well. Of course, such a request for information is not entirely unreasonable; one does want to know something about the general expectations. Yet, too often, the issue becomes the expectation and the need to meet it in the most expeditious way possible. This tendency to foster compliant forms of behavior is often exacerbated by programs that use behavior modification techniques. I was in one third-grade classroom in a wealthy San Francisco suburb where I noticed that on the wall of the room there was a chart on which each student's name was listed. Next to each name was a set of twenty boxes and in every fifth box was a picture of a smiling face. I asked one of the children what the chart was for, and he replied that after they completed reading a book they colored in one of the boxes. I then asked what the smiling faces were for. He replied that when they had read five books and therefore reached a smiling face, they got a goldenrod ticket, three of which were good for leave to go to lunch five minutes early.

There are a host of educational issues that could be identified and discussed concerning the use of such a reward system, but for now the point will remain with the fostering of compliant behavior. Such a reward system holds out to children something they apparently want and fosters a willingness to perform. In using such a system, the teacher or the school can, of course, increase or decrease the size or attractiveness of the reward to bring out the desired behavior at the lowest cost. Regardless of the type or size of the reward, the point remains the same: the school seeks to modify the child's behavior to comply with goals that the child had no hand in formulating and that might not have any intrinsic meaning.

Some interesting and useful research has been done in the hidden cost of reward. Lepper[6] and his colleagues have found in a number of experiments that the use of extrinsic rewards can create a set of expectations on the children's part that dampens their future interest in activities if extrinsic rewards are not provided. In other words, if a group of children are consistently led to expect that they will receive a reward for engaging in an activity—even an activity that is inherently enjoyable—they are less likely to engage in that activity if they believe that an extrinsic reward will not be provided.

What this line of research implies for the use of rewards in schools is significant. Do we intentionally habituate children to satisfactions that are not a part of the process itself when we emphasize an extrinsic reward structure? Do we create "reward junkies" out of our children by using such a payoff system?

Now, in some respects, the use of rewards to reinforce or control behavior is a ubiquitous part of our culture, indeed of all cultures. Insofar as there are conventions, mores, customs, sanctions, and the like in culture, there will be forms of behavior that are positively rewarded and others that are sanctioned negatively. The question is not whether there should or could be a cultural institution without procedures for monitoring, rewarding, and punishing those who are a part of that institution. The major question deals with the pervasiveness of such conditions and their appropriateness, given the institution's explicit mission. If an institution utilizes expedient means for the management of students that, while doing so, interfere with the realization of some of its primary purposes, there is reason for questioning such "expedient" means.

. I would not like to give the impression that the use of such rewards is the primary way in which compliant behavior is elicited and sustained. The factors that sustain such behavior are in a significant sense built into the ways in which roles are defined in schools. Take, for example, the expectation that students must not speak unless called on, or the expectation that virtually all of the activities within a course shall be determined by the teacher, or the fact that schools are organized hierarchically, with the student at the bottom rung of the ladder, or that communication proceeds largely from the top down. What does such a system teach the young, who must spend up to 480 weeks of their childhood there? What does it mean to children to engage in a wide array of tasks that often have little or no intrinsic meaning to them in order to cope with the school successfully?

For those who have analyzed the implicit curriculum of the school and what it teaches, these lessons are among the most important ones that children learn. It is pointed out that most children will not have jobs in adult life that are intrinsically interesting. Most jobs do not afford an individual the opportunity to define his or her purposes. Most jobs depend on the use of extrinsic motivation to sustain interest. Most jobs do not provide for high degrees of intellectual flexibility. Most jobs depend on routine.

From the standpoint of the type of work that most Americans will engage in during the course of their careers, one could argue that schools provide excellent preparation. Schools prepare most people for positions and contexts that in many respects are quite similar to what they experienced in school as students: hierarchical organization, one-way communication, routine; in short, compliance to purposes set by another.

Compliant behavior is only one of several kinds of behavior that schools foster. Some of these might be considered positive. I use compliance here simply for illustrative purposes. Take as another example competitiveness. Do schools teach children to compete, and do they encourage competitiveness? One way, and perhaps the most obvious way in which competitiveness is fostered, is through athletic competition. Athletic leagues engender a need to win by beating the other person or team. The metaphor is apt. One succeeds only at a price paid by another. But there are other forms of competition that are not as obvious that are also at work in schools. One of these is formal grading practices. When students are assigned grades based on the expectation that the distribution of scores or performance will be statistically normal, the relationship students are forced into is one of competition. If only students with the highest 10 per cent of scores can receive an A grade, then clearly one student's A is another student's B. Again, one wins only at the cost of beating another. When the stakes are high, as they are when students are seeking admission to universities, medical schools, and law schools, it is not unheard of for some students to destroy the work of others or to check out or mutilate books needed by other students to compete successfully. Knowing well what will count, some students use whatever means necessary to gain an advantage.

Because it is extreme, such behavior is not characteristic in schools and universities and, depending on one's social vision, competitiveness could be viewed as the engine of human progress, something that schools would be well advised to encourage.

Competitiveness is not only fostered by the grading system: it is also fostered by the differentiation of classes into ability groups. For example, most comprehensive secondary schools and even a large percentage of elementary schools differentiate students into three or more ability groups, in, for example, Mathematics or English. Students who successfully compete for grades are rewarded not only by grades, but also by admission to honors classes. This assignment to classes in which one is honored by being in an honors class often becomes something highly valued by parents and students. Yet, why should students whose background or genetic makeup is advantageous be rewarded in this public way? Is it the case that the less able are less honorable or less worthy? This is not far from a cultural truth. The word *virtuoso* means someone who is good at something. The word *virtue* means good. The association historically and culturally between being good at something and being good is of long standing. Thus, combined with the Calvinist tradition of associating failure with sin and success with goodness, it is not surprising that quicker students are honored by being assigned to honors classes. Increasingly, school districts are providing a differential credit system for students who are enrolled in courses in different tracks within the school curriculum. Thus, the student in the highest track is given more credit for a grade than a student who receives the same grade in a lower track. What we do when we employ such a procedure in schools is to convert formally grades into commodities that have different exchange values for different students. We have, of course, been doing this for a long time. Different grades have different values. But this formalized procedure tells the A student in a second-level English class that his or her A grade is worth the price of a B or C for students in the first- or honors-track English course. Perhaps this is the message we want to give students. Perhaps the sooner they learn to cope with the competitiveness of the "real world" the better. Yet, I would hope that the values that animate education were rooted in soil a bit richer and more humane than those of the marketplace.

Consider as still another example of the implicit curriculum the impact of time on the students' perception of what counts in school. In planning school programs one of the decisions that must be made is when various subjects will be taught and how much time will be devoted to them. Although such decisions are not intended to reflect to students value judgments about the significance of various subject areas, in fact, they do. Students learn in school to read the value code that pervades it. One of these coded qualities is the use and location of time. Take as a specific example the location and amount of time devoted to the arts in school programs. Virtually all elementary school programs devote some attention to the arts. But if one asks about how much and compares it to the amount of time devoted to, say, social studies, reading, mathematics, or the sciences, the proportion is quite small. But if one looks further to determine when the arts are taught, one will find that they are generally taught in the afternoon rather than in the morning and often on Friday afternoon.

What this conveys to the student is that the arts are essentially forms of play that one can engage in only after the real work of schooling has been finished. In the morning, students are fresh; they can cope at this time with the rigors of reading and mathematics. In the afternoon, the arts can be used as a reward, as a break from the demands of thinking. This reinforces the belief that the arts do not require rigorous and demanding thought and that they are really unimportant aspects of the school program. The idea that the arts deal with feeling and that reading and arithmetic deal with thinking is a part of the intellectual belief structure that separates cognition from affect, a structure whose consequences are as deleterious for educational theory as they are for psychology.

The major point I am trying to make here is one of illustrating the fact that schools teach far more than they advertise. Function follows form. Furthermore, it is important to realize that what schools teach is not simply a function of covert intentions; it is largely unintentional. What schools teach they teach in the fashion that the culture itself teaches, because schools are the kinds of places they are.

The recognition of the impact of the hidden, implicit curriculum is relatively new. Aside from Willard Waller's *The Sociology of the School,* in 1932, there was little interest in the educational consequences of schooling, per se, until the 1960s. It was during that decade that work by Dreeben, Jackson, and Sarason was first published. What students of education began to recognize was what Lewis Mumford was talking about in 1934 in his *Technics and Civilization.* At that time Mumford wrote:

> One may define this aspect of the machine as "purposeless materialism." Its particular defect is that it casts a shadow of reproach upon all the non-material interests and occupations of mankind: in particular, it condemns liberal esthetic and intellectual interests because "they serve no useful purpose." One of the blessings of invention, among the naive advocates of the machine, is that it does away with the need for the imagination: instead of holding a conversation with one's distant friend in reverie, one may pick up a telephone and substitute his voice for one's fantasy. If stirred by an emotion, instead of singing a song or writing a poem, one may turn on a phonograph record. It is no disparagement of either the phonograph or the telephone to suggest that their special functions do not take the place of a dynamic imaginative life, nor does an extra bathroom, however admirably instrumental, take the place of a picture or a flower-garden. The brute fact of the matter is that our civilization is now weighted in favor of the use of mechanical instruments, because the opportunities for commercial production and for the exercise of power lie there: while all the direct human reactions or the personal arts which require a minimum of mechanical paraphernalia are treated as negligible. The habit of producing goods whether they are needed or not, of utilizing inventions whether they are useful or not, of applying power whether it is effective or not pervades almost every department of our present civilization. The result is that whole areas of the personality have been slighted: the telic, rather than the merely adaptive, spheres of conduct exist on sufferance. This pervasive instrumentalism places a handicap upon vital reactions which cannot be closely tied to the machine, and it magnifies the importance of physical goods as symbols—symbols of intelligence and ability and farsightedness—even as it tends to characterize their absence as a sign of stupidity and failure. And to the extent that this materialism is purposeless, it becomes final: the means are presently converted into an end. If material goods need any other justification, they have it in the fact that the effort to consume them keeps the machines running.[7]

Mumford was concerned with the quality of life that technologically advanced societies were rapidly developing, and he believed that technology would get out of hand, becoming master rather than servant to man. Forty years later we find Ivan Illich expressing a similar concern.

Speaking of the distinction between convivial and anticonvivial tools, Illich holds that most tools used in industrial societies restrict rather than expand human freedom. He believes their impact on society to be socially devastating and calls therefore for a reconstruction of society in a form that would make convivial life possible:

> A convivial society should be designed to allow all its members the most autonomous action by means of tools least controlled by others. People feel joy, as opposed to mere pleasure, to the extent that their activities are creative; while the growth of tools beyond a certain point increases regimentation, dependence, exploitation, and impotence. I use the term "tool" broadly enough to include not only simple hardware such as drills, pots, syringes, brooms, building elements, or motors, and not just large machines like cars or power stations; I also include among tools productive insitutions such as factories that produce tangible commodities such as those which produce "education," "health," "knowledge," or "decisions." I use this term because it allows me to subsume into one category all rationally designed devices, be they artifacts or rules, codes or operators, and to distinguish all these planned and engineered instrumentalities from other things such as basic food or implements, which in a given culture are not deemed to be subject to rationalization. School curricula or marriage laws are no less purposely shaped social devices than road networks.[8]

Illich, a leading critic of formal schooling, is concerned with what he believes are the pervasive use of anticonvivial tools. He believes such tools—and the term *tool* refers to anything that can be used—impose themselves on the lives of individuals and groups in such a way as to close rather than open options, divide rather than unify the polity. The tool becomes a master that manages the lives of people. Furthermore, tools interlock and reinforce their power to control. If one is caught in a traffic jam, one misses one's plane at the airport. If this happens, the connection in Denver is also missed, which means that one cannot make an obligatory meeting in New York, which, in turn, will have other consequences.

Although Illich is writing about technological societies at large, the points he makes about them can be applied to schools. We divide time to create schedules that produce a degree of neatness and predictability for the use of school resources. When a school has two thousand students, as many schools have, it is important to develop an organizational pattern that avoids chaos. The timetable and computerized class schedule regulate operations. At the same time, such procedures impose a kind of rigidity that requires that regardless of what one is doing, regardless of how well it is going, one must stop working and move on to the next class. Another class is waiting to move in. Every fifty minutes, an entire school population of two thousand students and sundry teachers plays musical chairs.

Now, clearly, one must weigh the benefits of using time this way against the costs. It might very well be that the benefits outweigh the costs. I am not arguing now that they do not. The point however is not whether such a schedule constitutes an educational vice or virtue: it is that the structure of the school day itself has educational consequences for both students and teachers. The timetable teaches. What the timetable teaches is interesting to speculate about. For one thing it may teach students to be cognitively flexible, to be able to shift problems and adapt to new demands on schedule. It may teach students not to get too involved in what they do because to become too involved is to court frustration when time runs out. Such a schedule may teach students the importance of punctuality: they need to be where they are supposed to be, on time, eight times a day.

These aspects of the culture of schooling no school district advertises; indeed, there are few teachers or school administrators who conceptualize the latent lessons of school structure this way. The culture one is immersed in is often the most difficult to see. Yet, because these aspects of the life of schooling are so pervasive, their effects might be especially important. After all, the westward movement is studied for only a few weeks in the fall of the fifth grade, but the impact of school structure does not cease until one leaves graduate school.

It is usual to consider the implicit curriculum as having an entirely negative impact as far as education is concerned. But this is not necessarily true. The implicit curriculum of the school can teach a host of intellectual and social virtues: punctuality, a willingness to work hard on tasks that are not immediately enjoyable, and the ability to defer immediate gratification in order to work for distant goals can legitimately be viewed as positive attributes of schooling. They form no formal part of the curriculum, yet they are taught in school. Indeed, I believe that parents know they are taught, not perhaps at a critically conscious level, but more or less intuitively. This is perhaps best illustrated by two examples: the attractiveness of prestigious universities and the recent interest in more structured forms of elementary education.

What is it that makes Princeton, Yale, Harvard, Stanford, Swarthmore, University of California at Berkeley, Smith, and Radcliffe attractive places for so many aspiring middle-class students? A part of the reason might be the perceived excellence of the faculties at such institutions. The extensiveness of the libraries might also play a role. But one cannot easily discount the tacit appreciation of the general culture that pervades these schools. Colleges and universities with lesser reputations also teach most of the courses offered at these institutions. Indeed, the explicit curricula across universities in the United States are very much the same. But what does differ is the recognition that universities also present students with a way of life, a set of standards, a distribution of students coming from particular social classes, and levels of academic achievement that will have an important impact on entering students. If one visits university campuses across the country, one is struck by both their sameness and their differences. Some universities monitor or attempt to monitor students' behavior in much the same way as some high schools. Others give the impression that within their hallowed walls reside the seeds of social revolution. Still others have a kind of cool intellectual pride, a sense of scholarly self-esteem that sets the institution aside from the more prosaic forms of cultural life. Such environments, developed through tradition, have selection procedures for staff as well as students that provide an implicit curriculum whose specific goals are not articulated and might not even be consciously recognized. It is something one senses. Many parents as well as students recognize such qualities and guide their children to places whose implicit curriculum is compatible with their values and with the levels of social, economic, and academic achievements to which they aspire.

Similar factors are at work in the motivation among parents to create within school districts more structured forms of elementary education. Although the return to the so-called basics movement is a part of this motivation, the back-to-basics movement cannot be easily separated from larger, more general values. For example, in a suburb near Stanford University a small group of parents petitioned the school board to create a structured elementary school for their children. As a result of this petition and because some school board members were supportive of the proposal, the board offered to make a part of one elementary school a structured school, with a principal who was sympathetic to such a program. However, the board said that parents who did not want their children in such a program would have the option of having them attend parallel, nonstructured classes within the same school. This proposal by the board was not good enough. The parents seeking a more structured elementary school argued that what was necessary was for the entire school to be structured, not just a part of it, because "what happens to students on the playground is as important as what happens in classes." What the parents were correctly pointing out was that in order for the school to be optimally effective, in their terms, the entire environment needed to be taken into account. They did not want the values they thought would be fostered within the classroom vitiated by those that their children would encounter in the schoolyard.

The implicit curriculum of the school is not only carried by the organizational structure of the school and by the pedagogical rules that are established in school—in some high schools students must carry a pass to show hall guards that they have permission to use the washroom—but is also manifested in more subtle ways. Consider for a moment school architecture and the design of school furniture. Most school rooms are designed as cubicles along corridors and have a kind of antiseptic quality to them. They tend to be repetitive and monotonous in the same way that some hospitals and factories are. They speak of efficiency more than they do of comfort. Where, for example, aside from the teacher's lounge, can one find a soft surface in a secondary or junior high school? Schools tend not to be designed with soft surfaces. They tend to look like most of the furniture that goes into them. Most of the furniture is designed for easy maintenance, is uncomfortable, and is visually sterile. Plastics can be used in attractive ways, but instead wood-grained formica is used to make desks that restrict the ways in which one can sit and that yield to no form of body pressure. Rooms seldom have a soft relief; there are few places for enclosure or for privacy. The point here is not so much to chastise school architects but to point out that the buildings that we build do at least two things: they express the values we cherish, and, once built, they reinforce those values. Schools are educational churches, and our gods, judging from the altars we build, are economy and efficiency. Hardly a nod is given to the spirit.

Thus, the implicit curriculum of the school is what it teaches because of the kind of place it is. And the school is that kind of place through the ancillary consequences of various approaches to teaching, by the kind of reward system that it uses, by the organizational structure it employs to sustain its existence, by the physical characteristics of the school plant, and by the furniture it uses and the surroundings it creates. These characteristics constitute some of the dominant components of the school's implicit curriculum. Although these features are seldom publicly announced, they are intuitively recognized by parents, students, and teachers. And because they are salient and pervasive features of schooling, what they teach may be among the most important lessons a child learns.

The Null Curriculum

There is something of a paradox involved in writing about a curriculum that does not exist. Yet, if we are concerned with the consequences of school programs and the role of curriculum in shaping those consequences, then it seems to me that we are well advised to consider not only the explicit and implicit curricula of schools but also what schools do *not* *teach*. It is my thesis that what schools do not teach may be as important as what they do teach. I argue this position because ignorance is not simply a neutral void; it has important effects on the kinds of options one is able to consider, the alternatives that one can examine, and the perspectives from which one can view a situation or problem. The absence of a set of considerations or perspectives or the inability to use certain processes for appraising a context biases the evidence one is able to take into account. A parochial perspective or simplistic analysis is the inevitable progeny of ignorance.

In arguing this view I am not suggesting that any of us can be without bias or that we can eventually gain a comprehensive view of all problems or issues. I do not believe that is possible, nor do I believe that we would be able to know whether our view was comprehensive, for to know that would require that one know everything that was applicable to the problem. Such a perspective requires omnipotence. Yet if one mission of the school is to foster wisdom, weaken prejudice, and develop the ability to use a wide range of modes of thought, then it seems to me we ought to examine school programs to locate those areas of thought and those perspectives that are now absent in order to reassure ourselves that these omissions were not a result of ignorance but a product of choice.

In identifying the null curriculum there are two major dimensions that can be considered. One is the intellectual processes that schools emphasize and neglect. The other is the content or subject areas that are present and absent in school curricula.

Consider first the intellectual processes that are now emphasized in school programs. Discourse in education, both in the public schools and in university schools and departments of education, has placed a great deal of emphasis on the development of cognitive processes. Cognition is supposed to be contrasted with affect, which in turn is contrasted with psychomotor activity. This trilogy is believed to exhaust the major parameters of mind. Cognition, the story goes, deals with thinking, affect with feeling, and psychomotor activity with acting or skill performance. Once these distinctions are made they tend to become reified, a process that is encouraged by the use of taxonomies for the formulation of behavioral objectives within each of the three "domains": cognitive, affective, and psychomotor. Aside from the problems inherent in the reification of distinctions among thinking, feeling, and acting, cognition itself has come to mean thinking with words or numbers by using logical procedures for their organization and manipulation and not thinking in its broadest sense. The term *cognitive* originally meant the process through which the organism becomes aware of the environment. *The Dictionary of Psychology* offers this definition: "a generic term used to designate all processes involved in knowing. It begins with immediate awareness of objects in perception and extends to all forms of reasoning."[9] Yet, in the literature of education the term has been impoverished, and in the process what we consider to be thinking has also been diminished. Thus there is the irony of cognition becoming increasingly important in educational discourse while it is being robbed of its scope and richness.

What school programs tend to emphasize is the development of a restricted conception of thinking. Not all thinking is mediated by word or numbers, nor is all thinking rule-abiding.

Many of the most productive modes of thought are nonverbal and illogical. These modes operate in visual, auditory, metaphoric, synesthetic ways and utilize forms of conception and expression that far exceed the limits of logically prescribed criteria or discursive or mathematical forms of thinking. When attention to such intellectual processes, or forms, of thinking is absent or marginal, they are not likely to be developed within school programs, although their development might take place outside of school. But the consequences within schools for students when such modes of thought and expression are absent or given low priority are significant. The criteria that are employed for assessing intellectual competence must of necessity focus on the forms of thinking and experience that are available and salient. Thus, not only does the neglect or absence from school programs of nondiscursive forms of knowing skew what can be known and expressed in schools; it also biases the criteria through which human competence and intelligence are appraised.

When we look at school curricula with an eye toward the full range of intellectual processes that human beings can exercise, it quickly becomes apparent that only a slender range of those processes is emphasized. When one also considers the fact that some of the most interesting work going on in the field of brain physiology is pointing out that the hemispheres of the brain are specialized, that the right and left hemispheres perform different intellectual functions, and that those functions can atrophy or strengthen with use or disuse, the neglect of what are erroneously referred to as affective processes is particularly significant. Researchers studying brain functions have demonstrated that the left hemisphere is the seat of speech—a fact known since the nineteenth century. But they have more recently demonstrated that what in previous years has been regarded as the minor hemisphere is not minor at all. The right hemisphere provides the location for much of the visualization processes; it is the seat of metaphoric and poetic thought, and it is where structure-seeking forms of intellectual activity have their home. Writing cogently about research on hemispheric specialization, Gabrielle Rico says:

> These findings bespeak a partial redundancy in the two halves of the brain, operating to prevent the individual from being totally incapacitated should disaster strike one or the other hemisphere. But beyond redundancy of function, such evidence lends credence to Bogen's suggestion that a more fundamental distinction between the two hemispheres is not so much a distinction between material or content specificity (speech or faces) as between process specificity. How, then, can these differing capacities best be characterized? A question certainly far from resolved. But there are signs pointing the way:

> 1. If the left hemisphere is better able to process sequentially ordered information, the right is better at simultaneous patterning. Special tests by Levy-Agresti (1968) show a right hemisphere superiority for matching spatial forms, suggesting to her that it is a synthesis in dealing with information. Furthermore, one of the most obvious symptoms to follow right hemisphere damage is the patient's inability to copy block designs (Bogen,

1970) or to arrange blocks in a required pattern. There is also evidence that the left hemisphere tends to classify objects according to related linguistic categories, whereas the right tends to connect objects which are structurally isomorphic. Nebes (1975) writes "the left hemisphere tends to choose items which are similar in their use—i.e., if shown a cake on a plate it might pick out a fork and spoon, while the right selects objects unrelated in use but structurally similar—a round straw hat with a brim" (p. 16).

2. If the left is better able to cope with familiar, learned, habitual configurations, the right is better able to handle unfamiliar configurations: in tests those which were unfamiliar and therefore not susceptible to verbal labels—random shapes, unusual textures—were processed by the right hemisphere, totally baffling the left. Furthermore, shapes easily categorized by language, such as $\heartsuit$ or $\rightarrow$ were readily processed by the left (Nebes, 1975, p. 14).

    In addition, the right hemisphere is better able to reconstitute the whole of a figure after being exposed to only a small number of its elements (Bogen, 1972, p. 52).

3. If the left hemisphere is better able to handle time-ordered stimulus sequences, the right is superior for processing time-independent stimulus configurations (Gordon and Bogen, 1975). Carotid amytal injection is a method in which a drug is injected into one or the other hemisphere to immobolize it for 3–5 minutes. This method has confirmed that the left is specialized for time-ordered sentences, paragraphs, phrases which were retrieved according to grammatical rules and ordered into a specific temporal arrangement. In contrast, the right hemisphere was better able to retrieve songs and melodies which are remembered and produced as intact wholes (presentationally), not as units pieced together tone by tone, word by word. Gordon and Bogen suggest that the ability to store and recall intact such large units may be an important aspect of those tasks for which the right hemisphere of most individuals is dominant.[10]

What Rico is pointing out are some of the major conclusions of a body of research on the functions of the brain that has been going on over the last twenty years. The research provides a useful perspective for examining what school programs provide, what they cultivate, and what they neglect. If we are concerned in schools with the development of productive thought, if we are interested in strengthening those processes through which invention, boundary pushing, and boundary breaking occur, then it seems reasonable that school curriculum should provide children with the opportunitites to use those processes in the course of their work. It is not beyond the realm of possibility that every course that now occupies a position within schools could foster such processes. This would, of course, require that the curriculum activities planned, and particularly the kinds of tests that are used, elicit and reward such processes. The cultivation of imagination is not a utopian aspiration.

The neglect of such processes within schools, assuming they are not adequately fostered outside of schools, can lead to a kind of literalness in perception and thought that impedes the appreciation of those objects or ideas that best exemplify metaphorical modes of thinking. Take as an example the reading of poetry or literature. What will a strictly literal construction of the following poem render?

> *you shall above all things be glad and young,*
> *For if you're young, whatever life you wear*
>
> *it will become you; and if you are glad*
> *whatever's living will yourself become.*
> *Girlboys may nothing more than boygirls need;*
> *i can entirely her only love*
>
> *whose any mystery makes every man's*
> *flesh put space on; and his mind take off time*
>
> *that you should ever think, may godforbid*
> *and (in his mercy) your true lover spare:*
> *for that way knowledge lies, the foetal grave*
> *called progress, and negation's dead undoom.*
>
> *I'd rather learn from one bird how to sing*
> *than teach ten thousand stars how not to dance*[11]

Now take the last couplet in that poem,

> *I'd rather learn from one bird how to sing*
> *then teach ten thousand stars how not to dance.*

To penetrate the meaning of that couplet, to grasp the allusions it contains, requires one to free oneself from literal perceptions of meaning and to apprehend the import of the images in the poetry itself. Although these images are not literally translatable, there are a lot of things we can say about them.

Learning is a humble thing compared to teaching. To teach puts one in a superordinate position, to learn in the position of a subordinate. Learners are seldom philanthropists. But who would the poet rather learn from: not Einstein, or Marx, or Darwin, but from a bird. And what would he rather learn: to understand the universe, to be able to turn dross into gold, to be able to create atomic fission? No. He'd rather learn to sing. He'd rather learn to do something that gives joy to life from one of the most fragile of God's creatures than to teach the largest bodies of our universe itself how not to dance.

But who teaches stars not to dance? How does one teach stars not to do something? Astronomers do. Astronomers teach us that stars do not dance. What we see are simply the light waves that flicker as they traverse the atmosphere. The poet E. E. Cummings chooses joy over knowledge. But to know *that,* no literal reading will do. An ability to allow one's imagination to grasp and play with the qualitative aspects of Cumming's impression is a necessary condition for recovering the meaning the poet has created.

Schools have a role, it seems to me, to offer the young an opportunity to develop the kinds of intellectual processes that will be useful for dealing with the likes of E. E. Cummings and other poets who have given the world its poetry.

Such processes are not restricted to poetry; they function in any sphere of human activity in which new patterns must be perceived, where literal perception will not do, when multiple meanings must be understood, where intimation, nuance, and analogy are at work. Consider the following passage from Aleksandr Solzhenitsyn's *Gulag Archipelago:*

> Spring promises everyone happiness—and tenfold to the prisoner. Oh, April sky! It didn't matter that I was in prison. Evidently, they were not going to shoot me. And in the end I would become wiser here. I would come to understand many things here, Heaven! I would correct my mistakes yet, O Heaven, not for them but for you, Heaven! I had come to understand those mistakes here, and I would correct them!
>
> As if from a pit, from the far-off lower reaches, from Szerzhinsky Square, the hoarse earthly singing of the automobile horns rose to us in a constant refrain. To those who were dashing along to the tune of those honkings, they seemed the trumpets of creation, but from here their insignificance was very clear.
>
> In the first place, it was very interesting to try to figure out the layout of the entire prison while they were taking you there and back, and to calculate where those tiny hanging courtyards were, so that at some later date, out in freedom, one could walk along the square and spot their location. We made many turns on the way there, and I invented the following system: Starting from the cell itself I would count every turn to the right as plus one, and every turn to the left as minus one. And, no matter how quickly they made us turn, the idea was not to try to picture it hastily to oneself, but to count up the total. If, in addition, through some staircase window, you could catch a glimpse of the backs of the Lubyanks water nymphs, half-reclining against the pillared turret which hovered over the square itself, and you could remember the exact point in your count when this happened, then back in the cell you could orient yourself and figure out what your window looked out on.[12]

To understand this passage requires an ability and willingness to make the connection between spring and promises, to recognize its sense of growing life, and to appreciate how the experience of an April sky can be caught in "Oh, April sky!"—the tempo of the passage, the contrast of life and death, of heaven and prison, of the cacophony and the din of motor cars outside where life bustles and the cool systematic efforts to sustain that life in oneself by counting the turns en route to one's cell. An educational program that provides little or no opportunity for students to refine the processes that make such understanding possible is likely to yield a population ill prepared to read the world's great literature. But, perhaps even more importantly, it is likely to withhold from students the joys of intellectual discovery.

The major point I have been trying to make thus far is that schools have consequences not only by virtue of what they do teach, but also by virtue of what they neglect to teach. What students cannot consider, what they don't know, processes they are unable to use, have consequences for the kinds of lives they lead. I have directed my attention in the preceding section to the school's general neglect of particular intellectual processes. Let me now turn to the content or subject matter side of the coin.

Why is it that the vast majority of schools in the United States at both the elementary and secondary levels teach virtually the same subject matters? Let us assume for the moment that basic reading skills, basic arithmetic skills, and basic skills of writing, including spelling, grammar, and punctuation, are necessary parts of virtually all elementary school programs. But even given this assumption, why are time, space, and energy given over to advanced forms of mathematics, history, the sciences, and physical education? Why do most secondary schools require three years of English, two years of mathematics, and one or two years of science? Why do they require two or three years of U.S. history or social studies? Why is it that law, economics, anthropology, psychology, dance, the visual arts, and music are frequently not offered or are not required parts of secondary school programs? Why do so few schools offer work in filmmaking, in the study of communication, in the study of war and revolution? In raising these questions I am not now making a brief that these particular subject matters replace those that now occupy a secure place in school programs. I am trying to point out that certain subject matters have been traditionally taught in schools not because of a careful analysis of the range of other alternatives that could be offered but rather because they have traditionally been taught. We teach what we teach largely out of habit, and in the process neglect areas of study that could prove to be exceedingly useful to students. Take, as an example, economics.

Economics is presently taught in less than 10 per cent of all secondary schools in the United States. Now economic theory is not something one is likely to learn simply through the process of socialization. One does not counter economic theory as one might encounter various forms of social behavior. Yet economics provides one of the frames of reference that enables one to understand how our social system operates. Indeed, to take advantage of the economic opportunities that this nation affords, it is useful to know something of the economic structure of the society, to understand how capital can be used to increase income, to know how to read a stock market report—in short, to have what is needed to make the most out of the resources one has. Yet such problems and the subject matters within which they appear seldom receive attention within schools, say, in comparison to sentential calculus or advanced forms of geometry. The null curriculum includes the study of economics.

Take as another example the study of law. What does a lay person need to know about the law to understand his or her rights, the basic ways in which our legal system works, the rights and obligations incurred in the signing of a contract? What does it mean to be arrested? What is the difference between a criminal and civil suit? What is a tort and when has a crime been committed? Although I realize that such seemingly simple questions are extraordinarily complex, the same holds true for virtually all other fields in which a student works. Students could be introduced to the study of law first because the problems that it poses are interesting and rich—there is much that could be related to their lives in a fairly direct fashion—and second because it is important for citizens to know something about the legal system under which they live so that at the very least they will be in a position to understand the obligations of a contract and the remedies for its violation. At present, such knowledge is almost entirely within the province of the legal profession.

Take as still another example the study of what might be called the vernacular arts. In our society, a wide variety of visual forms are used to shape values, to influence aspirations, and in general to motivate people to do or not do certain things. The design of shopping centers, the forms of the displays that are created, the kinds of images that are shown in the mass media, on television and on film, those images are, as Vance Packard aptly called them, the "hidden persuaders" in our culture. They are designed with skill and serve the interests of the manufacturer and merchant, politician, industrialist, builder, and salesman. How do these images work? In what ways do they impose themselves on our consciousness? Are we or can we become immune to their messages, or do we delude ourselves into thinking so? Are there ways students could be helped to become aware of such forms and how they function? Could they be enabled to learn to "read" the arts of the vernacular, to understand how they themselves use such arts to persuade and motivate? Is there a grammar to these images, a syntax that, although not following the forms of logic used in verbal and written discourse, nevertheless exists and can be revealed through analysis?

The study of popular images, the arts of the vernacular, could of course be offered as part of the school's program. The study of such arts would, at least in principle, help develop a level of critical consciousness that is now generally absent in our culture. Yet, as ubiquitous and as powerful as such popular images are, there are hardly any schools in the country that pay serious attention to them or help students learn to read the messages they carry at a level that subjects them to critical scrutiny. Writing about these images, Edmund Feldman says:

One reason for this difference between the perception of visual and verbal imagery lies in the fundamentally sequential structure of speech and writing as opposed to the almost simultaneous perception of visual forms. Second, because of our phylogenetic heritage, the visual image established connection with different—one might say "older"—portions of the brain than verbal structures. The feelings experienced in the presence of visual images are more difficult to control or resist than those dependent on language. Because language (especially the complex linguistic forms of modern man) evolved after the development of visual perception in the phylogeny of our species, we are equipped with older, possibly less sophisticated, biological equipment for the apprehension of images. We cannot so readily defend against what a picture seems to tell us to do or feel. Third, our knowledge systems and our educational institutions have been organized almost exclusively for the transmissions and reception of linear structures. It is obvious that these institutions find themselves in crisis when nonlinear, that is, visual, sources of imagery are perfected and made cheaply and instantly available. To complicate the problem further, it is possible that the most technically sophisticated mental operations on which an advanced civilization depends cannot be learned except through linear, sequentially organized meaning structures. But for the engineering of public assent, the encouragement of nonreflective behavior, visual imagery is ideal.

If visual images are relatively invulnerable to logical and semantic scrutiny, how can we account for the extraordinary influence of verbal slogans in religion, politics, and advertising? The explanation is simple, and it reinforces our argument concerning the compelling power of the visual image: the effectiveness of a slogan depends on repetition, and the function of repetition is to convert a logical sequence into an image. In fact, the repeated slogan becomes a motor image—one that we find difficult to forget, like the lyrics of a bad song or a frequently heard advertising jingle. So long as a slogan can be analyzed semantically it can be resisted. But once it has been drilled into the popular consciousness in the form of a patterned reenactment, there is no way to prevent many compelling transactions, that is, automatic acquiescence, from taking place. Thus the slogan becomes part of our involuntary behavior.[13]

It becomes clear that what we teach in schools is not always determined by a set of decisions that have entertained alternatives; rather, the subjects that are now taught are a part of a tradition, and traditions create expectations, they create predictability, and they sustain stability. The subjects that are now taught are also protected by the interests of teachers who view themselves as specialists in particular fields. There is no national lobby of teachers of law, or of communications, or of anthropology. Indeed, in the words of one individual who tried to bring an anthropology curriculum into secondary schools, it was necessary to fly under false colors. In order for anthropology to be taught, it has to come disguised as history, a field already established and serving a well-defined professional interest group.

> The strategy that we finally elected was chosen because it looked as though it might work, because it was consistent with our definition of the faults of the traditional social studies, and because it made sense in terms of what anthropology as a discipline had to offer. We decided to subvert a course very commonly taught in the ninth or tenth grade—the world history course. More specifically, we intended to offer materials that could be rationalized as world history and which would, in effect, substitute for a substantial segment of the traditional course. Many supporters of anthropology in the high schools urged us to design a high school level anthropology course. We resisted this advice; we knew that such a program would never become a required course and we knew what happened to elective courses. The elective route was no way to bring large numbers of students into a meaningful encounter with anthropology.[14]

Take as still another example the general neglect of the arts in elementary and secondary schools. Although elementary schools are generally supposed to provide programs in the arts, few well-thought-out and competently taught art programs exist at this level. Elementary school teachers have little background in the arts and, in general, are not well prepared to teach them.

At the secondary level, where there are art specialists, the arts are taught in about half of all secondary schools and only 20 per cent of the school population enrolls for as little as one year. This neglect of the arts, compared to, say, the sciences, leaves students unable, by and large, to deal meaningfully with sophisticated forms of the serious arts. One need not have special tuition to appreciate "The Love Boat," "Hawaii Five-O," or "Family Feud." When it comes to the music of Stravinsky, the films of Bergman, the paintings of Matisse, the architecture of Corbusier, the sculpture of Brancusi, the dance of Cunningham, tuition is needed. Yet, schools do not provide programs that develop such abilities, and, because such abilities do not develop on their own, millions of students leave schools each year without access to what such artists have contributed to the world. If in hundreds of years some archeologist wanted to understand something of the aesthetic level our culture had achieved, no more representative artifacts could be dug up than the Sears Roebuck catalogue and the *TV Guide*.

Law, anthropology, the arts, communication, economics: these are just a few of the fields that constitute the null curriculum. I am not here making a brief for these particular fields or subject matters, for in fact I believe that there can be no adequate conception of appropriate curriculum content without consideration of the context in which it is to be provided and the students for whom it is intended. I identify these fields and subject matters for purposes of exemplification and to highlight the point that what we offer the young in schools is largely bound by tradition. One could hope for more.

When we ask, therefore, about the means through which schools teach, we can recognize that one of the major means is through the explicit curriculum that is offered to students. But that is not all. Schools also teach, through the implicit curriculum, that pervasive and ubiquitous set of expectations and rules that defines schooling as a cultural system that itself teaches important lessons. And we can identify the null curriculum—the options students are not afforded, the perspectives they may never know about, much less be able to use, the concepts and skills that are not a part of their intellectual repertoire. Surely, in the deliberations that constitute the course of living, their absence will have important consequences on the kind of life that students can choose to lead.

Thus far we have examined not only the major orientations that have guided thinking about what shall be taught in school, but we have also examined what schools teach that teachers do not realize they are teaching and what they neglect teaching, as well. The consequences of school programs emanate from values that are explicit and operational as well as those that are tacit and covert.

In the following chapter, we will deal with the problem of how curriculum objectives can be formulated, a problem that has been the center of great controversy during the last fifteen years.

References

1. Robert Dreeben, *On What Is Learned in School,* Addison-Wesley Publishing Co., Reading, Mass., 1968.
2. Phillip Jackson, *Life in Classrooms,* Holt, Rinehart and Winston, Inc., New York, 1968.
3. Seymore Sarason, *The Culture of the School and the Problem of Change,* Allyn and Bacon, Boston, 1971.
4. Elizabeth Vallance, "Hiding the Hidden Curriculum," *Curriculum Theory Network,* 4:1 1973–74.
5. Michael W. Apple, *Ideology and Curriculum,* Routledge & Kegan Paul, London: 1979.
6. Mark Lepper and David Greene eds., *The Hidden Cost of Reward,* New York, Halsted Press: 1978.
7. Lewis Mumford, *Technics and Civilization,* Harcourt, Brace and Co., New York, 1938, pp. 20–21.
8. Ivan Illich, *Tools for Conviviality,* Harper & Row, New York, 1973, pp. 20–21.
9. *The Dictionary of Psychology* (Warren, Howard, and Crosby, eds.), Houghton Mifflin, Boston, 1934.

10. Gabrielle Rico, *Metaphors and Knowing: Analysis, Synthesis, Rationale,* Doctoral Dissertation, Stanford University, 1976, pp. 41–44.
11. E. E. Cummings, *Collected Poems,* Harcourt, Brace and Co., New York, 1926, p. 315.
12. Aleksander Solzhenitsyn, *Gulag Archipelago,* trans. by Thomas P. Whitney, Harper & Row, New York, 1973, p. 212.
13. Edmund Feldman, "Art, Education and the Consumption of Images," in *The Arts, Human Development, and Education* (Elliot W. Eisner, ed.), McCutchan Publishing Co., Berkeley, Calif., 1976, pp. 137–148.
14. Robert Hanvey, "The Social Studies, the Educational Culture, the State," in *Confronting Curriculum Reform* (Elliot W. Eisner, ed.), Little, Brown and Co., Boston, 1971, pp. 143–153.

6

Educational Aims, Objectives, and Other Aspirations

Finally, there should grow the most austere of all mental qualities; I mean the sense for style. It is an aesthetic sense, based on admiration for the direct attainment of a foreseen end, simply and without waste. Style in art, style in literature, style in science, style in logic, style in practical execution have fundamentally the same aesthetic qualities, namely, attainment and restraint. The love of a subject in itself and for itself, where it is not the sleepy pleasure of pacing a mental quarterdeck, is the love of style as manifested in that study.

ALFRED N. WHITEHEAD

No concept is more central to curriculum planning than the concept of objectives. The argument for its importance is straightforward. I will try to provide it.

Behavioral Objectives

Objectives are the specific goals that one hopes to achieve through the educational program that is provided. In order for educational planning to be meaningful not only must goals be formulated, but they must also be formulated with precision and with clarity. To formulate them with precision and clarity it is best not to use words that have referents that are difficult to observe. Words such as *understanding, insight, appreciation,* and *interest* refer to qualities that cannot be observed directly; they require one to make inferences about their existence through the observation of manifest behavior. Thus, useful objectives should be stated in behavioral terms or, in more current jargon, performance terms. When objectives are stated behaviorally, it is possible to have specific empirical referents to observe; thus, one is in a position to know without ambiguity whether the behavioral objective has been reached. An objective that seeks to help students appreciate the insights of great poetry needs to be recast into terms far more specific and precise. What would a student *do* to demonstrate that such appreciation has occurred? What behavior would he or she display? What task is he or she to perform?

It should be noted, as it is by those who advocate the use of specific behavioral objectives in curriculum planning, that the objective is to be stated in terms of desired *student behavior*. It should not describe what the teacher is to do. If an objective stated that "The objective of the course is to introduce students to great ideas of the Western world," not only would the behavior be obscure—the term *introduce* for a behaviorist is vague—the objective would logically be achieved when the teacher introduced the material to the students. The objective in this case is stated in terms of teacher behavior, not in terms of the desired behavior of the students.

A further condition for formulation of meaningful behavioral objectives is that both the behavior and the content be identified. Appreciation, for example, is always of some thing or idea. Understanding always has a subject matter. One does something to something else and in some context. Thus, objectives that are adequately behavioral will not only refer to student rather than teacher behavior, will not only minimize the need for inference—the closer to manifest behavior the better—but meaningful objectives will also identify the particular subject matter in which the behavior is to take place. For example, the student will be able to identify the major causes of the Westward movement in the United States during the period 1840–1870.

Even with these criteria, for hard-line behaviorists, the foregoing objective is still too diffuse. What is missing is a statement of the specific criterion level the student will have to meet in order to demonstrate that the objective has been attained. There might be five major causes for the Westward movement. How many of these must a student identify—one, two, three, four, or all five? Thus, not only must an objective have the characteristics I have already described, but also, perhaps most importantly, it must specify the criterion level that must be achieved to demonstrate competency in reaching the objective. Perhaps the best spokesman for this view is Robert Mager:

> An objective is an *intent* communicated by a statement describing a proposed change in a learner—a statement of what the learner is to be like when he has successfully completed a learning experience. It is a description of a

pattern of behavior (performance) we want the learner to be able to demonstrate. As Dr. Paul Whitmore once put it, "The statement of objectives of a training program must denote *measurable* attributes *observable* in the graduate of the program, or otherwise it is impossible to determine whether or not the program is meeting the objectives."

When clearly defined goals are lacking, it is impossible to evaluate a course or program efficiently, and there is no sound basis for selecting appropriate materials, content, or instructional methods. After all, the machinist does not select a tool until he knows what operation he intends to perform. Neither does a composer orchestrate a score until he knows what effects he wishes to achieve. Similarly, a builder does not select his materials or specify a schedule for construction until he has his blueprints (objectives) before him. Too often, however, one hears teachers arguing the relative merits of textbooks or other aids of the classroom versus the laboratory, without ever specifying just what goal the aid or method is to assist in achieving. I cannot emphasize too strongly the point that an instructor will function in a fog of his own making until he knows just what he wants his students to be able to do at the end of the instruction.[1]

What Mager and others holding this view are trying to do is to develop a highly precise technology for statements of objectives that they believe will improve the quality of teaching and learning. For many behaviorists, one of the major problems of goal statements is that they are vague, and because they are vague they tend to be educationally meaningless. To have a meaningful objective, and by inference a useful one, one should be able to determine, usually through measurement, whether it has been achieved. To the extent that there is ambiguity in the statement, its meaningfulness and utility are diminished. Furthermore, if a curriculum planner knows exactly what kind of behavior he or she wants students to display, it is easier to select content and formulate activities that are instrumental to the desired end.

The Roots of the Objectives Movement

The tendency toward high levels of behavioral specificity is, of course, not new in American educational planning. Franklin Bobbitt, whose ideas we encountered earlier, listed ten areas for such objectives in his book *How to Make a Curriculum,* which was published in 1922. Although Bobbitt's objectives, too, are vague by today's standards, the spirit of behavioral specificity is the same. Indeed, the general thrust toward the study of behavior rather than experience has been characteristic of American educational psychology since the turn of the century. Thorndike, Watson, Hull, and Skinner participate in that tradition, and it provides the theoretical backdrop for this approach to the formulation of behavioral objectives.

There are two other traditions associated with the behavioral specification approach to objectives; one of these is found in industry, the other in military training. They have two features in common: the characteristics of the performance to be produced are known in advance, and, ideally, the specifications of the objectives and characteristics of the individual performance are isomorphic—i.e., a perfect match between objective and behavior is desired. In industrial settings, such as in automobile production, the same conditions hold. A prototypical form is created for the cars to be assembled. This form is described both physically and mechanically for each model. Subsequently, a component analysis is made of the prototype, a task analysis follows that prescribes the steps to be taken in production and their sequence, and production begins. The manager of the assembly line has the task of ensuring that all operations are performed in the order specified. The goal to be achieved is the creation of an isomorphic relationship between the original prototype and each car coming off the line. If these cars do not match, there is a call-back, and the problem is identified and readjustments are made. An efficient and effective assembly line produces identical cars day after day that in every aspect match the model that was originally created.

Military training programs have similar features. New recruits are processed through a program that specifies in almost every detail what is to be done and how. The slogan "There is a right way, a wrong way, and an Army way" is not altogether inappropriate. When one has a training program, a program that intentionally attempts to help another acquire a known, specific performance system to be used to achieve a known goal, the acquisition of known behavioral routines might be appropriate. Personal ingenuity and idiosyncratic behavior are discouraged both on the assembly line and in the boot camp. The armed forces justify such an approach on the basis that it is of paramount importance for soldiers to learn to follow orders: prediction and control of troops are required in time of war. Industry employs such an approach because it is efficient; more cars can be produced in better fashion when systematic, routinized procedures are followed.

It is interesting to note that the earliest efforts at specifying goals and prescribing the methods through which those goals could be attained occurred during the so-called efficiency period in American education from about 1903 to 1925.[2] During this period, school administrators were being criticized in the press for running slack schools, schools that had much waste, that did not give the public a fair return on its investment. These men, vulnerable as they were (and are), sought what they could to make schooling more rigorous and in the process discovered the work of Frederick Taylor, an industrial management consultant and the father of time and motion study. Taylor would go into industrial plants with a team of colleagues and study the movements of the work force, measure the current level of productivity, and then prescribe minute steps to be taken by workers to eliminate excess waste in movement. By utilizing his methods, companies such as Bethlehem Steel were able to increase their level of productivity significantly. Raymond Callahan, a historian noted for his work pertaining to this period, writes:

> The first element in the mechanism of scientific management listed by Taylor was time and motion study and the development of unit times for the various components of any job. This Taylor regarded as "by far the most important element in scientific management," and it was the basic element in achieving his first principle of the development of a true science for a particular job. Frank Gilbreth testified on this point by stating that "any plan of management that does not include Taylor's plan of time study cannot be considered as highly efficient. We have never seen a case in our work where time study and analysis did not result in more than doubling the output of the worker." Not only was time and motion study thus conceived by the engineers themselves, but also it was apparently identified in the mind of the average American as the key element of the system. Milton Nadworny notes, "Although scientific management employed many identifiable and characteristic mechanisms, its most prominent tool was a stopwatch, the popular symbol of the scientific management movement. The stopwatch symbolized the new approach to management: 'management based on measurement.'[3]"

It is not surprising when one is in a vulnerable position, as superintendents of schools were and are, that one should embrace any new idea that promises to reduce that vulnerability. Scientific management, as Taylor called it, appeared to provide the mantle of scientific respectability that schoolmen needed and wanted. By wrapping themselves in a scientific cloak, they believed they could protect themselves from the criticism that they were inefficient stewards of the schools. One superintendent said:

> One may easily trace an analogy between these fundamentals of the science of industrial management and the organization of a public school system. For example: (1) The state as employer must cooperate with the teacher as employee, for the latter does not always understand the science of education; (2) the state provides experts who supervise the teacher and suggest the processes that are most efficacious and economical; (3) the task system obtains in the school as well as in the shop, each grade being a measured quantity of work to be accomplished in a given term; (4) every teacher who accomplishes the task receives a bonus, not in money, but in the form of a rating which may have have money value; (5) those who are unable to do the work are eliminated, either through the device of a temporary license or of a temporary employment; (6) the differential rate is applied to the teacher, quantity and quality of service being considered in the rating; (7) the result ought to be a maximum output at a low relative cost, since every repeater costs as much as a new pupil; (8) the teacher thus receives better wages, but only after demonstrated fitness for high position; (9) hence we ought to have the most desirable combination of an educational system—relative cheapness of operation and high salaries.[4]

It is, I think, particularly important to take note of the language that was used during this period. The society was viewed as the consumer of the school's products. The children were the raw material to be processed according to specifications laid down by the consumer. And the teachers were the workers who were to be overseen by supervisors. All of this was to take place under a superintendent. Although the modern concepts of quality assurance and quality control were not used then, a similar spirit was at work in those "good" old days.

The analogy between industrial processes and educational processes is a deceptive one. When one is working with inert material for ends that are uniform and prespecified, the task of determining effectiveness and locating inefficiency or ineffectiveness is comparatively simple. After all, when one thousand pounds of pressure is placed on thirty-gauge steel within a one-inch diameter, the reaction of the steel to the pressure is quite predictable. As long as there is no human error or mechanical failure, the results will be the same time and time again. Industrial managers bank on it. Such conditions, however, seldom obtain in the classroom. Children are far from inert, so are teachers. They respond differently to the "same" stimuli, because how the stimuli are perceived—indeed, *whether* they in fact stimulate—depends as much on the characteristics of the student as it does on the objective characteristics of the stimuli themselves. Furthermore, the realization of outcomes that are common to all students, the production of educational products all having identical features, at best suits only a small array of those aims that most educators seek in the course of teaching. One major problem I see in the admonition to teachers and curriculum planners to specify their aims in behavioral terms is that the limitations of such objectives are seldom acknowledged. They are offered as though one were not really professionally competent without a list of objectives that one could pull out for each set of curriculum activities formulated.

In identifying what I believe to be an oversimplified view of the character of educational aims, I am not taking the position that there is no place for clearly defined behavioral objectives in a school curriculum. When specific skills or competencies are appropriate, such objectives can be formulated, but one should not feel compelled to abandon educational aims that cannot be reduced to measurable forms of predictable performance. Conceptions of method should serve as tools and as heuristic devices for improving the quality of educational experience, not as constraints on teachers, teaching, or what students have an opportunity to learn.

Limitations of Behavioral Objectives

Let me provide a description of some other limitations behaviorially defined objectives have in the design of educational programs. I identify these limitations not as a wholesale condemnation of their use but as an attempt to increase the sophistication of the dialogue about them.

One limitation of discursively defined behavioral objectives deals with the limits of discourse itself. Much, perhaps most, of what we aspire to and cherish is not amenable to discursive formulation. Take, for example, our image of human sensitivity. Although we could describe discrete behaviors that were intended to characterize a sensitive human being—say, one who was responsive to the feelings of others and compassionate—discrete forms of human performance would ultimately fail to capture what we are able to recognize in others. Language is, after all, a surrogate for experience. We try to articulate in words what we know in nonlinguistic ways. For much of our experience, discursive language performs rather well. But for the subtleties of human experience, for our knowledge of human feeling, for modes of conception and understanding that are qualitative, discourse falls far short. How many words would it take to describe insight, perceptivity, integrity, self-esteem? How would one describe how water tastes? How would one describe the qualities of a late Beethoven quartet in precise, unambiguous, measurable terms?

The point here is not an effort to inject the mystical into educational planning but rather to avoid reductionistic thinking that improverishes our view of what is possible. To expect all of our educational aspirations to be either verbally describable or measurable is to expect too little.

A second problem with the use of specific behavioral objectives is that those who evaluate them often fail to distinguish between *the application of a standard* and *the making of a judgment*. Dewey makes this distinction quite clear when he says the following:

> There are three characteristics of a standard. It is a particular physical thing existing under specified physical conditions; it is *not* a value. The yard is a yardstick, and the meter is a bar deposited in Paris. In the second place, standards are measures of definite things, of lengths, weights, capacities. The things measured are not values, although it is of great social value to be able to measure them, since the properties of things in the way of size, volume, weight, are important for commercial exchange. Finally, as standards of measure, standards define things with respect to *quantity*. To be able to measure quantities is a great aid to further judgments, but it is not itself a mode of judgment. The standard, being an external and public thing, is applied *physically*. The yard-stick is physically laid down upon the things measured to determine their length.
>
> Yet it does not follow, because of absence of a uniform and publicly determined external object, that objective criticism of art is impossible. What follows is that criticism is judgment; that like every judgment it involves a venture, a hypothetical element; that it is directed to qualities which are nevertheless qualities of an *object;* and that it is concerned with an individual object, not with making comparisons by means of an external preestablished rule between different things. The critic, because of the element of venture, reveals himself in his criticisms. He wanders into another field and confuses

values when he departs from the object he is judging. Nowhere are comparisons so odious as in fine art.[5]

Standards are crisp, unambiguous, and precise. A person can swim five lengths of the pool or cannot. Someone can spell *aardvark* or cannot. Someone knows who the twenty-seventh president of the United States was or does not. Someone can multiply two sets of three-digit figures correctly or cannot. For such performances, standards are specifiable and applicable by anyone or by any machine that "knows" the rules through which the standards are to be applied. But what about the rhetorical force of a student's essay? What about the aesthetic quality of her painting? What about the cogency of his verbal argumentation? What about her intellectual style, the ways she interprets the evidence in a science experiment, the way in which historical material is analyzed? Are these subject to standards? I think not.

But to say that such qualities cannot be measured by standards is not to say that judgments cannot be made about them. It is not to say that one can have no criteria through which to appraise them. Judgments can say much about such qualities, not by the mechanical application of prespecified standards, but by comparison of the qualities in question to a whole range of criteria that teachers or others making the judgment already possess. How much weight does one give to insight and how much to logical argument? How does one compare this essay, or this statement, or this project, or this painting, to the one or ones the student did before? Judgments about such qualities are not will-o-the-wisp, cavalier, irresponsible conclusions; they are complex appraisals that use an extraordinarily wide range of knowledge to arrive at what, on balance, is a warranted human judgment. The multiple-choice test is simply not adequate for everything.

A third problem with the demand that all objectives be behavioral and defined in advance deals with the assumption that the prespecification of goals is the rational way in which one must always proceed in curriculum planning. This assumption is rooted in the kind of rationality that has guided much of Western technology. The means-ends model of thinking has for so long dominated our thinking that we have come to believe that not to have clearly defined purposes for our activities is to court irrationality or, at the least, to be professionally irresponsible. Yet, life in classrooms, like that outside them, is seldom neat or linear. Although it may be a shock to some, goals are not always clear. Purposes are not always precise. As a matter of fact, there is much that we do, and need to do, without a clear sense of what the objective is. Many of our most productive activities take the form of exploration or play. In such activities, the task is not one of arriving at a preformed objective but rather to act, often with a sense of abandon, wonder, curiosity. Out of such activity rules may be formed and objectives may be created.

The relationship between action and the formation of purpose is well known to artists. In a particularly telling passage describing the work of the abstract expressionists, Harold Rosenberg, one of America's leading art critics, writes:

> At a certain moment the canvas began to appear to one American painter after another as an arena in which to act—rather than as a space in which to reproduce, re-design, analyze or "express" an object, actual or imagined. What was to go on the canvas was not a picture but an event.
>
> The painter no longer approached his easel with an image in his mind; he went up to it with material in front of him. The image would be the result of this encounter.[6]

What Rosenberg describes of the abstract expressionists is to some extent an echo of Aristotle's remark more than two thousand years ago. "Art," he said, "loves chance." "He who is willing to err is the artist." What both Aristotle and Rosenberg point out is that purpose need not precede action. Purposes may grow out of action. Unfortunately, our cultural tendency to eschew play and praise work makes it sometimes difficult to explain why play is justified in its own right and why in a broad sense it may be among the most productive forms of human activity.

Problem-Solving Objectives

What would a broader, more generous conception of educational aims look like? Are there ways of thinking about objectives and outcomes that are not constrained by the kinds of criteria that are prescribed for behavioral objectives? I believe there are. But before describing two other ways of conceptualizing educational aims let me reiterate that I believe behavioral objectives to be appropriate for some types of educational aims, even though I recognize that they are in no way adequate for conceptualizing most of our most cherished educational aspirations. When it is appropriate to formulate specific types of educational exercises that aim at particular definable skills, the use of such objectives may be warranted: one must be able to swim four laps of the pool to be able to swim in the deep end. But one should not, in my view, attempt to reduce all of our goals into such forms. To do so robs them of the very qualities of mind one may be seeking to foster.

In Figure 2, two types of objectives and one kind of outcome are presented that can be planned in the design and evaluation of educational programs. The first of these, the behavioral objective, has already been described, and I will not restate its feature here. The problem-solving objective differs in a significant way from the behavioral objective. In the problem-solving objective, the students formulate or are given a problem to solve—say, to find out how deterrents to smoking might be made more effective, or how to design a paper structure that will hold two bricks six-

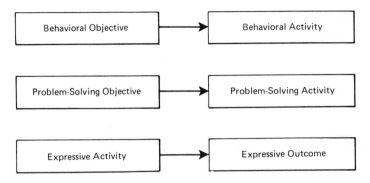

Figure 2   Relationship of Curriculum Objectives to Curriculum Activities

teen inches above a table, or how the variety and quality of food served in the school cafeteria could be increased within the existing budget.

In each of these examples the problem is posed and the criteria that need to be achieved to resolve the problem are fairly clear. But the forms of its solution are virtually infinite. Some students might increase food quantity and variety by finding new sources of supply or by establishing a student volunteer system to work with the kitchen staff. Others might decide that the most effective solution would be for interested students to set up their own kitchen facilities on school premises, and others might formulate an ordering system so students could place orders for some good Chinese and Italian food at a local inexpensive restaurant.

The point is that the shapes of the solutions, the forms they take, are highly variable. Alternative solutions to problem-solving objectives could be discussed in class so that the students could begin to appreciate their practical costs.

This form of objective is not unknown in the design field and in science laboratories. Designers, for example, are almost always given a set of criteria or specifications and asked to create a product that will satisfactorily meet those criteria. Often they are asked to create several solutions so that the client can compare alternatives and decide which suits his or her needs best.

In architecture, the client provides the architect with a set of specifications—budget, site, personal life-style, preferred architectural style—and the builder and municipal code present others. Finally, engineering requirements impose their demands: the building has to stand, the cantilevered deck must not fall, the foundations must not sink. Within these design constraints, the architect must create viable and constructive solutions.

In such situations the potential answers are not known beforehand.

What is known is the problem; what constitute appropriate solutions remains to be seen after the work has been done.

In the sciences this type of problem-solving activity is characteristic, at least for most scientists. The concept of "normal science," a term coined by Thomas Kuhn, aptly describes the work of the typical scientist. Such a person works within a given theory, a theory that he or she does not question. The problem is to find solutions to problems posed within the terms of the theory. Kuhn writes:

> Mopping-up operations are what engage most scientists throughout their careers. They constitute what I am here calling normal science. Closely examined, whether historically or in the contemporary laboratory, that enterprise seems an attempt to force nature into the preformed and relatively inflexible box that the paradigm supplies. No part of the aim of normal science is to call forth new sorts of phenomena; indeed those that will not fit the box are often not seen at all. Nor do scientists normally aim to invent new theories, and they are often intolerant of those invented by others. Instead, normal-scientific research is directed to the articulation of those phenomena and theories that the paradigm already supplies.[7]

Like the architect, the scientist tends not to redefine the givens, in this case the basic theoretical premises by which he or she has been professionally socialized and that serve to define not only the problem, but also the scientist's expertise.

One very important difference between the problem-solving objective and the behavioral objective is that the solution to the problem in problem-solving objectives is not definite. The problem is, in a significant sense, a genuine one. Behavioral objectives have both the form and the content defined in advance. There is, after all, only one way to spell *aardvark*. Given the same set of behavioral objectives for a class of students, the successful teacher elicits homogeneous behavior at the end of an instructional period that is isomorphic with the objective. This is not the case with a problem-solving objective. The solutions individual students or groups of students reach may be just as much a surprise for the teacher as they are for the students who created them.

The issue concerning the form statements of objectives are to take is far wider than the character of the forms themselves. Although it is said that form follows function, the opposite is equally true: function follows form. The form, in large measure, reflects an underlying set of assumptions that might not themselves have been examined. The idea that goals should be specifiable in advance and that success in teaching consists primarily of bringing about predictable outcomes are themselves what is at issue. Such a set of beliefs, fostered not through an explicit educational rationale but rather embedded in the very techniques that one is encouraged to use, can have significant effects on the way the teacher's role is conceived and what educators believe they are after. Surreptitiously but inexorably, techniques that go unexamined with respect to the ideology that they reflect can be debilitating. Training comes to be substituted for education.

The use of problem-solving objectives places a premium on cognitive flexibility, on intellectual exploration, on the higher mental processes. It tends toward the formulation of curriculum activities that are likely to be taken seriously by scholars. The reason I make these claims is that not only have I seen this happen in classes where students had such objectives, but also it is reasonable to expect that when students have a set of clear criteria and are free to meet those criteria in ways that require ingenuity, they will take a deeper interest in coping with the problem. The opportunity to use ingenuity breeds interest.

Expressive Outcomes

A third type of educational aim is what I have called, in previous writing, expressive objectives.[8] Because I now see that the term *objective* implies a preformulated goal, something out of reach but to be attained, I think it desirable to change the term to *expressive outcomes*. Outcomes are essentially what one ends up with, intended or not, after some form of engagement. Expressive outcomes are the consequences of curriculum activities that are intentionally planned to provide a fertile field for personal purposing and experience. Take, for example, much of our ordinary activity— say, going to the movies. There is no one I know who formulates specific behavioral objectives before going to a movie. Nor do I know anyone who formulates a problem-solving objective. Most of us go to the movies because we think something interesting or exciting will happen to us there. We do not formulate specific goals that describe what our behavior will be after we leave. We do not establish criteria that the director and actors will have to meet in order to be successful. The fact of the matter is that we already have such criteria in ample abundance and retrospectively select from the ones we have those that appear appropriate for the particular movie we have just seen. If the movie is a comedy, we apply comedic criteria, if an adventure, dramatic criteria, and so forth.

But the problem of appraising the qualities of expressive outcomes is more complicated than I have just described, even in life outside of schools. If the movie we have just seen was billed as the year's funniest comedy or if it is being shown in the finest first-run theater charging the highest prices in town, we come to expect more than we would otherwise. If our favorite actor or actress is in the film or if it was directed by Fellini, Bergman, or Houston, we might make a more complex appraisal. If we have had the bad fortune of seeing a series of poor films during the last two months, our receptivity toward a somewhat better than mediocre film may be higher than it would otherwise be. The point here is that the appraisals we make as a result of activities we engage in are clearly complex and highly rational, employing a wide range of criteria that, although not explicit, operate in our judgments. The same holds true in classrooms.

I believe that it is perfectly appropriate for teachers and others involved in curriculum development to plan activities that have no explicit or precise objectives. In an age of accountability, this sounds like heresy. Yet surely there must be room in school for activities that promise to be fruitful, even though the teacher might not be able to say what specifially the students will learn or experience. Parents do this all the time. The trip to the zoo, weekends spent camping in the woods, the bicycle ride after dinner: no specific objectives or problems are posed prior to setting out on such activities, yet we feel that they will be enjoyable and that some "good" will come from them.

Curriculum planning and schooling in general need not always be single-minded in their pursuits, forever focusing on objectives that are by definition always out of reach. Purposes need not precede activities; they can be formulated in the process of action itself.

In Figure 2 not only is a distinction made among educational objectives, problem-solving objectives, and expressive outcomes; they also are related to different types of curriculum activities. What we see in Figure 2 is that in both behavioral objectives and problem-solving objectives the formulation of the objectives precedes the curriculum activity. In this respect, they both participate in the standard means-ends approach to planning. However, expressive activities precede rather than follow expressive outcomes. The tack taken with respect to the generation of expressive outcomes is to create activities that are seminal; what one is seeking is to have students engage in activities that are sufficiently rich to allow for a wide, productive range of educationally valuable outcomes. If behavioral objectives and behavioral activities constitute the algorithms of curriculum, expressive activities and expressive outcomes constitute their heuristics.

These are not the only forms of language that are significant. The modifiers around the word *objective* have themselves changed significantly. In Tyler's[9] curriculum monograph published in 1948, *objective* was preceded by the word *educational*. Thus, what one was to formulate was an *educational* objective. Later the term was shifted by other writers to *instructional*. Still later the word became *behavioral*, and even later it was a *performance* objective that was to be formulated.

This shift in modifier is not an accident, it reflects an increased emphasis on the manifest behavior of the student and on discrete forms of student activity. It gradually moves from the general to the specific. But it is significant in other ways, as well. An educational objective supposedly has something to do with *educational* outcomes. An instructional objective, although not strongly normative, still participates in the context of education. But behavioral or performance objectives may or may not be educational; the normative aspect of education no longer is a part of the term. One can have a behavioral objective that aims at creating racists or paranoids. Such an aim could hardly be regarded as educational, unless, of course, racism and paranoia were a part of one's conception of education.

These shifts in language are, in my opinion, no mere minor modifications. Words, of course, have connotations as well as denotations, and it is often the connotative meanings that influence significantly the way we come to think about things. For new students of education, students who do not have the benefit of perspective, the new term, normatively void as it is, might appear as a natural entity. History sustains our memory and provides for depth of field.

It would be erroneous to assume that some fields, such as the fine arts, have a monopoly on the use of expressive activities. This is not the case. Any activity—indeed, at their very best, activities that are engaged in to court surprise, to cultivate discovery, to find new forms of experience—is expressive in character. Nothing in the sciences, the home or mechanical arts, or in social relationships prohibits or diminishes the possibility of engaging in expressive activities and in the process of achieving expressive outcomes. The education problem is to be sufficiently imaginative in the design of educational programs so that such outcomes will occur and their educational value will be high.

What I hope comes through in the foregoing is the view that there is no single legitimate way to formulate educational aims. I have described three approaches or conceptions of objectives. Each has its virtues and utilities. The point of making the distinctions I have made among types of objectives is to expand the array of options that those who plan curricula can use in their work. Once a conception of problem-solving objectives is formulated, it is possible within each subject field—social studies, mathematics, art, English, physical education, and so forth—to plan activities related to such objectives. The same holds true for expressive outcomes. Such outcomes *are not* the exclusive domain of the arts. Even in a field that appears as rule-governed as arithmetic, expressive activities designed to yield expressive outcomes are possible.

A second utility of these three conceptions of educational objectives or outcomes is to ameliorate the unrelenting force and narrowness that a single view of what counts as a legitimate objective tends to have. If there is only one correct way to do something, those who hold other values or envision other means are going to be left out. If the scope of what is legitimate is broadened, the degrees of freedom for teachers and for others who plan curricula will be wider than would otherwise be the case. Indeed, it is reasonable to believe that the types of objectives, outcomes, or aims that can be formulated are not exhausted by the three types I have described. It is reasonable to expect that as our conceptual ability and creativity are applied further to this important aspect of curriculum planning other options will emerge.

With the distinctions that have been made it is, as I have already indicated, possible to use them to plan curricula in the various fields that constitute the program of the school. It is also possible to use these conceptions as criteria for analyzing existing curricula, both teacher-made and commercial. To what extent are problem-solving objectives and expressive activities included? What is the ratio or rhythm among these types of objectives within a curriculum? Do the evaluation methods that are employed in the classroom or school district provide students with opportunities to deal with all three types of tasks, or do these evaluation methods provide only for behavioral objectives to be assessed?

At present in American education, criterion-referenced testing is becoming increasingly popular. Criterion-referenced testing is a procedure that directly relates the test content to the specific behavioral objectives that have been formulated for a course or a school district. The aim of criterion-referenced tests is to help educators determine whether or not students within a school or school district have achieved course objectives. Unlike the norm-referenced test, which is designed to differentiate among students by sorting them out in relation to a normal distribution, the IQ test and most standardized achievement tests are norm-referenced. The criterion-referenced test is designed not to compare students with each other but rather to indicate which students have met the criteria—i.e., the objectives. Since the objectives that are usually employed in school districts are behavioral in character, the use of criterion-referenced tests could inadvertently reinforce an emphasis on a limited conception of objectives. Testing for outcomes whose form and content are not easily predictable complicates the evaluator's task, yet it would surely be unfortunate to have educational aims determined by the technology of testing that is presently available. The educator who understands the alternatives and the issues involved in curriculum planning and educational evaluation is in a much better position to provide educational leadership with a school or school district than one who believes that there is only one way to plan curricula or to evaluate legitimately the outcomes of educational practice.

Some General Questions About the Use of Objectives in Designing Educational Programs

After all of the analyses of the various types of objectives and the criteria that each should meet, one is still left with some basic questions about their utility in curriculum development and teaching. One of the questions deals with the matter of specificity and the educational "unit" for which they are appropriate or necessary. How specific should objectives be? Should they be formulated for the entire course, for parts of a course, for each curriculum activity that is formulated? It is clear that answers to these questions will differ depending on the view of educational planning that one holds. If one views curriculum planning and teaching, as, in their idealized form, an error-free type of program that moves a student as swiftly as possible from one condition at entry to another at exit—I use the technical jargon intentionally—it is likely that specificity in objectives and a large number of objectives would be desired. Yet I believe that in general one would do well to think through a set of objectives in some detail, particularly when one is not clear about the purposes or aims of teaching or when one needs for matter of public record a set of specific statements of educational goals. In other words, on the whole I see no compelling need for a teacher to formulate or to have formulated for him or her a highly specific set of behavioral objectives. For one thing, such a list, especially if prepared at the level of specificity that would satisfy a behaviorist, could easily run into hundreds of items for an elementary school teacher in a self-contained classroom. Assume for a moment that a teacher taught seven subject areas each week. Suppose further that the teacher divided the class into three ability groups and had one objective each week for forty weeks during the school year for each of the three groups in each subject area taught. Such a teacher would have $7 \times 3 \times 40 = 840$ objectives. Obviously no teacher is able to make explicit 840 objectives or be in a position to remember them if they were presented in the form of a guide or manual. How many objectives are feasible? Which ones should be omitted? For what scope of curriculum content are they appropriate? At present there are no quantitative research data that are adequate for answering such questions, nor do I believe there are likely to be.

What I want to claim is that teachers during the school year deal with far more than 840 objectives in the classroom. These objectives are not found in lists. They are not written (although some school districts have compiled such lists of objectives in notebooks the size of the New York City telephone directory). These objectives are a part of the personal and psychological repertoire that teachers draw on each day when working with students.

What I am referring to is the kind of intelligent activity that teachers typically employ in working with students, the kind of intelligence that gives motive and purpose to their teaching, that tells them when they should help a child feel better about himself, when she needs to work harder, when he needs a richer set of resources to work with, when a closer analysis of the text is appropriate. In thousands of ways, teachers draw on images of human virtue as criteria for the direction of their activity as teachers and for the directions they should take with their students. The storehouse of such images is large, and it needs to be. It is modulated according to circumstances and context and with regard to the particular student with whom the teacher interacts.

From this point of view, 840 objectives is a paltry sum. Consider for a moment the range of problems, content, contexts, and individuals with which a teacher must deal. Not only must there be some sense of purpose or direction to the activities in which teachers are engaged, but also the priorities among those projects must be considered, altered, or sustained. When does a teacher, for the time being, wisely forget about the goal of helping a student learn to spell a set of words correctly or learn how to punctuate an adverbial clause and instead attend to other aims, aims that are also a part of his or her aspirations for the student but not an explicit part of that particular segment of the curriculum? When does a teacher choose to make educational capital out of unexpected opportunities in the classroom—an offhand remark by a student or a keen insight by another—and in so doing depart from his or her previously specified objective? All of these happen in classrooms, at least those that are not rigidly tied to a set of single-minded aims. In particular, elementary school classrooms often acquire their own tempo; the students become immersed in what was to be a casual short-term project; and teachers often yield to such tempo, recognizing the need for an organic as contrasted to a mechanical treatment of time.

Thus, from one point of view, 840 objectives are far more than any teacher can reasonably be expected to focus on—420 would be equally difficult. Yet, at the same time, teachers operate with thousands of objectives in the form of their aspirations for the students with whom they work. The major difference is that their latter aims are implicit and contextual rather than explicit and prepared prior to the specific context in which they are to teach.

References

1. Robert Mager, *Preparing Instructional Objectives,* Fearon Publishers, Palo Alto, Calif., 1962, p. 31.
2. See Raymond Callahan, *Education and the Cult of Efficiency,* University of Chicago Press, Chicago, 1962.
3. Ibid., p. 28.
4. Ibid., pp. 103–104.
5. John Dewey, *Art As Experience,* Minton, Balch and Co., New York, 1934, pp. 307–308.

6. Harold Rosenberg, *American Painting Today,* Horizon Press, New York, 1965, p. 25.
7. Thomas Kuhn, The Structure of Scientific Revolutions, University of Chicago Press, Chicago, 1962, p. 24.
8. Elliot W. Eisner, "Instructional and Expressive Objectives: Their Formulation and Use in Curriculum," in *AERA Monograph on Curriculum Evaluation: Instructional Objectives* (W. James Popham, ed.), Rand McNally, Chicago, 1969, pp. 1–18.
9. Ralph W. Tyler, *Basic Principles of Curriculum and Instruction,* University of Chicago Press, Chicago, 1950.

7

Dimensions of Curriculum Planning

*We need, that is, both a way of passing from naked propositions
and their logical connections to the human activities that give
them their sense, and beyond those activities to the features of the
world and human life within which they are at home; and also
a reverse road, back from "forms of life" in the world to the
specific activities in question, and so eventually to the original
propositions again.*

STEPHEN TOULMIN

Thus far, a variety of ideas, concepts, and theories have been discussed pertaining to the design and evaluation of educational programs. The ultimate test of these ideas is determined by the extent to which they make educational planning more intelligent. As I have already indicated, education is not a field that will yield to simple prescriptions or recipes. Each situation in which educational decisions are made is significantly unique, not simply unique in the sense of time and place—all situations are unique in that sense—but unique in the sense that the goals, methods, people, and context differ from each other in important ways and must be treated with respect to those differences if decision making is to be effective. What we can expect of ideas about curriculum planning is not that these ideas provide formulas, but that they sophisticate our deliberations in planning programs and, hence, contribute to educationally richer programs than might otherwise be provided. In short, we ought to view ideas as tools, not as blueprints; they are things to use, not things to follow.

What Is Curriculum Planning?

Curriculum development is the process of transforming images and aspirations about education into programs that will effectively realize the visions that initiated the process. I use the term *images* and *aspirations* intentionally. The initiating conditions of curriculum development are seldom clear-cut, specific objectives; they are, rather, conceptions that are general, visions that are vague, aspirations that are fleeting. Much of what we value, aspire to, and cherish is ineffable; even if we wanted to, we could not adequately describe it. Furthermore, what we value and seek is often riddled with contradictions—even within the context of schooling—and must be compromised or negotiated in context. We want children to master "the basic skills"; we would like them to be supportive and cooperative with their peers and with adults, yet we also would like them to take initiative, to be able to compete and not feel bound by rules that might stifle their imagination, curiosity, or creativity. Our images of virtue are in flux; because images can never be translated wholly into discourse, to that degree they are always somewhat beyond the grasp of written or verbal expression.

Curriculum development in the context of education is, in this sense, a process that seeks the realization of certain ineffables. It is a process that is engaged in by anyone who attempts to make that translation. One group continually engaged in that process is teachers. Teachers inevitably have a range of options that they can exercise in the selection, emphasis, and timing of curricular events. Even when they are expected to follow certain guides or books in which activities and content have already been determined, there are still options to be considered and choices to be made by teachers with respect to how those materials will be used and the ways in which what is done in one particular area of study will or will not be related to what is done in other areas of the curriculum. These decisions are, of course, decisions bearing on the curriculum; they influence the kind of opportunities for learning and experience that children will have.

Who Plans Curriculum: The Teacher's Role

But more typically the scope of teachers' freedom regarding what skills are to be taught, when, in what order, and how, is far wider than what the most highly structured programs provide for. Typically, the teacher will have a general guide of topics in a subject field, a sequence among topics, a general set of aims, textbooks, and other instructional resources. With these materials and within the constraints set by time, school culture, and the characteristics of the students, the teacher builds an educational program. The decision making for that program may be a species of long-term, highly systematic planning; a teacher might try to develop a calendar of topics and activities that extend throughout the year, or the teacher might plan on a week-to-week basis, without making any attempt to follow a specified timetable. The extent to which one or the other plan is selected can depend on the teacher's need for order and predictability and on the teacher's view of the educational process. For example, if a teacher believes that students should play a role in the development of curriculum, that they should have opportunities to decide what they study and what ends they seek, then it is not so likely that it will be possible to predict where a class or an individual student is likely to be a month or two in the future. The point in such a view of educational planning is to encourage the student to develop increasing amounts of competence and initiative and thus to assume greater responsibility for planning his or her educational program. The control of student progress and the prediction of learning at specific intervals over time are, given this view of teaching, beside the point. But even so, the teacher plays an important role in curriculum decision making, because it is the teacher who decides to give or not to give students the opportunity to assume curricular responsibility, and it is the teacher who decides what kind of encouragement and guidance to provide in the selection of topics and areas of study.

In contrast to such a currculum plan, consider the increasing tendency among school districts to specify particular performance objectives for students at intervals within each grade level. In such a system the scope for teacher or student flexibility in curriculum decision making is reduced significantly because the specified objectives define expected levels of student performance. The teacher and the students know what these expectations are, they know that they (both students and teacher) will be tested to determine their success in meeting these objectives, and hence their choices are circumscribed by the objectives. Options that might have otherwise been pursued are relinquished in favor of school- or district-wide goals.

Whether one works within a system that encourages truly individualized educational programs and that supports high levels of student planning or within one where grade-level expectations and curriculum content are specified in great detail, the role of the teacher in curriculum decision making is always important. It is important because the teacher serves as the interpreter of educational policy and because the teacher is the major mediator of what shall be taught—if not learned—in the classroom.

Although curriculum development can and often does take form in the creation of materials, curriculum development more frequently yields no materials but, rather, plans that might be no more than sketchy notes. For example, a teacher might decide that a particular activity would be educationally beneficial in a classroom, say, a discussion of a book or film that students have read or seen. And the teacher might also decide that after the discussion he will ask the students to express their ideas about what they have read or seen in a painting or short story, a poem or a play. What the teacher wants to do is to help children recognize that ideas can be expressed in different ways and that they can have a choice in the way in which they choose to express what they know. Suppose further that the teacher thinks that it might be interesting and useful to follow up this activity by having a poet or a painter visit the class to talk with the children about her work. In this episode, the teacher is engaged in curriculum planning, but no materials are being created. It might be that the teacher prepares some notes to himself or develops a fairly elaborate lesson plan, but the latter is not a necessity. Teachers engage in such planning most of the time, and to do so is to make curriculum decisions, to engage in a form of personal curriculum deliberation. This, too, is one way in which curriculum development occurs. Indeed, it would not be possible to have a school without some form of curriculum development. The form might be as "loose" as is used in a neoprogressive school or as "tight" as a highly systematic training program that leaves virtually nothing to chance. The point here is not the form that curriculum planning takes, but the fact that it must occur.

District-wide Curriculum Planning

A second group involved in curriculum development is that working under the aegis of school districts. Many school districts appoint committees made up of subject specialists and teachers to work jointly in the creation of curriculum materials that are considered particularly suitable for their particular school district or some portion of it. A school district under the leadership of the assistant superintendent for curriculum and instruction might decide as a result of the activities of a lay group that curriculum materials are needed in the area of human relations. The district serves a community that has a wide array of ethnic and racial minority groups and after having conducted a national search for available curriculum materials decides to create its own materials, materials that will draw on the talents and resources of people living in the community. A committee is appointed by the superintendent to work on such a project, and a budget is made available to compensate teachers and others for the additional work that they will be required to do.

Such a group might work two afternoons each week after school for six months to develop the structure and format for the curriculum, to create the activities, and to secure the necessary materials so that what is created can be used in the classrooms. At the end of its work this committee will have prepared written, visual, and perhaps audio material relevant to the children living in the community the school district serves. Such work might be followed up with in-service education programs for principals and selected teachers, so that the aims of the project are gradually realized. If as a result of such a trial the materials are found to need revision, revision will occur. The expectation is that these materials, especially created for this particular school district, will become a regular part of the curriculum of each school. The materials represent the vehicles through which the initial aspirations of the lay group will be realized.

It is obvious that it is one thing to create plans for oneself and quite another thing to create plans and materials that others are to use. All teachers do the former; relatively few do the latter. What one can consider in developing materials for others to use will be described in detail later. For now it is important to recognize the difference.

State Curriculum Planning

A third major group to engage in curriculum development are the staffs of state departments of education or the committees that work under the aegis of the chief state school officer.

Curriculum development at the state level can take the form of specific curriculum materials to be used in the classroom, or, as is more typically the case, it can take the form of curriculum outlines that can be used as guides by local school districts. In California, for example, the state superintendent of schools appoints committees to develop new state guidelines, or, as they are called in California, State Curriculum Frameworks, for the teaching of particular subject areas prescribed in the state education code. These committees, made up of representatives from professional groups in education and lay people, might be appointed for a one- to three-year period to meet, say, monthly, and to carry out the deliberations, consultations, and preparation of a new framework for teaching mathematics, social studies, art, music, the humanities, and so on.

The function of such statewide curriculum committees is to make use of knowledgeable people in the subject field in order to upgrade the quality of educational programs in the various fields of study. It provides an opportunity for the state to update what it offers school districts and in the process be instrumental in guiding the direction of educational change.

In developing a statewide framework for a field, a curriculum committee is faced with a variety of difficult decisions. How specific should the materials be? If they are highly specific, they might be inappropriate for particular populations within the state. If they are very general, the translation from the guidelines to practice might be very difficult. Who should be consulted in preparing such guidelines? In a statewide framework committee on which I served, a circuit of hearings was held throughout the state with relevant professional groups. We wanted reactions to the ideas we as a committee had created and we wanted the groups to feel that they, too, participated in the process of planning the framework they would eventually use. As it turned out, this process was a form of in-service education for those of us on the committee as well as for those who participated in twenty-odd meetings that were held throughout the state. We learned a great deal about what teachers and university professors regard as appropriate goals and content, and they had the opportunity to reflect on some ideas about the content and goals of curriculum that they might not have otherwise considered.

This planning process lasted about three years, at the end of which a statewide framework for the visual arts was published by the state department of education and disseminated to all public schools and colleges in California. In addition, the work of the state curriculum framework committee was given a central place in regional and statewide conventions in art education. What occurred was a spinoff whose effects were much wider than the work that the committee did on the written document itself. The position the committee developed with respect to the curriculum for teaching art in the state had an intellectual set of consequences for the way in which art education was conceptualized.

One should not underestimate the importance of state-endorsed programs or curriculum materials. The ultimate legal responsibility for education belongs not to the local school district but rather to the state. The constitutions of the various states assign that responsibility to the state board of education, which in turn develops a state education code that provides the guidelines, standards, and mandates for local school districts. The state superintendent of schools, through his or her staff, and with the assistance of the county school superintendent, is responsible for monitoring local school districts to assure that the requirements of the state education code are met. Although relatively few county superintendents execute primarily a monitorial function, the authority of the office and that of the state department of education carry weight. In many states, the withholding of funds to local school districts is possible if the mandates provided in the state education code are not heeded.

The point of all of this is to underscore the importance of state sanctions in the area of curriculum policy, particulary when a statewide educational policy is backed up by funding options that the state department of education holds.

It should be noted also that the state board of education is in some degree guided by the advice of the state superintendent of public instruction, particularly with respect to matters dealing with what should be taught and for what amount of time. In some states, the education code specifies which subjects will be taught at each grade level and how many minutes of instruction will be provided for these subjects each week. In addition, the state prepares a list of acceptable textbooks or provides state-adopted textbooks for the local school districts. Because many teachers build their programs around them, these resources have a great impact on the content with which students come into contact. If a textbook in science devotes three chapters to ichthyology, students using that textbook study ichthyology. If a textbook on the social studies presents a black perspective on the civil rights movement, students study that material. Because access to content is a condition to learning that content, questions of content inclusion–content exclusion are extremely important. In effect, they define much of the opportunity students will have within the school to deal with certain topics and ideas.

Research and Development Center

A fourth group that engages in curriculum development are those working in university research and development (R&D) centers and in regional educational laboratories supported by the National Institute of Education. Research and development centers, all of which are affiliated with universities, conceive of their mission as conducting research and facilitating educational development by devising products and programs that are primarily experimental and, in principle, related to ongoing research. Educational laboratories do, however, engage in the creation and testing of curriculum materials, the marketing of which is handled by commercial publishers.

Educational laboratories such as CEMREL engage in the development of curriculum materials in mathematics and in the area of aesthetic education. The main function of educational laboratories is to use federal funds to pioneer new methods and programs that require the skills of sophisticated curriculum specialists and others and the kind of risk capital that commercial publishers would be unwilling to provide. Thus, with average annual budgets of millions of dollars, the laboratories conceptualize, develop, test, and document these materials for use in classrooms throughout the country. In addition, some laboratories have created teacher centers to train teachers in the use of the materials they have designed. The materials once produced are often published commercially, and school districts, with the aid of federal funds, may purchase from a commercial publisher what has been developed through the support of federal funds at the laboratory or the university-related R&D center.

Educational laboratories are generally larger and have larger budgets than R&D centers; they occupy often elaborate and at times sumptuous quarters and have a staff that consists not only of curriculum specialists, but also social scientists, designers, photographers, managers, secretaries, and the like.

In their ideal form, educational laboratories and university R&D centers should undertake programs of curriculum development that are high risk, forward looking, and based on the highest professional standards of the field. Agencies supported by the taxes of citizens have a special obligation that, in my view, exceeds that of commercial publishers. Unfortunately, the competition for federal funds has created in both laboratories and R&D centers a need to "look good," to project an image of success that too often hampers candor. Laboratories and R&D centers should be places where it is all right to fail. Indeed, a laboratory without failure is a contradiction in terms.

Commercial Publishers as Planners of Curriculum

A fifth group, and in many respects the most influential group aside from the classroom teacher in the area of curriculum development, are commercial publishers. And the most influential material published is the textbook. Textbooks are not typically looked on as curricula, but they are certainly important curriculum materials. In the first place, textbooks are, for many teachers, the hub around which programs are built. When a school or school district adopts a textbook in social studies, science, or mathematics, this book, de facto, defines a significant portion of the content of what students will study. Textbooks in these areas also contain suggestions to students and teachers for supplementary activities and in this way further define what students will do in the classroom. In addition, teacher guides are prepared for many textbooks that provide guidance to the teacher regarding the kinds of questions or issues that can be used for discussion, and some contain tests that can be used to determine if the students have learned what the textbook taught.

Increasingly, however, publishers are developing not only textbooks, but also multimedia kits designed to teach what publishers believe will sell in schools. Most of these materials—and they come in video cassettes, filmstrips, audiotapes, computer software, graphic displays, and educational games—are designed to provide short-term units rather than semester or year-long programs. The creation of these materials originates from at least three factors: the possibilities that new technology provides, the marketability of the materials to schools and hence their profitability for publishers, and the realization that the channels through which students learn are multiple and the range of sensory modes that can be used for facilitating learning is wide. Yet, despite the plethora of such materials—a visit to a national convention of teachers and school administrators will provide a mind-boggling array of such materials displayed by publishers—the single most important resource influencing what children study in school, aside from the teacher, is still the textbook.

Federal Influences on Curriculum

There is another source that while seldom involved in planning curricula nevertheless has a significant effect on the curriculum that is offered.

That source is the Federal Government. The government has access to two important resources for influencing the curriculum: money and publicity. When the government adopts a policy that will infuse $400,000,000 into the teaching of science and mathematics in the schools and when the President of the United States speaking to the nation says that science and mathematics education is a national priority, the conditions are created for bringing about a new emphasis in these fields in the nation's schools. With such funds, new curriculum development projects can be initiated, institutes for teachers to be retrained in these fields can be created, scholarships to encourage students to select these fields of study can be provided, and increased salaries for science and mathematics teachers can be offered. These are not trivial considerations. But perhaps even more important is the rationale for more science and mathematics in the schools. The President provides the nation with an economic rationale: we must emphasize science and mathematics in school curricula in order to remain economically competitive with Japan, Germany, and other competitive nations. The reason is an instrumental one; students need to study in these areas for the economic well-being of the nation. There are, of course, other bases on which to justify the teaching of mathematics and science. One might wonder what a purely economic justification does to the public's understanding of education when such rationales are provided from the high office of the President of the United States.

Furthermore, what will happen to other aspects of the school curriculum when only two subjects receive such massive support? How is a balanced curriculum to be sustained—assuming one wants balance in the curriculum? Such questions and issues need to be asked and addressed by school boards and professional educators, even when they are neglected by policy makers in Washington. The Federal Government, despite our commitment to state control of education, plays an extremely important role in shaping the school curriculum.

What we find, then, when we look at who does curriculum development and where and when it is done are a variety of groups engaged in the task. Teachers develop curricula when they plan for their classes, school districts engage in curriculum development through the creation of materials to be used in classrooms, and professional and lay groups develop curricula when they create state frameworks for teaching in particular subject fields. Educational laboratories, R&D centers, and commercial publishers engage in curriculum development through the production of materials such as *Man: A Course of Study*, SRA Reading Kits, DISTAR, CEMREL's Aesthetic Education Program, and SWIRL's Basic Reading Series. Finally, the Federal Government is very influential in reshaping what schools teach. All of these groups and individuals engage in curriculum development as they attempt to transform aspirations and images of educational virtue into plans and methods they believe are useful for realizing such ends.

Dimensions of Curriculum Planning

What are the factors that one might consider in the design of an educational program? What can one take into account in curriculum planning? As I have already indicated, I do not believe it possible in the field of education to prescribe formulas that one is to follow, but it is possible to provide concepts and generalizations that can heighten one's sensitivity to issues, problems, and possibilities to which one might attend. What follows is the identification and discussion of some dimensions of curriculum planning that can be considered by those attempting to design educational programs. *The sequence of these dimensions is, to a large degree, arbitrary. One need not begin or end with the factors or aspects as they appear here.* Because for the purposes of writing some ordering is necessary, the sequence that follows seems to me to be reasonable, but one may proceed in curriculum development with a very different order.

It should be noted at the outset that the study of the processes of curriculum development as it actually occurs for individuals or groups is rare. It has only been quite recently that the process has been studied empirically. The reason for the general neglect is fairly clear. Individuals and groups interested in developing curriculum materials or formulating curriculum policy have had those goals as their major priorities. The study of the processes through which decisions are made is seldom a part of their mission. Hence, what groups actually do in different contexts and circumstances is at present largely known through recollection rather than through, say, naturalistic observation as an ethnographer might study the process. What is clear from the case studies of curriculum decision making that have been published is that the process is far more convoluted, circuitous, and adventitious than one might be led to believe by reading the formal literature on curriculum planning. In the next chapter, a description of the planning processes of one curriculum development group will be described in some detail. For the present, we will examine some of the aspects that can be considered in the creation of a curriculum.

Goals and Their Priorities

Perhaps the area in curriculum planning that has received the most attention in the literature is that of how objectives should be formulated. If one looks into the literature in curriculum, one will find distinctions that are made among aims, goals, and objectives. Aims are the most general statements that proclaim to the world the values that some group holds for an educational program. "The aim of this school is to help students learn to participate effectively in the democratic way of life." From aims we sense a direction, a point of view, a set of values, to which the community or group subscribes. These statements form a kind of educational manifesto of cherished values, and, although such statements have been regarded by many as meaningless, if one were to contrast the statement of aims made in school districts in the United States with those found in the written material produced in China, Cuba, or the Soviet Union, one would note significant differences in the spirit and outlook of what has been written. What such statements provide is an articulation of educational faith, in a sense in the way in which the Preamble of the Constitution or the Declaration of Independence expresses general but still meaningful beliefs about the individual and his or her relationship to the society.

A second kind of aim is referred to as a goal. Goals are statements of intent, midway in generality between aims and objectives. Goals describe the purposes held for a course or school program. "The goal of this course is to help students understand the causes of social revolution." "The goal of the course is to develop skills in copper enamel jewelry making." These statements are considerably more specific than aims, but insufficiently specific for, say, instructional objectives. Goals are intended to provide a greater focus on anticipated outcomes and to provide curriculum planners with the basis for the selection of curriculum content. In the standard curriculum literature, goals are supposed to be deduced from aims. Having deduced goals, one then deduces objectives. Having deduced objectives, one then proceeds to formulate curriculum activities. The planning process is supposed to be a step-by-step process from the general to the specific; from ends to means. The problem with this view, as I have indicated earlier, is that it assumes that curriculum activities that are educationally significant always have explicit goals or objectives, which they do not, and that the formulation of goals must precede activities, which is not always true.

Objectives are typically specific statements of what students are to be able to do after having experienced a curriculum or a portion of one. Objectives of the instructional variety are supposed to state with little ambiguity what particular forms of behavior the student will be able to display. Thus, "The student will be able to create a clay bowl on a potter's wheel that is at least twelve inches high, having walls no thicker than one-half inch," would be an example of an instructional objective.

Now the thrust of these comments is not essentially to restate the forms in which educational intentions are couched or even to describe their levels of generality but rather to point out that intentions are appropriate to consider in the development of an educational program and that priorities among goals must be determined.

The determination of priorities is influenced by the context in which programs are to function. For example, a school board, a community, or a school faculty might be convinced that a particular set of goals is of the utmost importance but at the same time recognize that the realization of those goals in this particular context is not possible at this time. Thus, goals, even those holding high status, are shifted in their operational importance. A faculty might believe that the critical study of local politics is crucial to the sound education of adolescents but might also recognize that the community would not allow such studies to be taught, or that there is in fact no one on the faculty who has the professional competence to teach such a course well. In this case, other areas and goals become practically more important.

Thus far I have discussed goals as they relate to and across subject matters, but within fields, too, there is a host of competing goals. What kind of goals should be emphasized in mathematics: comprehension of the structure of mathematics as a system or skills in computation? What kind of social studies should be provided: those that emphasize history or those that emphasize the methods of inquiry of the social sciences? What sort of art program should be offered to students: one that enables them to appreciate the most significant works of art that have been created or one that aims at the development of skills needed to create art? Competent curriculum deliberation will consider the options within as well as between fields of study. In such consideration, educational values obviously come into play, and it is here that basic orientations to curriculum emerge among those who deliberate. But the ultimate resolution of these priorities always takes place within the constraints of the context. What one finally puts into practice is a function of the interaction of aspirations and existing constraints.

Although acquiescing to existing constraints in educational planning can lead to an inert form of educational conservatism, regard for the constraints of the context is necessary for an intelligent form of curriculum deliberation. Curriculum planning cannot adequately be treated in a simple piecemeal fashion; there are always tradeoffs in time, expected outcome, human and fiscal resources, community support, and the like. To neglect "the big picture" is to court disaster, yet to regard the context only as a set of constraints rather than a set of opportunities is to embrace a maintenance model of educational management. Negotiating the balance between the desirable and the possible is one of the arts of school administration as well as curriculum planning.

The Content of the Curriculum

Because goals seldom prescribe the content that can be used to achieve them, attention to the selection of content is always an important curriculum consideration. If a curriculum development group working on the development of a curriculum in, say, biology agrees that the major aims of the program are to help students understand (1) that scientific inquiry always yields conclusions that are tentative and (2) that living organisms depend on the environment to survive, the specific content as well as the teaching methods that may be instrumental to such purposes is still not yet given. What the group must do is to identify the variety of potential content areas within biology or within the students' experience outside of biology that will help them grasp these ideas. A curriculum development group might, for example, choose a variety of content ranging from simple forms of plant life to complex forms of human behavior for exemplifying the relationship between organism and environment. Or the group might decide to create some analogies to nonbiological entities such as cities or nations in order to illustrate how similar principles operate in "nonliving phenomena."

The point here is that groups concerned with curriculum planning have options in content selection. The problem is one of deciding which of the possible content options should be selected. One possible criterion for content inclusion, in addition to whether there is some relationship between the content and the aim, is whether the content is likely to be meaningful to the children for whom the program is intended. Children bring to school wide varieties of experience that originate from the homes and communities in which they live. The kind of biological content that children living in a rural area might find meaningful can differ significantly from that which inner-city urban youngsters might find meaningful. One way of dealing with such diversity is to include in one's curriculum material options from which teachers and students can themselves choose. In other words, by providing different kinds of content to make the same point, the flexibility of the materials is increased.

In Sweden new curricula are being developed under the auspices of the Ministry of Education. Curriculum developers identify significant concepts and generalizations within particular subject areas. For example, in the social studies the concept might be *role*. Generalizations are then provided about role: "Societies tend to differentiate the roles people perform in order to deal with problems and social needs efficiently." Given the concept of role and the generalization in which it is embedded, the teacher, or the faculty of the school, works out the particular curriculum activities and specific curricular content that will make this concept and generalization meaningful to students. For students living in rural areas, exemplars of role may very well be different than exemplars for students living in urban areas. Thus, once the important concepts and generalizations are identified at a national level for a particular field of study, the way in which they are transformed into an operational curriculum for students is a task for the teacher or the faculty of the school. In this way both national and local needs can be met.

There are, of course, limitations on the number of options that can be provided. The physical size of the syllabus, for example, is not a trivial consideration—nor is the amount of materials teachers should be asked to read. More will be said about these considerations later; for now, the major point to be made is that goals do not prescribe content. Content selection, like goals, can be considered against a backdrop of options. Furthermore, curriculum developers, within the limits that seem reasonable, can provide teachers with the content of options that are related to the aims of the curriculum.

Types of Learning Opportunities

Goals and content are necessary but not sufficient for the development of a curriculum. The educational imagination must come into play in order to transform goals and content to the kinds of events that will have educational consequences for students. This transformation requires that an event be conceptualized and have sufficient educational promise for students to be used in an educational program. I say that the educational imagination comes into play because it is this task—educational transformation—that draws most heavily on the expertise of the teacher or curriculum designer.

If a group of citizens wanted to know what the most significant concepts and generalizations were in some branch of biology, the individuals most likely to provide such information would be biologists who know their field well and who were aware of the most recent developments within it. But to acquire such information from biologists is not sufficient for the creation of an educational program. Some educationally appropriate means must be created to enable students to interact with problems or situations that will yield an understanding of these concepts and generalizations. A biologist who has not worked with adolescents, who does not understand what teachers are able to do in a secondary school classroom, is not necessarily the best person to make such a transformation. It is here that curriculum expertise is crucial. For it is here that educational events must be planned and curriculum materials prepared to enable teachers and students to grasp those concepts and generalizations and to do it in a form that is consistent with one's view of education. For example, if one believes that the major mission of the school is to introduce students to the products of the best inquiry in the arts and the sciences, one might decide to use a moderately didactic approach to instruction in, for example, the biological sciences. Such an approach would emphasize the big ideas and theories that biological greats have created. In such a view, the work of Mendel, Darwin, Wall, Muller and Dobzhansky would play a prominent role in content selection. The thrust of the curriculum would be to help students understand the theories and concepts these biologists created, say, within the context of their time. To do this one might provide lectures and films, and perhaps have students read excerpts from primary source material. But if one were interested in having students understand the relationship between biological ideas and the methods through which those ideas were created, if one wanted to help students appreciate the tentativeness of scientific conclusions, then the type of learning opportunities one might use would give students experience in the conducting of biological experiments. The transformation of the "same" content would take different forms because the basic orientation to education would differ significantly.

The options available to the curriculum designer are numerous with virtually any body of content, and in the curriculum field, as in education at large, there has been a longstanding controversy on the relative importance of process as compared to product. Those who emphasize the importance of process tend to formulate learning opportunities that stimulate children to active inquiry. Such individuals want the student to inquire, to think, to act, and in the process to learn. The outcomes of the process are what children learn from the engagement. It is to be hoped that the product of such activity will be consistent with valid substantive knowledge in the field in which the inquiry occurred. But that is not necessarily the major aim. The main aim is to teach children to think, to act, and to learn from the consequences of their actions.

Those who emphasize the product are more interested in what children learn of the conclusions of mature inquiry in specialized fields. Does the student understand the relationship between random mutation and natural selection? Does the student grasp the concept of dominant and recessive genes?

These views of what counts educationally have an extraordinarily important bearing on the kinds of learning opportunities that are created in the curriculum. The advocate, for example, of learning by discovery will frequently be interested in helping children "learn to think like scientists." For such people the curriculum should be built around problems. The task of the curriculum designer is to create activities that help children either formulate problems or try to resolve the problems posed within the materials.

Although I have emphasized the relationship between one's orientation to curriculum and the kinds of learning opportunities that might be provided, in practice the relationship between activities and goals is neither linear nor unidirectional. Indeed, teachers are more inclined to focus on what they might *do* than on what goals they intend to accomplish.[1] This is because practical decisions always relate to the utility of action. What teachers want and need are ideas that have practical payoffs; ideas that for the most part lead to action. Projects that appear interesting, activities that seem heuristic, events that will be attractive and engaging to students are valued by teachers. Once students are fully engaged in such activities, one can guide them so that various goals and aims are achieved.

But goals and aims, unless they can be transformed into educational events within the classroom in a form that is interesting to students, and within the capacity of teachers, are only empty hopes that have little educational reality. One means through which types of learning opportunities might be created is a matrix of intellectual processes. One such matrix has been formulated by J. P. Guilford, a psychologist long interested in creative thinking and in the structure of the human intellect. What Guilford has done is to conceptualize the variety of aptitudes or processes that the human mind is capable of. His scientific ambition has been not only to conceptualize these mental processes, but also to create instruments that can be used to assess them. We need not for our purposes try to evaluate the scientific validity of these intruments, but we can examine his model of intellect for its potential utility in the creation of learning opportunities within a curriculum. That is, we can use Guilford's model as a kind of mnemonic device to help us—if we so choose—to create learning opportunities that elicit different forms of thinking. These forms, once identified, could then be related to bodies of content considered important so that sophisticated forms of thinking could be used to deal with educationally significant content.

Related to Guilford's structure of the intellect are the intellectual processes identified in the taxonomy of educational objectives in the so-called cognitive domain. The cognitive taxonomy lists not 120 mental processes, as does Guilford, but six. They are:

1. Possession of Information.
2. Comprehension.
3. Application.
4. Analysis.
5. Synthesis.
6. Evaluation.

Although these terms refer to kinds of objectives that one can formulate and to the kind of test items or tasks on tests related to those objectives, the taxonomy can also be used to formulate types of learning opportunities that can be made available to students. For example, one could design learning opportunities that were intended to elicit each or all of these processes. Of course, there can be and often is a gap between intention and reality, but nevertheless the taxonomy can help focus attention to enable one to convert a learning opportunity from one that is parochial and prosaic into one that has intellectual significance.

A word must be said about the potential hazards of classification systems, taxonomies, theoretical models, and the like. Such conceptual devices can be extremely useful for helping one differentiate and classify. In performing this function, they increase intellectual precision by helping us bracket the world in useful ways, but one must not forget that such bracketing is a construction of mind, that there are other ways to classify, and that one should take care not to reify concepts into realities that eventually constrain our understanding. Some of this has already occurred in the case of the taxonomy of educational objectives. These taxonomies differentiate the cognitive from the affective, the affective from the psychomotor, and the psychomotor from the cognitive. Individuals in education and psychology sometimes conclude that so-called cognitive activities are independent of affective ones, or that psychomotor activities are neither cognitive nor affective. In actual experience, there is no clear line between cognition and affect, except within the definitions of the taxonomy. For example, to have a feeling and not to know it, is not to have it. To think about a feeling is to know it. In short, the affective and cognitive pervade each other. Although in our culture we do find it useful to talk about our thoughts and our feelings, in education such talk can lead to theoretically devastating ideas and to practically questionable results. Some schools, for example, teach "cognitive" subjects in the morning and "affective" ones in the afternoons. My point here is not to argue that conceptual devices should not be used in the formulation of types of learning opportunities but rather to state that unless they are treated as tools such devices can interfere with the ways in which aims and activities are conceptualized.

The Organization of Learning Opportunities

All educational programs occur over time. How events are planned within a period of time is one of the decisions curriculum planners can make. There are two images of curricular sequences that it may be useful to distinguish between. One of these is the "staircase" model already mentioned; the other is a "spiderweb" model.

The staircase model conjures up the image of a series of independent steps that lead to a platform from which one exits. This conception is one that conceives of curriculum activities as building on what preceded them, preparing for what is to come. The movement, as is true in the climbing of a staircase, is always upward.

This conception is metaphorically consistent with terms such as *entry skills* and *exit competencies*. The route is well defined, mechanical in construction, and efficient. There is little room for wasted motion or exploratory adventures. Perhaps the most pristine example of such a model in curriculum is to be found in linear programs used in computer-assisted instruction. The same image was used in teaching machine programs that were available several years ago. The task of the curriculum designer is to create a sequence of frames, that, like the staircase, leads the student to a predetermined destination whose features are known by the curriculum designer and the teacher. One of the major needs of educators who wish to use the microcomputer is to secure or create programs that are sufficiently flexible to respond to the purposes and decisions of the student. Most programs put the student in a responsive position; the task is presented, the student responds, and then, if the response is correct, he or she proceeds along a fixed path that has already been predetermined. Much of the work is drill and practice. As programs become intellectually demanding and computers for classroom-use more sophisticated, intellectual processes that are truly important will be cultivated through computer-use. We are, as yet, still far from such a goal for the vast majority of computers and programs that are now being used in classrooms.

The spiderweb model is one in which the curriculum designer provides the teacher with a set of heuristic projects, materials, and activities whose use will lead to diverse outcomes among the group of students. The assumption used in this mode of curriculum organization is that what is needed are projects and activities that invite engagement rather than control. With engaging projects or activities students will create ideas and develop skills that they want to pursue. The task of the teacher is then to facilitate the interests and goals that students develop as a result of such engagement. As children bring with them different experiential backgrounds, it is reasonable to expect that the kind of meaning they make will also differ. This is seen as a virtue rather than a liability, for it is in the cultivation of those interests that truly personalized education resides.

To be sure, the kind of personalized education that is implied in a spiderweb model of curriculum organization places great demands on the inventiveness of the teacher. In this model the teacher cannot rely on stock responses to identical problems or tasks among students. Some students will work independently, others will work in small groups, but all will require a teacher who knows what kinds of problems and interests the students have and who is prepared to provide or point them to the resources that they need to develop those interests or to resolve those problems.

I do not believe it possible to conclude that one mode of curriculum organization is more educationally beneficial than the other. It depends on one's view of education and on the readiness of students—regardless of their age—to cope with different types of problems or tasks. It requires, as Whitehead implied, attention to the rhythm of education:

> Life is essentially periodic. It comprises daily periods, with their alternations of work and play, of activity and of sleep, and seasonal periods, which dictate our terms and our holidays; and also it is composed of well-marked yearly periods. These are the gross obvious periods which no one can overlook. There are also subtler periods of mental growth, with their cyclic recurrences, yet always different as we pass from cycle to cycle, though the subordinate stages are reproduced in each cycle. That is why I have chosen the term "rhythmic," as meaning essentially the conveyance of difference within a framework of repetition. Lack of attention to the rhythm and character of

mental growth is a main source of wooden futility in education. I think that Hegel was right when he analysed progress into three stages, which he called Thesis, Antithesis, and Synthesis; though for the purpose of application of his idea to educational theory I do not think that the names he gave are very happily suggestive. In relation to intellectual progress I would term them the stage of romance, the stage of precision, and the stage of generalization.[2]

Yet, notwithstanding the argument that there is no intrinsic value in the abstract for either of these models of curriculum organization, I think that it is fair to say that the spiderweb model has more appeal to the progressives among educators, whereas the staircase model has appeal to those with the more conservative educational bent. Those holding a progressive, or child-centered, philosophy tend to emphasize the differences among children and the belief that children should be given ample opportunity to formulate their own educational aims. The image of the teacher in such a view is like that of the travel agent described earlier. The teacher is not to "stuff the duck" but rather to facilitate the achievement of aims born out of the interaction children have with the stimulating resources the teacher provides.

Those with a more conservative view of education believe that there is a body of content that children should learn and that the sequential organization of this material is the best assurance that it will be learned. The staircase model fits the view nicely because it is systematic, well organized, and linear. When this view prevails, providing for individual differences usually means varying the pace through which children proceed to climb the same stairways rather than building different stairways leading to different goals for different children.

Historically these alternative models or conceptions of curriculum organization have been the subject of much dispute. In his classic book *The Child and the Curriculum,* John Dewey describes these camps this way. One group says:

> Subdivide each topic into studies; each study into lessons; each lesson into specific facts and formulae. Let the child proceed step by step to master each one of these separate parts, and at last he will have covered the entire ground. The road which looks so long when viewed in its entirety, is easily traveled, considered as a series of particular steps. Thus emphasis is put upon the logical subdivisions and consecutions of the subject-matter. Problems of instruction are problems procuring texts giving logical parts and sequences, and of presenting these portions in class in a similar definite and graded way. Subject-matter furnishes the end, and it determines method. The child is simply the immature being who is to be matured; he is the superficial being who is to be deepened; his is narrow experience which is to be widened. It is his to receive, to accept. His part is fulfilled when he is ductile and docile.
>
> Not so, says the other sect. The child is the starting-point, the center, and the end. His development, his growth, is the ideal. It alone furnishes the stan-

dard. To the growth of the child all studies are subservient; they are instruments valued as they serve the needs of growth. Personality, character, is more than subject-matter. Not knowledge or information, but self-realization, is the goal. To possess all the world of knowledge and lose one's self is as awful a fate in education as in religion. Moreover, subject-matter never can be got into the child from without. Learning is active. It involves reaching out of the mind. It involves organic assimilation starting from within. Literally, we must take or stand with the child and our departure from him. It is he and not the subject-matter which determines both quality and quantity of learning.[3]

For Dewey, the solution to the problem of how to sequence learning opportunities was to be found not in orthodoxies or in dogmas but rather in the concept of experience itself. The central question for Dewey was, "What kind of experience is a mode of curriculum organization likely to yield for students?" For Dewey, the experience was to be educative, rather than non- or miseducative.[4] Yet differences of view as to what educational experience is and what conditions are likely to produce it still generate a considerable degree of acrimony in the field. Different parties may agree that students should have experiences in school that educate rather than its contrary, but they may differ radically in their conception of educational experience and in their judgment of what will bring it about. One task of the curriculum specialist is to facilitate the critical deliberations of such issues so that the choices that are ultimately made will rest on considered alternatives.

The Organization of Content Areas

One task of the curriculum specialist is to help curriculum planners consider the ways in which content areas within the curriculum should be defined. One can, of course, maintain the traditional subject matter fields and make decisions about content within these boundaries. One might continue to teach arithmetic, history, art, music, science, reading, and the like. But one could also choose to teach communication, the humanities, the social studies, or ecological studies, problems of contemporary society, popular culture, and other areas that redefine or cut across the traditional subject matter fields within the curriculum.

The definition of these areas of study is a matter of what Bernstein calls "classification." Classification can be strong or weak, it can invite integration or discourage it. Bernstein writes:

> Classification, here, does not refer to *what* is classified, but to the *relationships* between contents. Classification refers to the nature of the differentiation between contents. Where classification is strong, contents are well insulated from each other by strong boundaries. Where classification is weak,

there is reduced insulation between contents for the boundaries between contents are weak or blurred. *Classification thus refers to the degree of boundary maintenance between contents.* Classification focuses our attention upon boundary strength as the critical distinguishing feature of the division of labour of educational knowledge.[5]

If the model from which the curriculum is drawn is what is usually found among academic disciplines that occupy so central a place in the university, then it is likely that its classification will have strong boundary strength.[6] Discrete subject matters will constitute the content and organization of the curriculum. But if the curriculum of the secondary school is considered not primarily as preparation for the university or as an effort to prepare students to become scholars in discrete fields of learning, then it is more likely that other forms of content organization will be considered. To develop programs that depart from traditional subject matter disciplines is easier to say than to do. In the first place, certification requirements may deter the educators of teachers from preparing prospective teachers who can deal with a range of fields or with problems that are not within single disciplines. Second, there may be no individuals on existing school faculties who are interested in cross-disciplinary teaching or teaching in areas that do not closely approximate the field in which they have been trained. Third, the political situation of professional educators often parallels disciplinary lines, and they may not wish to have competition for time and resources coming from programs outside of their particular fields. Finally, testing programs might penalize students who did very well in, say, the study of mass media in high school, but who knew little about English literature. In short, there are many social, political, and intellectual impediments to the development of new forms of content organization within the curriculum.

Yet, notwithstanding the practical difficulties of developing new forms of content organization, this is an area in which theoretical options exist. If the grounds for developing new modes of content organization are sufficiently compelling, one could try to make the changes or secure the resources to support it.

It is interesting to speculate on the possible grounds for such change. One of the arguments that has supported conventional approaches built around the disciplines is related to the so-called structure of the disciplines argument.[7] It is argued that each formal discipline has a distinctive structure. The syntactical aspect of the structure of a discipline defines the mode and criteria through which inquiry proceeds. The conceptual or substantive structure defines the concepts and subject matters inquired into. Because disciplines have a history and are well defined compared to general fields of study and because they offer the student organized concepts and theory, knowledge in these disciplines is easier to acquire, to store, and to retrieve than that available in fields that are less well organized. The order disciplines provide, the methods they employ, and the criteria they use, make intellectual precision possible.

Yet it can be argued that the problems that citizens confront in their daily lives seldom come in the forms with which the disciplines can deal. Most practical problems of life are "messy." They require the use of diverse kinds of knowledge; they demand the application of practical judgment that is not rule-governed or accessible, using criteria that might be suitable for a single discipline. The argument proceeds that school programs, both elementary and secondary, should not be controlled by a propaedeutic theory of education. Schools should not decide what to teach or how to organize what they teach on the basis of what universities teach. What follows represents one secondary school's effort to offer courses that traverse disciplinary lines:

Junior and Senior Offerings

Courses in the upper two years are generally available to both juniors and seniors. Very few requirements are placed upon upper class students since they are expected to exercise mature judgment in choosing their areas of specialization. Students are expected to sign up for approximately 30 units of courses per year, except by special permission from the faculty scheduling committee.

Science

300   How to Fix It
Simple maintenance and repair of household items.   1 unit
301   Student Teaching In Science—3 W's or TBT (seniors only)
Students will teach science classes in consultation with science teachers.
Credit for mini-teaching.   2 units per trimester
303   Intermediate Biology
An inquiry into life and a study of the basic structures and functions of microorganisms, plants, and animals with emphasis on evolutionary steps, patterns of heredity, animal behavior, and ecosystems.   4 units
304   Advanced Biology   4 units
305   TBT I—(theories behind technology)
Inter-disciplinary course of physics and chemistry. Emphasis on scientific processes rather than accumulation of facts.   4 units
306   TBT II
An advanced continuation of TBT I   4 units

Social Sciences

310   Rebel
A study of the rebel in contemporary society—his reasons and his strategies.   4 units
311   Survival
Practical ways of understanding and surviving in the modern city.   2 units
312   Which Way America
An in-depth approach to key events and people that shaped America 2 or 4 units

313   Backgrounds of Contemporary America
Course starting with contemporary events as a springboard into their root causes. Use of historical factual data along with American literature to capture the American consciousness of today. Will include some emphasis on means of communicating these ideas. Can be used in partial fulfillment of State History and English requirements.   4 units
314   Black Humanities   To be announced
A study of the writing of the Afro-American people with emphasis on the period from 1900 to the present, oral interpretation of recent Black writing in America and the African nations. (Course design could be a project of the interested students and faculty.) A Black teacher is being sought for this course.   2 units

What we see here is a set of course titles that reflect an interest in relating course content to the interests of adolescents. The topics chosen to serve as titles for the courses are not, as they are so often, U.S. History and Math 1. They are rather "Which Way America" and "Survival." Such course titles are in a sense symbolic of the faculty's desire to develop programs that address in a meaningful way the interests of students who are likely to enroll in them. In this sense, the faculty is making an effort both to capitalize on what students already are interested in and to tantalize them with descriptions that it hopes will satisfy.

These course titles are, for the most part, out of fashion in 1984. They were taken from a list of courses offered in a secondary school in Chicago in 1968. Our fashion today is more academic, demanding "less pizzazz" and more convention. Whether one believes the shift from 1968 to 1984 is educationally beneficial or detrimental will depend on the way in which one views the purposes of the secondary schools and the needs of the particular population in a school or school district.

Mode of Presentation and Mode of Response

One of the least-considered options in curriculum planning deals with the modalities through which students encounter and express what they learn. For the vast majority of subject fields in schools, the mode of presentation that students encounter is either verbal or written language. The teacher talks or students read textbooks containing the information and ideas they are to acquire. To demonstrate what they have learned, the students are expected to write or to take examinations that are also presented in written form. Out of traditional expectations we have inadvertently allowed one mode to so dominate how expression is to occur in school that we have come to believe that to have any understanding at all the student must be able to demonstrate it in verbal or written terms.

Yet the forms through which knowledge and understanding are constructed, stored, and expressed are considerably wider than verbal or written discourse. What can be known, say, about Autumn can take form in scientific propositions that deal with chemical changes in trees, in astronomical propositions about the location of our planet in relation to the sun, in poetic expression disclosing the smell of burning autumn leaves, in visual images that present to our consciousness the color of a Vermont landscape, and in auditory forms that capture the crackle of leaves under our footsteps. Autumn, in short, is known in a variety of ways and the ways in which it can be known are expressible in a wide range of expressive forms.

Now the significance of this fact for the development of educational programs is considerable. What it implies is that educational programs that aim to help children gain an understanding of the world need to recognize that understanding is secured and experienced in different ways. What one is able to know through forms of musical expression cannot be known in discursive form, and vice versa. Humans employ different knowledge systems to acquire, store, and retrieve understanding, and they use different performance systems to express what they know about the world. For the curriculum designer this implies that if students are to understand phenomena in the variety of ways in which they can be understood, they need to have the opportunity to encounter forms that express ideas about those phenomena in different ways. Furthermore, it implies that if teachers are to understand what students know about something, then students should be given options in the ways in which they can express what they know. In short, students need not be restricted to one way of expressing what they have learned; curriculum designers need not use verbal forms of expression as the only means of presenting ideas to students.

When one also recognizes that there are aptitude differences among students with respect to the knowledge and performance systems they use best, the grounds for using diverse modes of presentation and response become even stronger. One could argue that by withholding such opportunities from students a significant proportion of them are denied equal educational opportunity and that certain modes of presentation and forms of response deny them the opportunity to display what they have learned in the forms that most suit their aptitudes.

Although this might seem farfetched, I do not believe it is. We have created a culture in schooling that is so heavily pervaded by verbal and written performance systems that we take such performance systems for granted. In the process we forget that the culture at large depends on a much wider array of human competencies. We regard alternatives that are nondiscursive as "enrichment activities." We assign them to the margins of our concerns; they are events that are "nice to have" but not really of educational significance. Furthermore, we do not often recognize the unique epistemological functions that different expressive forms make possible.

The appreciation of this epistemological diversity allows the curriculum designer to create activities that may be experienced in one mode and expressed by the student in another. For example, a student might read a short story and express what she has learned or experienced from it in a painting, film, or poem. Or, conversely, a student might see a film and express his reaction in a short story. Although such activities do occur at present, they are seldom created intentionally and are seldom based on a realization of the interaction between knowledge and performance systems. What I am suggesting here is that curriculum designers can intentionally exploit the variety of modalities humans use to conceptualize and experience the world and to express what they have learned about it.

It is true, of course, that fields do have indigenous expressive modalities. Historians write prose, physicists express what they have learned in equations, musicians perform with voice or instrument, painters create visual images. To know whether someone knows history, we ask the the person to speak or write. To determine whether someone knows physics, we ask the person to explain physical theory or to do a physics experiment. To the extent to which we would like students to express themselves within the mode that is indigenous to the discipline, *that* mode should dominate. But ideas secured from a discipline need not necessarily be limited to the mode indigenous to it. A study of history can lead to ideas that are best expressed by some students within the context of poetry rather than prose or within film or music. Ideas dealing with historical phenomena can be expressed in modes that are nonverbal. In addition, ideas that are not historical, per se, can be stimulated by the study of history, and, of course, these too can be expressed in modes that do not make use of what is indigenous to historical scholarship.

I use history only as an example. Other fields fit, a fortiori. Now this way of thinking about expression and response has some very interesting epistemological implications. We take history to be what has been written that meets, roughly, the criteria accepted within that field. By convention, historians expect history to be written and they expect historical scholarship to contain evidence, if not proof, of historical veracity. But such conventions need not necessarily foreclose other ways in which historical insight or generalization can be conveyed. Indeed, one might argue that written expression is a surrogate for what the historian knows in other ways, ways that often are not verbal. What I am suggesting is for curriculum designers to consider the potential of allowing students to use modes of response to historical ideas or experiences that might take shape in forms that are not indigenous to history as it is now conceived. I believe the exploitation of such possibilities has considerable potential for the education of the young. Indeed, to dramatize the limited scope of our expressive options, one has only to look at graduate programs. We seem to operate on the belief that the written word is the only means through which one can legitimately demonstrate that one knows something.

Types of Evaluation Procedures

Closely related to the type of presentation and response available to students is the type of evaluation procedures that are used to identify and assess what students have learned and experienced. Although subsequent chapters treat the problems of educational evaluation in detail, some preliminary remarks about the relationships between evaluation and curriculum development seem appropriate here.

In the first place, evaluation is a process that pervades curriculum decision making. Evaluation is not simply an activity that occurs after students have completed a unit of study. The very act of deciding on content, activities, aims, sequence, or mode of presentation or response requires one to consider the options and to evaluate the utility of the alternatives. Because more options exist than can be employed, selection is necessary. Selection requires choices, and choices require appraisals concerning strengths and liabilities of the alternatives with respect to some set of values; hence, evaluation occurs. The main issue with respect to evaluation centers around the care, the complexity, and the comprehensiveness with which the choices are made. In this sense, evaluation is a necessary part of any deliberate process. What we seek is that it be competent. Evaluation in the more traditional view often refers to the measurement of student performance. Here, too, there are important options that curriculum can consider. In terms of what I said earlier about the relationship between modes of presentation and response and student aptitudes, we may infer that how a student is able to express what he or she has learned will influence what the student can make public. What is made public in turn influences what conclusions teachers and others come to regarding how well the student has done. Although the provision of different student performance options for purposes of summative evaluation creates problems for classical test theory, I do not believe that the requirements of classical test theory should determine how we try to find out what students have learned and experienced at school. Let the test and measurement specialists follow our needs in education rather than we follow theirs.

With respect to the procedures for evaluation in the curriculum development process, groups often go thorugh several steps or stages. As I have already indicated, evaluation occurs throughout the process of curriculum development. The determination that a new program is needed is, in part, the consequence of having judged that a lack exists or that some new program holds promise for significant educational gain. Needs assessment, the process through which educators and others determine exiting needs, is itself pervaded by value judgments in the selection of items used on questionnaires and tests, of the format that is employed, and in the populations that are selected for assessment, not to mention the value-saturated process of interpreting the information once it is secured.

But even after the initial judgment has been made about the need for a new program, the selection of activities, goals, content, and the like require, as I have indicated, some form of evaluation. Any form of decision making requires judgment, and judgment requires evaluation of choices, options, and alternatives.

Stages in Evaluating Curriculum Materials

Taking this as a given, we can identify the stages or steps that many curriculum groups employ in the process of evaluating materials that are being developed. One such process is referred to as *hothouse trials*. In this stage, a group of curriculum developers will work with an evaluator to locate classrooms in which prototype materials may be tried. These prototype materials are usually in rough form, having enough finish for the teacher or, as is sometimes the case, a member of a curriculum development team to use them in a classroom. The purpose of the hothouse trial is to identify any major problems with the material, to determine if some important oversights have been made: Are the problems suitable for children of this age? Can a teacher have easy access to the materials the way they have been designed? Do the tasks take longer than was expected?

To engage in hothouse trials, a curriculum development group, say, one working within an educational laboratory, will have established a network of schools around the laboratory that have agreed to cooperate with the laboratory in testing new material. For the school, such cooperation provides stimulation to teachers and creates a form of in-service education. In addition, some laboratories give cooperating schools free materials after they have been tested. For the laboratories, the schools provide the field site that they need to reality-test the materials. A network of schools with which the laboratory has a good relationship diminishes the need to locate and contact new schools each time materials have to be tested. Thus, the relationship can be viewed as a kind of symbiotic one: all concerned appear to benefit by meeting the needs of the others.

The evaluator attached to the curriculum development group observes the materials being used in the hothouse trial. The evaluator's function is to locate difficulties that the teacher might not recognize and to feed back such information to the curriculum development team. Sometimes a member of the curriculum development team will actually teach with the materials in order to get a firsthand view of how the materials function, but even when this occurs, the evaluator may still be present to observe what the teacher might not see.

The function of the hothouse trials is to permit the curriculum team the closest possible scrutiny of how materials function in classrooms. The rapport between the member of the team and the teachers of the schools should be good: ideally they should see each other as colleagues. Although this rapport and relationship do not typify the field at large—teachers and curriculum developers are seldom seen as colleagues and they typically have no rapport—such a relationship is helpful for purposes of formative evaluation.

After hothouse trials have been completed and the necessary revisions made, the materials are then offered to a limited number of school districts for *field testing*. Field testing is done on a larger scale and is more impersonal in character than hothouse trials. In this stage of evaluations school districts agree to return to the laboratory their appraisal of the materials after they have had the opportunity to use them. Such appraisals might consist of evaluations that teachers complete or instruments that measure students' performance on achievement tests that the laboratory supplies. The function of the field testing is to approximate more closely the conditions under which the materials will be used but still to be in a position to modify the materials prior to their publication and dissemination. The materials at the field trial stage of development are often in a mimeographed or offset-printed form: they lack the kind of finished quality that they will receive when they are to be marketed.

As a result of field testing, final modifications of the material are done, and subsequently the materials are sent to a publisher who then mounts an advertising program to make their purchase possible by the 16,000 school districts in this country. This advertising program includes display of the materials at conventions attended by teachers and school administrators, mailing of brochures to school districts, placement of ads in journals read by teachers, and visits by salespeople to the school districts to demonstrate the materials at in-service meetings.

These procedures might give one the idea that testing curriculum materials is like testing new drugs before they are marketed, but the resemblance is slight. In drug testing, it is possible to isolate the relationships between the chemistry of a drug and the chemistry of individuals. For the testing of curriculum materials, the context and manner in which they are used by the teacher make a crucial difference in how they will be experienced by children. Poor teaching can render even the most attractive materials dull, and teaching that is imaginative can convert even the most banal materials into experiences that are stimulating. Curriculum materials are always mediated by the context, and the teacher plays a crucial role in that context. This is one reason why the notion of developing "teacher-proof" curriculum materials is suspect. Not only does it demean the teacher and the profession of teaching, it also simply cannot be done in educational situations: training programs, perhaps, but educational programs, no.

I make a point of this because I do not believe that we can have standards for the evaluation of curriculum materials as we have standards to appraise food and drugs. We can use criteria, but criteria imply judgments that are flexible, that consider relationships between the materials and the context in which they are to function. What might be right for one situation will be wrong for others. The creation of a bureau of standards for curriculum materials could work only for the identification of their most egregious faults; such a bureau might function as a screening agency but not as a selection agency. What I believe we can provide through the evaluation of curriculum are judgments concerning the qualities the materials possess, information about some of their effects in a particular context, but not guaranteed results or even the implication of such results. In educational situations we do not have the luxury of substituting rule for judgment.

What I have tried to do thus far is to identify some of the factors that one can take into account in the process of curriculum development, in particular in the design of materials that may be of help to the teacher in his or her work. These factors, or considerations, are to be viewed as heuristic: they are tools to be used, not rules to be followed. There are no rules or recipes that will guarantee successful curriculum development. Judgment is always required, and if this task is a group effort, sensitivity to one's fellow workers is always necessary. To provide a sense of how one such group actually functioned, I have prepared in Chapter 8 a description of Stanford's Kettering Project, a curriculum development project in elementary art education that I directed at Stanford University. I hope it provides you with a sense of the adventitiousness and flexibility curriculum development requires.

References

1. This point has been made with particular force by James McDonald. See his article, "Myths About Instruction," *Educational Leadership*, Vol. 22, No. 7, May 1965, pp. 613–614.
2. Alfred North Whitehead, "The Rhythm of Education," in *The Aims of Education and Other Essays*, Macmillan Co., New York, 1929, p. 29.
3. John Dewey, "The Child and the Curriculum," in *Dewey on Education* (Martin S. Dworkin, ed.), Bureau of Publications, Teachers College, Columbia University, New York, 1959, p. 95.
4. For a discussion of the differences among educative, noneducative, and miseducative experiences, see John Dewey, *Experience and Education*, Macmillan Co., New York, 1938.
5. Basil Bernstein, "On the Classification and Framing of Educational Knowledge," in *Knowledge and Content* (Michael Young, ed.), Collier-Macmillan Publishers, London, 1971.
6. Ibid., p. 49.
7. Joseph J. Schwab, "The Concept of the Structure of the Discipline," *Educational Record*, Vol. 43, July 1962, pp. 197–205.

8

Some Observations on a Curriculum
Development Project

---

*There is a simple job to be done. The task can be stated in
concrete terms. The necessary techniques are known. The
equipment needed can easily be provided. Nothing stands in the
way but cultural inertia. But what is more characteristic of
America than an unwillingness to accept the traditional as
inevitable? We are on the threshold of an exciting and
revolutionary period, in which the scientific study of man will be
put to work in man's best interests. Education must play its
part. It must accept that fact that a sweeping revision of
educational practices is possible and inevitable. When it has
done this, we may look forward with confidence to a school
system which is aware of the nature of its tasks, secure in its
methods, and generously supported by the informed and effective
citizens whom education itself will create.*

B. F. SKINNER

The intention in this chapter is to provide an intimate view of the work of
one curriculum and development project.[1] Although this work was done
several years ago, it is included in order to offer the reader some concrete
examples of the way in which ideas are used, altered, tested, and discarded
in the course of curriculum development.[2] Some of the assumptions and
ideas that are described are not ones I would use today, but because this
work represents my first effort to create a body of curriculum materials for

use on a national scale, I believe it appropriate to describe that work so that its assumptions can be compared and contrasted with those presented in earlier chapters of this book. Despite Professor Skinner's confidence in the state of educational technology, our work was not the assured execution of a set of known and tested procedures, but a halting and exploratory effort to give form to a vision.

In the first section of this chapter are described some of the salient characteristics of the field of art education at the time the project was started. In the second section of the chapter the specific purposes of the project and the way in which the work was organized are described. In the third section the theories and beliefs that gave direction to the curriculum development work are addressed and the limitations of theoretical ideas in the practical context of curriculum development are pointed out. Finally, the potential virtues of alternative approaches to the curriculum development process are discussed.

The Background and Aims of the Kettering Project

In September 1968, with the support of the Charles F. Kettering Foundation, I initiated a two-year project aimed at developing an art curriculum that would improve the quality of art education in American elementary schools. Although in 1968 the curriculum development movement was more than ten years old, the formal and systematic development of curriculum in the field of elementary art education was hardly begun. In mathematics, in the sciences, in the social studies, and in English, large-scale national projects had been launched. Yet in art education no national project had as yet been funded.

The need for curriculum development programs in art was, I believed, apparent to anyone familiar with the general quality of art education at the elementary school level in the United States. Most school districts in the country employed few or no elementary school art teachers, and the large urban districts that had trained art teachers used them as itinerants who had limited contact with both children and teachers. Thus, most of the art teaching provided in elementary schools was handled by teachers who possessed little skill or understanding in this area.

Because of their obvious lack of background either in art or art education, I was interested in developing resources—both written and visual—that elementary school teachers could use to improve the quality of art education they provided.

In the proposal to the Charles F. Kettering Foundation, a number of ideas that were to provide guidance in the development and organization of the curriculum development efforts were made explicit. First, it was made clear that the curriculum that was being proposed included what I have called in previous writing the productive, the critical, and the historical aspects of art.[3,4] The productive realm focused on helping children acquire the skills necessary for converting a material into a medium for artistic expression. The critical realm focused on developing students' ability to see what they looked at, to develop their ability to encounter visual forms from an aesthetic frame of reference and through such a frame to acquire aesthetic experience. The historical realm attempted to help students understand that art is created in the context of a culture that influences the form and content of art, and art in turn influences the culture.

A second feature of the proposed curriculum was that it was to have a sequential character. It was recognized that few elementary art programs provided continuity. Itinerant art teachers work with a class only occasionally and very often initiate class projects that can be completed in "one sitting." Regular classroom teachers tend to believe that the wider the variety of projects and materials they allow children to work with the better; hence they, too, offer children not so much an art program as a collection of unrelated art "activities" that are so brief in duration that children seldom have the time necessary for developing the skills that make artistic expression possible.

A third feature of the curriculum proposed to the foundation was that it should contain a wide variety of visual materials especially designed to develop the skills identified in the written curriculum guide. It was quite apparent that in the physical sciences, for example, curriculum developers had provided devices that visually illustrate, say, Newton's third law; why could not similar devices be prepared for teaching the visual arts? It seemed ironic that in a field concerned with vision so few especially designed visual materials were available. It was one of the goals of the project to prepare such materials and to relate them directly to tasks and objectives that appeared in the written curriculum guides.

A fourth feature of the proposal was its attention to the development of evaluation devices or procedures for each of the lessons and units that were to be created. I took the view—not one widely shared at that time in the field—that it was possible to determine the extent to which artistic learning had occurred. Evidence of such learning is manifested not only in the quality of products children create, but also in the insight, sensitivity, and relevance of their remarks about works of art and other aspects of the environment. In addition, I believed that it was possible to create exercises or tests that would in specific ways elicit such skill if it had been developed in the first place.

In sum, the Kettering Project was an effort to develop a sequentially ordered curriculum in art that contained both a written syllabus and a wide array of visual support materials that elementary school teachers could use to increase the quality of the art programs they provided to their students.

How Work on the Project Was Organized

Because the grant for the project covered a two-year period, it was within that period of time that a number of tasks had to be undertaken and completed. These included refining the ideas presented in the proposal, creating a structure for writing the syllabus, appointing a staff, creating and field-testing lessons, constructing the visual materials to accompany the lessons, evaluating and revising both written and visual materials on the basis of field testing, locating schools wishing to participate in the project, constructing evaluation instruments, and preparing a final report to the foundation. Had I, as project director, fully appreciated the complexity and magnitude of the curriculum development task, I would have requested funds to cover a five- rather than a two-year period. At that time, I did not, and it was with the two-year time frame that work was planned.

The first thing I did after being notified that support would be forthcoming was to select eight doctoral students, five in the field of art education and three in general curriculum at Stanford University, who were to work on the project during the two-year period. These students were joined by a student in product design who was to provide some of the artistic expertise for the construction of visual materials. The doctoral students and I formed the primary core responsible for the major decisions during the life of the project. This group of nine people would meet regularly each week to consider, for example, the way in which the curriculum would be structured, to write lessons, and to critique what each had created. I tried, during the two-year period, to fulfill two responsibilities: first to provide the leadership necessary for the project to succeed; second, to make the project one that could contribute to the education of graduate students. This meant that decisions I might have made on an arbitrary basis were made less efficiently with respect to action but more effectively in relation to the contributions that group deliberation made to the education of the students who worked with me. Furthermore, I wanted the students to feel that this was *our* project, not simply my project; hence, collective decision making was something that I encouraged. Only when preservation became acutely frustrating or grossly unproductive did I attempt arbitrarily to resolve an issue being discussed.

Once the core group had been formed, I shared with each member of the group the proposal that was submitted to the foundation and I described in detail the rationale for the project and some of the goals I hoped an effective curriculum would achieve. These sessions were used to orient members of the group to the kind of work that was ahead of us and to reemphasize and clarify through discussion the leading ideas constituting my thinking about the teaching of art at the elementary school level. It became clear to me that the kind of understanding I wanted the core group to secure could not be compressed and secured within three or four staff meetings. Such understanding needs time to grow and would, I hoped, occur during the course of the curriculum development work. Yet, I did want to lay enough groundwork concerning what the project was after and why, so that members of the group would feel intellectually secure in what they were trying to accomplish.

The work for the project was divided in two phases. Phase I was devoted to (1) conceptualizing the format, or structure, to be used for writing lessons and designing instructional materials, (2) writing lessons and having them critiqued by the group, (3) designing instructional materials to accompany the written materials, (4) securing teachers and classrooms for initial field testing, and (5) revising the materials, both written and visual, as a result of initial field testing. Phase II was devoted to the local dissemination of the use and effects of the materials developed.

The core group decided that it would be a good idea to invite four elementary school teachers to join the group as consultants and to use their classrooms as the places where the initial testing of the materials would take place. Four teachers, each of whom worked in a different elementary school near Stanford University, were subsequently employed as consultants to the project. Their role was to read the material that had been prepared and to let us know what aspects of the work were clear and useful. The teachers were, in a very real sense, our contact with educational reality, and, although we did not expect or want them to function as experts on art, they were informed about and sensitive to children and to life in their classrooms and were in a position to tell us whether what we were developing had any chance of succeeding in an elementary school classroom.

Thus, the staff of the Kettering Project for the first year of its existence consisted of a project director, five doctoral students in art education, three doctoral students in general curriculum, one master's degree student in product design, and four elementary school teachers. Meetings of the project director and the students were held two to four times per week, whereas meetings that included the teachers were held once every month to six weeks.

One of the first tasks that needed to be undertaken after the initial staff orientation session was completed was the development of a structure, or format, that could be used to organize our lesson writing and that could be read easily by elementary school teachers. Although the rationale for the project and the three realms of artistic learning had been formulated, the specific format that would provide the architecture within which our curriculum writing would occur had not been developed. I now believe, although I did not appreciate it at the time, that decisions about the character and structure of this format are crucial for the curriculum development process. This conceptual architecture reveals implicitly the assumptions and values embedded in a project and provides the constraints within which curriculum writers must work. It is clear that when eight to ten people come together to prepare written materials that are to constitute a syllabus for others to use, some common framework must be developed that all members of the group can use if the syllabus is to have continuity and cohesiveness. The first month of the project was devoted to the development of the categories that would constitute the format for our work. The categories for this format are as follows:

1. Concept.
2. Principle.
3. Objective.
4. Rationale.
5. Introductory motivating activity.
6. Learning activity 1, 2, 3.
7. Evaluation procedures.
8. Materials needed.

Concept refers to an idea, such as color or line, that was to be the focus of a unit. A unit consisted of seven to ten lessons. *Principle* refers to a general proposition about the concept that the curriculum was designed to help children understand in some way. Thus, "Color can express feeling" is a principle in which the concept *color* is embedded. *Objective* refers to instructional objectives that the children were intended to attain. *Rationale* provides the teachers with reasons that justify the importance of the concept, principle, and objective we had formulated.

The *introductory motivating activity* was a procedure we suggested could be used by the teacher to help the students get ready for the lesson. *Learning activity 1, 2, 3* refers to the fact that each lesson contained one to three learning activities, each of which we believed was instrumental in achieving the objective for that lesson. The availability of three learning activities was intended to provide teachers with choices regarding the learning activity that seemed most suitable for their particular class. *Evaluation procedures* describes how the effectiveness of the lesson or unit could be evaluated, whereas *materials needed* was a list of materials that we provided and those that the teacher needed to provide for use in the particular lesson.

As I have already indicated, each unit consisted of seven to ten lessons. This meant that once a teacher chose a unit he or she was committed to staying with it—to its culmination, we hoped. We did not want to encourage teachers to shift from lesson to lesson in different units, because we believed that this would vitiate any continuity that we were able to build

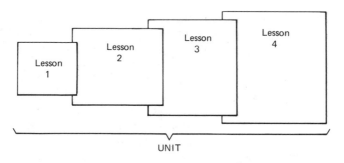

Figure 3

into our materials. The organization of lessons into a unit is schematically illustrated in Figure 3.

By use of this curriculum format, seven units were selected for the development of lessons. In the productive realm, units focused on drawing, graphics, and painting. In the critical realm, units dealt with line, color, and composition. In the historical realm, they focused on the general features of art history. Using these units, the core group of project staff produced sixty-seven lessons and about seven hundred pieces of specifically designed instructional materials that accompanied the lessons in the units. These materials, both written and visual, are sufficient for over two years of art instruction assuming that a teacher allocates about two hours per week to the study or creation of art.

At the time the project was undertaken, I was very intent on specifying goals or objectives so that teachers would know where they were heading. I was also intent on developing a structured sequence among lessons to counteract the fact that most elementary classrooms had no sequentially organized art programs. Although the objectives that were formulated were more general than formal instructional objectives, I would today provide a much more open-ended approach to objectives, using instructional objectives much more sparingly and placing more emphasis on problem-solving objectives and expressive outcomes. Similarly, I would not attempt to provide a sequence longer than three lessons; we used sequences of from seven to ten lessons in our work.

How the Group Worked

To produce the lessons within each of the units, the core group was organized into teams of two members each. These teams were responsible for writing ten lessons in each of the units and for conceptualizing the type of visual support materials that they believed would increase the effectiveness of the lessons. Our working procedures provided for each team to write a draft version of the lesson and to have it reviewed by either the project director or the total group. After this initial review, the material was revised and reviewed by the teachers who served as consultants. Following their recommendations, the lesson was used in the classroom of the teacher-consultant and subsequently further revisions were made.

It is important to note here that the process of group planning and review of curriculum materials is a complicated and time-consuming enterprise. Even seemingly minor decisions, such as whether to use slides of works of art or cardboard reproductions of works of art for a particular lesson, could require a full hour or more of discussion. These discussions appeared to some to be inefficient and frustrating, but I am convinced they are a necessary part of curriculum planning.

As already indicated, the teams that wrote curriculum were also responsible for conceptualizing the instructional support materials to accompany their written work. In most cases, members of the team also constructed these materials and made seven copies of each of them so that eight complete sets of materials were available for testing in classrooms. When the materials were especially complex or could not be efficiently fabricated by a team member, the student who served as our product designer undertook the responsibility for production. As I have already indicated, the project produced about seven hundred pieces of visual instructional materials, each having a code number corresponding to a number found within a lesson in a particular unit.

Phase I of the project, which extended from October 1, 1968, to August 1, 1969, culminated with the production of two large syllabi containing the units for each of the three realms of artistic learning that the project was interested in fostering. Also produced were eight pairs of "Kettering Boxes," which contained sets of instructional support materials. These materials, both written and visual, had been revised at least twice, and most of the lessons had been tried in the classroom by teacher-consultants or by members of the team who developed the material.

Phase II, the second year of the project, was one in which the tryout of the materials expanded from four teachers to twenty teachers working in five schools in two school districts near Stanford University. During this phase of the project, units that were not completed during Phase I were brought to completion and observations of the use of the curriculum and instructional resource materials were continued.

Because it was my aspiration as project director to develop materials that did not require extensive in-service education, only one formal in-service session was held for the twenty elementary school teachers who participated in the project during the second year. Whatever additional in-service education occurred was provided informally by the core staff as they observed teachers and students when they were using the materials in class.

This aspiration also reflected naiveté on my part. I had hoped to create material that needed little pedagogical expertise, but in retrospect—particularly in art—the need for in-service education in the use of the material cannot be circumvented. The teacher plays a crucial role in the ways in which materials are employed in the classroom.

In addition to the expanded field testing of the curriculum materials, Phase II became the period in which evaluation procedures and instruments needed to be developed. With the bulk of the curriculum development work completed by March 1968, the attention of the staff shifted to the conceptualization of aspects of artistic learning that were to be evaluated in ways not provided for in the evaluation procedures suggested at the end of each lesson. This effort required for its successful completion as much time and support as went into the development of the curriculum itself. The project staff obviously had neither the same amount of time nor the kinds of resources that would have been optimal. Nevertheless, the types of competencies the staff sought to assess and the procedures that were *conceptualized* were, in my opinion, promising and ambitious. These materials included the appraisal of the visual products that children in the classes produced, interviews with teachers, and analyses of the written comments they made in the curriculum syllabus they were using. Evaluation procedures also employed tests of comprehension that had been prepared. The staff of the project made every effort within the time constraints to secure a wide variety of evaluative information that would be useful in determining the effects of the projects on the students as well as those aspects of the curriculum that needed further revision. The data from these procedures and instruments were collected in May and June of 1969 and analyzed during July and August.

As the last formal task of the project, a final report was prepared for the foundation. This report was divided into eight sections and each member of the core staff was asked to prepare a chapter or portion of the report. As project director, I prepared both the introductory and concluding chapters of the report and reviewed all of the material prepared by the staff. In addition to the final report that describes the project in detail and presents a critical analysis of its strengths and weaknesses, a collection of sample lessons was prepared that was intended to provide those interested in the project with material necessary for understanding the format of the lessons and the level of detail with which they were written. Thus, two final written products were prepared during the summer and fall of 1969, a final report and a collection of sample lessons from each of the units that had been written.

Dissemination of the Work

One might ask, after a substantial fiscal investment,[5] not to mention the investment in time and energy, how the results of the project were disseminated to the field of art education, aside from the information provided in the final report and sample lessons. To disseminate information about the project to the field, a wide variety of channels became available, most of which were neither consciously sought nor anticipated. These channels emerged in part because there was a growing interest in the work we had done and in part because the ideas in the project were a "natural" part of ideas I had worked with professionally in the field. For example, I prepared two articles for two major art education journals.[6,7] One of these was published when the project was initiated and described its goals and rationale; the other was published after the project had been completed and provided a description of what we had learned. Other channels for dissemination included invitations to speak about the project at conferences and conventions. The *New York Times* and the *Christian Science Monitor* had articles about the project. One of the largest school districts in the United States invited me to make a videotape dealing with the project for in-service training of teachers, and the state of Hawaii invited the core staff there to work with elementary school teachers to develop materials similar to those used in the Kettering Project that would be appropriate for Hawaiian schools. When I was in England and Israel I described the project to various groups of educators. In addition, people in art education from various parts of this country had visited schools where the materials were being used. The opening chapter in *Program of Promise*[8] is devoted to a description of the Kettering Project, and my own book, *Educating Artistic Vision*,[9] describes the project in some detail. Finally, the materials and ideas used in the project are being used in my own teaching and training of teachers. Regarding the last point, the *California State Framework for the Visual Arts*[10] recommends an approach to curriculum development that, in significant measure, grew out of the curriculum development work done on the Kettering Project.

As I have indicated, these channels for dissemination were not contrived at any point during the life of the project. I knew, of course, that a final report would be written, but I did not plan the events or opportunities that flowed after the work had been completed. It is important to point out that in disseminating information about the project there was no attempt to offer the curriculum as a completed or a flawless program. Indeed, whenever lectures were delivered or articles published, every effort was made to point out the difficulties and limitations of the work we had done as well as the kinds of benefits it could offer. We did not attempt to market the materials, either literally or psychologically, to the professional public. Our main concern, in addition to developing the best materials we could produce, was to acquire a more adequate understanding of the problems involved in curriculum development work and to share such understanding with members in the field.

Theories Used to Develop Curriculum Materials

Thus far I have described the goals of the Kettering Project and the kinds of tasks that were undertaken in Phases I and II of its life, in order to clarify how the project was organized. It is to the theories used in its development that we now turn.

When one talks about theories underlying or guiding curriculum development work, there are at least two aspects of the term *theory* that need clarification. If by *theory* is meant a systematic set of interrelated statements that explain, through their power to predict specific consequences flowing from certain conditions, then theory in education generally and in curriculum particularly can be used only in the loosest sense. If ideas that are used to guide action—if general beliefs about what children ought to learn—are considered theoretical, then this is much more like the status of theoretical ideas in curriculum work than the type of theory referred to earlier.

A second necessary clarification deals with the referent of *theory*. In curriculum development work, *theory* can refer to ideas about the nature of the subject matter being taught, about how children learn, or about how a particular enterprise might go about its work. For example, aesthetic theory deals with explanations concerning the defining characteristics of art, and behaviorism presents ideas that purport to explain the conditions necessary for learning, whereas organizational theory is supposed to explain why an organization functions the way it does and by implication what sorts of changes might make it more productive.

In the development of the lessons and the visual materials, there was one particular theoretical idea in psychology that guided a great deal of what we produced. That idea deals with the process of visual differentiation: seeing is not identical to looking. For example, in grammatical terms *seeing* is an achievement verb, whereas *looking* is a task verb.[11] Seeing is an accomplishment, something that is learned; it is not an automatic consequence of maturation. Hence, in the development of materials and tasks, we were intent on providing visual images that students could compare and contrast and in this process attain better skills in visual differentiation. That is, they would gradually become able to see visual qualities in visual form that previously went unseen. To do this required that we produce tasks and materials whose differences from a visual point of view were at first obvious. Gradually, the differences between visual images students were asked to look at and compare became increasingly subtle. Many of the materials we developed, such as transparent overlay boards that were used to alter the quality of reproductions of works of art, were intended to foster visual differentiation.

The point here is that both beliefs about what is desirable from an educational point of view (developing greater visual differentiation) and beliefs about the ways in which such learning can be fostered played an important role in providing direction to our practical work.

Another important idea had to do with the importance of time and practice in the acquisition of the skills necessary for artistic expression. In my writing in the field of art education I have differentiated between expression and what might be called self-disclosure.[12] The former requires that an individual have sufficient control over a material to be able to use it as a medium for expression. Expression requires the application of intelligence for the purpose of converting a material into a medium.[13]

To be able to achieve expressive ends with materials requires from an educational point of view that the student have sufficient time and opportunity to acquire, practice, and refine the necessary skills. In the language of curriculum discourse, both continuity and sequence should be provided for in the materials developed. In practical terms, these ideas about the meaning of expression and the conditions necessary for its achievement function as the intellectual justification for the development of units as compared with a grab-bag or an ad hoc approach to the development of learning activities.

The significance of these theoretical beliefs in our curriculum development work can perhaps be better appreciated if some theoretical ideas that we did not employ are mentioned. The concept of reinforcement, a central idea in behaviorism, was nowhere purposefully employed in the preparation of written materials. We did not want teachers to use, for example, secondary reinforcers to sustain interest or to motivate children. The idea of giving "brownie points" for work completed would have been abhorrent to the group, and at no time did it emerge as an idea for consideration. Another idea not employed was that of using immediate as compared to delayed feedback to guide or reinforce the students' learning. This psychological idea simply was not a part of the intellectual body of beliefs that gave direction to our efforts.

In identifying the theoretical ideas that were central to and those that were absent from the project, I do not want to imply that ideas about visual differentiation and those dealing with continuity and sequence provided recipe-like prescriptions that were to be followed assiduously. Although some ideas were of greater significance than others, it is more accurate to say that these ideas were embedded in a constellation of more general ideas about art, education, and artistic learning that had permeated my writing for about a decade. These ideas formed what Decker Walker[14] has called a platform. They constituted a body of beliefs that were shared by members of the project staff and provided an almost unarticulated covenant that gave direction for our work.

It is both of interest and of significance to note that the beliefs that become a shared aspect of group endeavors often seem to be internalized by group members much in the way that social habits are learned during childhood. The language that becomes salient in a group, the way in which values are communicated, and the general intellectual style of the leading group members seem to create a climate—or a culture—to which group members adapt. In our case, there was no manifesto that presented the values and beliefs the group came to share. In the first place, an important characteristic of deeply held beliefs and values is their ineffable quality. Yet, this does not mean that they are not communicable, and I believe the total configuration of decisions within a group expresses and at the same time reinforces such beliefs and values.

Curriculum development on the scale with which we worked is inevitably a group enterprise; yet, despite this obvious feature, there is little in the literature that discusses curriculum development from the standpoint of group processes. In the types of theory that guide curriculum work, ideas about how people learn and about the nature of the subject to be learned often are prominent. For example, *Science: A Process Approach* is structured largely by ideas about the nature of cognitive operations and the conditions that will refine them, whereas *Man: A Course of Study* is based largely on certain large ideas about the nature of man believed important for children to learn and understand. These teaching ideas reflect the orientations to curriculum that each project embraces. When it comes to ideas that can be used to structure currriculum development groups in order to maximize their ideational fluency, social compatibility, or morale, little is available in the published material in the field of curriculum. Yet, for groups who organize their work as ours did, the importance of group process is enormous. We found that whereas psychological ideas, for example, could provide some general guidance when it came to making specific concrete decisions concerning a particular lesson or instructional support material, psychological ideas were too general to be of much use. Although we used such ideas as a general intellectual backdrop, sustained deliberation was required among members of the core group to arrive at a decision with which we could feel comfortable. There are several good reasons why these deliberations required so much time. First, we were trying to anticipate the likely effects of taking one course of action rather than another. Because theoretical ideas are by definition general, and because we were dealing with a specific instance, we could not confidently extrapolate from the theory to the consequence of the action we were considering. Consequently, we felt compelled to explore a wide range of possible consequences flowing from a particular action in order to avoid miseducational side effects. Blind alleys as well as direct routes need to be identified, and group deliberation is one way of doing this. Joseph Schwab's conception of the "practical" is, from our experience, both accurate and apt as a way of characterizing the process of curriculum planning.[15]

Second, through group deliberation, a variety of perspectives are presented. This variety makes it possible to see the problem from different angles, and hence the decision reached is much more likely to arise from the comparison of a host of alternatives. Paradoxically, "inefficiency" in group deliberation can be more efficient than efficiency. .

Third, it is often the case, as revealed in group deliberation, that more than one educational value attends to a variety of decisions being considered. In a sense, the decision finally reached is partly a matter of which group member has been most persuasive in the decision-making process. For example, there are assets and liabilities attached to the use of, say, cardboard reproductions of works of art as compared to colored slides. The former are easily movable, and there is no need to turn down the lights. However, the quality of such reproductions leaves much to be desired, and some might not possess the very qualities that one hopes children will learn to experience. Slides, although often of high visual quality, require a darkened room, a screen, and a projector. In addition, teachers might not want to take the time to set up this equipment if only a few slides are to be shown.

What happens in group deliberation is that the pros and cons, from an educational, practical, psychological, and social point of view, are discussed. The decision the group finally makes will depend not only on the "objective" evidence but also on the persuasiveness of a member who feels deeply and argues cogently about either slides or reproductions.

Because the actors in this drama are human, all of the human emotions come into play. Group members gradually learn how to couch their criticism in forms that are not so abrasive. There are times when someone's ego must be the primary consideration. In short, the viability of the group as a group is not a trivial consideration when curriculum development is undertaken as a group effort.

In an interesting way, the process of group deliberation in curriculum development has certain similarities to the kind of deliberation that goes on when juries decide the disposition of a case they have heard. In both situations, the evidence is weighed. And the metaphor *weigh* is a telling one. What is being considered and compared is not qualities or anticipations that can be put on a common yardstick and measured. Rather, it is more a comparison of incomparables. There are few curriculum problems that have one solution. For any problem there are usually several credible solutions; hence, the problem for the curriculum group is to weigh the various putative virtues *and* costs of each and finally to arrive at a decision that is then subjected to empirical test. This process includes not simply securing the facts—which are probably more difficult to secure in curriculum planning than in jurisprudence—it also includes assigning values to these facts. In both situations, the absence of recipe-like solutions is notable.

The various rationales and concepts that are found in the literature of curriculum and the empirical generalizations that are produced in the behavioral sciences should not, as I have said so often, be considered blueprints for curriculum construction but rather as devices that enable a curriculum construction group in its more passive and reflective moments to remember what might be an important consideration. The concepts of objectives, continuity, sequence, integration, and formative and summative evaluation and the categories describing the changing cognitive structure of the child provide only the most general criteria against which decisions about the curriculum can be appraised. And none by itself is adequate to resolve the range of diverse and at times competing values that can be justly claimed for different courses of action. There is not now, and I do not believe there can be, a single theory of curriculum capable of resolving and integrating the conflicts in interpretation, fact, and value emerging from different theories within the several social sciences. Theoretical consistency in curriculum development, even if it could be achieved, might in fact be an educational pyrrhic victory.

If one uses three commonplaces in the curriculum literature—the student, the society, and the subject matter—as criteria with which to identify what considerations were most prominent in our own curriculum development, in retrospect it appears that attention to the subject matter was easily the most prominent of the three. The student, although important, was simply too remote during the course of curriculum development to play a really central role in our work. In addition, we believed—or took comfort in the thought—that the classroom teacher would make whatever adaptations of our material that were necessary to suit the particular child or class or situation in which the curriculum would be used.

As for the society, it simply never appeared in our deliberations, perhaps because our value commitment toward the visual arts already implicitly embraced the belief that the development of children's artistic abilities would be important for the improvement of society. Whatever the reason, once the group was launched into the process of curriculum development, focused attention to the needs of society did not seem productive for meeting our immediate need: that of creating learning activities and instructional support materials that would teach nontrivial artistic content to elementary school children.

Possible Alternative Approaches to Curriculum Development

It is far easier for me to identify those aspects of the curriculum we created that need modification and improvement than it is for me to identify those aspects of the curriculum development strategies we employed that need improvement. We attempted to identify the strengths and weaknesses of the curriculum throughout the process of curriculum development and through "achievement testing." We did not try to identify the difficulties that might have resided within our style of curriculum development work. I do not believe that a style of work can be appraised legitimately outside the context, values, and purposes of the project for which it is an instrumentality. I believe that significant interaction occurs between the kind of orientation or platform one establishes for a curriculum and the working arrangements one formulates. The tool and the product are interdependent. What I sought was a program that would nurture the artistic development of children. I do not believe that such a program could be created within a set of working arrangements that were, for example, mechanical or authoritarian in nature. Furthermore, the context within which we worked was an educational one. I had an educational as well as an administrative responsibility for the people who worked in the core group. This educational responsibility necessitated, in my view, particular types of working relationships that might not be critical in, say, a regional educational laboratory.

In retrospect, I would not have made radical changes in the basic way in which we operated, given the conditions I laid down in the proposal that I prepared for the Kettering Foundation. Those conditions stipulated that there would be developed at Stanford University a set of curriculum materials, both written and visual, that could be used by elementary school teachers to increase the quality of art education in their classrooms. However, there are approaches to curriculum development that differ significantly from the model we employed. One of these, one that I used in the development of Kettering-like materials in Hawaii, is to bring groups of elementary school teachers together for workshops where examples of the lessons and visual instructional materials that have already been developed are presented and discussed. These materials are then used as prototypes for curriculum development by teachers. The teachers act as curriculum writers and as artists who produce instructional support material to accompany the written materials they prepare. As in the working arrangements used at Stanford, teachers can be grouped in teams of two or three, perhaps from the same elementary school. The major conceptual work—the format, its categories, and the development of exemplary lessons—will already have been completed. This aspect of curriculum development work is both difficult and time-consuming, and I have found when working with teachers that they are able to produce a great deal of promising material quite quickly. Of course, the supervision of such teams must be close, and people competent in art need to be available for consultation, especially with respect to the separation of ideas and skills that are trivial from those that are significant.

One of the potential strengths of such an approach to curriculum development is that it takes the responsibility off a single group of people for creating a complete "curriculum package." Instead, it uses the core team to conceptualize the basic curriculum structure to be used and to develop prototype materials. The structure and materials created are then resources for teachers to use in developing their own materials. In addition, the core team functions as consultants to the teachers.

This procedure for curriculum development also has the potential advantage of increasing the teacher's understanding of the project by putting him or her in the position of having to think through the project clearly enough to be able to prepare materials that others can use. This last condition for curriculum writing is an important one. Teachers must write their materials and develop their visual support devices with the criterion in mind that other people will need to be able to use such materials without direct consultation with the person who made them. Such a criterion provides a new frame of reference for teachers to use in curriculum writing.

This procedure for curriculum developments has, I believe, an important contribution to make to the in-service education of teachers. It has the virtue of being practical and concrete while asking teachers to consider concepts such as continuity and sequence as well as other matters that so often appear to teachers to be little more than educational slogans. In identifying this way of going about curriculum development as an alternative to the way our group worked, I am not suggesting that it is without liabilities. Our problems in education are not to be characterized as having ideal solutions. They are, rather, problems whose solutions are always imperfect and need to be weighed with respect to competing strengths and weaknesses. For example, although broadening the responsibility for curriculum writing is likely to yield products whose quality is uneven, at the same time, it is likely to increase motivation and comprehension of the project's objectives. What kind of tradeoff is most beneficial from an educational point of view? As far as I know, there is no metric that can be confidently applied to resolve such a problem: it's a matter of making a judgment rather than applying a standard. In making such a judgment, the image one holds of teachers and of schools comes sharply into play. If schooling is seen as a quasi-industrial venture and teachers as a workforce to be directed by management, the likelihood of being sympathetic toward a program that is "teacher-proof," one in which the teacher functions as a conduit for a totally prepackaged program, is higher than if one conceives of teachers as professionals who, with students and other teachers, jointly plan the educational program.

The work that we did in curriculum development was instructive because it provided an arena in which theoretical ideas could be employed and through use their utility and limitations appreciated. Some of the ideas that were embraced at the outset of the work were reaffirmed, whereas others were discarded. We erred in attempting to develop materials that needed little or no in-service education, that overemphasized instructional objectives, that paid too much attention to the development of technical skills and provided too little opportunity for the exercise of imagination, that were too prescriptive regarding sequence, and that underestimated the need for a syllabus to be attractively illustrated and printed. We also severely underestimated the amount of time needed to do work on the scale we aspired to reach. Yet, to be able to learn these things required the investment of time and energy that all those affiliated with the project expended. All in all, I believe that what we learned was worth the investment we made.

References

1. A modified version of this chapter appears in *Strategies for Curriculum Development,* (Jon Schaffarzick and David Hampson, eds.), McCutchan Publishing Co., Berkeley, Calif., 1975.
2. The final report of the Project is entitled *Teaching Art to the Young: A Curriculum Development Project in Art Education,* Stanford University, School of Education, 1969.
3. Elliot Eisner, "Curriculum Ideas in a Time of Crisis," *Art Education,* Vol. 18, No. 7, October 1965.
4. Elliot Eisner, "The Development of Information and Attitude Toward Art at the Secondary and College Level," *Studies in Art Education,* Vol. 8, No. 1, Autumn 1966.
5. The amount allocated to the project by the Kettering Foundation for the two-year period was approximately $70,000.
6. Elliot Eisner, "Curriculum Making for the Wee Folk: Stanford University's Kettering Project," *Studies in Art Education,* Vol. 9, No. 3, 1968.
7. Elliot Eisner, "Stanford's Kettering Project: An Appraisal of Two Years Work," *Art Education,* Vol. 23, No. 8, 1970.
8. Elliot Eisner, "Stanford's Kettering Project: A Radical Alternative in Art Education," in *Programs of Promise* (Al Hurwitz ed.), Harcourt Brace Jovanovich, New York, 1972.
9. Elliot Eisner, *Educating Artistic Vision,* Macmillan Publishing Co., New York, 1972.

10. *California State Framework for the Visual Arts,* State Department of Education, State of California, Sacramento, 1971.
11. For this distinction, I am indebted to the work of Gilbert Ryle, *The Concept of Mind,* Barnes and Noble, London, 1949.
12. This distinction grows out of John Dewey's writing, especially Chapter 13 of *Art As Experience,* Minton, Balch and Co., New York, 1934.
13. Ibid.
14. See the following by Decker Walker, *Strategies of Deliberation in Three Curriculum Development Projects,* Ph.D. Thesis, School of Education, Stanford University, 1971.
15. Joseph Schwab, "The Practical: A Language for Curriculum," *School Review,* Vol. 78, November 1969, No. 19.

9

On the Art of Teaching

First we see the hills in the painting, then we see the painting in the hills.

LI LI WENG

In the previous chapter and in those that preceded it, I have focused mainly on the problems of curriculum planning. In this chapter I wish to address another central aspect of the educational process: teaching. It is my thesis that teaching is an art guided by educational values, personal needs, and by a variety of beliefs or generalizations that the teacher holds to be true.

To argue as I will that teaching is an art is something of a paradox. We live at a time when virtually the entire effort of those who have attempted to study teaching has been devoted to the creation of a science of teaching.[1] Yet, most of those who teach—indeed, even those who study teaching scientifically—often regard their own teaching as an artistic activity. For some, to say that teaching is an art is to say that it is poorly understood and that when it is understood a science of teaching will have been developed.[2] I will have more to say about this issue a bit later, but for the present let us think about what it means to say that teaching is an art.

Four Senses of the Art of Teaching

There are at least four senses in which teaching can be considered an art. First, it is an art in the sense that teaching can be performed with such skill and grace that, for the student as well as for the teacher, the experience can be justifiably characterized as aesthetic.[3] There are classrooms in which what the teacher does—the way in which activities are orchestrated, questions asked, lectures given—constitutes a form of artistic expression. What occurs is a performance that provides intrinsic forms of satisfaction, so much so that we use the adjectives and accolades usually applied to the fine arts to describe what the teacher does while teaching.

Second, teaching is an art in the sense that teachers, like painters, composers, actresses, and dancers, make judgments based largely on qualities that unfold during the course of action. Qualitative forms of intelligence are used to select, control, and organize classroom qualities, such as tempo, tone, climate, pace of discussion, and forward movement. The teacher must "read" the emerging qualities and respond with qualities appropriate to the ends sought or the direction he or she wishes the students to take. In this process, qualitative judgment is exercised in the interests of achieving a qualitative end.[4]

Third, teaching is an art in the sense that the teacher's activity is not dominated by prescriptions or routines but is influenced by qualities and contingencies that are unpredicted. The teacher must function in an innovative way in order to cope with these contingencies. To say that prescription and routine do not dominate the teacher's activity is not to say that they are not present or play no part in teaching. Teaching requires for its artistic expression routines with which to work; the teacher must have available repertoires to draw on. It is through repertoires or routines that the teacher can devote his or her energies and attention to what is emerging in the class. Without such routines, an enormous amount of energy would need to be spent by the teacher to develop skills to use in the classroom. Thus, the presence of well-developed routines or teaching repertoires enables the teacher to deal inventively with what occurs in class. It is precisely the tension between automaticity and inventiveness that makes teaching, like any other art, so complex an undertaking. Without automaticity and the ability to call on stock responses, energies are lost and inventiveness is hampered. Yet, if responses are too automatic or routine, if they become too reflexive, the teacher's ability to invent is hampered. Teaching becomes a series of routine responses rather than an opportunity for ingenuity.

Fourth, teaching is an art in the sense that the ends it achieves are often created in process. Craft has been defined as the process through which skills are employed to arrive at preconceived ends. Art has been defined as the process in which skills are employed to discover ends through action. H. W. Janson, the noted art historian, has said, "Artists are people who play hide-and-seek but do not know what they seek until they find it."[5] In a similar sense, teaching is a form of human action in which many of the ends achieved are emergent—that is to say, found in the course of interaction with students rather than preconceived and efficiently attained. This is not to say that there are no situations in which preconceived ends are formulated; most of the arguments urging the clear specification of instructional objectives tacitly imply that the quintessence of teaching resides in the efficient achievement of such ends. It is to say that to emphasize the exclusive use of such a model of teaching reduces it to a set of algorithmic functions. Opportunities for the creation of ends in process or in the post facto analysis of outcomes require a model of teaching akin to other arts. Teachers do, at least in part, use such a model to guide their activities, not as a function of professional incompetence, but as a way of keeping their pedagogical intelligence from freezing into mechanical routine.

It is in these four senses—teaching as a source of aesthetic experience, as dependent on the perception and control of qualities, as a heuristic or adventitious activity, and as seeking emergent ends—that teaching can be regarded as an art.

Because teaching can be engaged in as an art is not to suggest that all teaching can be characterized as such. Teaching can be done as badly as anything else. It can be wooden, mechanical, mindless, and wholly unimaginative. But when it is sensitive, intelligent, and creative—those qualities that confer upon it the status of an art—it should, in my view, not be regarded, as it so often is by some, as an expression of unfathomable talent or luck but as an example of humans exercising the highest levels of their intelligence.[6] As Phillip Jackson has said, rather than complain about the art of teaching, we should try to foster whatever artistry the teacher can provide.[7]

The Role of Theory in Teaching

If we conceive of teaching as an art, does theory have a role to play in the guidance and conduct of teaching? Does artistic teaching vitiate the use of scientifically grounded theory? Theoretical frameworks, scientific or otherwise, are frames of reference that perform two extremely important functions. First, they serve as a means for identifying aspects of the reality to which they address themselves. Theories remind us of what to attend to by calling our attention to the theory's subject matter. For example, theories in sociology make vivid the social structure of the classroom, they illuminate class differences among pupils, they describe friendship patterns and formal and informal sanctions. Psychological theory (depending on the specific theory being used) might address itself to questions of self-esteem or forms of reinforcement or the need to provide students with opportunities to practice the behavior they are expected to learn. What theories do in this regard is to help us focus attention on aspects of classroom life that we might otherwise neglect. They are tools that help us bring the world into focus.[8]

But theories, in the social sciences at least, do more than this. They also provide rough approximations of what we might expect of certain pedagogical arrangements by the kinds of generalizations that they provide. Although no single theory in any of the social sciences is likely to be adequate to deal with the particular reality with which an individual teacher must cope, theories do provide generalizations that can be considered in one's reflective moments as a teacher. These moments, what Jackson calls "preactive teaching,"[9] occur prior to actual teaching: planning at home, reflecting on what has occurred during a particular class session, and discussing in groups ways to organize a program. Theory here sophisticates personal reflection and group deliberation. Insofar as a theory suggests consequences flowing from particular circumstances, it enables those who understand the theory to take those circumstances into account when planning.

In all of this, theory is not to be regarded as prescriptive but as suggestive. It is a framework, a tool, a means through which the world can be construed. Any theory is but a part of the total picture. Joseph Schwab describes the limits of theory this way:

> If, then, theory is to be used well in the determination of curricular practice, it requires a supplement. It requires arts which bring a theory to its application; first, arts which identify the disparities between real theory and theoretic representation; second, arts which modify the theory in the course of its application, in light of the discrepancies; and, third, arts which devise ways for taking account of the many aspects of the real thing which the theory does not take into account.[10]

The point in Schwab's observation is not, as some seem to believe, to excise theory from curriculum planning or from teaching, but rather to hold appropriate expectations for its utility. What is dysfunctional is to regard it as a formula to be followed or as utterly useless. The former overestimates its function, the latter underestimates it.

In one sense, all teachers operate with theory, if we take theory to mean a general set of ideas through which we make sense of the world. All teachers, whether they are aware of it or not, use theories in their work. Tacit beliefs about the nature of human intelligence, about the factors that motivate children, and about the conditions that foster learning influence the teacher's actions in the classrooms. These ideas not only influence their actions, they also influence what they attend to in the classroom: that is, the concepts that are salient in theories concerning pedagogical matters also tend to guide perception. Thus, theory inevitably operates in the conduct of teaching as it does in other aspects of educational deliberation. The major need is to be able to view situations from the varied perspectives that different theories provide and thus to be in a position to avoid the limited vision of a single view.

Thus far we have talked about teaching as an art and about some of the functions that theory performs in teaching. But what of the concept *teaching* itself? What does it mean "to teach?" What are the ways in which the term can be construed?

The Meaning of Teaching: Two Views

For John Dewey the term *teaching* was regarded as similar in form to the term *selling*.[11] That is, one could not teach unless someone learned, just as one could not sell unless someone bought. Teaching and learning were regarded as reciprocal concepts. Although it was possible to learn without having been taught, one could not be said to have taught unless someone had learned.

The reason this view of teaching was embraced was because the term *teach* implied an end-in-view—namely, learning. Teaching was goal-directed and represented, in Gilbert Ryle's terms, an achievement, not merely the performance of a task.[12] For example, to say that someone has run is to describe an activity—it is a task term. But to say that someone has won is to describe an achievement; it is an achievement term for Ryle. Thus, if a teacher attempts to teach but does not succeed in helping the student learn, then he or she may be said to have lectured, conducted a discussion, demonstrated, explained but *not* to have taught. To teach, in this sense, is known by its effects. Those effects are learning. Just as one could not be said to have sold something unless another bought, so too, one could not have been said to have taught unless another had learned.

When the study of teaching became a major interest among researchers in the early part of the 1950s, the view that teaching should be conceptualized in terms of its consequences presented something of a difficulty. To subscribe to this view of teaching means that one could study teaching only by first determining its effects on students, particularly with respect to the achievement of specified goals. This posed formidable problems in the study of teaching because it required that one must study two things: what teachers do and what students learn.

To simplify the research task, teaching was reconceptualized as a variety of acts performed by individuals called teachers as they work in classrooms with the intention of promoting learning. Whether they were successful was a matter to be studied separately. Thus, using this conception, it became possible to ask what teachers did in the classroom and to establish criteria, independent of their effects, that could be used to appraise the quality of what they did. Teachers, for example, lectured, demonstrated, explained, led discussions, introduced materials, and brought lessons to closure. All of these activities, regardless of their effects, could be evaluated by using criteria appropriate for each act. For example, the logic of lectures, the vividness of the examples provided, and the coherence of expression are considerations that could be used to evaluate aspects of teaching. The ability to ask questions in a discussion, to help the discussion move forward, to engage many participants, and to foster critical and analytical skills could be applied as criteria to appraise the teacher's skills as a discussion leader. It was believed to be too much to expect that both the quality of the acts of teaching and their consequences be studied simultaneously in a field just beginning to study teaching scientifically.

What we see here are two radically different conceptions of teaching. One regards teaching as a form of achievement directly related to learning. The other regards it as a set of acts performed by people we call teachers as they attempt to foster learning. To which of these conceptions shall we subscribe? Which one is "correct?"

It is both interesting and important to recognize that if we consider how we use the term *selling* it becomes clear that we do in fact use it not in one way but in two ways. Nel Noddings has pointed out that when we talk about someone engaged in selling, we describe a series of acts and not necessarily a series of achievements.[13] Someone is a salesman, is in the selling game, is selling cars. We use such phrases without necessarily implying that the individuals so engaged are successful. One is selling even though one might not have sold any cars today or even this week. Selling here designates a variety of actions that are guided by a set of intentions, not by a set of achievements. Similarly, we can talk about teaching as a set of acts guided by intentions, not as representing achievements.

At the same time, we also talk about teaching in the sense that someone has fulfilled an intention. Teaching also refers to the achievement of intended learning. We say, for example, "I taught you or I failed to teach you," implying that if one had not succeeded, teaching did not occur.

What can we do about this duality? I suggest that we can appropriately conceptualize teaching both ways. We do at present and have in the past used both conceptions of teaching, and I believe that they have served us well. We discern the meaning of the term *teach* not by referring to some operational or stipulated definition, but by recognizing how it functions in a context of other meanings. Much of our language functions in the same way. If under certain circumstances the context is insufficient to provide clarity of meaning, we can then stipulate what we mean by teaching so that others will know how we intend to use the term. In most cases, I believe, we can use the term *teach* in both ways—as an achievement term and as a task term—without a serious problem in communication.

Teaching and Instruction

There is, however, a tendency in our discussions to use *teaching* and *instruction* interchangeably. These terms, I would suggest, are not interchangeable. Their connotative meanings are sufficiently distinctive to warrant attention because what they connote can lead to different conceptions of education and educational practice.

Perhaps the best way to illustrate the differences between *teaching* and *instruction* is to relate an episode that occurred to me in 1972[14] when I was studying English primary schools. I was having tea in a common room of a London primary school with a group of primary school teachers. We were talking about how the school day was organized and in the course of the conversation I said that I was interested in the way in which they provided instruction. A group of incredulous expressions appeared on their faces. "Instruction?" they asked. I said yes, I was interested in how they provided instruction to the pupils. One of them said, "We don't provide instruction in this school, we teach. Instruction is provided in the church and in the army, but in this school we teach."

What they were conveying to me, and it was the first time I had reflected on the distinction, was that instruction was concerned with forms of training; it was harsher, less organic, more mechanical than teaching. To "teach" is softer than to "instruct." Perhaps this is why the term *instruction* is more likely to be used by those whose orientation to curriculum is technological and who want to maximize effective control over the content and form of what children learn in school. *Instruction* is a term more suited to a manual than is the term *teach*. Instruction is less apt to be associated with the adventitious, with what is flexible and emergent, in short, and what is artistic, than is teaching.

Now to draw this difference between terms might seem like quibbling, but it is not. It is precisely because we do not have clear-cut, stipulated definitions of these terms that their connotative meanings take on such importance. When terms are not formally differentiated, context and connotation significantly influence the kinds of meanings that individuals are likely to construe. To use the term *instruction* as an equivalent to the term *teach* is not to have an equivalent at all; each term carries its own conceptual baggage, and although there is some overlap, the significance of the terms resides in their differences because each implies a different image of what teaching should do.

It is significant, also, I believe, that the terms we use in educational discourse not only reflect different assumptions about the means and ends of education, but that terms cluster—that is, individual terms tend to have conceptual links to other terms. In combination, they generate a view of what is educationally desirable. Consider, for example, the term *individualized instruction*. Contrast this with *personalized teaching*. The term *individ-*

ualized is harsher and more bureaucratic in character than *personalized*. The latter is softer and more intimate. When combined with *instruction, individualized instruction* takes on a connotation that is more technological than *personalized teaching*.

Consider the following: "In this school system, individualized instruction is provided to learners after first having measured a learner's entry skills. Once these entry skills have been determined, appropriate exit skills are specified and measured at the end of the instructional period." Language of this sort communicates not only because of the specific denotations of the language used but because of the images that the language conveys. *Entry* and *exit* conjure up something of an assembly line in which products are processed according to specifications. Education in this context is something that one does to another through a process called instruction. When such terms permeate our discourse they shape our view of the character and aims of education.

When it comes to discourse about teaching, perhaps no concept has had greater currency than the concept of individualized instruction. I have already pointed out that the concept itself participates in a tradition that is more mechanical than organic. If we were to study the ways in which individualization is provided in classrooms, we would find that in many classrooms the variable that is individualized for students is time. Individualized instruction in a great many classrooms means allowing children to take different amounts of time to arrive at the same destination. Yet, individualization (or personalized teaching, if you prefer) can be provided by altering the teaching method so that it suits particular children, by altering content, and by altering the goals themselves. Time is but one factor of many that can be modified to accommodate the characteristics or aptitude of different children.

What is not recognized—even by teachers who provide it regularly—is that the use of different kinds of explanations for different children, the variety of questions and types of examples teachers provide, the different ways in which motivation is engendered, the modulation of one's tone of voice and one's tempo to suit individual children are examples of individualized instruction. To be sure, these forms of pedagogical adaptation use no mechanical means—no workbooks, test forms, color-coded boxes of reading material—yet they reside, I believe, at the heart of individualization, for they represent one person's effort to try to communicate with another. Each child, so to speak, is a custom job.

Because of our national tendency to seek prepackaged and field-tested devices to make education efficient, we sometimes fail to recognize the extent to which some of the teaching practices employed daily reflect the most straightforward examples of individualization. Mechanical images too often intervene and hamper our recognition of the excellent things we already do.

Artistry in teaching is not a common occurrence. It is an ideal. The reasons for its importance are not self-evident, and although I have described the senses in which teaching is an art, I have not said much about why artistic teaching is so important to the educational development of the young.

The Importance of Artistry

Artistry is important because teachers who function artistically in the classroom not only provide children with important sources of artistic experience, they also provide a climate that welcomes exploration and risk-taking and cultivates the disposition to play. To be able to play with ideas is to feel free to throw them into new combinations, to experiment, and even to "fail." It is to be able to deliteralize perception so that fantasy, metaphor, and constructive foolishness may emerge. For it is through play that children eventually discover the limits of their ideas, test their own competencies, and formulate rules that eventually convert play into games. This vacillation between playing and gaming, between algorithms and heuristics, between structure-seeking and rule-abiding behavior, is critical for the construction of new patterns of knowing. Play opens up new possibilities, whereas games exploit these possibilities within a set of defined parameters, something that mature intellectual models do with their work. Playing with ideas that are transformed and guided by rules is as prevalent in the art studio as it is in the science laboratory. Although each area has its own syntax, each its own form and rules, they share the need for play as a source of invention and discovery. But for such a disposition to be cultivated, teachers themselves need to feel free to innovate, to explore, and to play. Teaching is not an act modeled after the sequences of a highly efficient assembly line. Teaching is more like what occurs on a basketball court or on a soccer field. Let me develop this analogy.

Basketball is a game defined by certain rules in which its players seek an unambiguous outcome: to end the game with more points than their opponents. In the former characteristic, basketball and teaching are similar: both have rules that define the activities of their respective games. However, in the latter characteristic, having unambiguous goals, the teacher is generally unlike the basketball player. Goals change in teaching, they are not without ambiguity, and they are certainly not the same for all students. Still, basketball and teaching are alike in many ways. A basketball player must watch the court and understand emerging configurations; so must a teacher. A player must recognize productive possibilities and must know how to pass as well as to shoot: so must a teacher. The basketball player must also know how to slow down the pace, when to speed it up, and even when to stall for time: so must a teacher. He needs to know when to cut, how to slow down a pass, how to talk to his opponent, and how to provide support for his teammates; so must a teacher. The skills that he must have to play the game well require intellectual flexibility. Although good teams have a set of preplanned patterns, once they get on the floor they need to know both how to improvise within those patterns and when to give them up at a second's notice in order to exploit other options. Flexible purposing, Dewey calls it:[15] knowing when to alter the goal, when to explore new interactions and when to shift strategies. In this sense, neither basketball nor teaching is optimized by chaotic abandon or rigid adherence to pre-specified plans. Fluid intelligence, intelligence in process, is the hallmark of effectiveness in both arenas. Unlike the automobile assembly line where systemization, orderliness, predictability, and control serve the goals of efficiency, effective teaching, like effective basketball, profits from flexibility, ingenuity, and personal creativity, the last things desired on the assembly line.

To say that excellence in teaching requires artistry implies that the teacher is able to exploit opportunities as they occur. It implies that goals and intentions be fluid. But in many ways this is contrary to the belief that single-mindedness and clarity of one's ends-in-view are required for rationally guided activity. To be rational, one must be intentional. But what is not adequately appreciated is the limitation that such a conception of rationality places on the ways in which teaching can be undertaken. If teaching is regarded—at least in part—as a form of inquiry, as a process of exploring problems that one cannot always define or predict—problems of a pedagogical and substantive variety—the limitations of such a conception of rationality begin to become apparent.

Furthermore, the mandate to operationalize aims has the effect of frequently restricting the aims of teachers in curriculum development to those for which a technology of measurement is available. If such a technology is absent, the likelihood of relinquishing valued aims increases. The ability to measure provides a formidable restraint on what teachers come to believe they ought to do.

But perhaps the most insidious aspect of belief that aims should always be clear and measurable is the coercive impact such a belief has on our conception of rationality and intentionality.

What counts as an intention? Must an intention be capable of linguistic formulation? Is it necessary that the aspiration one seeks be statable in discursive language? Given the admonition that teachers state their objectives behaviorally, it would appear that objectives that cannot be articulated in discursive form are not objectives. Such a view is naive on several counts. First, much of what we aim for is held "in the mind's eye" as an image rather than as a proposition. The image is a visual form of knowing that is in many ways clearer than its discursive representation. Imagine an architect having to discursively describe the features of the structure she intends to create. Such a description is likely to fall far short of the architectural qualities she is after. The images of excellence in the arts and the sciences, in the social studies, and in the conduct of practice are often extremely difficult to articulate—and at times are ineffable. To expect all of what we prize to be capable of being translated into discourse is to make a second conceptual blunder: namely, failure to appreciate the modes of conceptual representation humans are capable of using.

One must ask further whether intentions must always precede action. Is it not the case that action breeds intention as often as intention leads to action? Regarding the relationship of action to ends, one of the foremost organizational theorists in the United States, James March, has this to say:

> Goals are thrust upon the intelligent man. We ask that he act in the name of goals. We ask that he keep his goals consistent. We ask that his actions be oriented to his goals. We ask that a social system amalgamate individual goals into a collective goal. But we do not concern ourselves with the origin of goals. Theories of individual organizational and social choice assume actors with pre-existent values.
>
> Since it is obvious that goals change over time and that the character of those changes affects both the richness of personal and social development and the outcome of choice behavior, a theory of choice must somehow justify ignoring the phenomena. Although it is unreasonable to ask a theory of choice to solve all of the problems of man and his development, it is reasonable to ask how something as conspicuous as the fluidity and ambiguity of objectives can plausibly be ignored in a theory that is offered as a guide to human choice behavior.
>
> There are three classic justifications. The first is that goal development and choice are independent processes, conceptually and behaviorally. The second is that the model of choice is never satisfied in fact and that deviations from the model accommodate the problems of introducing change. The third is that the idea of changing goals is so intractable in a normative theory of choice that nothing can be said about it. Since I am unpersuaded of the first and second justifications, my optimism with respect to the third is somewhat greater than most of my fellows.
>
> The argument that goal development and choice are independent behaviorally seems clearly false. It seems to me perfectly obvious that a description that assumes goals come first and action comes later is frequently radically wrong. Human choice behavior is at least as much a process for discovering goals as for acting on them.[16]

March's view of this matter seems clearly persuasive. Why then should a static, unidirectional conception of intentionality and rationality dominate our conception of responsible teaching and curriculum development? Largely, I believe, because we have taken our image of rationality from technologies that emphasize standardization, routine, and efficiency. As long as we conceive of the school as an institution with a static and common mission whose goals must be clearly specified, the belief that effective teaching must lead to the efficient attainment of such goals follows. The task of school administrators, or "program managers," as they are being called increasingly, is to see to it that teachers perform in ways consistent with those goals. Rational planning consists of articulating those goals, subdividing them into units, and casting them into operational forms. The next step is to attempt to discover or to create procedures known to be instrumental to the achievement of those goals. Once this has been accomplished, a monitoring system can be employed to control the performance patterns of teachers who, in turn, can control the performance patterns of students.

The failure to distinguish between education and training, between the school and the factory, between the algorithms and the heuristics of teaching accounts for the simplistic nostrums that are promulgated as ways of improving education. Intentions need not be statable to be held. Intentions need not precede action; they can grow out of action. Rationality includes the capacity to play, to explore, to search for surprise and effective novelty. Such activities are not necessarily contrary to the exercise of human rationality; they may be its most compelling exemplification. What diminishes human rationality is the thwarting of flexible human intelligence by prescriptions that shackle the educational imagination.

On the Relationship between Teaching and Curriculum Planning

Just what is the relationship between teaching and curriculum planning? For some, the distinction between teaching and curriculum is blurred. The argument is that if curriculum constitutes the content of what children learn, then it is not possible to separate the forms through which that content is conveyed from the content itself because form and content interact. How one teaches and what one teaches are inseparable.

This argument is not without merit. Indeed, one of the aims of this book is to encourage students of education to consider curriculum planning and schooling as an entity because each aspect of schooling has a bearing on other aspects. The timetable of the school, for example, influences the way in which teachers must plan the curriculum, pace lessons, and organize learning activities. Evaluation practices influence educational priorities as much as they reflect them. Yet, to say that teaching and curriculum interact or influence each other is to make a distinction between teaching and curriculum. I believe this distinction is a useful one for several reasons.

First, we already have a tradition of discussion regarding the term *teaching*. In the English language—despite the difficulties and differences in conceptions discussed earlier—we do talk about teaching and regard it as something other than curriculum. In the simplest terms—too simple to be sure—curriculum is the content that is taught and teaching is how that content is taught. This simple difference is important because all curriculum planning, insofar as it precedes its actual use in the classroom, requires a transformation of a set of plans or materials into a course of action. This transformation is what we regard as teaching.

Now it should be noted that in this view not all of teaching takes place when teachers talk to a group of students or lead a discussion. Teaching includes the setting up of conditions that do not require the teacher to be in an interactive relationship with students. Thus, a teacher who arranges a set of conditions, say a terrarium or a selection of books or art material with which students may work, and who provides a modicum of guidance to enable students to use these resources is engaged in teaching even though no lecture or discussion is provided. In short, teaching does not require either a didactic or a dialectic relationship between teacher and pupil. It can and does occur through the creation of an intellectually productive environment.

Earlier I pointed out that intentions and rational planning need not precede action, that intentions can develop out of actions as well as lead to them. How does such a conception bear on the relationship of teaching to curriculum?

The "standard" model of this relationship appears in Figure 4.

In this model, intentions are formed that set the direction and the constraints for curriculum planning. Once the curriculum is planned, it provides the aims, the content, and the resources that the teacher employs to transform intentions and curriculum materials into classroom conditions that promote learning. Although much pedagogical activity takes this route, not all of it does. Consider the diagram in Figure 5.

In this model, teaching, which always has a content because it is logically impossible to teach or to try to teach someone nothing, interacts with curriculum. One engages in teaching some content and out of action intentions develop that are then used as a basis for planning curriculum. In this

Figure 4

Figure 5

model, action is the initiating agent that leads to the formation of intentions, which in turn leads to curriculum planning.

Both of the models presented here are unidirectional. One starts with intentions and terminates with teaching. The other starts with teaching and terminates with curriculum planning. Perhaps a more adequate representation of the process is found in Figure 6.

In this model, the process is circular—that is, one can enter the circle at any point in the model. Intentions lead to curriculum planning, which in turn provides the content and structure for teaching, which through the course of action leads to the formation of new intentions. One might start with curriculum planning and through it provide the content and structure for teaching, which in turn leads to intentions; or one might start with teaching and through action formulate intentions, which in turn lead to curriculum planning.

With such a model, one can begin to study the sources of intentionality in teaching and speculate on the kinds of value orientations that are more likely than others to encourage teachers to use teaching to formulate intentions and vice versa.

There is another comment worth making about the relationship of curriculum to teaching that has to do with primacy of curriculum in this relationship. By this I mean that it is no virtue to teach well what should not be taught at all. Put another way, what is not worth teaching is not worth teaching well. Thus, if the content to be taught is without redeeming fea-

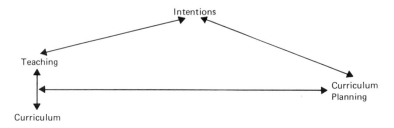

Figure 6

tures, it makes little sense to worry about how well it is being taught; teaching matters, so to speak, when what is taught is worth the student's time.

Looking at it from another angle, a curriculum composed of high-quality content and imaginative activities and materials can be scuttled by poor teaching. If the teacher is unable to use materials in the classroom effectively, regardless of how well planned they are, the virtues of the materials as far as the students are concerned go unrealized. But if the curriculum materials are without intellectual virtue, effectively teaching them constitutes a vice.

The virtues and vices of teaching are not only related to the quality of what is taught, but are also determined by criteria that are appropriate to the form of teaching that is provided. For example, the kinds of skills one needs to be able to give a lucid and coherent lecture are not the same as those needed to conduct a discussion. A teacher who is good at the former may be poor at the latter. To attempt to apply a single set of criteria to a wide variety of types and forms of teaching is to overlook what is distinctive about each type. Consider not only the giving of lectures and the leading of discussions, but the organization of small-group activity, individual counseling and guidance, and the ability to maintain a wide array of diverse but productive activities in the classroom; each of these forms of teaching requires the use of different skills. The criteria that are appropriate for appraising the quality of one kind of teaching are not necessarily appropriate for appraising the quality of another.

This admonition to apply to an art form the criteria appropriate to it is well known in the fine arts. We do not use criteria appropriate for tragedy to appraise the quality of melodrama and vice versa. What constitutes excellence in surrealist painting does not constitute excellence in impressionistic work. In teaching, too, excellence is related to the form of teaching being employed. It is probably too much to expect a high degree of excellence in all of the major forms of teaching that can be provided in a classroom. What we probably do want is a high degree of excellence in some.

I make this point—although it may seem obvious—because we often talk about excellence in teaching as though it were a single set of qualities. We sometimes tend to evaluate teaching with a single image of pedagogical merit. And research in teaching has tended to underplay the distinctive differences of different forms of teaching as well as the normative frames of reference or orientations to education that any set of criteria must in some way reflect. Yet these orientations are, in the last analysis, the crucial criteria for appraising the educational value of teaching. Excellence as a lecturer or as a discussion leader is not sufficient to constitute educational virtue if either the lectures or the discussions are regarded as educationally inappropriate. No judgment can be made about the quality of teaching as an educational event or performance without reference to some theory of education. It is ironic that the most neglected aspect in research on teaching is the very framework that would have made it possible for the researcher to say something about the educational significance of the findings.

In all of this discussion about the art of teaching, about differences between teaching and instruction, and about teaching as an independent or reciprocal concept, it is easy to neglect the fact that teachers have needs that must be met through teaching. Because teachers are *people* who teach, it is important that, in our efforts to develop self-instructional materials for students and prepackaged procedures for instruction, we do not eviscerate the classroom of those opportunities that teachers need to gain satisfaction from teaching. When such procedures begin to dominate classroom practice, opportunities to gain satisfactions from teaching can be seriously diminished. The teacher who wants the pride and satisfaction that come from having designed a reading program may be restricted from using such a program. Although schools do not exist primarily for the benefit of teachers, teachers who receive little or no satisfaction from what they do are not, I believe, likely to be educationally effective. The human need for pride in craftsmanship and being able to put something of oneself into work is recognized even by companies that sell packaged cake mixes.

The need to get something out of what one does, aside from student achievement, is still very great for most of us. The school should provide the conditions where such needs can be met. Unless the school can provide the necessary life-space for the teacher's growth, the existence of optimal conditions for the educational growth of students is not assured.

References

1. See, for example, the two volumes of the *Handbook of Research on Teaching*. (N. L. Gage, ed.), *Handbook of Research on Teaching*, Rand McNally & Company, Chicago, 1963; and Robert M. W. Travers, ed. *Second Handbook of Research on Teaching*, Rand McNally & Company, Chicago, 1973.
2. This is reflected in the phrase "The state of the art," which typically implies that a high state of refinement or understanding has not yet been attained.
3. That the quality of experience defines art is best argued by John Dewey in *Art As Experience*, Minton, Balch and Co., New York, 1934.
4. See David Ecker, "The Artistic Process as Qualitative Problem-Solving," *Journal of Aesthetics and Art Criticism*, Vol. 21, No. 3, Spring 1963.
5. H. W. Janson, quoted in *Meaning*, Michael Polanyi and Harry Prosch, The University of Chicago Press, Chicago, 1977.
6. Dewey writes of the role of intelligence in art as follows: "Any idea that ignores the necessary role of intelligence in production of works of art is based upon identification of thinking with use of one special kind of material, verbal signs

and words. To think effectively in terms of relations of qualities is as severe a demand upon thought as to think in terms of symbols, verbal and mathematical. Indeed, since words are easily manipulated in mechanical ways, the production of a work of genuine art probably demands more intelligence than does most of the so-called thinking that goes on among those who pride themselves on being 'intellectuals.'" *Art as Experience,* Minton, Balch and Co., New York, 1934, p. 46.

7. Phillip Jackson, *Life in Classrooms,* Holt, Rinehart, and Winston, New York, 1969.
8. See especially, Morris Weitz, "The Nature of Art," in *Readings in Art Education,* (Elliot W. Eisner and David Ecker, eds.) Blaisdell Publishing Co., Waltham, Mass., 1966.
9. Jackson, op. cit.
10. Joseph Schwab, "The Practical: A Language for Curriculum," *School Review,* Vol. 78, November 1969, p. 12.
11. John Dewey, *How We Think,* D. C. Heath, Lexington, Mass., 1910.
12. Gilbert Ryle, *The Concept of Mind,* Barnes and Noble, New York, 1949.
13. Nel Noddings, in a personal communication.
14. For a report on this work, see Elliot W. Eisner, *English Primary Schools,* National Association for Young Children, Washington, D.C., 1974.
15. John Dewey, *Experience and Education,* Macmillan Co., New York, 1938, passim.
16. James March, "Model Bias in Social Action," *Review of Educational Research,* Vol. 42, No. 4, Fall 1972, pp. 413–430.

IO

The Functions and
Forms of Evaluation

*Our discussion will be adequate if it has as much clearness as
the subject matter admits of, for precision is not to be sought for
alike in all discussions, any more than in all the products of the
crafts. . . . for it is the mark of an educated man to look for
precision in each class of things just so far as the nature of the
subject admits; it is evidently equally foolish to accept probable
reasoning from a mathematician and to demand from a
rhetorician scientific proofs.*

ARISTOTLE

Although many people regard evaluation as something analogous to the
giving of grades, in fact evaluation is used in education to perform a wide
variety of functions. This chapter identifies some of these functions and
describes the forms evaluation can take when directed toward various
ends. Of the functions of evaluation in education, five seem especially
important:

1. To diagnose.
2. To revise curricula.
3. To compare.
4. To anticipate educational needs.
5. To determine if objectives have been achieved.

Let's examine each of these different functions. Evaluation can be used
to diagnose—but what? Three subject matters, each of which will be dis-

cussed in detail later, can be identified now as being the potential focus of diagnosis. They are the *curriculum* itself, even before it is employed in a classroom, *the teaching* that is occurring, and *the student* and his or her learning and experience.

Diagnosis

Diagnosis as an evaluative technique is most often used in the context of student learning, and the term itself has a medical connotation. Students are "diagnosed" in order to "prescribe" a "treatment" that is educationally effective. The medical analogy has its uses: it suggests that treatments will be employed that fit the nature of the student's difficulties. But there are limits to such metaphors. Students are not patients and they don't normally have illnesses to be treated. Furthermore, although there are standard forms of medical technique, controlled pharmaceutical formulas for medicines, and routine procedures for medical diagnoses, virtually none of the rigorous tools, treatments, or techniques available to the medical practitioner is available to the educational practitioner. To be sure, there are intelligence tests and diagnostic tests in reading and in some other subject areas such as mathematics, but the confidence one can place in these tools is limited and, in addition, performance on them is greatly influenced by the cultural conditions in which students live. Having said this, we can still talk about diagnosis as a function in evaluation. To diagnose can represent the effort to locate or try to locate the sources of difficulties students are having with particular learning problems. In the field of reading, where many of the available diagnostic tools exist, it is possible to employ tests that assess word-attack skills, paragraph meaning, general comprehension, and vocabulary. The achievement profile secured from such instruments is designed to guide the teacher so that if a student is weak in a particular area instruction in that area can be provided.

It should also be pointed out that the diagnosis of learning difficulties does not require the use of tests, and at its most general level is used by virtually all teachers to identify whether their students understand what is being taught. For example, an art teacher can look at a student's work or watch the student while working in class and "diagnose" the sorts of strengths and weaknesses that the student possesses. One student might, for example, be unable to control the material adequately to use it as a medium of expression, another student might be neglecting attention to his work's formal features, still another student might be inadequately wedging the clay with which she is working. In each of the foregoing cases, the type of problem the student has requires a different type of "solution" or educational "treatment."

But even more generally, any teacher attempting to explain something to students in class would attempt to determine whether the explanation was understood. To do so requires some form of diagnosis: a request by the teacher to a student to explain, to demonstrate, to draw relationships. The questions students ask also provide diagnostic information to the teacher. Indeed, if one looks at teaching dialectically, much of what teachers do will be seen as a result of their understanding of where students are and what they need. The use of an example to clarify a point that is not understood requires some conception of what is likely to make more sense to students than the explanation just provided. The good example provides the necessary bridge between the student's current level of comprehension, his or her experience, and the aims toward which the teaching is directed. The selection of the right example is, one might say, the result of a diagnostic evaluation.

Perhaps the classic example of such diagnosis occurs in the sixth book of Plato's *Republic*.[1] Glaucon, after he asks about the nature of knowledge, is given an image by Socrates in an effort to help him grasp the hierarchy of truth that is used in Plato's epistemology. Glaucon fails to grasp the meaning of the image (in this case, a line divided into four segments intended to represent various degrees of truth), and so Socrates proceeds in the beginning of Book Seven to tell Glaucon the famous parable of the cave, which even more graphically depicts the relationships Socrates tried to explain earlier. What Plato gives us here is a telling image of both teaching and diagnostic evaluation.

Recognizing that Glaucon does not understand the abstract explanation he has provided, Socrates makes his explanation more concrete and uses the vivid imagery of the cave, the shadows, and the sun to help Glaucon grasp his point about the nature of knowledge. Like the good teacher, Socrates *individualizes* his example to help his pupil understand what he is trying to teach. To recognize the need for individualization, evaluation must occur. Evaluation here is used to diagnose and monitor. Thus, diagnosis in evaluation can be employed dynamically in the context of teaching or more formally in the context of specially designed tests that locate the students' strengths and weaknesses, and therefore it provides a basis for curriculum change.

Curriculum Revision

A second function of evaluation is to revise the curriculum. If for the moment we conceive of the curriculum as a set of materials to be used by students or by the teacher in order to have educational consequences, then it becomes clear that such materials will need modification and improvements from the point of initial inception to the point where they are ready for general dissemination to the schools. This process—what Michael Scriven refers to as formative evaluation[2]—has as its major aim the improvement of the program or curriculum that is being developed. In educational laboratories that develop curriculum materials, such evaluation goes through a variety of stages before the final product—in this case a packaged curriculum—is disseminated. One of these stages focuses on an evaluation of the content and aims of the curriculum.[3] Before learning activities are created, there is some appraisal of the content that has been selected and the aims that have been formulated. This process, which itself is a part of the curriculum development process, lays the groundwork for transforming content and aims into promising learning activities: events that have as their intended consequences educational outcomes related to the subject matter or content employed in the first place.

Once the content has been appraised and learning activities have been formulated, the materials are "hothouse tested," as described earlier. Among other things, this affords schools the opportunity to have contact with a developing educational enterprise that is stimulating to the school. It provides a type of Hawthorne effect for those teachers who elect to try the new material.

If the curriculum developer and an evaluator visit the classroom on appointment to watch the class use the materials and to observe the teacher and talk with him or her about the materials, the developer can gain some insight into the problems that exist and how they might be remedied. The materials might be too sophisticated for children of a particular age to use, the learning activities might turn out to be dull, the teacher might have difficulty handling the materials physically, the explanations might be misleading and therefore likely to be misunderstood, and so on. After the materials have been revised as a result of hothouse testing, the materials will be disseminated for field testing. Ideally, these stages of evaluation will yield curriculum materials that do not have major educational faults.

When the curriculum development movement got under way in the early 1960s, there was talk about the desirability of creating "teacher proof" curricula. That aspiration has, through the years, given way to the more realistic view that teachers are not mere tubes for curriculum developers. Teachers cannot and should not be bypassed. Materials guarantee nothing. What they do is to expand the range of resources with which teachers and students can work. They are not a substitute for teachers.

Using evaluation to revise the curriculum is in my view one of the central functions of evaluation. It is a type of feedback mechanism for educational improvement that diminishes the tendency to use evaluation practices simply as a means of classifying students, rewarding them, or selecting the able from the rest. Although classification, selection, and reward have been historically important functions of evaluation, when evaluation is used this way the responsibility for performance shifts almost wholly to the student rather than the school. If students fail to perform, under conventional assumptions the fault lies with the students.[4] However, when student performance is viewed as an index of program effectiveness, the likelihood of curriculum improvement increases and a major contribution is made toward improving the quality of education.

Comparing Programs

A third function of evaluation is to compare programs, teaching, and other aspects of schooling such as forms of school organization. Educational policy is supposedly made with an eye toward improving the quality of educational experience the school provides. This means that when a school board decides that new school buildings will be designed on an open plan, there is implicit in that policy the belief that such a plan will have beneficial effects on the students for whom it is intended. Many, but not all, policy changes in schools are based on certain values that the new policy is intended to realize. Often the "new math" was adopted because people came to believe that it was important for students to understand the logic, or structure, of mathematics. The use of peer tutoring is embraced because it is believed that students teaching each other provide benefits that cannot be secured from a student-teacher relationship. Team teaching is used in schools because collaboration by teachers is thought to make it possible for them to exploit their strengths as teachers. Related arts programs are developed because such programs are considered to help students appreciate the common elements among the arts. Comparative approaches to evaluation ask whether these beliefs are true. Does the new math do more than the old math in helping students understand the structure of mathematics? Does peer tutoring have benefits that more typical teacher-pupil relationships fail to provide? And so forth. Insofar as educational policy rests on evidence concerning the effects of the alternatives being considered, the comparative evaluation of these programs, in principle, is one vehicle for making such evidence available.

There is, however, a set of paradoxes regarding the use of comparative methods for curriculum policy making. In the first place, educational materials and modes of school organization are not susceptible to the kind of standardization that can be assigned to, say, light bulbs. If the electric company says that a light bulb will burn for about 740 hours, nine times out of ten its life will be close to that mark. Educational materials and new forms of educational practice cannot be standardized with the precision possible with materials that are inert; hence, a program evaluated as effective in one setting is not guaranteed to be effective in other settings. Moreover, the new setting will assuredly differ from the others in which the materials were originally used. Thus, a policy to adopt a new curriculum, to employ a new form of school organization, or to use a new procedure for scheduling must to a large degree be based on the attractiveness of such materials, modes of organization, and procedures rather than on "hard data."

Even if such data could be obtained, it might take several years to evaluate programs adequately to the point where hard data were available. By that time, the desire to implement the innovation might have run its course; its most ardent advocates might have left the district, the need for such innovation might have changed, or some new and even more promising innovations might have emerged on the horizon. Thus, comparisons of educational programs are difficult. They are difficult not only because of the reasons cited, but also because new programs most often tend to be aimed at the achievement of goals different from those that old programs were designed to achieve. It is seldom the case that the goals of existing programs are considered to be without merit. Hence, when one weighs the promise of a new program against that of an existing one, their effectiveness is found to be not strictly comparable. They aim at different ends. Because it is not a matter of one program doing better what another program does—that would be far easier—the problem of comparison is extremely complicated. Nevertheless, the effectiveness of different programs can be compared, if only in relation to their own goals and unanticipated consequences. Such a comparison will not provide simple and certain conclusions about what to adopt and implement, but it will expand the pool of considerations from which competent educational conclusions can be drawn.

Identifying Educational Needs

A fourth function of evaluation is to anticipate or identify educational needs. The concept of educational needs is directly related to the practice of needs assessment, in which various modes of data collection are employed with a community or school population in order to identify appropriate educational goals. For example, the U.S. Office of Education and later the National Institute of Education frequently required the writers of proposals for educational innovations first to do a needs assessment to demonstrate the existence of the need to be met through the proposed project. Writers of proposals would then employ tests of achievement and of attitude, conduct interviews, and determine public opinion by collecting statements from community leaders that there was a need for the program for which funding was sought. Needs assessment became the process for justifying the educational importance of educational innovation.

The practice of studying the community or the school population for which a program is intended is not unreasonable. At the same time, it is wise to be aware of the fact that educational needs are not like the clouds or the grass. They are not simply out there to be discovered by interview or tests. Educational needs are the products of judgments about what counts in educational matters. What constitutes an educational need depends on the educational values one holds. In Chapter 4, some of the values that animate educational programs were identified. Clearly, someone who embraces academic rationalism will perceive educational needs differently from someone who is a social reconstructionist. The academic rationalist looks at the school population and concludes that the students are without an appreciation of the past, are ignorant of the major intellectual works of man, and cannot adequately reason. The social reconstructionist exclaims that students need to know that the environment is being poisoned, that bigotry and race hatred are rampant, and that the world needs a common government if it is to survive.

The influence of the values one brings to a situation is manifest in how one describes that situation. The selection of tests, the identification of relevant populations to study, the way in which data are secured and analyzed: these all reflect the values one considers important. If one values curiosity, imagination, and sensibility, it is possible to describe educational needs in these terms. If one values reading skill, arithmetical competency, and neatness, one looks for other types of data. In short, we look for data with which to determine educational needs by selecting subject matters to which we are already commited. In part, we find what we look for.

Determining if Objectives Have Been Achieved

A fifth function of evaluation, and the one most traditionally employed in curriculum theory, is as a means for determining whether educational objectives have been attained. The theory underlying this function of evaluation is straightforward. Educational programs should be purposeful; therefore, they should have goals. To be meaningful, these goals should be sufficiently specific to make it possible to determine whether they have been realized. The objectives once formulated at a meaningful level of specificity are the criteria through which student performance is assessed. Evaluation in this function is designed to provide the tasks and identify the situations that make possible the acquisition of data relevant to the objectives. Evaluation therefore can be used as a type of feedback mechanism to "recycle" the student if he or she fails to achieve the objectives, to pass him or her on to the next level if the objectives have been attained, to revise the curriculum if it is not effective for a particular student or group of students, or to alter the objectives.

This emphasis on use of evaluation conceives of clearly formulated objectives as a central and necessary condition for meaningful evaluation. It is argued, erroneously in my view, that there can be no evaluation without a "clear" statement of objectives.[5] Objectives are the criteria for determining whether the program has been effective. Evaluation is the means of collecting the data and analyzing them.

There is, of course, a reasonableness in the desire to have objectives in order to evaluate the effectiveness of an educational program. Yet, the evaluative net one casts can and ought to be much wider than the particular objective or set of objectives specified by a particular curriculum. The outcomes of educational programs are not completely predictable, and hence to evaluate only for those goals one has intended can lead one to neglect equally important, and at times even more important, outcomes that were unintended. Using objectives to serve as criteria for evaluating educational programs has an important function to perform, but a conception of evaluation that limits itself to what has been preplanned in terms of goals or objectives is likely to be educationally thin.

It should be noted that the use of objectives as a basis for evaluation has given rise to particular conceptions of educational practice. Mastery learning[6] is one such practice. Mastery learning theory posits that schools should not be primarily concerned with sorting out people through instruments that compare students to each other. Schools have historically performed the sorting role for society, and the result has been both frustration for those students who did not succeed and a loss of talented resources that society could have otherwise secured. Rather than attempt to sort out the able from the less able through evaluation procedures that are designed to compare students to each other, the school should formulate specific levels of mastery—particular objectives—and should evaluate students in relation to their mastery of these objectives, regardless of the amount of time it might take for particular students to attain mastery. Such a theory of educational practice would give virtually all students a sense of achievement and, in the long run, would contribute to their mental health as well as to their competence.

In describing mastery learning, I am simply pointing out the function that evaluation performs in such a view of educational practice. In this view, the form of evaluation called for requires a specific, operationally defined conception of mastery; hence the need for a set of behavioral objectives.

The idea that evaluation should determine whether objectives have been achieved has given rise not only to the concept of mastery learning, but also to distinctions between two types of tests. These are *norm-referenced* and *criterion-referenced* tests.[7] In norm-referenced tests, of which IQ tests and most published achievement tests are examples, the performance of an individual or a group is compared to the performance of other individuals or groups. The test is constructed to discriminate between the performances of individuals and to enable the test maker or user to rank individuals within a group. Ranking can be individual or within groups, the most general being that of individuals whose performance places them in the upper half or in the lower half of a population of those who have taken the test. Rankings can be further refined into quartiles—the placement of individuals in the first, second, third, or fourth quarter of a population. Regardless of the particular scheme used, the distinguishing feature of norm-referenced tests is that the scores individuals achieve on such tests are reported and their meaning is interpreted in relation to the performance of others.

Criterion-referenced tests are designed to measure performance in relationship to some criterion.[8] The purpose is not to compare an individual with a group but to determine whether an individual has attained some criterion to which the test is referenced. An example might help illustrate this function.

When I was a boy of about nine years of age I attended a summer camp located on a small lake in Illinois. On that lake there were three areas marked off by floats that were to be used for swimming by the boys in the camp. One area was for nonswimmers, a second for intermediate swimmers, and a third, which had a small wooden raft anchored to the bottom of the lake, for advanced swimmers. To get permission to swim to the raft that was in deep water, a boy had to be able to swim two laps of the intermediate section of the lake. If he could swim one and three-quarter laps, he had to use the intermediate section. It didn't matter whether a boy could swim three or three hundred laps; all he needed to be able to swim to use the raft was two laps. That task, defined clearly in terms of a measurable competency, is an example of a criterion-referenced task or test. The issue was not one of comparing the swimming skills of the boys (although that inevitably happened)—it was to determine the presence of a competency.

Driver training programs, typing classes, and other skill-oriented courses use criterion-referenced tests. Indeed, contract learning—that form of educational practice in which teacher and student jointly form an agreement regarding the education task to be performed, the anticipated product, and the time of completion—is a not too distant relative of criterion-referenced testing, which itself is related to the use of defined objectives as a basis of evaluation.

The Major Subject Matters of Evaluation

As I have indicated earlier, evaluation is a process than can be directed toward three important subject matters: the curriculum itself, the teaching that is provided, and the outcomes that are realized. Attention to the curriculum is justified on rather straightforward grounds. Unless one appraises the quality of the content and learning activities that constitute the curriculum, one has no basis for determining whether it is worth being taught. To paraphrase Plato, "The unexamined curriculum might not be worth learning."

Significance of the Content

But what are the aspects of the curriculum that can be evaluated, even prior to its implementation in the classroom? First, one can make some judgment about the educational significance of the content to which students will be exposed. Now the significance of the content can be determined only with criteria that flow from a set of values about what counts educationally. But whatever these criteria are, and they will differ for different groups and individuals, the application of such criteria is important for appraising the value of the curriculum in the first place. Some example of how such criteria are applied might be helpful.

For years state boards of education and local school districts have engaged in the process of textbook selection. Textbooks, a fundamental element in most curricula, were adopted on the basis of attractiveness and feasibility as a teaching tool. It wasn't until the civil rights and women's liberation movements that states adopted specific criteria dealing with race and sexism to be used for evaluating textbooks and other curriculum material. Regardless of how attractive and significant the educational content of a textbook is, if it places minority groups in an unfavorable light or undermines the image of one of the sexes it is to be rejected as suitable material for children in the schools. In California, the state department of education guidelines regarding the content of educational materials, including textbooks, state:

Male and Female Roles—Ed. Code 9240(a), 9243(a)
In order to encourage the individual development and self-esteem of each child, regardless of gender, instructional materials, when they portray people (or animals having identifiable human attributes), shall portray women and men, girls and boys, in a wide variety of occupational, emotional, and behavioral situations, presenting both sexes in the full range of their human potential.

Emotions—for example, fear, anger, aggression, excitement, or tenderness—should occur randomly among characters regardless of gender.

Traditional activities engaged in by characters of one sex should be balanced by the presentation of nontraditional activities for characters of that sex.

Ethnic and Cultural Groups—Ed. Code 9240(b) and 9243(a)
In order to project the cultural diversity of our society, instill in each child a sense of pride in his or her heritage, eradicate the seeds of prejudice, and encourage the individual development of each child, instructional materials, when portraying people (or animals having identifiable human attributes),

shall include a fair representation of white and minority characters portrayed
in a wide variety of occupational and behavioral roles, and present the contributions of ethnic and cultural groups, thereby reinforcing the self-esteem
and potential of all people and helping the members of minority groups to
find their rightful place in our society.[9]

Obviously, these particular criteria, while important, represent only a
limited range of those relevant to evaluate textbooks or curriculum. The
intellectual significance of the content itself is, or ought to be, an important focus for appraisal. In the teaching of science, for example, what are
the intellectual significance and validity of the concepts, generalizations,
and subject matters with which students will deal? If the concepts are intellectually marginal and the generalizations trivial or so remote as to have
little illuminative power for those other than specialists, it seems unlikely
that schools should use their students' time to deal with that material. If
ideas are being promulgated that are out of date, no longer valid, or simply
insignificant, it makes little sense to spend a great deal of energy trying to
help children learn such material. Some appraisal of the content of the
curriculum in terms of its intellectual significance and the covert messages
it might convey seems an appropriate focus for the evaluation of the
curriculum.

But because curricula are intended for people and because people have
different priorities, the appraisal of the curriculum needs also to be made
with an eye toward its appropriateness for the population for whom it is
intended. Determining the appropriateness of curriculum content takes at
least two forms. First, it is important to determine whether the content
and tasks the curriculum encompasses are within the developmental scope
of the children who are to deal with it. Some kinds of content are inappropriate from a developmental point of view for the children of certain
developmental levels. The concept of readiness, although at times abused
in schools, can be employed to make judgments about the relationships
between psychological tasks and content and the characteristics of the students.[10] Thus, content within a curriculum might fare well from the standpoint of its significance within a discipline and yet be rejected on the
grounds that it is developmentally inappropriate for particular groups of
children.

The second basis on which content may be evaluated deals with the
experiential fitness of the content to the experiential background of the
students. Curriculum content might be intellectually important and developmentally appropriate but still be ill-suited to the background or interests
of the students. The importance of this criterion will, of course, vary with
the curriculum orientation one embraces. To someone holding an academic rationalistic orientation, the need for students to be interested in a
particular subject matter is likely to be less important than it is to someone

concerned with personal relevance as a central condition of meaningful education. Yet this criterion can never be completely neglected. If the experiential background of students is so remote from the content encountered as to make it essentially meaningless, it is obvious that the curriculum, regardless of how defensible on other grounds, is inappropriate for that population. The point to remember here is that in evaluating the curriculum the educational significance of the content is a primary consideration. If the content is misleading or invalid, subsequent evaluation is not necessary. But even if the curriculum has been adjudged intellectually impeccable, one still has to appraise it both developmentally and experientially with respect to its suitability to the population for whom it is intended.

I have in the course of my work in education visited classrooms in Nigeria where eight-year-old Nigerian children were studying the Battle of Hastings. One can only wonder why out of all the possible subjects that those eight-year-old children might encounter they were studying the Battle of Hastings. There are good reasons why a former British colony should continue its traditions, but one might question the appropriateness and the meaningfulness of such content for those children. One does not have to travel to Nigeria to find similar situations in schools.

There are, of course, other criteria that can be used to evaluate the curriculum aside from the three already identified. As a matter of fact, any of the dimensions identified as relevant for curriculum development are also relevant for evaluating the curriculum after it is developed. Two examples should suffice.

You will recall that the forms used to display content and tasks to students and the forms through which their responses were elicited were identified as dimensions to be considered in curriculum development. If it is true that different forms of presentation provide different types of information, and that different forms of expression convey different types of understanding and insight, and if it is further assumed that the nurture of a wide range of human abilities is an educationally desirable goal, then it seems reasonable that educational materials, those materials that constitute a central portion of the curriculum, should employ the range of means available for both display and expression. This means in practical terms that curriculum materials can be evaluated with respect to the extent to which they employ visual, auditory, and kinesthetic modes of presentation as well as linguistic ones. It means also that the forms through which the students' competency is to be displayed can have a similar range. There is no intrinsic reason, except tradition, why curriculum materials must require a verbal mode of presentation and a linguistic form of response. Once we are willing to grant that the forms one uses to express oneself influence what one is capable of "saying" and that individuals differ with regard to their aptitude for using different sensory modalities for processing and expressing what they know, feel, or believe, the first steps are laid for justifying the use of diverse modes of presentation and response in the curriculum and classroom. To the extent to which we value this diversity and try to nurture it, it becomes important not only to construct, but also to evaluate materials with an eye to these values.

Quality of Teaching

The second major subject matter for evaluation is the quality of teaching that is provided. Although some educational theorists make no distinction between teaching and curriculum, I believe the distinction to be useful for several reasons. First, one can and usually does plan curriculum prior to using it in the classroom. Thus, curriculum development is a process, at least during some of its stages, that occurs outside of the classroom.[11] Second, and most important for the purposes of this chapter, the intellectual significance of the curriculum can be appraised independently of how well it is taught. A teacher might do a brilliant job of teaching, but the ideas or skills being taught might be trivial, biased, or invalid. Conversely, a teacher might be using a faultless curriculum with respect to its intellectual merit and its appropriateness both developmentally and experientially for students, but that teacher might be teaching so poorly that only confusion and frustration result for the students. The educational problem in each of these cases is different, and without a distinction between curriculum and teaching I fear they will fail to emerge.

To evaluate the quality of teaching is, of course, easier to say than to do. Efforts at identifying the qualities that make for effective teaching have been many but for the most part have not proved very illuminating. The approaches that have been taken to study and identify effective teaching have been scientific in character. The need for quantification, for explanation, for replicability, and for generalization has often led to a highly reductionistic approach to the study of teaching, one that attempts to locate specific causal relationships. The assumption is that by identifying specific causal units, eventually a holistic view of teaching will result. As yet this has not happened.[12] I will have more to say about the study of teaching later, but I would like to say now that there are aspects of teaching that can be evaluated by a sensitive student of classrooms: the type of relationships teachers establish with their classes, the clarity of their explanations, the level of enthusiasm they display, the kinds of questions they raise. Although these specific qualities have not been demonstrated through quantitative empirical research to make for effectiveness, I believe that they are relevant considerations in evaluating what teachers do when they teach.

In stating that I believe they are relevant for evaluating teachers even though quantitative empirical research has not as yet demonstrated their efficacy, we approach the hub of an epistemological issue in education.

What is true? What counts as evidence? It is clear that scientific evidence about teaching or about most other aspects of educational practice is quite limited. There is very little in the way of hard data that can be used to justify educational practices, and even the little there is requires a non-scientific leap of faith because the sample from which the original conclusions were drawn is not likely to be identical to the population to whom the conclusion is to be applied. Indeed, if educational practitioners *had* to base their educational practices on hard data we would have to close our schools. Yet, to assume that the only source of understanding is the laboratory is to render oneself helpless. There is much—to provide a gross understatement—that is useful from seasoned experience and critical reflection on that experience. The aspects of teaching that I have identified are only a few of the relevant dimensions that can be attended to and evaluated. Without evaluating teaching as well as the curriculum, one is not in a position to know, when there are difficulties, what their sources are.

Outcomes Achieved

The third major subject matter for evaluation and the most characteristically attended to is the evaluation of student outcomes. The selection of the term *outcomes* as opposed to *objectives* was not a casual one. Objectives are intended goals; they are the destinations one hopes to arrive at through the educational program. But roads taken do not always lead to the destination one intends, and even when they do, much can be learned en route. Thus, *outcomes* is a broader term than *objectives*. The achievement of objectives can be included in the outcomes, but there is often much more to include as well.

Figure 7 presents a simple trichotomy of the kinds of outcomes that might be realized in a classroom. One segment of the circle deals with the

Figure 7

outcomes that are subject-specific; a second segment deals with outcomes that are teacher-specific, and a third segment refers to outcomes that are pupil-specific.

Subject-specific outcomes are directly related to the content that is taught. Such outcomes can be, but are not necessarily, related to the objectives for the course. There are several reasons why subject-specific outcomes need not necessarily be related to course objectives. First, many courses in a field of study have no articulated objectives yet are educationally effective. Second, even when objectives are specified, outcomes may be realized that, although within the context of the subject studied, are not defined by the objectives. To evaluate with respect to subject-specific outcomes means to focus one's evaluation on the learning of the subject matter of a course or segment of the course. This is often done through the use of standardized or teacher-made achievement tests. Generally, such assessment focuses on outcomes within a subject that are common across students. A multiple-choice test, for example, presents to a population of students a common set of test items. Such items allow no scope for a personally constructed response; the alternatives are provided in the distractors from which the student must select. Thus, what such a test reveals is determined by the choices the test maker made during test construction. Hence, what one finds out about student understanding when such tests are used is what has been selected by the test constructor as being relevant. These are items sampled from the universe of content that the course has provided. And because in "objective" or multiple-choice tests little or no scope is provided for students to demonstrate their understanding of aspects of the course or content not sampled, those aspects simply fail to emerge for consideration.

Attention to what students learn about specific content within a course has been a primary and traditional concern of achievement testing. To find out what students have learned has almost always meant to find out what about the content taught they have learned. Such a focus is useful for evaluation, but it represents only one segment of a much more complex picture. Students learn not only what was intended, they learn not only what is related to the content of what has been studied, they also learn because of the unique intellectual relationships they make between the content and their other interests. They may be stimulated by the content of a course to learn things that are only tangentially related to the content. These outcomes, outcomes that are ripe for educational evaluation, are student-specific.

If one raises the question "What has a student learned in my class or course that is not about what I have been teaching?" one begins to move into student-specific domains. And if one begins to develop procedures for obtaining some understanding of such outcomes, one is engaged in a student-specific mode of evaluation. Obviously, so long as the options presented to a student or group of students present no opportunity for the display of what might be called personalized learning, such outcomes will not be manifest. If we want to know what the personal spinoff is from the content or courses we teach, the tasks or methods used for evaluation have to be sufficiently open-ended to allow such personalized learning to emerge. Interviews, open-ended essays, and projects whose parameters provide opportunities for students to reveal what personal meanings they have constructed for themselves need to be made available. Such procedures will, of course, not be focused on providing comparative data. They are focused on the revelation of idiosyncratic outcomes.

Procedures that elicit idiosyncratic outcomes—in other words, personalized learning—are methodologically distinct from procedures normally used in the construction of achievement tests. Typical procedures for the construction of achievement tests require not only that a common set of items be applied to a population of students, but also that items on which most of all students do well or items that systematically differentiate male from female performance be eliminated. The aim of typical achievement tests is to provide scores that make possible the differentiation of students. The type of differentiation sought arises from differences in performance on the same set of items for all students. In general, the closer the population's performance is to the normal curve, the greater the likelihood the test is statistically reliable.

Yet, applying a common set of items to assess a common content across a population of students can vitiate efforts to individualize teaching or to foster the development of students' aptitudes and interests. We often say that it is educationally desirable to encourage students to pursue particular interests within school and that teachers should be flexible and imaginative in developing programs particularly appropriate for the individuals with whom they work. However, the use of tests that seek only common outcomes from a content area common to all students can be and often is inconsistent with such aims. If we are really serious about curriculum differentiation for students, the need for student-specific forms of evaluation will become increasingly important.

The third segment of student outcomes is represented by those that flow from what the teacher teaches about him- or herself. The intellectual style the teacher displays, the standards that he or she upholds, the willingness to take risks, the tolerance for nonconformity, the type of precision and punctuality he or she values: these aspects of the teacher as a person are not necessarily trivial aspects of teaching. Indeed, because these features are likely to be more pervasive than the content studied, it might be that they have important consequences for what students learn. Studying with a really great teacher, whether in elementary school or at the highest levels of the university, can help a student more than exposure to some particular body of content.

What do the personal qualities of teachers mean for the elementary-school age children with whom they spend five or more hours each day for forty school weeks? At present these questions are not answerable. Conventional conceptions of educational evaluation have seldom included them in the procedures used to assess the effects of schooling. Yet, these questions and others that could be raised, it seems to me, are nontrivial aspects of schooling. Unless one is aware of the possibility of educationally significant effects issuing from the characteristics, values, and interests of teachers it is not likely that answers to such questions will be obtained. It would be interesting to ask students to characterize the contributions, other than those provided by course content, that their teachers made to them. What would students say about those contributions? Do those who work with particular teachers over extended periods of time display particular characteristics, interests, attitudes, or styles of inquiry that derive from characteristics of their teachers? A comprehensive theory of educational evaluation would include teacher-specific outcomes as at least one of three that warrant examination.

How Can Educational Evaluations Be Reported Artistically?

How can what occurs in a classroom or school be made vivid to a public that wants increasingly to know what it is getting for its investment in schools? The typical procedures for reporting the educational efficacy of schools have been twofold. First, parents have been led to believe that the grades their children receive adequately portray how well their children are doing in school and by implication how well the school is doing by the child. Good grades mean that the child is doing well; poor grades mean that the child is doing poorly, although as educational consumerism increases, poor grades might come to mean that the school rather than the child has done poorly.

The other major vehicle for reporting to the public how schools do is through the use of standardized testing. In many states, standardized achievement tests are mandated by the state legislature, and in some cities newspapers publish the mean performance by grade of students in schools within the school district.[13] Parents and other citizens read such reports and draw conclusions about the educational quality of the school or school district by the rank that a school or school district occupies in some regional or national distribution. These scores are usually "unencumbered" by socioeconomic considerations or by any other factors or conditions that could influence test scores. Thus, the public has before it an array of test scores that provide a deceptive sense of educational precision.

Although no competent educator would claim that performance on standardized reading and math tests adequately represents educational quality, these test scores, for all practical purposes, have become the major indices the public uses to judge the effectiveness of schools. And because the public uses such scores, school administrators feel the need to focus their teachers' attention onto activities that are likely to lead to higher standardized test scores. A school that succeeds (and by extension an administrator who is effective) is one whose students receive high standardized test scores.

Thus, we have something of an educational irony. Most educators would say that neither letter grades nor standardized test scores capture the richness of educational experience, nor do they adequately disclose the quality of education provided and experienced in the school. Yet schools do reward students with honors classes and deans' lists based on such grades and therefore legitimize the importance of grades while recognizing their limitations. Although educators point out that standardized test scores do not necessarily represent what students are learning, the administration of such tests proliferates and the subsequent publication of their results has consequences that are as often as misleading as they are informative.

This state of affairs stems from several sources. First, the aspiration for precision in evaluation has manifested itself in the quantification of student performance, which in turn is translated into grades. Somehow a type of precise objectivity is implied when complex forms of learning are reduced to a single score or letter. Second, parents often want an unambiguous indicator of their child's or the school's performance. To suggest contingencies or qualifications concerning the performance of students or the school is for many parents to inject an uncomfortable degree of uncertainty and complexity. Simplicity, even if it is misleading, is often preferable to the kind of complexity that an educational connoisseur might perceive.

This preference for the simple and the neat is not unrelated to the correct assessment that parents make of the criteria that their children must meet if they are to have upward educational mobility. Admission to universities is heavily influenced by the rank students hold in high school. And class rank is a function of the grades received. In short, the criteria applied to students for purposes of selection and retention in the hierarchy of schooling reinforce the use of a grading system that can be easily translated into simple, numerical indices. Grade-point average, class standing, college board scores: these are far easier to compare in a competitive educational market than widely diverse, even if illuminating, forms of educational disclosure. We seek to reduce diversity in order to have a uniform scale on which comparisons can be made.

A third reason standardized test scores and grades have become the basis for judging educational quality is that we have not provided the public with alternatives. By neglect of such alternatives, a tradition of grading practices has been established. The public expects it. Yet, if we think about the reporting problem—helping parents and others to understand what has taken place in schools—a wide array of possibilities comes to mind.

The problem of disclosing the character of educational events and the quality of what children are learning can, I am arguing, be conceived as an artistic problem. How can the results of educational evaluation be communicated so that the complexity *and* ambiguity *and* richness of what happens in schools and classrooms can be revealed?

Part of the answer to this question depends on the recognition that people communicate through different expressive modalities and that each modality has the power to convey different types of understanding. Quantitative indices are useful for some purposes but not for all. Written descriptions are helpful for understanding some events, but they cannot duplicate visual images for some purposes. Statistically derived norms are helpful for locating trends but neglect the unique occurrence. In short, if one considers the range of ways through which people come to express and understand and compares it with the range used for reporting the results of educational evaluations, it becomes apparent that only a slender slice of educational life is likely to be captured by the forms of reporting that are typically used. To capture this richness and therefore to help the public understand and appreciate the problems as well as the achievements of a classroom or school requires the construction of an evaluational landscape. Such a picture will probably employ a wide range of information secured from a variety of sources and revealed through different types of reporting procedures.

One of these procedures is likely to be what I referred to as educational criticism.[14] Such criticism would be aimed at helping parents, let us say, understand what has happened during the course of a school year in a particular school. What were the key events in the school? How did they come into being? In what ways did students and teachers participate? What consequences for the school did such events have? How could such events be strengthened? What do such events enable children to learn?

What is Mrs. Jones' classroom like? In what sorts of activities have the children engaged? What does Mrs. Jones provide that is uniquely hers? What is the character of the school day for children in her class? What are children deriving from her class that is not likely to be revealed by standardized testing? Questions such as these, if answered by a competent educational critic, would give parents an understanding of the school and the classroom that most at present do not have. Even parents who value education very highly have only the vaguest ideas about the kind of educational experience provided by the school their children attend. In the first place, report cards, if they are used, give no indication of the sorts of events I have described. The major focus of report cards is on how "well" the child is doing according to some criterion that itself is vague. And if the school is one where parent-teacher conferences are held in lieu of formal report cards, even then the discussion between parent and teacher is more likely to focus on the student's performance than on the program in which he or she is participating.

Another vehicle for disclosing the richness of educational programs to parents is through the use of film and videotape. One can capture on film or tape aspects of educational life that give a vivid picture to parents and others of what the school actually provides. The creation of such tapes and films will of course demand skills that most evaluators do not at present possess. Yet, the absence of such skills is no argument against developing them. The use of film and videotape, even the use of still slides and photographs, can be extremely informative if they have been taken with an artistic, educationally informed eye. The task of making such visual materials the sources of educational disclosure has scarcely been touched. There have been films made of schools, such as *High School* by Frederick Wiseman, that are powerful statements about the quality of life in an urban high school, and by extension in others. That film is extremely skillful in portraying certain aspects of high school life, but its strength is at the same time a source of its weakness. It exaggerates to make a point—it is a visual polemic. It does not attempt to disclose the strengths of the school it portrays, but instead accentuates its oppressive, mindless, military character. Informed educational criticism and the informed educational use of videotape and film would aim at a more circumspect view of educational life. Supplemented by critical narrative, such visual materials considerably expand the channels for communication.

The use of still photography is also potentially powerful in revealing aspects of educational life that measured achievement and even artful criticism cannot capture. Paradigm cases of such visual renderings already exist, perhaps the most notable being Alfred Stieglitz's *The Family of Man.* Since Stieglitz created that exhibition, numerous other portfolios of visual reporting have appeared. What these portfolios offer us, and what they could portray about the educational quality of life in schools, is a nondiscursive mode of disclosure capable, when artistically created, of helping us vicariously participate in the life that the school provides. At present, the use of such vehicles as an explicit form of educational reporting is virtually absent from the scene in American education. When it does occur, it is by accident, connected to a student yearbook or newspaper but not as part of formal resources the school uses to understand and report what it is doing.

During the past few years, increased attention has been focused on the use of nontext materials to portray schooling. This interest among educators parallels the relatively recent interest among anthropologists in what is called *visual anthropology.* Implicit in this new-found interest in both education and anthropology is the recognition that the form one uses to represent the world defines the parameters within which the content of expression and communication occurs. Not everything, even through the efforts of a highly talented writer, can be expressed in words. Some things, for example, need to be expressed thorugh visual images. Pictures portray what words may never be able to reveal. Hence, to limit one's expressive options to words, particularly to propositional language, is to limit what can be conveyed about the world in which we are interested.[15]

Educational criticism and the use of videotape, cinematography and still photography can be supplemented with still other types of information that would provide a more comprehensive and adequate picture of school life. One of these supplements is tape-recorded interviews of both students and teachers that deal with their work and its aims, their satisfactions, the situations and problems they encounter, their ideas about educational improvement, their aspirations in the school, the outcomes they value most and least, and so forth. Taped interviews on cassettes could be produced and edited in a way that would deal with ideas, beliefs, and feelings that seldom get expressed on written questionnaires and are never possible to express on achievement tests. The spontaneity of the interview, when it is conducted by a skillful interviewer, one who knows both interview techniques and education theory and practice, could yield data that are at present simply unavailable.

It should be noted that listening to tape-recorded interviews may itself require a type of connoisseurship that needs to be developed. What is said and what is not said, how something is said, the tone of expression, and so forth—all of the nonlinguistic cues that possess meaning—need to be penetrated if what one says is to be fully appreciated. Nevertheless, all of us have developed such skills to a considerable degree—they are survival skills—and even if they are not refined to an optimum level, we have learned how to listen sufficiently well to get much of what others say.

Additional information that could be used to construct an adequate evaluation of a school or classroom would include an analysis of the work that children produce. In typical evaluation procedures, examination scores, grades received on essays, and ratings of projects undertaken and completed are the data that are reported to parents about the progress their children are making in school. When this is done, it is seldom clear whether, for example, a grade of B on an essay refers to the quality of the essay in relation to some external standard, whether it refers to the quality of the essay relative to other essays produced by students in the class, whether it is based on the efforts put forth by the student in writing the essay, whether it represents the amount of growth the student has achieved since the beginning of the semester, or whether it is based on a combination of all of these criteria. These procedures for grading are not the ones I am referring to as an analysis of what children produce in school. The problem with such procedures is that they provide conclusions rather than disclosures about the character of the work done and the sorts of progress and problems children encounter. To do the latter would require, first, close attention to what a given child or class has created. If the work is an essay, one might describe how a child has organized his or her essay, the quality of the arguments or evidence he or she employs, the extent to which his or her imagination has been used to create the work. These aspects of the work could be treated comparatively with other work created by the child or the class and could be accompanied by a critique that would help adults or children understand what has been accomplished. If, for example, one wants to help a school board or a group of parents understand that human development is uneven, that children of the same age are at quite different places with respect to skills or understanding, it would be useful to display the range of work—not just the best work—that the children in class create. The display of only the best conceals the range of differences and distorts the real educational picture with which teachers must work. The visual display of such range when critically described and analyzed would do much to make apparent to a school board, for example, some of the realities of classroom performance.

The major point I am attempting to make here is that the problem of communicating to some public—parents, school board members, students, state agencies—about what has happened in schools, the problem of making known what is strong and what is weak, what needs support and what does not, can be usefully conceived as an artistic problem. It is a problem of putting together an expressive, sensitive, and revealing picture of educational practice and its consequences. The construction of such a picture can exploit both the various modalities that people have always used to communicate and also the new technology that can capture and hold even the most evanescent happenings in classroom life.

That this approach to educational evaluation is rare can be appreciated by examining evaluation studies. These studies virtually always are characterized by the attempt to be quantitatively "objective" and impersonal and to focus on measured achievement with no attention paid to the relationship between what was done (the process) and what ensued (the product). Conventional training in evaluation still bears the imprint of psychometrics. Although psychometric techniques are useful for describing some aspects of education performance, they by no means embrace the entirety of what counts educationally. When young evaluators are trained in psychometrics and neglect the normative and theoretical aspects of educational practice, the problem is compounded. Education is a normative enterprise. What counts educationally depends on one's educational values. The reduction of educational evaluation to a set of limited quantitative methods, ones that harbor their own values, which often go unacknowledged or unappraised, is to reduce educational evaluators to technicians and evaluation to a technical process. Educational evaluation is more than that, however. No narrow range of technical skills applied to educational settings is likely to reveal the richness of their context. To interpret the meaning of even that which is secured through parochial means requires some vision of educational virtue and some understanding of the history of educational practice.

It might seem strange to mention the importance of the history of education and educational theory in the context of discussing educational evaluation. These subjects are seldom found in such discourse, and when they occur as a part of the educational program of prospective evaluators, more often than not they are there to meet institutional requirements rather than because they are considered important. Yet I hope I have made the point that educational evaluation requires a sophisticated interpretive map not only to separate what is trivial from what is significant in educational settings, but also to understand the meaning of what has been seen. Without a normative and historical perspective, the interpretation and appraisal of educational events are impoverished.

References

1. *The Republic,* transl. by B. Jowett, The Modern Library, New York, 1956.
2. Michael Scriven, "The Methodology of Evaluation," in *AERA Monograph Series on Curriculum Evaluation,* No. 1, Rand McNally, Chicago, 1967.
3. Not all development processes start with aims and content. Curriculum activities themselves can provide a starting point for aims.
4. This assumption is widely prevalent in England and on the continent, where evaluation practices are designed to select the most able for the assignment to different forms of secondary schools and for university admission.
5. This assumption is embedded in much of the material on evaluation sent to school districts by state departments of education.
6. Benjamin Bloom, *Human Characteristics and School Learning,* McGraw-Hill, New York, 1976.
7. For a description of norm- and criterion-referenced test theory, see Gilbert Sax, "The Use of Standardized Tests in Evaluation," in *Evaluation in Education: Current Applications* (W. James Popham, ed.), McCutchan Publishing Co., Berkeley, Calif., 1976, pp. 243–308.
8. Ibid.
9. *Guide Lines for Evaluation of Instructional Materials for Compliance with Content Requirements of the Education Code,* California State Department of Education, Sacramento, 1975.
10. The work of Jean Piaget is often used to support this view.
11. Phillip Jackson refers to this as "Pre-Active Teaching." See his book, *Life in Classrooms,* Holt, Rinehart and Winston, New York, 1968.

12. Barak Rosenhine and Norma Furst, "The Use of Direct Observation to Study Teaching," in *Second Handbook of Research in Teaching* (Robert Travers, ed.), Rand McNally, Chicago, 1973.

13. State-mandated achievement tests are used in fifteen states as of 1973. Source: Phyllis Hawthorne, *Legislation by the States: Accountability and Assessment in Education,* Report No. 2, Wisconsin Department of Public Instruction, August 1973.

14. Although Chapters 11 and 12 describe the theoretical aspects of educational criticism and provide examples of it, those wishing to consult other works should see Elliot W. Eisner, "On the Uses of Educational Connoisseurship and Educational Criticism for Evaluating Classroom Life," *Teachers College Record,* Vol. 78, No. 3, February 1977, and "The Forms and Functions of Educational Connoisseurship and Criticism," *Journal of Aesthetic Education,* Vol. 10, Nos. 3 and 4, July–October 1976. Also see the following doctoral dissertations completed at Stanford University.

  W. Dwaine Greer, *The Criticism of Teaching,* Doctoral Dissertation, Stanford University, 1973.

  Elizabeth Vallance, *Aesthetic Criticism and Curriculum Description,* Doctoral Dissertation, Stanford University, 1975.

  Leonard Davidman, *A Formative Evaluation of the Unified Science and Mathematics in the Elementary School Curriculum,* Doctoral Dissertation, Stanford University, 1976.

  Gail McCutcheon, *The Disclosure of Classroom Life,* Doctoral Dissertation, Stanford University, 1976.

  Robin Alexander, *Educational Criticism of Three Art History Classrooms,* Doctoral Dissertation, Stanford University, 1977.

  Betty Sternberg, *What Tokens and Trophies Teach,* Doctoral Dissertation, Stanford University, 1977.

  Tom Barone, *Inquiring into Classroom Experiences: A Qualitative Holistic Approach,* Doctoral Dissertation, Stanford University, 1978.

  John Fielders, *Action and Reaction: The Role of an Urban School Superintendent,* Doctoral Dissertation, Stanford University, 1979.

  Hilma Hagberg, *Don't Be Teachin Jouita Wrong: An Exploration of Reading Instruction in Four Urban Third Grade Classrooms, Doctoral Dissertation,* Stanford University, 1983.

15. See, for example, *Communication Strategies in Education,* (Nick L. Smith, ed.) Sage Publications, Beverly Hills, Calif., 1982.

II

The Forms and Functions of Educational Connoisseurship and Educational Criticism

The transition from a paradigm in crisis to a new one from which a new tradition of normal science can emerge is far from a cumulative process, one achieved by an articulation or extension of the old paradigm. Rather it is a reconstruction of the field from new fundamentals, a reconstruction that changes some of the field's most elementary theoretical generalizations as well as many of its paradigm methods and applications.

THOMAS S. KUHN

It is the function of this chapter to identify and discuss some of the assumptions, principles, and procedures used in educational connoisseurship and educational criticism. This form of educational inquiry, a species of educational evaluation, is qualitative in character[1] and takes its lead from the work that critics have done in literature, theater, film, music, and the visual arts.

Interest in qualitative forms of research and evaluation has increased in recent years, but little of the work that has been done has been related to the fine arts. Most of those who have used qualitative approaches have related their work to ethnography. Yet, there is no area of human inquiry that epitomizes the qualitative more than what artists do when they work.

Thus, it seems to me that if we seek to know what qualitative inquiry consists of, we can do little better than analyze the work of those who use it the most.

Artists inquire in a qualitative mode both in the formulation of ends and in the use of means to achieve such ends.[2] The result of their work is a qualitative whole—a symphony, poem, painting, ballet—that has the capacity to evoke in the intelligent percipient a kind of experience that leads us to call the work art. My claim is that the paradigmatic use of qualitative inquiry is found in the arts.

Another form of qualitative inquiry is found in the work of those who inquire into the work of artists, namely the art critics. The art critic finds himself or herself with the difficult task of rendering the essentially ineffable qualities constituting works of art into a language that will help others perceive the work more deeply. In this sense, the critic's task is to function as a midwife to perception, to so talk about the qualities constituting the work of art that others, lacking the critic's connoisseurship, will be able to perceive the work more comprehensively. "The end of criticism," wrote Dewey, "is the reeducation of the perception of the work of art." The critic's task in this view is not primarily the issuance of a judgment but rather the difficult task of "lifting the veils that keep the eyes from seeing."[3]

There are two important points to be made about criticism. First, criticism is an empirical undertaking. The word *empirical* comes from the Latin *empiricus,* meaning "open to experience." Criticism is empirical in the significant sense that the qualities the critic describes or renders must be capable of being located in the subject matter of the criticism. In this sense, the test of criticism is in its instrumental effects on the perception of works of art. It is not abstraction that one understands through criticism but rather qualities and their relationships.

It is interesting to note that the studies we usually call empirical are studies whose findings are couched in terms that are not in the strict sense empirical at all. Take, for example, studies that report significant differences in variances or in means between groups of students. What we have in such studies are conclusions that may be four or five orders removed from the empirical qualities from which the conclusions were drawn. We tend to forget that individual students confront individual test items and answer them correctly or incorrectly. From the individual's response to individual items, a raw score is calculated for each student. This raw score is itself an abstraction that significantly limits the information on each student's performance. Two students, for example, can receive the same raw score for entirely different performances on the same test. These raw scores are then summed and averaged, a second-order abstraction. Following this procedure, variances are computed and compared and a probability is calculated to determine the relationship between variances across groups. These represent third- and fourth-order abstractions. In no way is it possible to reconstruct an individual student's test score from knowledge of a mean or from the differences between means. These latter quantities are in fact abstractions that, although derived from empirical performances, are not themselves empirical. One cannot locate a mean by looking for it in the world.

The second point I want to emphasize with respect to criticism is that *anything* can be its subject matter. Once again, by *criticism* I do not mean the negative appraisal of something but rather the illumination of something's qualities so that an appraisal of its value can be made. Although *criticism* is a term that is most frequently used in the arts, it also is used in sports, in the assessment of research, in the appraisal of human behavior, particularly in social settings, and in a host of other areas in which humans have intercourse with the world. There is nothing, in principle, that cannot be the object of criticism.

Although teaching is frequently referred to as an art, and although in our vernacular we recognize the artistic aspects of educational practice— the beautiful lesson, the exciting discussion, the well-made point, the elegant exposition—when it comes to our attempts to describe or understand educational practice, criticism is seldom appealed to as a possible method or approach. The reason for the neglect of criticism as a potentially useful vehicle for the description, interpretation, and evaluation of educational practice is, I think, a result of the ways in which educators have been professionally socialized, particularly those holding doctorates and working in universities.

Doctoral programs socialize students to believe that the most dependable procedure one can use to obtain knowledge is through science and that respectable inquiry in education, at least respectable empirical inquiry, is scientific in character. To use other methods, to employ metaphor, analogy, simile, or other poetic devices, is to lack rigor. Jeffreys tries to make the point this way:

> No matter what the subject matter, the fundamental principles of the method must be the same. There must be a uniform standard for validity for all hypotheses, irrespective of the subject. Different laws may hold in different subjects, but they must be tested by the same criteria; otherwise we have no guarantee that our decisions will be those warranted by the data and not merely the result of inadequate analysis or of believing what we want to believe. . . . If the rules [of induction applied in scientific inquiry] are not general, we shall have different standards of validity in different subjects, or different standards for one's own hypotheses and somebody else's. If the rules of themselves say anything about the world, they will make empirical statements independently of observational evidence, and thereby limit the scope of what we can find out by observation. If there are such limits, they must be inferred from observation; we must not assert them in advance.[4]

Jeffrey's argument proceeds beyond the rejection of critical language; it also tends to include all forms of inquiry that do not translate the phenomena of interest into quantity. This is so pervasive a belief in educational research that educational research itself is identified not just with empirical inquiry but with quantitative empirical inquiry.

I mention this not as a condemnation of statistically oriented inquiry in education but rather as an example of its pervasiveness and of the relative neglect of other forms of inquiry that could be useful to the field. I believe that the creation of educational criticism, a form of criticism not unlike that found in the arts but directed to educational matters, could provide a kind of utility that scientific studies and quantitatively treated phenomena neglect. Indeed, I hope that one day we will have journals of educational criticism and critical theory that will seek to refine the quality of educational criticism and the methods and assumptions with which those doing such criticism work. During the past decade progress has been made toward that end; for example, *Curriculum Inquiry* and the *Journal of Curriculum Theorizing*.

The Relationship of Educational Criticism to Educational Connoisseurship

Effective criticism, within the arts or in education, is not an act independent of the powers of perception. The ability to see, to perceive what is subtle, complex, and important, is its first necessary condition. The act of knowledgeable perception is, in the arts, referred to as connoisseurship. To be a connoisseur is to know how to look, to see, and to appreciate. Connoisseurship, generally defined, is the art of appreciation. It is essential to criticism because without the ability to perceive what is subtle and important, criticism is likely to be superficial or even empty. The major distinction between connoisseurship and criticism is this: connoisseurship is the art of appreciation, criticism is the art of disclosure. Connoisseurship is a private act; it consists of recognizing and appreciating the qualities of a particular, but it does not require either a public judgment or a public description of those qualities. The perception and appreciation of a particular requires a sensory memory. For example, if one is to develop connoisseurship of wine, one must drink a great deal of wine, learn how to attend to its qualities, and be able to recall from one's gustatory memory— and in the case of wine, the olfactory and visual memories also come into play—the qualities of other wines in order to have a backdrop against which the particular qualities of the wine being tasted can be compared and contrasted. In the case of music, the auditory mode provides the backdrop. A connoisseur could compare Arturo Toscanini's performance of Beethoven's Seventh Symphony with that of Herbert von Karajan. Only after a range of experiences are had in a mode of expression will sophisticated levels of connoisseurship be developed.

The same considerations apply with respect to educational connoisseurship. One must have a great deal of experience with classroom practice to be able to distinguish what is significant about one set of practices or another.

In saying that experience counts in the development of connoisseurship, whether in education or in the fine arts, it is important to recognize that the length of time spent in a classroom or the number of museums visited or the frequency with which one attends sports events is not necessarily an indication of the level of connoisseurship someone has achieved. Let us distinguish between recognition and perception, and let us agree with Dewey that recognition is perception aborted: looking is engaged in simply to be able to see enough to classify.[5] That is an oak tree, the other is an elm, that dive was a half-gainer, that was a full twist with a somersault, and so forth. Perception based on recogniton alone stops with assigning the particular to the class to which it belongs; it does not proceed to the sensory exploration of the ways in which *this* particular oak tree differs from other oaks, it does not locate the specific characteristics of *this* elm, *that* half-gainer, *this* full twist with a somersault. Recognition is not exploratory; it is focused on classification.

If one looks within a classroom primarily to recognize rather than to see, the number of years one spends in a classroom will contribute little to the development of connoisseurship. To develop connoisseurship one must have a desire to perceive subtleties, to become a student of human behavior, to focus one's perception. Looking is a necessary condition, but looking is essentially a task one undertakes; it is seeing that is an achievement.

It would be difficult to overemphasize the importance of connoisseurship in the creation of educational criticism. Connoisseurship provides the fundamental core of realization that gives criticism its material. Because it is so central to any understanding of practice, it is rather surprising that it has received so little attention. We tend to take it for granted, or we seem to believe that with the use of an observation schedule the problem of seeing what goes on in classrooms is cared for. This is simply naive. What is significant in a social setting might have little to do with the incidence of a particular activity or statement but a lot to do with a single act or statement or with the organizational structure of the classroom or with the character of an assigned task or with the way in which a reward is given. Observation schedules are tools that can guide one's attention, but their mechanical use can blind one to what is significant.

It may be that the neglect of connoisseurship is due to the fact that relatively few people doing educational research spend much time in classrooms. The general tendency in educational research is to use instruments that can be easily administered and scored and that are not susceptible to confounding through bias or long-term exposure to the vicissitudes of classroom life. The rigorous experiment in education is "clean." To achieve such cleanliness, experiments in educational research tend to be brief. The modal amount of time for educational experiments reported in two years of the studies published in the *American Educational Research Journal* is less than one hour. For fourteen experimental studies reported during this period, six used a treatment period of less than one hour, three from one hour to one day, three from one day to one week, and one for over one year. No time was reported for one study. It is my view that such a conception of clean experimentation in education is likely to lead to work that has little significance for educational practice.

The development of educational connoisseurship requires an ability not only to perceive the subtle particulars of educational life but also to recognize the way those particulars form a part of a structure within the classroom. Erickson's discussion of the chess game is most apt.[6] To understand a chess game, one must do much more than measure or even describe in qualitative terms the character of the physical movements made by each player. One must be able to perceive the structure of the game within which the physical movements take on social meaning. One must eventually be able to conceptualize the rules that give structure to the enterprise and define it as the game.

Similarly, the development of educational connoisseurship requires the ability to perceive the "rules" through which educational life is lived. Such a task is what Gilbert Ryle refers to as "thick description," about which more will be said later.[7]

The work that my students and I are doing at Stanford University is aimed at the development of educational connoisseurship and the ability to create useful educational criticism. Educational connoisseurship is to some degree possessed by virtually everyone who has spent some time in schools as a student or as a teacher, but it can be refined and developed. What is involved in the development of educational connoisseurship is, first, the opportunity to attend to happenings of educational life in a focused, sensitive, and conscious way. Second, it requires the opportunity to compare such happenings, to discuss what one sees so that perceptions can be refined, to identify events not previously perceived, and to integrate and appraise what has been seen. This is being done at Stanford through the direct observation of classrooms and through the careful viewing of videotapes of classroom life. When students jointly view such tapes, the basis for description and discussion is provided. Over time, descriptive language becomes less mechanical, more incisive, and increasingly literary or poetic as students try to get at the essence of what is occurring. To talk about essences and significance in the observation of educational events requires, of course, not only a sensitivity to the emerging qualities of classroom life, but also a set of ideas, theories, or models that enable one to distinguish the significant from the trivial and to place what one sees in an intelligible context. This process is not serial: we do not see and then assess significance; the very ideas that define educational virtue for us operate within the perceptual processes to locate among thousands of possibilities what we choose to see. The essence of perception is that it is selective; there is no value-free mode of seeing.

Given the impact of our theories on our perception, the development of educational connoisseurship is much more complicated than simply a species of discrimination training. The problem of developing connoisseurship of the complex life of classrooms is not simply one of identifying the equivalent of Boeing 707s or DC-10s. Plane spotters have a comparatively simple task. The forms of such planes can be known in advance, and interaction effects are minimal. A 707 is a 707 is a 707. But in classrooms, interaction effects are the rule, not the exception. To discern what an event means requires an understanding of the context in which it occurs; that context requires not only some knowledge of the people involved and the circumstances within which the event occurs, but in many situations also something about the past, against which the particulars of the present can be placed. Again, memory is indispensable.

What we begin to recognize when we consider what connoisseurship entails is that the perceptual processes operate within an array of values and theoretical concepts that influence perception. Indeed, in both the social sciences and philosophy we use theories to organize our conception of the world. Individuals working with different theories—whether normative or descriptive—will attend to different phenomena within the "same" setting and interpret their significance differently. For the development of educational connoisseurship, an understanding of different social sciences, different theories of education, and a grasp of the history of education is not simply an intellectual ornament to be acquired within a graduate program but an essential working tool.

The cognitivist view that I am expressing with respect to the perception of educational practice has eloquently been expressed by a major American aesthetician concerning the role of theory in the perception and appraisal of art. Morris Weitz points out that although previous attempts to define the necessary and sufficient properties of art have been unsuccessful (because art is an open rather than a closed concept), the work of the great aestheticians is not useless. He writes:

> In spite of the fact that all of them [theoreticians] fail to accomplish what they set out to do—to give a true definition of works of art—these definitions are nevertheless helpful and well worth intensive study. For behind every one is a redefinition of "work of art"; i.e., an attempt to get us to concentrate on certain criteria or properties of works of art as against others. If we attend to these criteria or properties and forget the unsuccessful attempts as true, essentialist definitions, we can learn a great deal from the theories, especially

as to what we should look for in works of art and how we should look at them. Indeed, the great contribution of theories of works of art is precisely in their teachings, not in their definitions, of art: each of the theories represents a set of explorable criteria which serve to remind us of what we may have neglected or to make us see what we may not have seen. To do this, I should think, is the primary job of teaching. Here, then, is the relation between teaching and the nature of art or, to use the title of your conference, the nature of art and its implication for teaching: that the great theorists of the nature of art have served as the great teachers as well, in telling us, through their definitions of art, what we are to learn from them about the arts.[8]

The same argument can be made—a fortiori—for theories of human behavior, culture, and education.

What Do Critics Do?

As I have already indicated, educational connoisseurship is a necessary condition for doing useful educational criticism. But what is it that critics do? What do they write about? And what kind of validity and generalizability does criticism have? Criticism is the art of disclosing the qualities of events or objects that connoisseurship perceives. Criticism is the public side of connoisseurship. One can be a connoisseur without the skills of criticism, but one cannot be a critic without the skills of connoisseurship. In using language to make public qualities and meanings that are not themselves discursive, something of a paradox exists. How can words express what words can never express? The successful resolution of this paradox lies at the heart of the critical act. To accomplish this feat, critics do not aspire toward a translation of an event from one modality to another. For in fact no such translation, at least in the literal sense, can be made. It is one thing to translate from one language into another. And even between languages there are difficulties. But to expect to translate what is known in a visual mode into a discursive mode is to use the term *translate* metaphorically. A more appropriate word, coined by Kozloff, is *rendering:*

> For what criticism proposes to give, I think, is essentially an account of an experience, and never, as is sometimes supposed, a substitute for an experience. Though ideally it must be self-sufficient as prose, it can never be a stand-in for what has been perceived, lest it compromise a metaphorical with a literal fiction. Indeed, criticism's merit lies exactly in the fact that it is neither a work of art nor a response, but something much rarer—a rendering of the interaction between the two. Best, then, that it reconcile itself to virtual rather than actual meanings, the ambiguity of symbolic reference as opposed to the pidgin clarity of signs.[9]

What critics do or should try to do is not to translate what cannot be translated but rather to create a rendering of a situation, event, or object that will provide pointers to those aspects of the situation, event, or object that are in some way significant. Now what counts as significant will depend on the theories, models, and values alluded to earlier. But it will also depend on the purposes of the critic. For example, an educational critic focusing on the learning patterns of a particular student will attend to qualities and circumstances different from those he or she would attend to if interested in the critical rendering of the character of classroom discourse, the qualities of the classroom's visual environment, or the meanings embedded in the treatment of time in the classroom. The point here is straightforward: What is rendered by someone working as an educational critic will depend on his or her purposes as well as the kinds of maps, models, and theories being used.

Discursive and Nondiscursive Knowledge

Of particular importance in understanding how critical language is illuminative is the distinction between discursive and nondiscursive forms of knowledge and that between representational and presentational symbols.

The conception of nondiscursive modes of knowing is not a new distinction among those schooled in philosophy, but it is new to those raised in the traditions pervading American educational research and its offspring, educational evaluation. American educational research has, since the early work of E. L. Thorndike, been largely behavioristic in its psychology and operationalist in its philosophy. To "know" has meant to make statements couched in the form of propositions and that therefore can be appraised by logical criteria. But because logic is essentially a tool for determining consistency between propositions, something more is needed if relationships between propositions are to be more than merely consistent. If propositions are to make true statements about the world, referents for those statements have to be located in the world. And because in empirical matters observation is subject to biases of one sort or another—biases in perception, in selection of population, and the like—observations need to be operationalized through standardized procedures that are reliable and quantitative and therefore supposedly least likely to suffer from unreliability and subjectivity. For generations, this conception of the meaning of knowledge has dominated inquiry into educational matters. Indeed, to do educational research has come to mean, by custom, to engage in inquiry having these characteristics. The idea that there are multiple ways in which things are known—that there is a variety of expressive modalities through which what is known can be disclosed—simply has been absent from the conversations that animate the educational research community.

A distinction between the respective contributions of the sciences and the arts to human understanding is made by Ernest Cassirer in *An Essay on Man*. Cassirer points out that a scientific perspective without an artistic one or an artistic perspective without a scientific one leads to monocular vision; both are necessary to have depth perception. Science, writes Cassirer, focuses on what is general and common across particulars, whereas art focuses on the unique characteristics of the particulars themselves.

> The two views of truth are in contrast with one another, but not in conflict or contradiction. Since art and science move in entirely different planes they cannot contradict or thwart one another. The conceptual interpretation of science does not preclude the intuitive interpretation of art. Each has its own perspective and, so to speak, its own angle of refraction. The psychology of sense perception has taught us that without the use of both eyes, with a binocular vision, there would be no awareness of the third dimension of space. The depth of human experience in the same sense depends on the fact that we are able to vary our modes of seeing, that we can alternate our views of reality. Rerum videre formas is no less important and indispensable task than rerum cognoscere causas. In ordinary experiences we connect phenomena according to the category of causality or finality. According as we are interested in the theoretical reasons for the practical effects of things, we think of them as causes or means. Thus, we habitually lose sight of their immediate appearance until we can no longer see them face to face. Art, on the other hand, teaches us to visualize, not merely to conceptualize or utilize, things. Art gives a richer more vivid and colorful image of reality, and a more profound insight into its formal structure. It is characteristic of the nature of man that he is not limited to one specific and single approach to reality but can choose his point of view and so pass from one aspect of things to another.[10]

Cassirer's plea for binocular vision through complementary forms of inquiry is one that I would echo. One mode of conception and one form of disclosure are simply inadequate to exhaust the richness of educational life.

The notion that knowledge can be conceived and experienced in non-discursive as well as discursive forms has been perhaps most eloquently expressed by an American aesthetician who was influenced by Cassirer's work, Susanne Langer. Langer argues that although propositions are among the most useful of cultural tools for expressing ideas about factual states of affairs, they are virtually useless when it comes to expressing what we know about the life of feeling:

> Yet even the discursive pattern has its limits of usefulness. An expressive form can express any complex of conceptions that, via some rule of projection, appears congruent with it, that is, appears to be of that form. Whatever there is in experience that will not take the impress—directly or indirectly— of discursive form, is not discursively communicable or, in the strictest sense,

logically thinkable. It is unspeakable, ineffable; according to practically all serious philosophical theories today, it is unknowable.[11]

Discursive language, the type used in science and in much of our ordinary speech, is our most powerful tool for classification, but when particular qualities of life must be revealed we have to appeal to a language more intimate, or, in Langer's terms, a language that presents to our consciousness what the feeling of those qualities is. Literature is, of course, a prime example of the nondiscursive use of language. So is poetry. What enables us to participate empathetically in the events, lives, and situations that the writer portrays is not mere factual description. If this were the case, everyone who could describe the facts would be a Dostoevsky, a Shakespeare, or a Bellow. What gives literature its power is the way in which language has been *formed* by the writer. It is the "shape" of language as well as the perceptive recognition of the metaphorical, connotative, and symbolic character of particular words and phrases that makes written language literature. What the writer is able to do, as is the painter, composer, dancer, or critic, is to transform knowledge held in one mode into another, namely the mode within which the artist or critic works. Somehow the artist finds or creates the structural expressive equivalent of an idea, a feeling, or an image within the material with which he or she works. The material becomes the public embodiment—a medium, in the literal sense of the word—through which the life of feeling is shared. The arts are not a second-class substitute for expression, they are one of the major means people throughout history have used both to conceptualize and express what has been inexpressible in discursive terms.

Now the talk of the critic is in many respects similar to that of the artist. Both work within the limits of the material to create a form that expresses what has no name. The *particular* qualities of joy, grief, enchantment, irony, perseverance, or courage are never adequately revealed through the ordinary verbal classification of these terms alone. What was the character of this man's courage? What is the particular quality of her joy or grief? How does this classroom lead its life? What kind of personage does this teacher represent to his class? To reveal these particulars, to capture these "essences," one must not only perceive their existence but also be able to create a form that intimates, discloses, reveals, imparts, suggests, implies their existence. In this process of transformation, metaphor is, of course, a centrally important device. Metaphor breaks the bonds of conventional usage to exploit the power of connotation and analogy. It capitalizes on surprise by putting meanings into new combinations and through such combinations awakens our senses. Metaphor is the arch enemy of the stock response.

The use of metaphor is not restricted to the creation of literature and the writing of poetry and criticism; it plays an extremely important role in our vernacular language. Take, for example, slang. "Cool it," "right on," "hot-shot," "you know it," "into it," "heavy" are only a few examples of metaphorical usage. We don't ask of such language what it literally means because literally its meaning is either absurd or nonexistent. Yet we all sense the rightness of the phrase when used in an appropriate context. Indeed, we use such language not simply because it is more economical than its discursive "equivalent" but because it has no discursive equivalent. Fresh conceptions find their expression in the inventive use of language. Even our discursive language is filled with words that once were metaphorical or had visual referents but through conventional usage have lost their initial power: Someone feels low, or high, or depressed; he has an inflated ego; she is being defensive; he is being slick; that painting is well balanced. The symphony is melancholy. Such words are so pervasive a part of our language that we seldom stop to reflect on the way in which they acquired meaning.[12]

What is ironic is that in the professional socialization of educational researchers, the use of metaphor is regarded as a sign of imprecision; yet, for making public the ineffable, nothing is more precise than the artistic use of language. Metaphoric precision is the central vehicle for revealing the qualitative aspects of life.

The revelation of the qualitative aspects of life, particularly those aspects that deal with what individuals experience in various situations, has been a major focus of artists through the centuries. Let's assume for a moment that we wanted to know something about life in, say, a concentration camp. How would we find out? We could try to locate psychological and sociological studies of the inmates and of the organization of such camps, and if we could find such studies we might learn something about how new inmates were socialized, how they adapted to the conditions of the camp. We might learn something about social mobility, stratification, and class, about the various roles assumed, and about achieved and assigned status. We might learn about the use of sanctions and about the destruction of the ego. Such knowledge is, of course, useful. Based as it would be on concepts and theories within the social sciences, it would describe, through the concepts the theories employ, the various features of camp life and how they function.

But let us say we wanted to know what it was like to be taken to such a camp, to go through the initial screening, to work fourteen hours a day in bitter cold, to have a wretched diet. To know these aspects of life in a concentration camp, one must go to the forms of expression that convey the qualities of such life to the reader. One could do little better than to read Solzhenitsyn's *A Day in the Life of Ivan Denisovich*.[13] Through literature and through effective criticism we come to know what it feels like to be in prison, to be in ecstasy, to be in a particular classroom in a particular school. Through the arts we have the opportunity to participate vicariously in the lives of others, to acquire an empathetic understanding of situations, and therefore to know them in ways that only the arts can reveal.

If I dwell on these matters, it is because I believe they are crucial for understanding why educational criticism is such an important complement to the existing modes of inquiry in education.

The language of criticism, like the language of the arts, is essentially nondiscursive; that is, it informs not by pointing to the facts of the world but rather by intimation, by using forms to *present* rather than to *represent* conception or feeling. Representational symbols, the type used in conventional discourse, are like signposts: they point one toward qualities but are not themselves intended to possess expressive qualities. "Listen, listen to the bird" is a literal discursive expression, but "Hark! hark! the lark!" contains an energy absent in the former. The former is representational; it directs our attention so that a certain kind of experience can be had. The latter presents us with a form that itself generates the excitement of the experience. The former is a conventional utterance, the latter is poetic.

Thus far I have tried to identify the functions of qualitative inquiry in education and to distinguish between educational connoisseurship and educational criticism. Before describing in greater detail the major dimensions of educational criticism, it will be useful to examine a brief segment of art criticism written by the distinguished American critic Leo Steinberg. From it, we can get a better sense of what one critic does in the course of one of his criticisms.

PAUL BRACH'S PICTURES

They are very near invisibility.

Invisibility is of various kinds, and to list its varieties while the pictures are up helps to focus attention.

Invisibility by disappearance. An object absent, remote or indistinct leaves a leftover emptiness and a straining to see. This seems relevant to Brach's pictures. Their vacant geometry suggests depleted voids, voided containers. Their huge suspended circles can look like extinguished suns. Solar cult emblems snuffed out. Empty icons.

Then, invisibility by extinction of light. This too seems relevant. Not actual darkness—which conveys a specific degree of reduced illumination—but a consistency or opacity that can be neither brightened nor deepened.

And invisibility due to dimmed vision; whether through blindness or the sightlessness of inattention. Brach makes his pictures easy to resist. They court unseeing indifference or disinterest; as if to remain invisible to the averted mind.[14]

Although this constitutes only the first portion of Steinberg's criticism we can use it to try to understand what he does. Consider first the title, "Paul Brach's Pictures." Steinberg does not write a long, complex title but a simple one, one that we shall find is in keeping with the works that he will criticize. Notice also that Steinberg does not refer to "Brach's Paintings" but rather to "Paul Brach's pictures." "Pictures" suggests more of illusion, of image, of icon. "Paintings" suggests a medium, the qualities of the material used, or technique, and as we find as we read on, paint and technique are not essential aspects of Brach's work; his are indeed images of a mysterious kind: *pictures* is more apt than *paintings*.

Steinberg's opening sentence, "They are very near invisibility," hangs there by itself. In some ways, it's an awkward sentence, yet it possesses some of the mysterious magical qualities of the paintings Steinberg is attempting to render. A lesser critic might have written, "Brach's paintings are nearly invisible." But such a sentence does not possess a spell.

Steinberg sets the mood of the work in his opening line and then shifts pace to suggest, in somewhat Aristotelian terms, that the classification of types of invisibility will be helpful to us in seeing Brach's work. And, abruptly, he repeats the fragmented tempo of the opening line, "Invisibility by disappearance." Because the issue is not grammar but mood and insight, the tempo works; it sets up a backdrop for the longer, more expository sentences to follow. Notice the nice contradictory quality of "leftover emptiness." Leftovers usually imply overabundance, not emptiness. Yet this, too, combined with "a straining to see," as Steinberg says, is relevant to Brach's pictures. What Steinberg is doing is depicting by implication and suggestion the pervasive quality of Brach's work. He is preparing the reader psychologically to see the point of the pictures, not only by specific verbal cues (which come later in the criticism), but also by the ambience in his language.

Steinberg then describes the "vacant geometry" of Brach's work, "depleted voids, voided containers," "huge suspended circles" that "look like extinguished suns." He then stops the paragraph as he began it, with a terse nonsentence: "Empty icons."

Again the illusion of Steinberg's language has its parallel in the works to which the language refers, not as an attempt to translate their visual qualities but rather, as Kozloff has suggested in his own writing, "to render" the works. Criticism works by implication, "the most appropriate devices at my disposal have been innuendo, nuance, and hypothesis, because what is peripheral to direct statement in language is often central to a pictorial encounter or its meaning." Steinberg would surely agree.

Steinberg continues in his criticism of Paul Brach's pictures to combine nuance and innuendo with more literal references to the qualities of the work, but always the tempo of the writing epitomizes the suspense and mystery of the work itself. Steinberg ends the criticism as he began, tersely as though it were suspended in space. His last paragraph reads, "They are beautiful pictures, solitary and serious."

Three Aspects of Educational Criticism

Educational criticism is composed of three major aspects or dimensions. One of these is descriptive, another interpretative, and another evaluative. Each of the distinctions that I make I am making for analytical purposes—

to illuminate differences in language and intention—but the distinctions are sharper on paper than in fact. All description is in some degree evaluative inasmuch as only a fool would choose to describe the trivial. All evaluation is interpretive to the degree that one seeks to make some sense of what a situation or an experience means. Nevertheless, the distinctions are useful to the extent that they sharpen perception of the foci of criticism and therefore enable us to read or create criticism more intelligently.

The Descriptive Aspect of Educational Criticism

The descriptive aspect of educational criticism is essentially an attempt to identify and characterize, portray, or render in language the relevant qualities of educational life. Such qualities may be the general environment or cultural style of a particular classroom or school. How is life lived in Miss Held's fourth grade? What kind of tempo pervades Mr. Marco's algebra class? Or the descriptive aspects of educational criticism might focus on more limited or molecular characteristics. How does this particular child relate to his peers? What covert messages does the teacher give her students through the tone of her voice? What is the quality of the visual environment of the school, and what does it convey to the student about life in school? Although it is a piece of literature rather than a piece of criticism, the following passage from *Pilgrim at Tinker Creek* illustrates how a perceptive and skillful writer can portray the sensory qualities of a complex environment:

> It was sunny one evening last summer at Tinker Creek; the sun was low in the sky, upstream. I was sitting on the sycamore log bridge with the sunset at my back, watching the shiners the size of minnows who were feeding over the muddy sand in skittery schools. Again and again, one fish, then another, turned for a split second across the current and flash! the sun shot out from its silver side. I couldn't watch for it. It was always just happening somewhere else, and it drew my vision just as it disappeared: flash, like a sudden dazzle of the thinnest blade, a sparking over a dun and olive ground at chance intervals from every direction. Then I noticed white specks, some sort of pale petals, small, floating from under my feet on the creek's surface, very slow and steady. So I blurred my eyes and gazed towards the brim of my hat and saw a new world. I saw the pale white circles roll up, roll up, like the world's turning, mute and perfect, and I saw the linear flashes, gleaming silver, like stars being born at random down a rolling scroll of time. Something broke and something opened. I filled up like a new wineskin. I breathed an air like light; I saw a light like water. I was the lip of a fountain the creek filled forever; I was ether, the leaf in the zephyr; I was fleshlike, feather, bone.[15]

What the author has succeeded in doing is to enable the reader to participate vicariously in the auditory and visual qualities of the layered web of life at the creek. Such writing is in no sense a catalogue of the number of trout, jays, or oak trees that populate the region; it is not a chronicle of happenings; it is the artistic reconstruction of events that may be more vividly experienced through that distillation called a work of art than in direct contact with the creek. This point is an important one, and one that is frequently overlooked. The artist, like the educational critic, does not write about everything that exists in a situation but rather about what he or she brackets, what he or she chooses to attend to. This bracketing of perception and its incisive rendering in an expressive medium allow the percipient of the artist's or critic's work to see, in part, through the bracket what the artist has created. Many have walked through places like Tinker Creek, but few have seen them with the clarity and sensibility of Annie Dillard.

The perception of both the pervasive qualities—those qualities characterizing a situation or object such as the upward thrust of gothic interiors, the scintillation of light in a Monet landscape, the vacuous mechanical regularity of an assembly line—and component qualities—those particular qualities within a whole, such as the tonal passages in the second movement of Sibelius's First Symphony, the supportive quality of a teacher's smile—are only two important subject matters for critical description. The nature of the "game" that is played is also a proper object of critical description. What are the rules by which educational life in this classroom operates? What are the regularities, the underlying architecture of social life in this school? What is the core value within this mode of school organization, or teaching, or evaluation? The description of these underlying qualities blends into the process of interpretation as well as description. Nevertheless, such structures can be conceptualized and described, and in a certain sense the effort to do so is reminiscent of the structuralist's attempt to locate the basic architecture underlying language. Again, Erickson makes this point well:

> There are many ways of describing what happens in a social event other than in functionally relevant terms. We could, for example, describe the playing of chess in terms of movement in millimeters forward, backward and sideways on a plane. The behavior of chess pieces on the board could be coded by observers this way with high inter-coder reliability, and the resulting data could be manipulated statistically. Yet such description and analysis would by itself tell us nothing about what was going on in terms of the game of chess. The descriptive categories would have no relevance to the game being played. For that we need descriptive categories with functional relevance for the game—checkmate, defense—terms that are meaningful in terms of an understanding (working theory) of the game as a whole.[16]

All in all, the descriptive aspects of criticism can be regarded as making the most artistic demands on the critic. I say this because it is in the descriptive aspect of criticism that the critic's verbal magic must be most acute. Recall Steinberg's phrase, "An object absent, remote or indistinct leaves a leftover emptiness and a straining to see." To be able to express such an idea, one must not only be in touch with the qualities of a painting and one's response to it, but also be able to capture such qualities through the possibilities within words; a poet must speak. Such demands are not easy to meet, but they are not insurmountable. Indeed, one of the most striking things that has emerged in working with doctoral students at Stanford in educational criticism is the sensitive way in which they have been able to write such criticism. Even students who have had considerable difficulty writing in the traditional academic mode have produced educational criticism of impressive literary quality. To say this is not to imply that all will be the Leo Steinbergs, Max Kozloffs, or Susan Sontags of education. It is to say that the skills of critical writing can be developed and that there may be a good many students for whom this mode of writing is more compatible than the modes that many of them feel compelled to use in order to complete their dissertation.

It is of interest to speculate why some students take to this mode of writing and conceptualization more than others and why some students who do not do well in one mode do well in the other. It *might* be that the kinds of intellectual processes that nondiscursive forms of conceptions and expression require are possessed to different degrees by different students. Present work in the study of the hemispheric specialization of the brain might be relevant to such an explanation. As mentioned earlier, it has long been known that the left hemisphere is the seat of speech, and in the last twenty years neurophysiologists have determined that the right hemisphere plays a distinctively important role in dealing with nonlinear, nondigital, nonconventional forms of conception and expression. Gabrielle Rico distinguishes between the functions of the hemispheres this way:

> I suggest this fundamental difference lies in the left hemisphere's susceptibility for *order-abiding* capacities and the right hemisphere's susceptibilty for *structure-seeking capacities.* The distinction I have in mind which may underlie all the others is clarified by a look at the etymology of "order" and "structure," two words often incorrectly used interchangeably.
>
> *Order,* from the Latin, *orde, ordini,* literally means "in a straight row, in a regular series." The definition of order encompasses anything from "arrangement," "a regular or customary procedure," "established usage," "settled method," to "a precept or command," or "a regulation." Order, therefore, like discourse defined in Chapter I, suggests receptivity to linear, established, regularly patterned, rule-governed activity. Order is imposed from without. Wrote Wittgenstein: "Following a rule is analogous to obeying an order. We are trained to do so: we react to an order in a particular way. . . . When I obey a rule I do not choose."
>
> *Structure,* on the other hand, from the Latin *struere,* means "to heap together" to give the quality of wholeness, totality. Structure does not imply seriality or linearity; it does imply coherence, holism. Structure can be discerned even when only a limited number of relevant elements become apparent, as in a motif of a Beethoven sonata or as in a configuration of a Street

Figure Completion test item. Moreover, structure can be independent of a linear sequence between what comes before and what comes after because it is simultaneously grasped.[17]

Perhaps those students who are best able to work in a critical mode are those whose strongest aptitudes are located in the right hemisphere. At present, the case cannot be demonstrated, yet it is striking that some students take to educational criticism with a sense of ease and competence that seems to fit almost naturally the way in which they encounter the world. Indeed, one student told me that until he encountered the notion of educational criticism and the possibility of doing it within the School of Education at Stanford, he was living two lives. One was the life he led outside Stanford, which was responsive to the arts, to the poetic and romantic aspects of experience, and the other he encountered at Stanford, which presented a different view of reality and required that he substitute Stanford's reality for his own. He now finds he can draw on his sensibilities and on the modes of thinking with which he is most comfortable for doing his work at Stanford. A cognitively schizophrenic existence is no longer necessary.

The Interpretive Aspect of Educational Criticism

Although there is no sharp and clear line to be drawn between the descriptive and the interpretive, there is a difference in emphasis and focus. The interpretive aspect of criticism asks: What does the situation mean to those involved? How does this classroom operate? What ideas, concepts, or theories can be used to explain its major features?

In the interpretive aspect of criticism, ideas from the social sciences most frequently come into play. These ideas form the conceptual maps that enable the educational critic to account for the events that have occurred and to predict some of their consequences. For example, let's assume that someone functioning as an educational critic observes a classroom in which the use of contracts is pervasive. What we have are children of eight or nine years of age signing written agreements with teachers to plan and monitor their assignments in school. The use of such contracts creates a particular level of involvement in the classroom that the critic characterizes with sensitivity and vividness. But what do these contracts mean to the students and to the teacher? And what are their long-term effects? What kinds of concomitant learning are the children experiencing? What type of social relations do contracts create, and how do contracts, when they are ubiquitous in a classroom, affect a child's concept of purpose in school?

To answer these questions, one can refer to a host of theoretical ideas within the social sciences to explain the ancillary consequences of contractual relations in face-to-face groups. One can refer to reinforcement theory to explain why contracts might increase dependency rather than autonomy. One can use cognitive field theory to deal with the importance of ambiguity in learning and the effects of contracts on the student's ability to tolerate ambiguity. The point here is not that there is one theory to be used to interpret the meaning of events within classrooms, but that there is a variety of theories. No one is interested in the facts by themselves but rather in the facts interpreted. What theory provides is not single-minded, certain conclusions regarding the meanings secured in school but rather frameworks that one can use to gain alternative explanation for those events. If theories in the social sciences can be regarded as games consisting of rules or structures one lays upon a field of phenomena for purposes of making some sense of the phenomena, the interpretive mode of criticism can be regarded as the application of those games in whatever numbers appear to be useful for getting on with the business of education.

To be able to apply a variety of theories from the social sciences to the events occurring within schools and classroom is no simple task. First, one must know the theories that are to be applied. Second, one must be in a position to determine that this particular instance or situation is one for which a particular theory is appropriate. In legal theory, the process of recognizing that a particular case falls within the province of a law is called casuistry. And casuistry is a complex art that melds both theoretical knowledge and practical wisdom. No less is called for in seeing the connection between, say, Maslow's stages of human development and the kinds of social situations created in classrooms. In the education of teachers and educational researchers, practice in making such applications has been rare. We seldom use films or videotapes of classrooms, for example, in the education of doctoral students, despite all of our talk about the importance of "multimedia." We do not typically use case material as is used in schools of law, social work, and schools of business to which theory in the social sciences could be applied. We operate as if the ability to apply the theoretical ideas one learns in university classrooms is automatic, that no practice is necessary, that such skills take care of themselves. I wonder on what theories such beliefs are based.

The role of interpretation in criticism is related to the concept of "thick description" as used by Clifford Geertz in anthropology:

> Ryle's discussion of "thick description" appears in two recent essays of his (now reprinted in the second volume of his Collected Papers) addressed to the general question of what, as he puts it, "Le Penseur" is doing: "Thinking and Reflecting" and "The Thinking of Thoughts." Consider, he says, two boys rapidly contracting the eyelids of their right eyes. In one, this is an involuntary twitch; in the other, a conspiratorial signal to a friend. The two movements are, as movements, Identical; from an I-am-a-camera, "phenomenalistic" observation of them alone, one could not tell which was twitch and which was wink, or indeed whether both or either was twitch or wink. Yet the difference, however unphotographable, between a twitch and a wink is vast; as

anyone unfortunate enough to have had the first taken for the second knows. The winker is communicating, and indeed communicating in a quite precise and special way: (1) deliberately, (2) to someone in particular, (3) to impart a particular message, (4) according to a socially established code, and (5) without cognizance of the rest of the company. As Ryle points out, the winker has not done two things, contracted his eyelids and winked, while the twitcher has done only one, contracted his eyelids. Contracting your eyelids on purpose when there exists a public code in which so doing counts as a conspiratorial signal is winking. That's all there is to it: a speck of behavior, a fleck of culture—and voila!—a gesture.[18]

The distinction between thick description and thin description is a useful one. Geertz regards it as the anthropologist's work to explicate social phenomena. "It is explication I am after, construing social expressions on the surface enigmatical."[19] Seeking the deep structure of social events, the rules or modes that give them order, is what ethnographers should do, according to Geertz. It is an enterprise that has its place in the interpretive aspects of educational criticism as well.

The Evaluative Aspect of Educational Criticism

It is, perhaps, the evaluative aspects of educational criticism that most clearly distinguish the work of the educational critic from that of the social scientist. Education is, after all, a normative enterprise. Unlike schooling or learning or socialization (all of which are descriptive terms), education is a process that fosters personal development and contributes to social well-being. This is not necessarily the case with respect to learning, schooling, or socialization, to use only three examples. One can learn to become neurotic, be schooled to become a scoundrel, or be socialized to become a bigot. Education implies some personal and social good. But to say this is to raise the knotty question of what kinds of values to apply to phenomena that aspire to be educational. On this matter there is a wide range of different views. The five orientations to curriculum described in Chapter 4 represent some of the values that different groups bring to the development of educational programs and the assessment of educational practice. Yet, even though different individuals and groups hold different conceptions of educational virtue, and even though their judgments of the value of the processes and outcomes of schooling might differ, the need to make these judgments is inevitable. One must inevitably appraise the value of a set of circumstances if only because, in the process of description, selective perception has already been at work. Evaluation, as I have already indicated, pervades the perceptual processes themselves.

But even if this were not the case, the point of educational criticism is to improve the educational process. This cannot be done unless one has a conception of what counts in that process. Are the children being helped or hindered by the form of teaching they are experiencing? Are they acquiring habits of mind conducive to further development or are these habits likely to hamper further development? What is the relative value of direct learning to ancillary learning within this classroom? Questions such as these require the use of *educational* criteria. The educational critic, unlike the social scientist who has no professional obligation to appraise the educational value of a culture or group, has this obligation as part of his or her work.

To make such judgments requires, as I have already indicated, the application of educational criteria. Where can such criteria be found? They can, of course, come from arbitrary, uncriticized preferences. But the truly competent educational critic is aware not only of the educational values to which he or she subscribes, but also of the values that are rejected. The educational critic will be able to provide grounds for the value choices made while recognizing that others might disagree with these choices.

The grounding of such values not only requires knowledge of the history and philosophy of education, it also benefits from practical experience in the schools. Many things the pedagogically uninitiated might be quick to criticize negatively would give an experienced teacher pause. Teaching tactics that might appear inappropriate to someone fresh out of a graduate school of education and untouched by the trials and tribulations of classroom life might be viewed with greater sympathy by one who has taught. One of the first things that the teachers whose classrooms have been the subject of educational criticism want to know is whether the critic has ever taught. Some things can be known only by having acted. Teaching, like swimming, is one of them.

One of the questions that often arises when the evaluative aspects of educational criticism are discussed is whether the critic should make his or her values known in advance. Should one's educational values be laid out—up front, so to speak? To this question I have a mixed response. On the one hand, it might be useful in preparing an educational criticism to describe the kinds of values that the critic holds so that readers can understand where the critic is "coming from." A manifesto of one's educational position insofar as it is describable could, in principle, be provided as a critical prologue to educational criticism. On the other hand, the values one holds permeate the writing one does, just as they permeate the conversations people have about value-saturated issues. After a while those values, even when not explicit, become clear, and after several contacts with a critic's work a prologue might seem redundant. Those who read William F. Buckley, James Kilpatrick, or John Kenneth Galbraith know where these men stand on political and economic matters. I suspect that the same will hold true in reading educational criticism. Indeed, the issue is not whether such values are present but rather whether they should precede the writing of the actual criticism. At this stage in the development of educational criticism as a species of educational evaluation, it appears to me reasonable to have it both ways.

The fact that two critics might disagree on the value they assign to a common set of educational events is not necessarily a liability in educational evaluation; it could be a strength. For much too long, educational events have been assessed as though there were only one set of values to be assigned to such events. The drop in test scores is perceived as a problem, the increase in grade-point average is believed to be a problem, but little or no analysis or few countervailing views are offered. Thus, through a lack of professional leadership, the public takes our lack of analysis and debate on the meaning and significance of such events as tacit assurance that they are indeed indicators of poor-quality schooling. One of the virtues of differences among educational critics with respect to the meaning and significance of educational events is that they could open up the kind of discussion that educational practice should but does not now receive. Virtually every set of educational events, virtually every educational policy, virtually every mode of school organization or form of teaching has certain virtues and certain liabilities. The more that educational criticism can raise the level of discussion on these matters, the better. What I believe intelligent and professionally responsible deliberation calls for is the application of multiple perspectives on an issue or policy, perspectives that view the phenomena from different angles, weigh the costs and benefits, and lead to the core considerations as well as to the ramifications of alternative policy decisions. The denial of complexity, in educational matters, as in politics, is the beginning of tyranny. Educational criticism could contribute to the appreciation of such complexity and therefore provide a more adequate basis for the making of educational judgments.

What then can we say about the characteristics of educational criticism and how it differs as a mode of qualitative inquiry from the kind of quantitative inquiry that is conventionally used in educational research? First, educational criticism is focused essentially on the events and materials that purport to be educational. Its function is to expand one's awareness of such events and objects so that they are more fully appreciated. Appreciation in this context does not refer to the liking of something, although one might like what one sees, but rather to the achievement of a heightened awareness of the subject matter.

To achieve such ends, an educational critic must possess a high level of connoisseurship within the area that he or she criticizes. Connoisseurship is the art of appreciation, and criticism is the art of disclosure. Criticism can be only as rich as the critic's perceptions. To create such criticism, educational critics prepare material having three major aspects: description, interpretation, and evaluation.

Although there is no sharp line between these aspects of educational criticism, there is a difference in focus and emphasis. The descriptive aspect aims at the vivid rendering of the qualities perceived in the situation. The interpretive attempts to provide an understanding of what has been rendered by using, among other things, ideas, concepts, models, and theories from the social sciences and from history. The evaluative aspect of educational criticism attempts to assess the educational import or significance of the events or objects described or interpreted. The major function of the critic here is to apply educational criteria so that judgments about such events are grounded in some view of what counts within an educational perspective. In the performance of this task, knowledge of the history and philosophy of education is crucial. The former provides the context necessary for purposes of comparison and the latter the theories from which grounded value judgments can be made. An understanding of the variety of orientations to education makes it possible for the educational critic to appreciate what he or she rejects as well as what he or she accepts within educational practice.

Differences between Quantitative and Qualitative Modes of Inquiry

Given these characteristics of educational criticism as both a species of educational evaluation and a qualitative inquiry, we can now ask what the distinctive differences are between qualitative and quantitative modes of inquiry in education.

It is patently clear that quantitative- as well as qualitative-oriented inquirers attend to qualities emerging within educational settings. For example, the investigator who is interested in the incidence of teacher approval in the classroom must attend to qualities in order to detect approval and secure data. Furthermore, both quantitative and qualitative inquirers interpret the information they secure from the classroom, and both will, in general, make some value judgments about its educational meaning—although the qualitative inquirer may be more likely to do this than the quantitative inquirer, whose scientific orientation is less likely to emphasize *explicitly* the appraisal or valuative aspect of the inquiry.

I believe the major differences between quantitative and qualitative inquiry to be two. *The more important difference resides in the language of disclosure that each uses.* The quantitative inquirer is obliged to transform the qualities perceived into quantitative terms so that they can be treated statistically. In this translation the information is altered; differences between qualities are placed on a common scale to make them comparable. This process requires the use of a coding system—number—that is not structurally analogous to the forms that were initially perceived. The number symbol is a representational rather than a presentational symbol.

The qualitative inquirer uses a mode of disclosure that allows the percipient to participate vicariously in the qualities described because the symbols used to describe such qualities are structurally analogous to the event or object. The qualitative description allows the reader to envision and experience what he or she has not experienced directly. Poetry and literature are linguistic paradigms of such description, whereas the other arts—painting, music, dance—provide knowledge in other modes. What most radically distinguishes qualitative from quantitative inquiry is not that the former attends to qualities and the latter does not; they both do. What most sharply differentiates them is how they choose to inform the world about what they have seen.

The second feature that distinguishes quantitative from qualitative inquiry is the tendency of the former to prescribe procedures and to define in advance what shall be attended to. For example, the experiment in education has sought as its ideal procedure one in which all of the variables that might influence an outcome are brought under control. The lack of such controls is considered a confounding factor that makes interpretation difficult. Surprise and uncontrolled variation in educational experimentation are regarded as an epistemological liability.

Take as another example, not the experimental model, but that of systematic observation. Observation schedules are used to predefine what one is to look for; they prescribe to a very high degree what counts and what is to be counted. A qualitative approach to classroom observation is more open ended and flexible; the investigator or critic, rather than the prestructured schedule, is the major instrument through which observations are made.

In distinguishing between qualitative and quantitative approaches to education, I am in no way attempting to argue that one approach is always superior to the other. One approach *is* superior to the other, but only with respect to the nature of the problem one chooses to investigate. Quantitative methods have clear-cut virtues for some types of questions for which qualitative approaches would prove to be weak and inappropriate. And vice versa. It is this judgment—when and for what purposes each mode of inquiry is appropriate—that poses the toughest intellectual task in laying out a strategy for the investigation of educational problems. It is precisely around such judgments that disagreement is the greatest, because the tools investigators are skilled in using also serve to determine the parameters of their perception and thus how they define the problem itself.

Reliability, Validity, Generalization, and Other Matters of Inference

One of the central reasons given for scientific inquiry is that such inquiry makes it possible not only to secure warrant for belief, but also to establish empirical generalizations. Such generalizations, a product of drawing inferences from a sample, help one anticipate the future. Description, explanation, and prediction are the trinity that scientific inquiry makes possible.

But what of qualitative forms of inquiry that do not employ a scientific model? Can such forms of inquiry yield generalizations? To what extent are the claims they make valid? How is reliability determined? How can we know if educational criticism can be trusted?

The conceptual tools, the statistical procedures, and the research designs available for testing the inferences, reliability, and validity of conclusions in the social sciences are of long standing and highly elaborate. Donald Campbell and Julian Stanley's classic monograph[20] on experimental and quasiexperimental design is an example of existing canons for the conduct of scientific inquiry in education. Distinctions between Type I and Type II errors, between internal and external validity, between random selection and random assignment, between experimental and quasiexperimental designs, among construct, content, predictive, and concurrent validity, between stability and reliability—these are some of the technical terms that have been created to make scientific inquiry into human affairs more rigorous. Does inquiry in the qualitative arena have similar tools? If so, what are they?

Let's examine first the question that is most frequently raised concerning qualitative inquiry in general and educational criticism in particular: Is it objective? Perhaps the first response that should be raised is another question: What is meant by "objective"? Does objective mean that one has discovered reality in its raw, unadulterated form? If so, this conception of objectivity is naive. All of us construct our conception of reality by interacting with the environment. What we take to be true is a product not only of the so-called objective conditions of the environment, but also of how we construe that environment. And that construction is influenced by our previous experience, including our expectations, our existing beliefs, and the conceptual tools through which the objective conditions are defined. To hold that our conceptions of reality are true or objective to the extent that they are isomorphic with reality is to embrace a hopeless correspondence theory of truth—hopeless because to know that our conceptions correspond or deviate from reality would require that we have two conceptions operating. One is an unmediated view of reality, the other our conception of that reality. Only in this way would we know anything about correspondence. If we knew the former, however, we would not need the latter.

What so-called objectivity means is that we believe in what we believe and that others share our beliefs as well. This process is called consensual validation. It operated as powerfully in once held beliefs in the existence of phlogiston, ether, and a geocentric universe as it does in the religious convictions held by the religiously orthodox. Although a scientifically oriented individual might object and say that scientific beliefs are testable and religious beliefs are not and that the differences therefore are crucial, the religiously orthodox would counter by pointing out that scientific criteria do not exhaust the means through which beliefs can be held to be true. Indeed, they would argue—correctly, I believe—that scientists themselves hold beliefs, even within science, that cannot be warranted by scientific methods. In the social sciences, this most clearly is the case. The differences in basic assumptions among Freudians, Rogerians, Skinnereans, Heiderians, Eriksonians, Piagetians, and the like are not resolvable through science. The fundamental theoretical structures through which each defines psychological reality differ, and there is no critical test that will resolve the truth or falsity of their respective belief systems. Each has a community of believers who reaffirm the beliefs of those working within the system.

My point here is simply this: objectivity is a function of intersubjective agreement among a community of believers. What we can productively ask of a set of ideas is not whether it is *really* true but whether it is useful, whether it allows one to do one's work more effectively, whether it enables one to perceive the phenomenon in more complex and subtle ways, whether it expands one's intelligence in dealing with important problems.

Given this view, what can we say about the means through which educational criticism receives consensual validation? Two processes are important here. One is called structural corroboration and the other referential adequacy.

Structural Corroboration

Structural corroboration is a process of gathering data or information and using it to establish links that eventually create a whole that is supported by the bits of evidence that constitute it. Evidence is structurally corroborative when pieces of evidence validate each other, the story holds up, the pieces fit, it makes sense, the facts are consistent. Take as an example of structural corroboration the work of Inspector Poirot in Agatha Christie's *Murder on the Orient Express.*[21] The inspector finds himself with a dead man, murdered on a train, and the problem of solving the puzzle of who murdered him. Little by little, Poirot succeeds in putting the pieces together so that there are no contradictions, the pieces support one another, and the problem of who killed the man is solved. In the case of the Orient Express, the murdered man once had contact with everyone on the train. The final scene in the book finds Poirot presenting his case to the murderers in the lounge car of the train as it speeds toward Calais. Poirot's brilliant use of evidence works; his conclusions hold up.

The use of structural corroboration is found in jurisprudence as trial lawyers attempt to present to a jury the evidence that will exonerate or convict a defendant. The prosecution tries to create a structurally corroborative set of facts that will persuade a jury to convict, while the defense tries to construct a set that will convince it not to convict. In such circumstances, one has a combination of both *structural corroboration*—the evidence that the respective attorneys try to muster—and *multiplicative corroboration*—the use of a jury of peers to pass judgment on what has or has not been structurally corroborated. The jury in this case provides the consensual validation for the cases that the attorneys have presented.

When we write or read educational criticism we can ask about the extent to which the facts presented or the interpretation of those facts is corroborated by the way in which they support one another. Does the teacher really play favorites in class or was his behavior in that particular circumstance atypical? Is the teacher genuinely supportive of the students or is she merely using a superficial stock response that gives the illusion of caring? These questions and questions like them can be adequately answered only by securing other evidence that would structurally corroborate the conclusions one has drawn from observation.

The process of structural corroboration is not some exotic process that is used in special circumstances in courtrooms and in doing educational criticism, but it is a ubiquitous part of our daily lives. We all use such processes to make judgments about people, to determine whether they are fake or authentic in their relation with us, to understand their limits so that we can effectively relate to them and to cope with the situations in which we find ourselves. We use this process to negotiate the environment. It is a far more characteristic way of dealing with the world than conducting a controlled experiment. In the flux of events and in encountering new situations—a new classroom, for example—we try to read its code, to find evidence for our impressions, to structurally corroborate our initial observations so that our expectations for that situation are appropriate.

Referential Adequacy

Nevertheless, structurally corroborated conclusions can be false. As Geertz points out, nothing is so persuasive as a swindler's story.[22] Something more must be added to validate the observations of the educational critic. That something more is the determination of referential adequacy. The end of criticism, as I have already indicated, is a reeducation of the perception of a work of art. For *educational* criticism the end-in-view is the education of the perception of the educational event or object. We can determine the referential adequacy of criticism by checking the relationship between what the critic has to say and the subject matter of his or her criticism. What the critic does, whether in painting, drama, or schooling, is to write or talk about the object or event he or she has seen. If the talk or writing is useful, we should be able to experience the object or situation in a new, more adequate way. We use the critic's work as a set of cues that enable us to perceive what has been neglected. When the critic's work is referentially adequate we will be able to find in the object, event, or situation what the cues point to. It is in this sense that criticism is a highly empirical undertaking. We look to the phenomena to test the adequacy of critical discourse.

Now it might be objected that the critic might lead us to see certain things in a situation because the criticism biases our perception, that criticism is in a sense something like a self-fulfilling prophecy. I would point out that we all bring to events, situations, and objects certain preconceived ideas; none of us approaches the world with a blank slate. The issue is not whether we come to the world empty-minded, because we have no alternative, but whether what we bring to the world is useful for the purposes we consider important. Criticism is a kind of advance organizer, just as theory in general is an advance organizer.

Others might object and say that educational criticism may lead us to neglect aspects of the situation that the critic might not see or write about. This can occur. We never know when we have a comprehensive view of things, because, as in the correspondence theory of truth, we would need to know the thing itself in its comprehensive form to know whether our view of it was comprehensive. Again, if we knew the former, we would not need the latter. Yet, criticism might lead us to neglect certain aspects of the situation, but that is true of any theory, set of cues, or road map. Take as an example the services of a good travel agent.[23] He or she provides the client with information about what can be seen, but that does not foreclose the possibility of seeing other things as well. In the process of providing such guides, the travel agent readies us for sites and sights that we might otherwise overlook if left to our own devices. When the terrain is new or complex, guideposts help. Effective criticism provides such guideposts.

It is frequently pointed out that critics disagree on the characteristics and merits of the events and objects to which they attend. This claim is in some respects exaggerated. Critics in general achieve a high degree of consensus on objects or situations that have a reasonable amount of variation in quality. When critics do disagree, it is usually because the objects or events constituting the group to be judged present to critics a narrow range of unusually high-quality work.

But even when this occurs, the issue of differences among critics with respect to, say, the characteristics of classroom life is not crucial. In standard statistical procedures, interjudge agreement is critical. Low levels of interjudge agreement make a study invalid. What one usually does to ensure such agreement is to simplify the phenomena to be counted and to train the judges extensively. If judges are asked to count the incidence of, say, negative verbal statements given by the teacher, the probability of achieving high interjudge agreement is good. The tendency to focus on what can easily be counted is used as a way of achieving high interjudge agreement, even when what is easily counted might be of marginal educational importance.

The need for unanimity among critics is not characteristic of criticism, because it is recognized that complex phenomena—works of literature, painting, film, and the like—have several layers of meaning and that the greatest works seem inexhaustible in the meanings one can secure from them. What is sought is not the creation of one final definitive criticism of a work; rather, the goal is to have our perception and understanding expanded by the criticism we read. Classrooms and schools are at least as multilayered as works of art, and we should seek, therefore, not a single definitive criticism but rather criticism that is useful. Indeed, we should anticipate that critics with different educational orientations and interests will find in situations as phenomenologically dense as classrooms different things to describe, interpret, and evaluate. The cultivation of such productive diversity is a virtue, not a vice. As in education itself, we do not seek to create an army marching in step to the same tune but individuals who follow their own drummer as long as the beat is interesting.

The specter of having to consider for purposes of educational evaluation a variety of educational criticisms is likely to frighten some people. There is often the temptation to seek simple, clear-cut, unambiguous answers to complex problems. Having to consider alternatives, to deal with dilemmas, to resolve contradictions, to think in a complex way about complex issues may seem to be more of a challenge than some are willing to take. The seductiveness of simplicity is worth resisting. Not everything— whether we like it or not—can be punched on an IBM card.

These two processes, the determination of structural corroboration and referential adequacy, are the two major procedures with which to determine the validity of educational criticism. Structural corroboration seeks to determine the extent to which criticism forms a coherent, persuasive whole. It seeks to determine if the pieces of the critical story hold together, make sense, provide a telling interpretation of the events. Referential adequacy is the process of testing the criticism against the phenomena it seeks to describe, interpret, and evaluate. Referential adequacy is the empirical check of critical disclosure.

The task of determining the referential adequacy of a critical description of a piece of sculpture, painting, or work of architecture is to some extent different from determining the referential adequacy of a criticism of a classroom or other social situation. Works of art such as paintings, sculptures, and buildings do not change over time; classrooms do. How can one be sure that what the critic has created actually fits the phenomena a month or two later? How can a piece of criticism be tested against something that has a dynamic, changing quality? This problem is not unique to educational criticism. Ethnographers face similar problems, and even in the arts, such as in music and theater, two performances are never identical. What one assumes in doing educational criticism, as in doing ethnography, is that the salient and significant characteristics of a situation do not radically alter over brief periods of time. Classrooms and schools do have idiosyncratic characteristics that distinguish them from other classrooms and other schools. One of the reasons why it is important for someone functioning as an educational critic to have an extended contact with an educational situation is to be able to recognize events or characteristics that are atypical. One needs sufficient time in a situation to know which qualities characterize it and which do not.

This need for familiarity with the educational situation before a dependable critical account can be rendered is something that virtually all teachers recognize. Teachers do not believe it fair for someone to make a judgment about their teaching on the basis of one fifteen-minute visit or even one full day's visit. Teachers, like everybody else, have good and bad days. One cannot know which is which on the basis of one observation.

To say that competent educational criticism requires familiarity with the classroom or school to which the criticism is directed is to say that criticism as a form of educational evaluation is not a quick and easy procedure. Unlike the administration of standardized tests that are machine-scored and computer-analyzed, educational criticism requires time. But from my point of view, we have underestimated the amount of time useful educational evaluation requires. Easy test administration and test scoring have been seductively simple tools for evaluating what children learn and experience and what teachers and schools teach. We might very well have to face up to the fact that the kind of evaluation that will be useful to the teacher will need to pay attention not only to the outcomes of teaching and learning but also to the processes. Without careful attention to those processes, we will not be in a position to account for the consequences of our activities. Indeed, the sooner educators help the public to understand the need for forms of evaluation that attend to the processes of teaching and learning, the better. The more we legitimize forms of evaluation that we really believe to be inadequate, the more difficult it will be to provide children with the kind of educational programs to which they should have access.

Can Generalizations Be Drawn from Educational Criticism?

Scientific inquiry yields generalizations that help us to anticipate the future. What can be learned from a form of inquiry that is not scientific in its aims and procedures? What lessons can be learned from doing educational criticism? I believe educational criticism yields two types of generalizations. One of these is the generalization of more refined processes of perception. The other is the creation of new forms of anticipation.

The consequence of using educational criticism to perceive educational objects and events is the development of educational connoisseurship. As one learns how to look at educational phenomena, as one ceases using stock responses to educational situations and develops habits of perceptual exploration, the ability to experience qualities and their relationships increases. This phenomenon occurs in virtually every arena in which connoisseurship has developed. The orchid grower learns to look at orchids in a way that expands his or her perception of their qualities. The makers of cabinets pay special attention to finish, to types of wood and grains, to forms of joining, to the treatment of edges. The football fan learns how to look at plays, defense patterns, and game strategies. Once one develops a perceptual foothold in an arena of activity—orchid growing, cabinet making, or football watching—the skills used in that arena build on themselves for other objects and events within that arena. One does not need the continual expertise of the critic to negotiate new works, or games, or situations. One generalizes the skills developed earlier and expands them through further application. Once having learned that there is something to see or to do, one attempts to see and to do. A child does not need to be taught everything. Once a child learns that there is something to be learned in an area, the child not only learns those things but also learns that he or she can learn even more. This process is not unlike what John M. Stephens refers to as "spontaneous schooling."[24] If you teach children half of the names of the state capitals of the United States, it won't be long before they know most of the other half.

The point here is that skills generalize. Their use becomes more flexible and sophisticated. As educational criticism contributes to the development of connoisseurship, the generalization of skills occurs. Indeed, that is what is meant by connoisseurship. It is not the ability to appreciate a single object or event but the ability to appreciate a range of objects or events within a particular class or set of classes. No one is regarded as a connoisseur if only one particular object can be appreciated. What generalizes, therefore, in the case I have just described is a process rather than a proposition. This process we refer to as connoisseurship.

The other type of generalization that is fostered by educational criticism is in the acquisition of new forms of anticipation. Educational criticism illuminates particulars, but it is through particulars that concepts and generalizations are formed that are then applied to new situations. What educational criticism does is to help us appreciate the uniqueness of a set of circumstances; but this uniqueness can be appreciated only if we consider it against a backdrop of other instances and circumstances. For example, to recognize the distinctive or unique quality of mind displayed by a particular student we must be able to recognize the ways in which that distinctiveness manifests itself. To do this, some conception of typicality is required. Once having recognized distinctiveness, we are in a position to look for it in subsequent situations. Thus criticism creates forms of anticipation by functioning as a kind of road map for the future. Once having found that such and such exists in a classroom, we learn to anticipate it in other classrooms that we visit. Through our experience we build up a repertoire of anticipatory images that makes our search patterns more efficient.

The potential liability of such a repertoire is that classification and recognition abort perception. We may overlook what is unique by the precocious application of preconceptions. To avoid this, what we seek is a balance between the inclination toward perceptual exploration and the use of a repertoire of expectations that makes exploration fruitful. Kant put it well when he said, "Concepts without percepts are empty, and percepts without concepts are blind."

The kinds of generalizations that criticism yields are much more like those created during the course of ordinary life than those produced through controlled scientific inquiry. In the first place, no one ordinarily sets up the conditions for producing generalizations by randomly selecting objects or events and then randomly assigning them to some treatment. This is not to say that such procedures are not useful. It is to say that we do not negotiate the world in that way, and yet all of us form generalizations. The central question deals with the dependability of the generalizations we form. As a basis for dealing with complex problems of practical decision making, ordinary experience is far more effective than the attempt to design scientific procedures for creating generalizations from situations whose characteristics might no longer be the same after the scientific work has been completed. The point I wish to argue here, however, is not primarily about the virtues and vices of the practical and the theoretical; rather, I wish to argue that useful generalizations are made from particulars all the time. Criticism is one of the means through which the particular situation can be more effectively experienced and from which useful generalizations can be drawn.

Who Is the Educational Critic?

Although school districts, universities, and other institutions concerned with the practice of education might eventually employ on their staffs an individual designated as an "educational critic," educational criticism is, as I conceive of it, not so much a role as it is a function. Anyone—student, teacher, supervisor, school administrator, university professor, school board member—might provide educational criticism to enable a colleague or institution to pursue aims more effectively. In fact, to some degree, each of such individuals now provides an incipient type of educational criticism. The teacher provides it when feedback is given to fellow teachers or principals on the character and quality of their work. Supervisors are professionally responsible for such criticism when they consciously attempt to provide pedagogical guidance to teachers. Principals provide it as they appraise the teaching competency of the school staff, and school boards provide it when they attempt to assess the work of the school administrator.

Although the perception and appraisal of such work are not considered forms of educational criticism, the roots of criticism are present. The supervisor, for example, tries to see what goes on in a classroom and attempts to provide useful feedback to teachers. When principals meet their responsibilities as educational leaders, they, too, attempt to perceive, describe, and assess so that the quality of educational practice is increased. What has been lacking is a model with which such practice could be conceptualized, legitimized, and refined.

In making the point that existing forms of professional colleagueship provide incipient forms of educational criticism, I am not suggesting that what is now done is always adequate or useful. It is to say that both professional and lay people responsible for the improvement of educational processes have relied on their own perceptions, sensitivities, and ability to articulate what they see as a way of improving those processes. The refinement of such dispositions is something that should be encouraged. I would prefer this to the formal designation of an "educational critic" within a school or school district. I would prefer the broad utilization of the concept as a tool for educational improvement that all involved in the process could learn to use with skill and sensitivity.

I make this observation because schools are already sufficiently bureaucratized and teachers already too isolated from one another to create the kind of environment that breeds trust and respect. The nonspecialized use of educational criticism within classrooms, schools, and school districts might contribute to the kind of community among staff, students, and parents that would help make schools the kind of supportive and humane places that they can and should become.

Although most of what I have had to say about the subject matter of educational criticism has focused on the activities of teachers and students, educational criticism can be applied to any set of objects and events that one considers relevant to the aims of educational practice. For example, Elizabeth Vallance focused her efforts on the educational criticism of textbooks used in the social studies. The aim of her work was to identify the ways in which textbook writers and publishers conveyed messages to students, messages that were not simply explicit but instead a function of the ways in which books were designed, color was used, words were employed, emphasis was given in the text, and the like. She writes of one textbook:

Lacking any central focus other than the general subject-matter, the text develops meanings primarily through the images it creates. These general impressions are perhaps the strongest messages conveyed by the materials. There are several of these, some created by the visual qualities of the text and some by the written content itself. The first and strongest is the image of the city as a clean, well-scrubbed, nicely lighted world. It is an image created entirely through the illustrations. The cheerful colors, the comic-book flavor of fantasy in the drawings, the rich photographic tones, and the wholesome scenes which these portray—all contribute to a feeling of good cheer. Most (though not all) of the few pictures of urban grime manage to look clean and tonally rich, and the factory in the drawing of air and water pollution is quite likeable—the gray, thick and bulbous smoke puffing from the smokestack looks as friendly as the smoke of *The Little Engine That Could.*[25]

What is curious is that all of us living in the United States in the latter half of the twentieth century know firsthand how design, packaging techniques, forms of advertising, and types of emphasis given to certain products influence our own behavior and attitudes. The advertising industry is built on the fact that the forms used to market a product have an enormous influence on its success. Exposure, although important for a product, is not enough; the way in which that exposure occurs is important and the characteristics of the qualities that constitute the advertisement are critical. Yet these considerations have, until quite recently, never been applied by educators to textbooks, or, as far as I know, to other instructional tools. The recent exceptions, of course, are in the areas of race and sex stereotyping. But there is considerably more that can be attended to in order to discover the covert messages of the materials that children use in school. These, too, are proper subjects for educational criticism.

Take, as an example, the kinds of images used in illustrations for texts. What sort of men and women are portrayed? What kinds of settings do they work in? What type of emphasis do they receive? How much white space, how much color, what kinds of layouts are used to give emphasis to various aspects of the book? The use of such qualities might seem trivial, but they play on and with the images we hold of people, places, and ideas. The portrait of George Washington on a dollar bill and his heroic image at the bow of a small boat crossing the Delaware amid ice and threatening sky, surrounded by his weary but loyal soldiers, have created an indelible image in the minds of many Americans. Such images influence the ideas we hold, and as such they should warrant our professional attention; yet, educators have given these matters little conscious attention.

Consider as still another example of the objects that ought to receive critical attention the school buildings that we design for students and the furniture we use to fill them.

Buildings represent our ideals about the ways we want to live. State capitols throughout the nation hark back to Greek architecture to express the

ideals of government—justice, stability, and historical presence—that citizens believe are conveyed by domes, columns, and white marble. Factories
are most often designed with a no-nonsense quality about them. They present an image of work; surfaces are hard, right angles predominate, little
is done to refine, embellish, or soften the forms within which people spend
a major portion of their waking hours. The factory building expresses what
it is, a place of work. Consider bank buildings as another example;
although there are exceptions, of course, bank buildings tend to look like
the Rock of Gibraltar, having massive shapes and often Greek columns so
that they, too, can reap the benefit of association with the past. People who
bank their money want a place that looks solid; a fly-by-night image will
not do.

And what of schools? What image do schools present to children and
parents and the teachers who work there?

School architecture has come a long way since the days when many
urban elementary and secondary schools were built, during the 1910s and
1920s. The best of contemporary school architecture is as congenial to the
senses as almost anything else that has been built. However, most school
buildings, particularly those in cities, are characterized by long vacant halls
with nests of well-insulated rooms opening onto them. The rooms are usually identical: strong, rectangular boxes, drab in color and not given to
amenities. The rooms speak of functionality but do not address themselves
to the aesthetic needs of either students or teachers. They are not places
in which one would choose to spend a lot of time.

What do such places say to students? What values do they convey? How
do they affect the student's image of the school itself and the experience
of schooling? These questions, too, are appropriate ones for educational
criticism.

And what of the furniture used in schools? Why the ubiquitous use of
formica? Where in the school can one find a soft surface? Where can one
encounter a cozy place, somewhere where it is quiet? Where can a student
create a place of his or her own? Is a desk large enough for such a purpose?

When in the 1920s the German Bauhaus gave us machine-made furniture that exploited the aesthetic as well as functional possibilities of steel,
glass, chrome, and plywood, the concern for proportion, detail, finish, and
comfort was critical. The modern furniture of *that* era was so classic in its
proportions and style that it is still being sold. What is used in most school-
rooms today is furniture that is neither comfortable nor aesthetically sat-
isfying. What passes for modern furniture is too often so unattractive that
we learn how to avoid looking at it. Instead of using the environment of
the classroom as a source of psychological nourishment, we try to shut it
out of our consciousness. The same environmental qualities exist in most
college classrooms. The critic of education who can help us to see what we
have learned to shut out may be helping us acquire the kind of critical
consciousness that is necessary for bringing about change.

Finally, it is appropriate to direct our attention to the works and performances of the student as proper objects of educational criticism. One of the characteristics of standardized testing is that it describes student performance on a common scale. On norm-referenced tests students are differentiated from one another on a common scale of test items and on criterion-referenced tests in relation to their ability to perform at criterion level. In either case, a set of criteria common to all students taking the test is applied and differentiations are made in relation to those criteria.

But what is the distinctive style of a student's ideas, his or her verbal expression, the quality of his paintings, her analytic abilities, the way in which students respond to new opportunities? Is the student perceptive? Is he sensitive to the implications of new ideas or to the feelings of others? Is her written expression lean, logical, and classical or is it romantic, analogical, and baroque? What qualities of mind differentiate this student from the rest? What is it that uniquely characterizes the student's mode of thinking?

Surely attention to the qualities that uniquely distinguish a student from his or her peers is an appropriate consideration for educators to attend to. Surely what we want to know about students and what we wish to cultivate are not only those qualities that they share with every other student, but also the qualities that give them individuality. Because educational criticism focuses on the particular, because it does not require that the particular be characterized on a common scale, its potential for rendering these qualities in a language that makes them vivid is especially great.

In these pages I have tried to describe what I believe qualitative inquiry is in the context of education. The work needed to demonstrate the promise of such inquiry is under way not only at Stanford but elsewhere in various parts of the world. My hope is that in the near future educational criticism as a species of educational evaluation will become a useful complement to the quantitative procedures that have for so long been our dominant means for evaluating the process and consequences of educational programs.

References

1. John Dewey, "Qualitative Thought," in *Philosophy and Civilization*, Minton, Balch and Co., New York, 1931, pp. 93–116.
2. John Dewey, *Experience and Education*, Macmillan Publishing Co., New York, 1950, passim.
3. John Dewey, *Art As Experience*, Minton, Balch and Co., New York, 1934, p. 324.
4. H. Jeffreys, *Theory of Probability (Third Edition)*, Oxford University Press, London, 1961.
5. Dewey, op. cit., p. 52.

6. Frederick Erickson, "Some Approaches to Inquiry in School/Community Ethnography," in *Workshop Exploring Qualitative/Quantitative Research Methodologies in Education, Far West Laboratory for Educational Research and Development,* in cooperation with the National Institute of Education and Council on Anthropology and Education, Monterey, Calif., July 1967.
7. Clifford Geertz, *The Interpretation of Cultures,* Basic Books, New York, 1973.
8. Morris Weitz, "The Nature of Art," in *Readiness in Art Education* (Elliot W. Eisner and David Ecker, eds.), Blaisdell Publishing Co., Waltham, Mass., 1966, p. 10.
9. Max Kozloff, *Renderings: Critical Essays on a Century of Modern Art,* Simon and Schuster, New York, 1969, p. 10.
10. Ernst Cassirer, *An Essay on Man: An Introduction to a Philosophy of Human Culture,* Doubleday & Co., Garden City, N.Y., 1953.
11. Susanne Langer, *Problems of Art,* Charles Scribner's Sons, New York, 1957.
12. Rudolf Arnheim, *Visual Thinking,* University of California Press, Berkeley, Calif., 1969.
13. Aleksandr Solzhenitsyn, *A Day in the Life of Ivan Denisovich,* transl. by Max Hayward and Ronald Hingl, Praeger, New York, 1964.
14 Leo Steinberg, *Other Criteria: Confrontations with Twentieth Century Art,* Oxford University Press, London, 1972, p. 286.
15. Annie Dillard, *Pilgrim at Tinker Creek,* Harper's Magazine Press, New York, 1974.
16. Erickson, op. cit., p. 23.
17. Gabrielle Rico, *Metaphors and Knowing: Analysis, Synthesis, Rationale,* Doctoral Dissertation, School of Education, Stanford University, 1976.
18. Geertz, op. cit., p. 6.
19. Ibid., p. 5.
20. Donald Campbell and Julian Stanley, *Experimental and Quasi-experimental Designs for Research,* Rand McNally, Chicago, 1966.
21. Agatha Christie, *Murder on the Orient Express,* William Collins Sons and Company, Ltd., London, 1974.
22. Geertz, op. cit.
23. I am indebted to Gail McCutcheon for this example.
24. John Mortimer Stephens, *The Process of Schooling: A Psychological Examination,* Holt, Rinehart and Winston, New York, 1967.
25. Elizabeth Vallance, *Aesthetic Criticism and Curriculum Description,* Doctoral Dissertation, School of Education, Stanford University, July 1975, pp. 174–176.

12

Some Examples of
Educational Criticism

Technique is the means to the creation of expressive form, the symbol of sentience; the art process is the application of some human skill to this essential purpose.

The making of this expressive form is the creative process that enlists a man's utmost technical skill in the service of his utmost conceptual power, imagination.

SUSANNE K. LANGER

In Chapters 10 and 11, I dealt with some of the important general considerations in the design of educational evaluations. Chapter 11 presented a conceptual overview of educational connoisseurship and educational criticism. In that chapter I tried to provide the rationale underlying this approach to educational evaluation, to make clear its purposes, and to identify the "parts" that constitute the approach. From Chapter 11 you should understand that educational connoisseurship and educational criticism are related, but not identical, to the approaches to criticism used in the fine arts, that educational criticisms are directed to different audiences, that the way in which an educational criticism is written will depend upon the audience for whom it is intended, and that criticism includes writing that is descriptive, interpretative, and evaluative in character.

But as you well know—if you have grasped the underlying theme of this book and the two preceding chapters especially—words do not tell all. Between words, sentences, and stories, there often exists an unbridgeable chasm. Hence, one important way to grasp the meaning of educational connoisseurship and educational criticism is to encounter examples of them, to read them, and then to reflect on how they are constructed. This chapter provides five examples of educational criticism, one written by an educational psychologist who "enrolled" in a medical school as a second-year student in order to learn about the ways in which future physicians were trained. A second criticism was written by a professor of education whose specialty is curriculum and evaluation. He was asked to write an educational criticism about a school that had an art program judged by experts to be particularly outstanding. A third criticism was written by a graduate student at Stanford School of Education who attended high school for a full two weeks, every day and all day, in order to "shadow" a low-achieving senior male student. The other two criticisms, also written by graduate students in the School of Education at Stanford, are observations of visits to classrooms at the middle and senior high levels. The criticism written by Marshall was written as a class project. In the case of Porro and Catford, the criticisms were written as a part of an evaluation project with which they were affiliated. In each case the audience for whom the educational criticisms were intended consisted of their peers and their professors in the School of Education at Stanford.

Barone's educational criticism was prepared at the request of *DAEDA-LUS, Journal of the American Academy of Arts and Sciences*. It was prepared for publication in *DAEDALUS* in the summer of 1983. Cohen's criticism of a second-year medical school program was initially prepared for a presentation at a symposium at the American Educational Research Association meeting in New York City in 1981.

As you read these works it will become clear that they differ not only in focus but in style. Unlike most research articles appearing in psychological journals, educational criticism does not display a single legitimate style of writing: there is no dogma of form to which writing must pledge allegiance. On the contrary, the particular visions and views of the writer, the specific manner in which the piece shall be done, the desirability of leaving one's own thumbprint upon the work created are encouraged rather than discouraged. Critics in the fine arts are not voiceless creatures who have gone mute in the service of objectivity. In educational criticism one wants space for one's own subjectivity to operate, for it is from the subjectivities of the world that we learn. The vision of an officially sanctified form or style (the ubiquitous *we* in impersonal "objective" social science writing is largely sham) is an anathema. Let there be but one criterion: the criticism as written and read should provide insight and understanding. Through its form and content (the two cannot in the last analysis be separated) it should broaden and deepen our view of what is going on: it should help us get on with the processes of education.

It has been suggested to me several times during lectures in America and Europe that it would be wise to provide a framework—a set of dimensions or variables—that writers of educational criticism could use to observe and describe classrooms. It would not be a difficult task to provide such a framework, or indeed even a matrix. One can readily make a list of criteria to include: the quality of teaching, the intellectual character of the curriculum, the nature of classroom discourse, the forms of evaluation, and so forth.

One can as easily imagine a scale on the horizontal axis that might easily be converted into a matrix, a scale from 1 to 7. Such a grid or matrix would again be a vehicle for the kind of reductionism that educational criticism is intended to replace. Counting the incidence of behaviors or assigning numerical ratings on a scale of 1 to 7 is not what educational criticism is about, and although there might be a place for such schemes in conventional approaches to classroom research and *even as a part of educational criticism,* there is no exhaustive set of categories, dimensions, or variables that needs to be employed by those who go to classrooms, schools, or communities hoping to learn what their own perceptivity reveals. Well-prepared observers of educational practice already have a head full of grids! The observers take into account far more than can ever be portrayed within a simple classification scheme or taxonomy. More important is the ability to judge wisely which aspects are relevant to which situations, and what in any particular situation is important to see, know, and comment upon. Conjure up the image of an art critic or a literary critic approaching a painting or a novel with a mimeographed form affixed to a clipboard. Imagine the critic assigning appropriate numbers to parts of the work. If such an image appears strange, it is because it is. In the end, what I have sought is an approach that exploits rather than buries one's unique perceptivity, that makes educational capital out of the subtle but significant, that recognizes that what is significant can very well be unique to particular situations, that places a premium upon the inventiveness of the writer (or photographer) to reveal through the skilled use of word and image what he or she has seen. There are no recipes, no rules to follow, no formulas for writing a report. In educational connoisseurship and educational criticism we start with our own freedom. The work stands or falls, like all criticism, on its capacity to open our eyes and to help us understand. I believe the five criticisms that follow make important contributions to this end.

Meta-criticism is the criticism of criticism. What has a critic done? What has he or she intended? How does the critic convey meaning? What has been emphasized? In Chapter 13, I shall examine one of the educational criticisms in order to reveal how the critic's language, tone, and structure perform work within the criticism itself.

Playing the School System: The Low Achiever's Game

BARBARA PORRO

"So much of adolescence is an ill-defined dying,
an intolerable waiting
a longing for another place and time,
another condition."

ROETHKE[1]

1.   As part of my recent training at Stanford, I was sent to Claremont High to follow Bob and to discover what high school is like for a low-achieving sophomore. I came to this experience having spent nine years as an elementary teacher in non-public schools. So although I have an insider's view of education, both the high school level and the public school setting were new territories for me.

2.   I was first introduced to Bob on the side lawn, that place on the Claremont High School campus designated as the smoking section. Students who meet on the side lawn are drawn together for a number of reasons. Besides the fact that they smoke, many of the students are close friends who enjoy being together. I was immediately struck by how friendly and playful these students are toward one another. They share food, bum cigarettes, play cards, swap personal stories, keep each other warm on cold days, flirt, joke and generally have a good time. As one student from the side lawn put it: "We have a reputation of being tough, but really we probably have better friends than any one else on this campus. The thing about the side-lawners is—we hang together. If somebody messes with one of us, they'll have to take on the whole side lawn."

3.   In addition to being stereotyped as 'tough', members of this group are also characterized as the low achievers, those students who will never amount to much academically because they lack the skills, the interest, or both. The low achiever label, like the 'tough' label, fits this group of students from an outsider's perspec-

tive. If you ask the side-lawners what they are about, however, you will find with a high degree of consensus that they are seriously engaged in getting through high school by doing the least amount of academic work necessary to pass their courses. I came to realize in my two weeks as a pseudo-side-lawner that not only does this require a substantial amount of concentrated effort, but also that they are highly successful at achieving their goal. It is quite possible to get through high school without doing much, at least at Claremont. I was lucky to have been paired with Bob because of his uncanny knack at playing the low achiever's game and because of his willingness to share "inside" information. You can't tell by looking at Bob how bright and perceptive he really is. He's bigger and older than the other sophomores and has a sloppy but "cool" look about him. Typically he wears a baseball cap, "shades," jeans, and a t-shirt that says "The Moose is Loose." His peers and teachers are naturally attracted to his warm, playful spirit and charming sense of humor. His savvy is perceivable only if you discover how masterful Bob is at playing every situation to his advantage. By following Bob, I gained access into the kind of high school experience most teachers and administrators would rather sweep under the carpet. Bob, in his single-minded effort to avoid school work, pointed out all the loopholes in a system loosely designed to educate.

The district office calls low achieving students "terminal," meaning that their education will terminate with a high school diploma.

Me: What's going on in school?
Side-lawner: Nothing . . . it's boring . . . same thing every day . . . excitement level zero.
Me: So, you're trying to get through high school the easiest way possible?
Side-lawner: Actually it'd be easier if we just did the work . . .
. . . the work's not so hard. I'd just rather not do it.

Bob is a Title I student, which means he is two years behind in reading and math according to test scores. Bob's counselor told me that Bob is a capable student, but he's never really tried very hard. "He took over my office one day and did a fine job. He's really quite perceptive and smart."

The Outside Game

4. High school is played in two main areas—outside on the patios and lawns, and inside the classrooms. Like many of the side-lawners, Bob prefers the outside area because it is here he can avoid school work most effectively. School officials permit students to legitimately visit the outside area for 15 minutes during "brunch," 30 minutes during lunch, and five minutes between classes. There are, however, many additional ways to stay outside if one is clever enough to know when to skip class. "Stealing" additional outside time is one of Bob's strong suits.

5. At first I carefully noted the details surrounding Bob's "cutting" behavior in an effort to discover a pattern. Then, one day, while snacking with the side-lawners, I asked them outright: "How do you decide which classes to go to and which classes to cut?" They collectively offered these general cutting tips: (1) Seventh period is a good one to cut because Edwards (the dean who prowls the campus looking for delinquent students) is never around; (2) don't skip second period because that's when the roll is sent to the office and if you're absent, they call your home to find out if you're really sick; (3) forge a note from your parents saying you have a doctor's appointment, show it to the teacher, and then cut the class; (4) get an appointment card from the counseling office, write yourself an appointment for the period you wish to cut, present it to the teacher, and walk out; (5) determine which teachers do not penalize you for an "unexcused" absence and cut their classes at your own discretion. (Penalties include lowering your grade or sending you to detention.) Bob used this last strategy most frequently because he had several teachers who accepted his cutting behavior without penalty. In the eight days I followed Bob, he cut six classes and was late to five.

> Several teachers remarked that the rainy weather had helped promote good attendance. On sunny days students are more inclined to go to the beach than to class, especially in the afternoon.

> Mr. Edwards, dean: "Skipping class is the most difficult problem of all to control. When I have time, I pop up unexpectedly in different places around the campus and send students to class. This creates the illusion that I'm always watching."

6. The only other way to get out of class is by being suspended. None of the students recommended this method because you can only be suspended for committing a serious offense and this is often upsetting to parents. The students quickly pointed out how counter-intuitive suspension is as a punishment: "It's stupid to kick you out of school when you do something wrong. We don't want to be here anyway, and you can't learn anything when you're not at school." I saw the logic in this a few days later when Bob was suspended for getting into a fight. Although he was suspended on Tuesday at 10:30 in the morning, he had no way of getting home so he spent the rest of the school day lounging on the side lawn, talking and smoking with his friends. The lecture he missed in Health class that afternoon described the damaging effects of smoking on the body. When Bob and I met back at school Thursday morning, he informed me that he had made $30 mowing lawns on his "day off." Because Bob's absence was "excused," none of his teachers penalized him for missing nearly two days of class.

The Inside Game

7. Teachers and students meet in an assigned room to conduct class seven periods each day for 45 minutes each. The first thing I noticed about most of the classrooms is that no one seems to live in them. The rooms are furnished with the bare essentials: 30–35 desks lined up facing a teacher's desk, chalkboard, clock, filing cabinet, an occasional stack of dusty books, bulletin boards. None of the bulletin boards contain information that is currently relevant to the material being presented to students; some of the information is not even relevant to the class. For example, in the room where Psychology meets, the walls are decorated with a map of Vietnam, a poster of San Francisco, and a picture of a girl dancing. Perhaps it is because the rooms are shared by a number of teachers that no one has bothered to set up a learning environment.

8. Students, too, move in and out of the space without regard for the mark they leave. Although there seems to be a generally accepted set of ground rules for appropriate classroom behavior, whether the rules are enforced or not depends on individual teachers. In one classroom the rules are posted on a wall. Even in this room, however, desks are scribbled on and food wrappers often litter the floor.

PLEASE!
*Do not eat in class.
*Do not drink soft drinks or hot chocolate in class.
*Do not write on the desks.
*Do not bring skateboards or tape decks to class.

---

9. The most colorful aspect of classroom life is the students themselves, who are generally accepted on a "come as you are" basis. Students wear their culture proudly—miniskirts, sweat shirts, punk rock mohawk hair-dos, baseball caps, sneakers. Everyone carries a comb and uses it. The girls have additional beauty aids they apply regularly—lipstick, eye makeup, perfume, nail polish. Students saunter into class, take a seat with friends (which sometimes involves moving furniture), and do their own thing: the fun-loving types toss paper balls and peanuts across the room; the hungry ones eat apples, bananas, and potato chips; the sexy students massage each other's hands in the back of the room; the new-age adolescents arrange dope deals. Whatever students bring to class gets passed around—lollipops, candy bars, cans of coke, magazines. Then the bell rings, the teacher calls for quiet, and (for students like Bob) the waiting begins.

Bathroom Graffiti
"This school system is going down the tubes."

"Does anyone know how it feels to be pregnant?"

"Yeah, I've already had 4 kids and I'm only a sophomore."

"at least you don't get your period"

"When you're p.g. you feel kind of sick in the morning, sometimes all day. You get some cramps, and you feel tired."

Thanks!

10. Although there is a fair amount of variation in what takes place during the forty-five minutes between bells, watching the clock is a popular activity in all classrooms. This was perhaps most obvious in Bob's math class where the clock was broken. Whenever students wanted to know the time they asked Bob, the only person in the room with a watch. During the last twenty minutes of one class, students asked Bob on five occasions for the time. Bob's answers were direct and to the point: "only twenty more minutes," "ten minutes to go," and finally "9:28 school time," at which point students stood up and walked toward the door. It was not uncommon for students to stand up one or two minutes before the bell, even while the teacher was talking. Teachers respect this as a signal to stop talking, and wait with students for the bell to ring. The clock, it seems, controls teachers as well as students.

Cartoon on the chalkboard
in math class:

"School time" is five minutes slower than time outside of school. The clocks have been set back five minutes to help students be more punctual. Students still come late to class, however, since they know the clocks are slow and they also know how to tell time.

11. The classes Bob attends are different in a number of ways, depending on how individual teachers interpret their role. The teachers have different perceptions of what school is about, different modes of conducting class, and different expectations of students—all with different effects upon Bob's behavior in the classroom. When I asked myself the question, "What's going on in this room?" I discovered that the classes fell roughly into three broad categories that sketch a continuum.

   12. *Pretend School.* The first category, marking an extreme end of the continuum, is "Pretend School," which describes those classes in which teachers and students go through the motions of conducting school without considering educational consequences. These teachers seem to gear their courses in response to the attitudes of the low achieving students rather than to their academic ability. The predominant teaching style used in these classrooms is lecturing, though I use the term loosely to refer to teacher talking, students listening. (Films are often substituted for the teacher at the front.) The "Pretend School" classes are a good match for Bob because it is in these rooms that teachers are most cooperative in helping Bob "get by without doing much."

   13. Three of Bob's classes fit the "Pretend School" category. The first class, Mythology, is taught by Mr. Arnold. Although this course counts as an English credit, students read/wrote on only one of the eight days I observed. The rest of the time students listened. During three class periods Mr. Arnold told the story of the Greek myth *Odysseus,* and on three different days students watched the full-length film of the same story. These listening activities accomplished the goal Mr. Arnold had set for himself—to expose students to Greek mythology in an exciting way. As he put it, "You've got to be realistic when teaching a group of students who are terrible at writing and who don't put out much. Even though these students can't read, they can appreciate a good story, and if you're a good performer, they'll be good listeners." Mr. Arnold was an outstanding storyteller and the students responded by sitting quietly. Not only was he well-informed about Greek mythology, but also his delivery was entertaining. He brought the stories to life by inserting dialogue, often in the students' vernacular, and by acting out the exciting battle scenes.

Me: What do you like least about teaching?
Mr. A: My salary . . . any other professional who gives four shows daily gets paid much more that I do.

---

   14. Another priority of Mr. Arnold's is to relate to students in an open, easygoing way. "If you don't maintain good relations with students," he cautioned, "they'll turn off." Mr. Arnold remained cheerful and friendly even when students came late to class, socialized at inappropriate times, or chose not to work on class assignments. During one in-class assignment, Mr. Arnold circulated among half the students who were working, while the rest of the class openly talked, looked at magazines, combed their hair, or sat quietly doing nothing. Mr. Arnold made no attempt to bring the nonproductive students to task.

   15. Mr. Arnold also was lenient when it came to homework. The "major paper" he assigned asked students to write three diary entries that might have been written by one of the people involved in the Trojan War. When he introduced the assignment, he let students know that "if you weren't here when I told the story, you'll have to read the book because the movie version isn't accurate."

> This was my fourth day of observation and the first time I heard a book mentioned in this class. Mr. Arnold later explained that he was basing the course on Hamilton's *Mythology,* but unfortunately there weren't enough books for every student to have one.

16. The day the assignment was due, one week later, Mr. Arnold reminded students that he would be filing progress reports on the following day, and since this was the only paper he had assigned that term, it was important that they turn in something. He gave students the period to work on their papers and circulated among them doing whatever was necessary to get students working.

17. Bob had no paper, no pen, and no idea what the assignment was. When Mr. Arnold realized his predicament, he gave Bob a piece of paper, offered him a pen, and suggested he write his diary from Hector's perspective. "Was Hector on the Trojan or Greek side?" Bob asked, hoping for additional clues. "Hector was the greatest of the Trojan fighters," said Mr. Arnold in a friendly tone, and with that he began to dictate a few lines from Hector's diary. "Can you do it now?" Mr. Arnold asked in the end.

> During my two-week stay, this was the only class in which Bob was assigned a piece of homework.

18. Twelve minutes before the assignment was due, Bob made his first mark in the page. Although he did not hand in a paper at the end of the class, Bob later informed me that Mr. Arnold had not sent him a negative evaluation. "How did you get away with that?" I asked Bob. He smiled wide: "I just told him that I had to work and didn't have time to do the paper. [Bob works 20 hours per week at a sandwich shop.] Besides, Mr. Arnold likes me." Bob had taken a risk and won. He figured Mr. Arnold would not grade him down on the mid-term evaluation even though he did not write the "major paper," and he was right.

> Me: What do you think about Mythology?
> Bob: It's boring but O.K. because it's not hard. You don't have to read the book . . . just listen to the lecture and watch the movies . . . Mr. Arnold is a nice guy.

19. Bob's General Science class, taught by Mr. Cleary, is easier than Mythology in that less is expected of him, but harder to sit through because it is "dead boring." Although the period often begins with students reading from the science textbook, Mr. Cleary usually dominates class time by telling personal stories that are unrelated to the lesson in the text. As one student put it, "I like science, but Mr. Cleary gets off the track real easy." Dr. Pinot, a visiting scholar at Stanford in the area of science education, accompanied me to class one day and shared these observations: "The lesson consisted of two parts: A student read aloud a page and a half devoted to genetic counseling and then the teacher began to talk, telling all kinds of stories on marginal issues such as his acquaintance with a genetic counselor and with epileptic people. There was no discussion of the real issues and no attempt to explain the biological principles presented in the text. In fact it was clear that the teacher himself knew very little about these biological principles. I had the impression that initially the students were interested in what they read, but when the teacher began to talk they 'switched off.' "

20. In an interview with Mr. Cleary, I learned that he does not expect students to take notes during class, and that he does not assign homework. When I asked how he determined grades, he said he does not give tests because "they don't tell me anything I don't already know. I grade on what I think they've learned and if they're involved."

> Mr. C had recently received notice that he would not be asked to return the following year. Mr. C has been teaching science for 25 years.

21. Mr. Cleary's perception of low achieving students reveals his priorities and helps explain why he teaches in this way. In his mind the students' low self-esteem is the primary cause of their academic failings. Mr. Cleary said that, more important than teaching science, he wants to change the way students feel about themselves. "I'd like to break the chain that goes back a long time with these students . . . that they're no good. I want them to learn that the authority is not cruel and unreasonable, that they are not helpless, that they can affect the outcome."

22. Mr. Cleary's manner of conducting class demonstrated a sincere concern for students. He repeatedly told students how much he respected their opinions, listened carefully to what students had to say, and responded to their comments in a caring manner. Unfortunately, Mr. Cleary's affective agenda did not have much to do with science and often lost students' interest and attention along the way. It was not uncommon to see students whispering to their neighbors, reading other books, passing notes to friends, or sitting with their heads down.

> During one class meeting Mr. C reached down from where he was sitting and gently roused a sleeping boy.

23. Bob often skipped science class because "we never do anything. He just sits up there and tells stories like an old lady." Bob could easily get out of class by telling Mr. Cleary that he was working on a project he was making in Woodworking II, the class Bob attends the period before. On one of the days Bob skipped class, Mr. Cleary explained to me that although he supported Bob in his shop work, Bob had been "overdoing it lately."

24. The third class that fits the "Pretend School" category is Health, 7th period. This is a particularly difficult class to teach, according to Ms. Morton, because it's the last period in the day and "no one wants to be here." Ms. Morton usually begins class by reminding students how to behave: "Stop talking please . . . take your feet off the table . . . the next time I see food in here I'm going to ask you to leave . . . put the ball away please." Ms. Morton often relies on audio-visual materials to keep students focused during this difficult period. Films, videotapes or slides were shown in over half the classes I attended, including two full-length movies about schizophrenics, lasting three days each. The films, "Sybil" and "Five of Me," were presented to students at a time when the class was studying Red Cross First Aid techniques. When I asked Ms. Morton why she was showing "Sybil" she said that if she showed it earlier when they were studying mental health, the students would have nothing to look forward to.

> Bob: I'm cutting 7th.
> Me: Why?
> Bob: Why not.

> At the end of class one day, Ms. M put in one final request: "Will you please remember to go to the bathroom *before* you come to class tomorrow?

25. When students were not viewing audio-visual materials, they either listened to Ms. Morton lecture or worked on assignments and tests. Both activities served to run students through the course; rarely did the exercises allow students to discuss the material. For example, on two occasions students were asked to fill out a questionnaire prior to a lecture. Five minutes later the teacher read the true-or-false answers without reading the question or presenting any kind of explanation. In a similar way, lectures were formally delivered without any attempt to involve students, even when the material seemed relevant to their personal lives. In one lecture on alcoholism, for example, she named groups of people who experience problems with drinking, statistically speaking. Included in her report was the fact that alcoholism is the "biggest teenage health problem today." The teacher listed the nine signs of being an alcoholic on the board and asked students to copy the list because "it will be on your quiz tomorrow." When she read the list out loud to students, she mentioned that one of the items—"drinking alone"—may not apply to them because "you're underage and can't legally drink in public . . . so if you drink alone, it does not necessarily mean you have a problem." Although Ms. Morton seemed to be aware that students in the class probably drank alcohol, she was not interested in opening up the topic for discussion. Her tacit acknowledgment that the students drank alcohol and her unwillingness to deal with the issue almost seemed to condone the activity.

> One day when we arrived late to class, we found a note on the door: "In library, 7th period." Bob ripped the note from the door and stuffed it in his pocket explaining, "Here's another way to cut class. When she says— 'Didn't you read the note that we were meeting in the library?'—I'll say, what note?"

26. There appeared to be two types of students in Ms. Morton's class: those who did what the teacher said and those who didn't. Academic work was completed on time by the diligent students, while the others (including Bob) generally ignored the assignments. Ms. Morton responded to the nonworking students by extending all deadlines in the hope that they would eventually turn something in. Even tests were negotiable. On one day, for example, students who were not ready to take a quiz were invited to go to a neighboring room to study. The ten students who remained in the room were apparently the only ones in the class who were running the course on time. (Twenty-one students are enrolled.) Ms. Morton later warned students who were "getting behind" that if they hadn't turned in 60 per cent of the assigned work by the following week, they would receive a negative progress report. Although Bob did receive a failing mid-term evaluation, he invented an excuse that convinced Ms. Morton to change her report. Once again, Bob had managed to remain in good standing as a student without doing any academic work.

> A poster on the wall reads:
> SILENCE is the only successful substitute for brains.

> "Are you going to study?" I asked Bob as he raced out the door. "Are you kidding?" Bob replied, lighting a cigarette and walking to the side lawn.

27. *High Standards Classroom.* A second broad category of classroom types, positioned at the opposite end of the continuum, is the "High Standards Classroom" or "Simulated College." Unlike "Pretend School" teachers who take their cues from the reluctant learner's attitude, the "High Standards Classroom" teacher bases the curriculum on some external consideration—what students *should* be able to handle, for example, or what students will need when they go to college. This type of classroom is not a good match for Bob because the curriculum is delivered above Bob's head. Fortunately Bob is taking only one "High Standards" class, Psychology. Bob was forced to take this Psychology course because it is the only class he could get into that would fulfill the "History" requirement. (Bob's first choice, Film Literature, was already filled.)

28. Mr. Kelly's goal in teaching the course is "to expose students to all the different areas of psychology that they might be interested in pursuing in college." The instructional style Mr. Kelly uses is similar in some ways to Bob's other teachers. Lectures were used to deliver the bulk of course material. During Mr. Kelly's classes, however, students were expected to take notes and participate in discussion (though Bob didn't do either). Mr. Kelly dictated his lectures slowly enough for students to copy the material verbatim, even spelling out the more difficult psychological terms for students. Mr. Kelly was quite willing to interrupt his lecture to answer students' questions. He always switched from psychological jargon to students' lingo in addressing their remarks, and often succeeded in getting a discussion going with students. This was the only class I observed where dialogue between teacher and students lasted more than a few moments.

> Mr. Kelly: We're trying to get this course to be a senior elective again. There's a real mix in here now, and it's impossible to meet all their needs . . . the problem with public education is they're trying to educate *everybody*. As a result, all the programs have to be watered down.

29. Mr. Kelly also relied heavily on films to fill class time. In fact, he showed two of the same films we saw in Health—"Sybil" and "Five of Me." Unlike the Health showing, however, Mr. Kelly related the films to the "Abnormal Psychology" unit they were currently studying. Mr. Kelly liked these films about schizophrenics because they vividly showed a wide variety of bizarre behavior. Although the students were obviously fascinated with these psychotic characters, I couldn't help but feel that the teacher was exploiting a sensational aspect of psychology for the sake of keeping his audience's attention. Why should teenagers be asked to learn the difference between hebephrenic and catatonic forms of schizophrenia when they are experiencing their own pubescent problems? (The syllabus indicated that the unit dealing with abnormal psychology took up nearly half of the nine week course.)

> This was not the only class in which the curriculum overlapped. Near the end of my visits, sex education was introduced in both Science and Health.

30. Mr. Kelly expected students to attend class, participate in discussion, and perform well on tests in order to pass the course. According to Mr. Kelly, Bob is in danger of failing the course because "he doesn't do anything; he just shows up." Bob does show up because he knows his grade will be lowered if he doesn't. According to Bob, Mr. Kelly is hard to outfox because he's young and "knows how kids are these days." Although Bob recieved a negative evaluation from Mr. Kelly in the mid-term report, Bob later got a "B" on the abnormal psychology unit test. "How did you manage to do that?" I asked Bob. "It was an easy test," he explained, "multiple guess and true/false, the kind made up by the textbook. I just skimmed the chapter before taking the test." Part of playing the low achiever game skillfully is knowing when to become involved in the academics to secure the long-range goal: passing the course. The failing mid-term report had alerted Bob to the fact that it was time to start acting like a student.

> Bob worked out an arrangement with his sister to intercept the "progress report" from the mailbox before his parents got home from work.

31. *Real School.* The last category of classes is where "Real School" takes place. By this I mean that the majority of students spent a fair amount of time actively engaged in academic learning. The two classes that fit this description are different from Bob's other classes in several ways: the teachers gear instruction to the students' actual academic ability (rather than the students' lackadaisical attitude or some external standard); the teachers' instructional mode is private, 1:1 tutoring (rather than lecturing); and in both "Real" classes, students spent the majority of time doing an activity (rather than passively listening). In General Math and Woodworking II, the two classes where these conditions were found, Bob stopped playing the low achiever's game and became a real student.

32. Why does Bob choose to work in math rather than goof off? The most obvious answer is that in math, unlike most of his other classes, there is something for Bob to *do*. The teacher, Ms. Golden, organizes class time around a daily assignment she has specially designed for low ability students. Each period follows the same pattern: Ms. Golden announces the assignment for the day, places it on a shelf, and circulates among individuals, offering help and encouragement; students pick up the assignment, work independently or with friends, and call on Ms. Golden for assistance.

33. Another way in which math differs from Bob's other classes is that the teacher does not adjust her expectations of students in response to their attitude. Her approach to students communicates a clear sense of her role and theirs: "It's your responsibility to do the work, not mine to make you do it. If you want to pass this course, that's up to you. I'm here to help those who are here to learn." Ms. Golden's expectations of students are stated in the syllabus and are non-negotiable: students must complete 75 per cent of the assignments or they will receive an incomplete; students who do not finish the assignments in class are expected to finish them as homework; students with unexcused absences or tardiness must make up the missed time or they will lose points; students may not leave the room to go to their locker or to the bathroom after the bell rings.

> Ms. Golden: Math I and II are really the same course, but students can take it twice for credit. This is Bob's second year with me.

> Bob: I tried to take Algebra I but it was all lecture, and the homework you had to do at home. I don't do homework, so I flunked Algebra and switched back into Ms. Golden's class.

34. Establishing clear expectations with students does not wholly account for Ms. Golden's success, however. When I asked Bob why he worked in Ms. Golden's class, he said, "because she deserves it." Bob is one of many students who describes Ms. Golden as his favorite teacher. What is it about Ms. Golden that students like? Students responded to the question in this way: "because she cares about you," "because she knows what she's doing," "because she helps you learn," "because she's not too hard and not too easy." Ms. Golden seemed to have the right combination of qualities as a person and as a teacher to win her students over.

35. As I listened to Ms. Golden's conversations with students, I realized that she treated them individually and related to them on two different levels—as their teacher and as their friend. The way she talked to students depended on what the situation called for. To one student she issued an ultimatum: "We went over this stuff yesterday. If you feel you know it well enough to cut, you can figure it out yourself." In the next moment she complimented a boy on his new mohawk haircut. To the student who does a good job, she gives a pat on the back, "oh yes, you're so smart." And always, very patiently, Ms. Golden answers whatever question students ask. During one class period, I heard her explain how to do the assignment to five different students. When I asked why she repeated the directions to individuals rather than insist that students listen the first time, she explained that "only a few students get it from the lecture; the rest need to hear it individually." In this sense, Ms. Golden had adjusted her style to meet the needs of students who habitually "tune out" teacher talk, except in answer to a direct question.

36. Ms. Golden lectured one time, on the day she introduced new vocabulary words for the geometry unit they were beginning. She spoke slowly, used simple language, demonstrated her main points on the board, maintained eye contact with students, and asked them repeatedly if they understood the material. Her remarks were addressed to this particular group of students. Students listened attentively and were obviously "with it."

Ms. Golden: O.K. If I asked you on a test to circle the "endpoints," show me what you'd do.

---

37. Bob never skipped math and worked hard on the daily assignments. When Bob got behind in completing one of his assignments, he finished the work at home. This was the only class in which I observed Bob taking a test. Before my very eyes, Bob had transformed himself into a real student.

38. The other class where Bob consistently worked is Woodworking II, taught by Mr. Teicher. Like Math class, students spent the period actively applying the skills they have learned to a specific task. In shop class, however, the projects are chosen and designed by the students themselves. Some of their projects included building dressers, bookcases, skateboards, and wineracks. Bob was making a kitchen cupboard for his neighbor who often takes him fishing. It is easy to sense the students' high level of involvement. They are busy with their hands and bodies the entire class period—sawing, hammering, sanding, staining. While students work, Mr. Teicher circulates among them, answering questions, checking the quality of their work, offering suggestions for improvement. He takes time to lead the students through the thinking process rather than simply telling students how to solve their construction problems.

39. The students respect Mr. Teicher's skill as a craftsman and as a teacher. When I asked students what they thought about Mr. Teicher they said: "He's a real good teacher. He knows what he's doing. He'll let you make a mistake and then he'll teach you how to fix it. He can fix anything. And he jokes around a lot." Bob never skipped Mr. Teicher's class and on a few occasions worked overtime on his project. Although it is true Bob used his shop work as an excuse to get out of science, it was also obvious that Bob was wholly invested in constructing his cupboard.

What Does It Mean?

40. The close-up view Bob has provided says a number of things about the high school experience. Perhaps most obvious is the fact that Bob is winning his game. During the two weeks I observed, he carried no books, he seldom had paper, he rarely read or wrote (except numbers in math class), he almost never knew what the teacher was talking about, he skipped many classes, and he's passing his courses. You may find this difficult to believe, as I did at first. You may wish to call Bob the exception. But, in fact, Bob is one of many students I observed who is opting out of learning and is "getting away with it." If you talk to people at Claremont High, you will find that this is not unusual. It is simply the way things are; everyone has adapted accordingly. The way they adapt varies from person to person, but generally speaking, all "ways" are acceptable. Some play pretend school, others maintain high standards, and a few provide real educational experiences. Students and teachers alike have the option of playing school whichever way makes sense to them without upsetting the status quo and without jeopardizing their personal goals. Thus we see Bob faking it at the same time we see pretend teachers keeping their jobs at the same time we see gifted teachers stimulating Bob. The two teachers conducting "Real School" are not responding to any pressure they feel within the system to do a good job, but rather to their own personal commitment to make something educational happen. These exceptional teachers are exceptional individuals.

Me: How did you get so good at avoiding school work?
Bob: It comes with experience.
Me: Oh yah? How long have you been doing it?
Bob: Ever since I figured out I could get away with it . . . about second grade.

Me: Are you trying to graduate?
Senior: I'm not trying, but I'm going to graduate.

> Me: How can you stand to sit here all day?
> Bob: You get used to it.

41. The Claremont High School system is not so exceptional, however. Although it appears to be running smoothly, like a good machine, the way in which it operates in not necessarily related to educating. The system merely sets up an opportunity for education to take place. Whether or not real education happens is up to individual teachers and students.

42. I brought Bob to Stanford one day to show him my school. At the end of the tour he told me he was thinking of going to Foothill College after he graduates. "What!" I said in disbelief. "Why would you go to school when you don't have to?" "Money," said Bob. "I can get a better job if I go to Foothill. The only problem is I hate to read."

> Me, during the Stanford tour: There's no way to fake it at this place.
> Bob: Yah? That's what they said when I was in junior high . . . 'wait til you get to high school, then you'll *really* have to work.' What a joke! High school turned out to be *easier* than junior high.

43. My guess is that Bob doesn't like reading because he can't read very well. Bob is not learning to read better in high school because he is not participating in the academic life there and because he has not been lucky enough to get an English teacher who knows how to motivate Bob to learn. The cost Bob will pay as a result of these unfortunate circumstances is high: many doors will be permanently closed by Bob's "terminal" high school diploma. Bob has not yet figured this out—that there may be something in school for him. He is too busy "beating the system."

> Me: What do you want to be when you grow up?
> Bob I don't know . . . maybe a machine operator like my Dad, or a truck driver like a friend of mine . . .

44. Why is Bob playing this self-defeating game? One possible reason is that school is so boring for Bob. He plays his game in order to liven things up. It is much more interesting to try to "get away with stuff" than to do what "they" want you to do. Bob's game adds a little challenge to an otherwise dull day, and because he is successful, it gives him a sense of personal power, a feeling of being in control.

> Me: What do you like to do at school?
> Student from the side lawn: Get away with stuff.
> Me: What can you get away with?
> Student: You name it.

> Me: Why do you suppose you're so good at getting away with stuff?
> Bob: because I am AWESOME, and the teachers are lame.

45. Another guess is that Bob doesn't want to do school work because it is not something he has personally chosen. School is compulsory. Bob doesn't like being told what to do, so he rebels in any way he can. Whatever "they" want becomes what Bob rejects.

46. My last hunch is that Bob plays his game because that is what he sees adults doing. It is quite possible that Bob is mimicking the approach to life we unconsciously teach through our actions. How do we play the game? By avoiding the unpleasant . . . by going through the motions for someone else's sake . . . by passively waiting for a better time, always in the future? (Life is compulsory, something we must all go through, but you'll get used to it.)

> "Not once had he been present for his life. So his life had passed like a dream.
>
> Is it possible for people to miss their lives in the same way one misses a plane?"
>
> (from Percy's novel, *The Second Coming*)[2]

47. Another way of life we endorse through our behavior is the success route. High-achieving students seemed to have picked up on this message. They fill their days worrying about being good enough, making the grade, getting into the right school. But like Bob they are putting off real life for now in the hope of finding a brighter tomorrow. How can we expect our youth to invest in their present lives when we are unwilling to do the same? How can we convince them to live in this moment when we act as if there's nothing in it for us?

(from Liften)

> "As long as success is our goal we cannot be rid of fear for the desire to succeed inevitably breeds the fear of failure."
>
> (Krishnamurti)[3]

> When Dr. Lewis looked closely at his personal experience with four dying friends, he became aware of the ways in which a total life style can be seen as a mechanism for avoiding the death issue: "I refer here to what can be thought of as a compulsive life style that so focuses on tasks, accomplishments, and productivity as to exclude a broader consideration of life's meaning."[4]

Ernest Becker, author of *The Denial of Death,* considers this preoccupation with trivial tasks a central defense against the fear of death.

48. What else can be said about Bob's high school experience? There is one more thing that stands out for me. Bob voluntarily stopped playing his game a few moments every day. Even Bob, under the right set of circumstances, is capable of rising to the occasion and bringing himself to task. This tells us it is possible to reach a student like Bob. He is not a hopeless case. When we examine the classrooms where Bob became a real student we find that teachers taught him on a personal level. The condition that seems to have made a difference is the feeling Bob received from his teachers that they cared enough to teach *him,* 1:1. Bob responded by working for them.

> Me: Why do you work in math?
> Bob: Because she deserves it.

49. I could see that other teachers also cared about their students. In fact, one of the most surprising aspects of life at Claremont was the feeling I got that teachers and students were "on the same side." Regardless of which schooling game they played, student-teacher relationships were warm and genuine. It was almost as if there were two levels of experiences running tandem—a formal schooling dimension and an interpersonal dimension. While the schooling experience was often ineffective, the human dimension was fully functional.

50. Maintaining positive relations was a priority for both students and teachers. For example, there was rarely any need for teachers to discipline or reprimand students. The tone of the class was informal, friendly. Students and teachers laughed at the same jokes. There was a feeling of mutual respect. Even when students rejected the curriculum, they were polite about it. Teachers accepted students as they are, rather than demanding that they become something else. There was no need for students to lie about what they were doing. There were no negative consequences for getting the wrong answer. Teachers respected the rights of students to work in school or not. They did not set themselves up as the adversary.

They did not use fear to control. They were simply there to help students get through school. Students and teachers were working together to accomplish the same goal. Their relationships were honest. The integrity was intact. The contrast between the way school looks—barren, cold, unkempt—and the "feel" of the place clearly indicates that the human experience is most valued here.

> "One of the dangers of discipline is that the system becomes more important than the human beings who are enclosed in it. Discipline then becomes a substitute for love . . . discipline guarantees a result . . . but the means determine the end."
>
> (Krishnamurti)[5]

> "Conformity and obedience have no place in the right kind of education. Cooperation between teacher and student is impossible if there is no mutual affection, mutual respect."
>
> (Krishnamurti)[6]

> Whenever teachers walked out of the room, I noticed that the students' behavior did not change.

> "I call it the paradoxical theory of change . . . that change occurs when one becomes what he is, not when he tries to become what he is not. Change does not take place through a coercive attempt by the individual or by another person to change him, but it does take place if one takes the time and effort to be what he is—to be fully invested in his current positions."
>
> (Beisser)[7]

51. As we have seen, warm, human relations between teachers and students do not necessarily mean that education is taking place. Only two of Bob's teachers were able to teach him in addition to caring about him. The appearance of positive teacher-student relations in the classroom, however, is nonetheless important. I do not believe it is possible to educate without genuinely caring about those we seek to educate. The fact that relations between students and teachers are based on mutual respect rather than fear may be the most promising aspect of Bob's schooling experience. That people are not going through the motions of being human is a significant step in the right direction.

> "Systems, whether educational or political, are not changed mysteriously; they are

transformed when there is fundamental
change in individuals . . .

teachers who are really interested
in education, the main problem is
how to develop an integrated individual.
To do this, the educator himself must obviously be integrated . . .

love is essential to the process of integration

without love no human problem
can be solved . . ."
(Krishnamurti)[8]

SEEING IS BELIEVING—
I wouldn't
have seen it
if I hadn't
believed it.
(Brilliant)[9]

References

1. Roethke, T. Random lines from "I'm Here," 1956.
2. Percy, W. *The second coming.* New York, Farrar, Straus, & Giroux, 1980.
3. Krishnamurti, J. *Education and the significance of life.* New York: Harper & Row, 1953.
4. Becker, E. *The denial of death.* New York: Free Press, 1973.
5. Krishnamurti, op. cit.
6. Ibid
7. Beisser, A. The paradoxical theory of change. In Fagan and I. L. Shepherd (Eds.) *Gestalt therapy now.* New York: Harper & Row, 1970.
8. Krishnamurti, op. cit.
9. Brilliant, A. *I may not be totally perfect but parts of me are excellent.* Santa Barbara, CA: Woodridge Press, 1979.

Things of Use and Things of Beauty

*The Story of the Swain County High School Arts Program**

THOMAS BARONE

"It is clear that children should be instructed in some useful things . . . (but) to be always seeking after the useful does not become free and exalted souls."

ARISTOTLE[1]

"Weaving, hit's the prettiest work I ever done. It's asettin' and trampin' the treadles and watchin' the pretty blossoms come out and smile at ye in the kiverlet."

"AUNT SAL" CREECH of Pine Mountain, Kentucky[2]

The Appalachian Mountains of western North Carolina are aging gracefully. Thousands of years ago (geologists tell us) they possessed the kind of brittle, angular, energetic majesty of the Rockies. But with an infinite patience Nature has rounded their formerly pointed peaks into gentle curves, and cushioned them with a lush green canopy. Underneath this blanket of vegetation, one can observe the aging process up close, as the mountain streams etch wrinkles into the face of the earth. The centuries of erosion have worn down this land, but strength and dignity clearly remain: even at their age they are still able to lift themselves into the grandeur of the clouds.

Somewhere within these ancient hills lives a young man named Donald Forrister.

* Reprinted by permission of DAEDALUS, Journal of the American Academy of Arts and Sciences, Vol. 112, No. 3. Summer 1983, Cambridge, Mass. pp. 1–28.

Every weekday morning around 7:30, he leaves his wooden frame house, climbs into his pickup truck and heads north. Down a narrow dirt road to the highway, he rambles, through the town of Bryson City and a few miles later, into the parking lot of Swain County High School.

Don is an art teacher—the only art teacher—at the school, and the old Smoky Mountains provide, in many ways, an apt metaphor for what he has accomplished here. Slowly, carefully, patiently, Forrister has succeeded in sculpting formless adolescent talents into aesthetic sensibilities of impressive maturity. Almost singlehandedly he has created a high school arts program that is not only outstanding, but (perhaps even more remarkable) cherished by both the school and county communities. Any such embrace is, we know, quite rare in an era in which the arts are often treated like (in Jerome Hauseman's phrase) "unwelcome boarders in a burgeoning household."[3] And so even though the Swain County story is, in many respects, a singular one, I believe that we might learn from its telling much that is pertinent to the general survival and flourishing of the arts in our schools.

An Introduction to the Program

It was on one spring morning in 1982 that I first met the central cast of characters in the Swain story: the students. That morning as usual they flowed down from the mountains like individual drops of dew that had coalesced into a stream. Along the way they were joined by teachers like Don Forrister, members of the Swain administration and staff, and me. Together we poured through the school doors.

The mountains looming above Swain County High School provide a sense of locale, but move inside and where are you? Many places you have been before. In the more-or-less standard Modern American School Plant circa 1978. The building's right-angled innards seem familiar to me: the variously sized cubicles of space that stare blankly at the newcomer, the prolonged rectangular corridors that invite without a hint of destination. I am surprised to find a school building from near where I reside, in the Cincinnati suburbs, here in rural North Carolina, partly (I confess) because of my preconceptions about the level of financial support for education in a county so rural and with such a small economic base. But there it is: the same charmless modernity, the refreshing lightness of the glass and brick, the airiness of the pleasingly massive open chamber that dominates the heart of the building and serves primarily as a reading area and media center. But a startling difference, so crucial to our story, becomes vividly apparent as one's eyes move inevitably to a boldly executed (and placed) 5′ by 5′ abstract expressionist painting on the brick wall near the lobby to the administrative offices. And in several other spots—from the cloth wall-hangings (stuffed tubes intertwined playfully into serpentine knots) that dangle above the stairwells, to a remarkable set of drawings displayed near a side entrance (including a carefully composed and brilliantly colored still life of red and green apples)—there is art. To be sure, space exists for many more pieces, but the presence of any student artwork of such quality adorning the inside of a high school is unusual and exciting. They serve to whet one's appetite for learning more about these students and their Arts program.

There are approximately 500 students in Swain County High School; an average of 80 (or 20%) elect to take Art. During their freshman or sophomore year (in Art I class) students are introduced to what Forrister considers the foundations of aesthetic awareness: line, form, design, color. These concepts are broached not only through examination of the works of major artists, but also through a number of individual projects completed under the critical eye of the teacher. The forms of arts and crafts offered in Forrister's program include these: macrame, pottery, fibers, weaving, drawing, photography, silkscreening, papermaking, batique, stitchery, quilting, lettering, and airbrush. According to Forrister and his students it is from this broad exposure to a smorgasbord of possibilities that a student will sense a proclivity towards one or more areas. The student will then usually select a set of major projects in those areas for Art II and III. It seems probable that the range of activities enhances the overall success of the program by increasing the chances of students finding an agreeable specialty.

But training in every area of the arts is certainly not provided in this program. Notice, first, that the emphasis is on the visual: musical talent is under the *aegis* of the school band, literary and theatrical performance are to be developed, if at all, by the English Department. The gaps in the list of visual art forms, including all forms of painting, are due to the primary source of funding for the program: it is largely federal vocational funds that pay for the supplies, equipment and the services of Don Forrister. Hence the emphasis on the commercial arts and crafts (although not a totally exclusive one, as we shall see) provides the program with a strong local Appalachian flavor. To paraphrase Oscar Hammerstein, "the hills are alive" in the Swain County High School Arts Program. This fact certainly accounts for some measure of the program's success as well as its local support. This vital link with the community deserves documentation, and to do that we move back outside into the hills.

Community Context: Natural Richness/Economic Poverty

Swain County, North Carolina, is by-and-large a national park. Or more precisely, over half of the county is situated in the Great Smoky Mountains National Park, and over half of the Park is in Swain County. As such, the county, in the western wedge of the state, borders on Tennessee. About one half of the Cherokee Indian Reservation, including the town of Cherokee, is also within the county lines, but, like the Park to the north, outside of the county's governmental jurisdiction. Since the Federal government controls 82% of Swain County, only 18% is left for local taxation.

In the lower third of the county sits Bryson City, the county seat by default, and hardly a city—it is a town of 1500 people, the only (except for Cherokee) municipality in the county. The texture of life in Bryson City is, of course, to some degree influenced by its locale, but in other ways seems quite typical of Small Town America. In evidence here are, no doubt, some of the qualities that Carol Kennicut, the protagonist of Sinclair Lewis' *Main Street,* found so dismaying in turn-of-the-century Gopher Prairie, Minnesota: perhaps a self-satisfied provincialism in values and mores, certainly a cultural bleakness that even rules out most forms of public entertainment (save a games arcade and one "last picture show").

There is, to be fair, this rebuttal by a local newspaper: "No, Bryson City ain't very fancy, but it's real."[4] And if that sounds like a cliché, it also has the ring of truth. I observed among the populace a genuinely courteous and friendly demeanor with no hint of pretense. And although much of the town's commercial property is incessantly drab, many of the residences exude a homemade charm lacking in the dour architecture of Gopher Prairie.

And further unlike the folks of *Main Street,* a curious ambivalence is detectable among some of Bryson City's natives concerning its small town status. The local press may insist: "If you're looking for a place with a lot neon (sic), fast food restaurants and crowds of people, don't come to Bryson City." And rightly so, for Bryson City has indeed managed to elude some of the cultural blight common to the twentieth century. But one detects a note of false bravado, perhaps even thinly-disguised desperation, in that quote. For one thing, there is an unmistakable feeling of pride among the locals in their newly-opened "Hardee's"—the first national fast-food chain to locate a franchise in Bryson City. But more importantly, consider the source of the quote: it is excerpted from an article in *The Smoky Mountain Tourist News.*[5] So its mock disdain of crowds is in reality an open plea for carloads of tourists, and a suggestion that in coming to Bryson City they will somehow manage to escape from each other. My clear impression is that there are those in Bryson City who would love nothing more than to see it swell to the size of Gatlinburg, Tennessee, the overwhelmingly commercialized tourist mecca across from the Park—no matter that currently Bryson City's major selling points are those virtues (the peaceful isolation, the wilderness sanctuary, and the small-town charm) that Gatlinburg has chosen to prostitute. But since the Bryson City area is on the edge of the tourist belt, miles from the nearest interstate, it must be carefully sought out by vacationers for the attractions it offers: hiking, picnicking, white-water rafting, and above all, the natural splendors of the mountains.

I was not really surprised to hear Don Forrister speak one night of the spirituality he perceives in these mountains, for in them, I too had experienced a rare communion with nature. Sitting on the porch of Forrister's mountain home after a twilight thunderstorm, I watched the fireflies painting in watercolor on a gigantic canvas, their speckled phosphorescent moments of light diffused and softened by the mist. I recalled a poem by William Cullen Bryant, "Thanatopsis," which I had been forced to memorize in high school long ago, but which was only now helping me to see and hear "the voice of gladness, the smile, the eloquence of beauty, the mild and healing sympathy" that is the lavish gift of Nature.

This natural richness must surely suffuse the lives of the inhabitants of these mountains and hopefully it compensates somewhat for economic poverty of so many of them. That poverty pervades Swain County. The average capita personal income in 1979 was $5,705, as compared with the national average of $8,773.[6] In April 1982, when the national unemployment rate was a whopping 9.2%, Swain County's jobless rate was 26.2%.[7] But poverty in Swain county has a long history— which may be why (as some Bryson City townsfolk insisted to me) "folks here is poor, but they don't feel poor." One suggested that, because of a tradition of self-sufficiency—including vegetable gardening, canning, building one's own furniture and often one's own home—hard times in these hills are less painful than in city or suburb. Perhaps. It is a sociological truism that the poor have less to lose to a depression. But many from the middle class are also out of work in Swain County, and the testimony of several (in a local newspaper article) concerning their emotional shock and alienation sounds like an echo from far off Detroit or Akron.

Of the 4000 in the labor force who *are* employed nearly half are either tradesmen or workers in furniture and clothing factories. (A blue-jean factory closed in early 1982.) Most of the others work in a level of government, or service-related businesses. The latter include the motels, gas stations, cafes, and gift shops that cater to the tourist dollar. The tourist business is seasonal, of course, but still important to the Swain County economy.

The Craft Heritage: Aesthetics and Functionality

The tourists are lured by the wilderness of the mountains and once there attempt to preserve their memories by purchasing souvenirs of the mountain culture. The countryside is speckled with craft gift shops—the River Wood Craft Shop, the One Feather Craft Shop, and (within a stone's throw of the pink and white Teddy Bear Motel), Miller's Groceries and Crafts. The shops contain tons of mass-produced bric-a-brac, but items handcrafted by the Cherokees and the white mountaineers also abound—baskets, pottery, quilts, rugs. The genuine handiworks are a fundamental part of the Southern Appalachian heritage. Recently popularized in the series of Foxfire books, the crafts of the white Southern Appalachia Highlanders have evolved for generations since the arrival of the first pioneers in the 1790's and the early 1800's. It is possible, I believe, to discern several qualities of life among these people by considering their cultural artifacts. I will suggest only three.

The first, perhaps the most obvious, has already been mentioned. It is an almost totally *self-sufficient* lifestyle, demanded of a people kept apart from the rest of civilization by distance and even isolated from neighbors by a rudely intervening mountaintop. Once, in these hills, everything was handmade: cabin, furniture, clothing, utensils . . . Secondly, one senses the enormous *care* invested in these artifacts. It is surely patient people who were (and are) willing, for example, to wash and straighten animal and vegetable fibers, to stretch, twist, and spin them, then to dye and weave the yarn into cloth. It could only be someone inspired to create a thing of beauty and excellence who would produce from that hard-earned cloth the intricately patterned Appalachian "Sunday Quilts." And that inspiration must surely have arisen, as did Bryant's, from the "various language" spoken by their natural surroundings. One senses a link between the aesthetic pleasure that must have pervaded the creation of these artifacts and the satisfaction derived from the beauty in these hills.

But ultimately, there is *pragmatism*—indeed, the traditional pragmatism of the American frontier. These early mountaineers were not artists in any full-blown technical sense—they were craftspeople. The aesthetic character of their work was clearly subordinate to its functional nature. Their generally harsh circumstances strongly suggested a utilitarian channel for release of any artistic tendencies: "direct your need for the creation of beauty toward the things of survival." And so their pride in a cabinet built or a basket woven must surely have sprung not only from aesthetics—an appealing form, a pleasing design, an interesting texture—but also, perhaps primarily, from the presence of more practical attributes, such as strength, and durability, and general usefulness.

The Official, Vocational Orientation

One escape route from the malingering poverty in Swain County nowadays is through the production and sale of arts and crafts. The people of Swain County are aware of this fact and a rationale for an arts program which rested on it should be viewed quite sympathetically, for it would be the latest manifestation of the pragmatism that has lived in this region (and indeed, this country) for decades. And the Swain County Arts Program does in fact have a strongly vocational nature. The program, as mentioned, is funded with Federal monies, and administered by the North Carolina Vocational Education Department. Its official *raison d'etre,* therefore, is to equip students with the knowledge and skills needed to become commercial artists, artisans, and craftspeople.

Within the school the thrust of the program is also seen as primarily vocational. Mr. Frizell, the school principal, for example, spoke of it strongly in those terms. Written documents also ascribe to the program's vocationally oriented aspirations. Consider the Swain County High School Arts Program booklet prepared for a school accreditation process. At one point, there is the unequivocal assertion that "Crafts as a Vocation is an individualized program concerned with occupations in the crafts industry. (Craft as a Vocation is taken as Art II and Art III by graduates of Art I who so choose). The greatest portion of time is spent in laboratory activities while increased emphasis is placed on developing skills for local crafts industries."[8]

And again in the booklet's description of the Commercial Art courses one reads: "At least 50% of the allocated time for this class will be used in the lab or shop for hands-on experience, *illustrating their relevance to the work world* (emphasis mine)."[9] And why are the "basics" such as color and line, design, layout, balance and proportion taught in that course? "In order for the student to develop competencies relative to the occupation."[10] Likewise, two of the major objectives of the Photography course (taken as Art III) are: "To prepare individuals for gainful employment in occupations relating to photography," and "To become aware of sales potential and prepare and practice selling photographs."[11] And so it goes: one cannot escape an awareness of the program's official orientation.

The Roots of Vocationalism   This curricular pledge of allegiance to commerce is, of course, hardly novel—whether in the area of the arts or in terms of the overall agenda of the American School. Indeed, one of the first influential Americans to suggest that schools should pay serious heed to the needs of the marketplace was Benjamin Franklin. Franklin's utilitarian approach was embodied in his plans for an Academy in which classical scholarship was to become a curricular bedfellow to subjects of a more commercial interest to the newly emerging middle class: natural science and its applications, agriculture, bookkeeping, the history of technology, and so on.

Franklin suggested that the study of art (especially drawing) be assigned a purpose in addition to developing creative expression, namely, as a useful tool for improving the design of the work of ship builders, engravers, cabinet makers, and mechanics. Franklin's Academy never became a reality but his utilitarian notions of the general curriculum—and the place of art within—were the beginning of a lasting trend. Schooling, especially on the secondary level, would gradually divest itself of a large portion of the classical curriculum, often in favor of subjects and approaches more vocationally oriented. Several years later there appeared perhaps the original arguments for actual course offerings of handcraft art such as embroidery, quilting, drawing, painting, and needlework, in terms of an expanded economic opportunity. These were in the form of newspaper advertisements for the private "English" schools that were favored in the mid-eighteenth century by many of the middle-class over the stuffier Latin grammar schools, and indeed, some of the logic in the Swain Arts Program booklet is reminiscent of them.

But only in the last half of the nineteenth century was the marriage of art and industry in the school curriculum finally consummated. These were the years of robust industrial development and expansion, decades that witnessed the rise of American iron and steel, the expansion of the textile industry, and the growth of railroads and shipping that opened up both foreign and domestic markets for American goods. It was also, if we are to believe a bulletin of the U.S. Bureau of Education (quoted in Eisner and Ecker), a time of increased opportunity for artists willing to serve as handmaidens to the newly crowned lord of manufacturing:

> In addition to the increased competition arising from the steam-car-riage, new and cheaper methods of manufacture and increased pro-ductiveness, another element of value has rapidly pervaded all manu-facturers, an element in which the United States has been and is woefully deficient—the art element. The element of beauty is found to have pecuniary as well as aesthetic value. The training of the hand and of the eye which is given by drawing is found to be of the greatest advantage to the worker in many occupations and is rapidly becoming indispensable. This training is of value to all the children and offers to girls as well as boys opportunity for useful and remunerative occupa-tions, for drawing in the public school is not to be taught as mere "accomplishment." The end sought is not to enable the scholar to draw a pretty picture, but to so train the hand and eye that he may be better fitted to become a bread-winner.[12]

Another indication of the importance of art training for industry during this time was the intense lobbying used by leading industrialists to insure passing of an 1870 Massachusetts law which required all cities with a population exceeding 10,000 to provide art instruction to teenaged boys.[13]

The last half of the nineteenth century was thus the heyday of the vocational rationale for the teaching of drawing and the crafts in the public school. John Dewey and the Progressive Education Movement finally provided a rationale for the fine arts as an activity central to the educational process, and both the justifi-cations for and the methods in courses of the fine arts and the practical (or indus-trial) arts grew more disparate, as they are today.

And so in Swain County (according to Mr. Frizell), "it was not easy to get the crafts and commercial art into the Vocational program" back in 1973. The school administration decided to make the attempt when the state-funded arts teacher/ counselor retired. The intercession of the State Superintendent of Public Instruc-tion was required, but the Swain County Commercial Arts and Crafts program was finally accepted by the state Vocational Education Department. Today only one other such program in North Carolina—a strongly craft-oriented one at Robins-ville—also receives funding through the state from the Federal government.

The Swain program must be resubmitted every year, with projections of courses to be taught and numbers of students, along with follow-up studies of program graduates. This last process is apparently crucial, for the survival of the program depends in large measure on the percentages of Art III graduates who choose to pursue arts and/or crafts as a vocation, or as a major in a technical school or four-year college. The required percentage fluctuates, but according to Ms. Alice Lance, the school's Vocational Guidance Counselor, it usually hovers around 50%. "It is totally up to the Vocational Education Deparment," said Ms. Lance. "They go by the numbers . . . what's saving the program is that the students have been using (their arts and carfts training) . . . but it's scary."

This number seems astonishingly high to me, especially considering the traditional disinclination of the region's people toward higher education, and it stands as testimony to Forrister's profound influence on the career choices of his students. So despite its slightly tenuous future status, the program has indeed proved successful in terms of its official mandate. And while that accomplishment itself is interesting, there are, I believe, achievements in the Swain High School Arts Program even more fascinating and compelling. To consider those we need to look closer at the program in action.

The Arts Program's Non-Vocational Outcomes

There are really three "arts and crafts" rooms presided over by Don Forrister. The main classroom is located fittingly in the school's Vocational wing, while the other two—the photography darkroom, and the weaving room—require considerable transit through those right-angled corridor tubes. Forrister's classroom is L-shaped (the lap of the "L" is an adjoining arts material storeroom), but its angularity is somewhat softened by the layers of student crafts and artworks that cover the horizontal surfaces and cushion the walls. Entering this room is like exiting from the building: one leaves the nowhere-land of the school plant and slips back into Appalachian hill country. The sense of place returns, thanks largely to the local flavor of objects like the baskets woven of birch twigs, the large intricately designed Sunday quilt and the drawings of hill country still life. Many of these exhibit the same curious blend of the aesthetic and the functional seen in the artifacts of the southern Highlands pioneers.

And the longer one remains the stronger wafts the aroma of the hills. Not only in the distinctive accents of the students, but soon also in the open and friendly demeanor that is a reflection of their elders on the sidewalks of Bryson City. And certainly the perseverance and the care one observes as the students tussle with their materials are the qualities one can observe fossilized in the artifacts of the mountain pioneers. It causes one to ponder whether the same fuel that fired the engines of the mountain craftsmen is moving these students in Don Forrister's classroom. Is it indeed a struggle for economic survival that motivates them? Are the scarlet threads woven into that rug merely to supply a tangential beauty, placed there primarily to catch the eye and only secondarily to please it? Not as an end in itself, but as a means of ringing the cash register?

Just what does motivate these teenagers? It is an important question because its answer can provide a clue to the *educational* meaning and significance of the Swain County Arts Program's outcomes—the character of its impact on the lives of these students. Having spent only four days in the school, I will avoid pronouncements, and instead share my reasons for some strong suspicions. They are based on observations of student comportment, on their informal comments, on mass "whole-class" discussions over which I presided, and on interviews with individual students.

An Eclecticism of Purpose   First, it is apparent that a motivational eclecticism exists here—as in most human endeavors there are a variety of prevailing causes and reasons for actions. There is indeed a degree of the career/economic/commercial incentive, although the amount seems startlingly small considering the program's stated intentions and sources of funding. Consider, for example, the case of Robert, the senior voted "most talented in art" by the graduating class, an adolescent whose sensitive and technically accomplished drawings are an emphatic testimony to that talent, and whose family (according to Forrister) is of extremely modest means. I was quite moved by one of Robert's drawings and was interested in acquiring it, but when I asked him if it were for sale, his refusal was absolute: "I like to keep all of my drawings." Don Forrister assured me that this disinclination to part with their work, even for money, is quite common among his students—and their parents. Only a few of them (including the craftspeople) will merchandise their handiworks. More often the creations will either adorn their homes or become gifts, providing lasting pleasure to themselves, their kin, and friends.

And their plans for future employment? The current crop of upper classmen appear to fit the pattern of the past: of the fourteen I surveyed eight (57%) expressed an intention to work at an arts-or-craft-related job. For some, following in the paths of former students like John Herrin, a truck driver who "moonlights" in macrame, crafts may provide a supplementary income. But for the preponderance of Forrister's students different motives seem to dominate. Their interest in their arts and crafts is not based primarily on the acquisition of a salable skill. Here is the question I posed to an assembly of sixteen Arts II and III students: "Suppose it were impossible to use what you have learned in this class in terms of a job, would you still have taken this class, and would you still enjoy it as much?" A show of hands indicated a nearly unanimous affirmative response.

So while the image among much of the Swain County public, members of the school administration and faculty, and the distant bureaucrats in Raleigh and Washington who administer and fund the program, may be of students learning to draw and weave for the primary intention of acquiring future economic self-sufficiency, reality begs to differ: the economic imperative, the prevailing practicality of their ancestors, is, for most of these students, clearly subordinate to motives more compelling. What are they?

A Personal Pride   One discerns a personal pride emanating from their accomplishments. There are several facets to this pride, including a degree of vanity from the attention their talents attract. Occasionally a sense of self-importance could be detected among some of Forrister's senior students, an awareness of a kind of privileged status usually associated with talented athletes, or found among high school thespians backstage before the senior play. This status, as far as I could tell, was certainly not flaunted—and part of it might be explained by the fact that so many of Forrister's senior students were already part of (in Philip Cusick's term) the school's "power clique."[14] But this status was also derived from the recognition of and admiration for their many awards and honors which the students (they readily admit this) welcome. That thrill of victory is heady stuff. The scent from a drop or two can apparently provide the momentum for many a painstaking and time-consuming project. This attention and excitement may be particularly impressive to the large percentage of Forrister's students who are (according to Ms. Lance) in other subjects less than academically able. Can we imagine the impact registered on the psyche of an eleventh grader who after years of frustration, boredom, and perhaps even derision in Math and English classes, is suddenly flown to New York to receive a national award for his drawings?

Nevertheless, many junior and senior students insisted to me that visions of plane trips to exotic locations, or even the regional trophies and blue ribbons, did not lure them into Art I. As freshmen or sophomores they could not imagine that they might possess such talent. Just a few years later, however, the pride in creating (in their words) a "thing of excellence"—or, more accurately, the accolades received from those creations—does seem to partially explain the students' reluctance to sell them.

An "Expression of their Art" But again, many students are unwilling to part with their "lesser" works as well. Could this perhaps indicate a more intrinsic satisfaction in their creation? In that regard, a closer inspection of the SCHS Arts Booklet contains a beguiling passage:

> A great many people work at crafts as a hobby or avocation and a growing number are becoming craftsmen and producing crafts as a vocation. For some, craft work is an "alternative" vocation which the craftsmen prefer above the nine-to-five job. For others it is their sub-occupation and expression of their art for which the benefits can seldom be (sic) calculated in dollars and cents.[15]

A priceless "expression of their art"? Is there really a nonvocational incentive producing outcomes infinitely more valuable when measured with the economic kind of yardstick implied in the program rationale? The phrase suggests a purpose more concerned with the needs and development of the individual, as opposed to an exploitation of the needs of the marketplace. There are, of course, many rationales for aesthetic education that pertain to the personal well-being of the individual, such as the development of artistic talent, aesthetic appreciation, the therapeutic value of the artistic process, and so on. "Expression of their art," in the context used here, however, inspires two thoughts in me: First, it is reminiscent of the aesthetic pleasure which was an important by-product of the time-honored process of crafts-making in these hills. And secondly, it is a phrase which evokes a particular branch of art theory—the expressivist. These theorists see art as an expression, an embodiment of the artist's inward feelings and images into an objective, outward "expressive" form. They often speak of a subjective "inner life"—"the life of feeling" is Susanne Langer's term for it—and the aim of art, in their view, is to promote insight into and understanding of this inner realm. As Wordsworth saw art, it is "emotion recollected in tranquility." But according to the expressivists, this recollection is also a publication: A work of art is a transmutation of personal feelings and imagery into a unique sensible form—an objectification of the subjective. Objects of art, said Langer, articulate and present "ideas of feelings" for our contemplation.

But aren't we placing an overwhelming burden on the shoulders of a single phrase in a single paragraph in a single program booklet? Is the development of the students' creative self-expression really a significant feature of the daily activities in Forrister's classes? The evidence leans strongly toward the affirmative, expecially for the more advanced students.

According to Forrister, the Art I students (perhaps reflecting their heritage) are more interested in functional items, or in decorating things to be used—like the silk screen designs for their "tee shirts." With maturity, however, expressing one-self through the creative process also becomes important: In the private conversations I had with senior students, several told me of how they inform their materials with "a part of myself." Perhaps most telling was a discussion with a verbally (as well as visually) articulate son of a Baptist minister. Jim was an Art III student then pursuing the art of "paper making," a process of sifting pulp through a wire screen painting it with colors, often including other materials such as straw, newspaper photos, and so on, for a kind of collage effect. In one sensitive piece a photo of a pensive old woman in a rocking chair sits among brooding clouds of purple, green, and yellow-grey.

Tom: Why do you like papermaking?
Jim: I like to be able to . . . it's not so defined. I like the freedom of it more than anything.
Tom: What do you mean by "it's not so defined," that you can make abstract sorts of things?
Jim: Yeah, like lots of times you'll make something that you're not sure why you're doing it, but when it gets finished, you really like it.
Tom: When you do your papermaking, do you ever think "well, that has a certain feeling to it"? . . . like it's expressing an emotion? . . .
Jim: Oh yeah, I think it depends on when I come into class what kind of mood I'm in. I think that comes out in some of my work.
Tom: Like, for example, the one that you're doing now of the old woman. What kind of feelings does that express?
Jim: Kind of a lost feeling. You see, I graduate in about a week . . . and I feel kinda worried about it. I guess that's coming out in it (the piece). At least I think so.
Tom: You probably wouldn't have done that one . . .
Jim: Earlier on? No, I wouldn't have done that one . . .
Tom: When was the first time you realized (you were expressing yourself through your art)?
Jim: Probably sometime last year when I was a junior.
Tom: But in Art I it . . . was just techniques?
Jim: Yeah.
Tom: Do you think other art students . . . also express themselves like that?
Jim: Oh yeah, a lot of them . . . 'cause basically you (are allowed in Forrister's class) to do what you want to.

By the freedom "to do what you want" I don't believe that Jim meant a license to angrily scratch and scrawl on a drawing pad, or to giddily splash paint on a canvas at random. While such behavior might be "expressive" in a primitive sense, it is not artistic expression. I believe that in Forrister's class the individual student is preem-inent, but the individualism that develops there has a distinctly Deweyan cast to it. In lieu of a mindless outpouring of unbridled emotion, there is a considered chan-neling of impulses into purposeful actions. Their artistic activity is in fact comprised of careful negotiations with their materials, ardent attempts to create forms that communicate ideas and images. Degrees of success vary, of course, but in this process qualitative forms of intelligence can clearly develop.

"Working Hard" at Self-Expression   Several students described this process as "fulfilling" and "enjoyable," but they also insisted that it was "hard work." No question that I asked of Forrister's class was greeted with more chuckles of affirmation than this one: "Is art as hard a subject as the others you take?" Some admitted to electing Art I with hopes of coasting through with minimal effort. They apparently harbored a notion quite common in our society—the one that associates crafts like basket weaving with extremely low rates of mental taxation. But to their astonishment, these students soon found Art, in their own words, "harder than other subjects." Reason: they had not anticipated a "striving for perfection." Who, after all, would have expected this newfound desire to "make your next project better than your last"?

But in Forrister's class the nature of the "work" is different from the Calvinistic notion of work implied in Max Weber's famous critique of the Protestant ethic, the conception which has prevailed throughout American schools for centuries and which remains today the image of educational virtue held by parents, schoolpeople (including many at Swain), and much of the general public. Such "work" demands a deferment of present interests and needs for a vision of future rewards, an imposition of self-discipline to doggedly outlast the tedium of (in today's educational lingo) the "time on task." The result is said to be the development of certain personal attributes, as noted in this description of the weaving process of the mountaineers by Frances Goodrich, an early twentieth-century preservationist of the hill country artifacts:

> In the younger women who were learning to weave and keeping at it, I would see the growth of character. A slack, twisted person cannot make a success as a weaver of coverlets. Patience and perseverance are of the first necessity, and the exercise of these strengthen the fibers of the soul.[16]

Patience and perseverance are indeed personal qualities helpful in overcoming the monotony of the production phase of the weaving process or the boredom of the assembly line. For further implied in this notion of work is the mindless replication of a prototype—and thus a personal distancing, an alienation from the process. Indeed, any intellectual engagement with one's materials could be harmful to the reproduction of a standardized end result. What is needed instead is the skill for precision in copying—and in the arts and crafts, the "training of the mind and eye" (mentioned in that Bureau of Education Bulletin) might provide such skill.

It is not surprising that during the late 1800's—the period of maximum coziness between art education and industry—this image of work was most clearly reflected in the methodology of art instruction. The methods originated, as did the Industrial Revolution, in Britain. The British National Course of Art Instruction (a.k.a. the Cole System, after Henry Cole, head of the South Kensington Training School for Art Masters) was transported to the United States and its aim was, indeed, to manually train students in copying.

Stuart MacDonald has described this Course:

> Exact uniformity was insured by the National Course of Instruction, each of which had several stages, the sum of which comprised the twenty-three Stages of Instruction. The Stages . . . were mechanical steps to the acquisition of 'hand-power.' Twenty-one were successive exercises in copying . . . intended . . . to be strictly initiated until States 22 and 23 were reached—a most unlikely eventuality.[17]

This manual training approach to drawing was brought to America by another Englishman, Walter Smith, and soon the art instruction in American schools was pervaded by these alienating exercises of meticulous reproduction of master designs.

The activities in Forrister's class, however, provide a stark contrast with the Cole System. Technique is indeed mastered there, but as a means to a greater goal, rather than as an end in itself. And the students do seem to be "working," but in a sense different from that implied in the Protestant ethic. Patience is certainly present, but it often seems less imposed than arising from a more immediate gratification. The effort appears to be generated from within the activities themselves, and directed toward an original transformation of the ideas and experiences of the individual student.

One can observe in this process a dialogue between the student and the materials being shaped, a qualitative problem-solving process in which the student/worker/ artist struggles with possibilities, tentatively moves upon the material, encounters resistance, manipulates the component parts. For example, at one point in "working" on his paper collage, Jim incorporated some torn pieces of white paper above the head of the woman in the rocking chair, hoping to achieve a daydreaming effect. The "product," however, spoke back to him: "Perhaps too bright, distracting the eye from the central figure." Jim listened, reconsidered, added a more yellowish cast that reflected the woman's sallow facial tones, and that skirmish ended successfully.

Thus was the aesthetic tension between creator and creation resolved, as Jim used his "freedom" to work hard" at publicizing through his artistic medium his own distinctive ideas, feelings, values, and ends-in-view. Aestheticians are prone to words like "authenticity," "self-actualizing," "liberating," and "emancipating" in describing the effects of this creative process. It is a process that celebrates individual growth, as the student wrestles with his materials in order to create meaning, to make sense of his life.

Expressiveness in Crafts The result of this process—a result Maxine Greene has called the "recovery of the self"[18]—is obviously a far cry from what one might expect in a vocationally oriented arts program—especially considering those of an earlier day. Nevertheless, this kind of "personal unfolding" occurs not only in the more obviously artistic endeavors of Forrister's students, but sometimes in their craftmaking as well. There are many similarities in the processes: the same attitude of caring, the personal attachment to their products, the pleasure in their creation. Of course in craft production the intended function or use of the object is a design source which imposes limitations on shape and form. Some aestheticians would disqualify most crafts from membership in the realm of fine art on this basis: they are not (in Langer's term) "virtual objects," objects whose only function is to "create a sheer vision, a datum that is nothing but pure perceptual form."[19]

Nevertheless, it is clear the craftmaking can involve aesthetic judgments, as argued by Edward Mattil, who could have been speaking of the early Southern Highlanders in this passage:

> We must assume that the earliest tools and utensils of man were restricted to the considerations of utility. As their efficiency improved, there was a steady evolution of form. In any situation where people were first required to produce the necessities of life by hand, the useful concern was of prime importance and as long as impoverished or stringent conditions continued, the art quality of the object rarely exceeded the functional design of the object. However, as soon as time and skill permitted, the craftsman was fairly sure to elaborate or decorate his objects and it was at this point in man's development where the matter of choice entered into the picture. For example, when man became able to create a variety of clay bowls, each good for holding grain or water, he found himself engaged in the process of making judgments—practical *and* aesthetic—in determining form and decoration.[20]

Today's Swain County High School students also often create meaning in their crafts—arranging elements of color, form, texture into imaginative relationships that communicate feelings. Indeed, they told me so: When I asked the assemblage of advanced students to divide into two groups—art students to the right, crafts people to the left—no one moved. There was a nearly unanimous insistence that any arts/crafts dichotomy would be an unimportant one. The students whom I had observed "working" at crafts like weaving, quilting, and batik-making, clearly perceived themselves as "doing art." Indeed, distressed by their inability to effectively respond to the question in a group setting, two such students sought me out later for private discussions, and one of them said this: that while some minor distinctions may exist, nevertheless, there is "art in crafts" and that she was able to "express my emotions" especially in the design phase of her weaving. (I was able to extract an admission that in the production phase, there was some "work" required, as Frances Goodrich has assured us, but even that process was often filled with the excitement of seeing one's design "come to life" with the personal qualities placed in it).

Interestingly, the Arts Program booklet suggests that it is those once tangential, individually-produced aesthetic qualities that today provide the craft products with their functional value:

> In our age of mass production where a certain "sameness" marks most products, there is a growth market for goods that are unique and distinctive. The craftsman who can design and produce articles that have aesthetic value and brings (sic) distinction to their owners, have access to a market with which mass production cannot compete.[21]

Thus the "functional" value of today's craft objects may be defined less by their practical usability than by their ability to visually persuade a prospective purchaser. (The mountain-folk of yore could have survived a winter under an ugly quilt, but today's Appalachian craftsmen must beware the frigidity of the disinterested consumer.)

Recall, however, that Forrister's students are generally disinterested in selling their wares, and are therefore freer to consult with their own personal aesthetic values in the construction of their objects. Individual self-expression thus seems central not only to the activities of Forrister's future artists but to the craftmaking as well and is surely one of the sources of a profound satisfaction which attracts them to Don Forrister's class.

Here then is what we have learned thus far about the Swain program: that there exists within the program major non-vocationally-related motivational factors, attributes, methods, and outcomes; that these include a thirst for self-esteem and a need for individual self-expression; that these are generally recognized (at best) as ancillary, and (at least) as officially unsanctioned facets of the program; but that these same outcomes are viewed by a preponderance of the students as the most compelling features of the program.

These findings are especially intriguing when viewed in the light of a particular ongoing dialogue among some educationists. Radical critics of schooling have long portrayed schools as extensions of the modern technocratic state, as agencies ideologically committed to the corporate social order. Through both the overt and covert (or "hidden") curriculum, it is said, the institution of the school transmits the dominant cultural system. Schooling thus promotes a subversion of individuality in favor of attitudes and a world-view that further the mechanistic purposes of business and industry. In the rather pessimistic critique of some of the radical determinists, any piecemeal reform of this monolithic apparatus of control is extremely problematical. Teachers in particular are seen as ineffective change agents, enmeshed as they are in the technocratic superstructure of the school.

The official vocational rationale of the Swain program would seem to pay homage to this point of view, but the program in action suggests the possibility of a more complex and attractive model—one in which the deviant values and beliefs of individual participants (in our case, a teacher) can, through an infestation of activities and events, yield personally liberating rather than oppressive outcomes. A further articulation of our counter-example to the radical critique will require a discription of this history of the program and the role of its chief architect.

An Appalachian Artist Designs an Arts Program

Donald Forrister knows these hills and their people, for he is one of them. Now a tall, slim, thirty-three year old, he was born and raised in Appalachia and attended college at Western Carolina University. And reflections of those qualities found earlier in the mountain artifacts are clearly visible in Forrister's personality. There is, for example, his strong *self-reliance* and independence of thought and action. These manifest themselves in a variety of ways, including personal appearance. The beard and long hair of a couple of years ago were perhaps for some of the teachers an unwanted reminder of the stereotypical mountaineer and helped to solidify Forrister's image among them (at least according to some students) as something of a "weirdo." The beard (though trimmed) remains today, but Forrister's consistent casualness of dress, as well as his general life style and values, are reminiscent of the "back to nature" movement among middle class youth in the late 60's and 70's. (The difference may simply be that Forrister never left).

But his independence is evidenced in other ways as well. He particularly disdains gossip and is intentionally uninformed about the politics within the school faculty and administration. Though Forrister does not seem disliked by other faculty members, some of them may mistake his aloofness for disdain. Forrister, for example, often lunches with students in the cafeteria rather than with his peers—perhaps only a slight breach of the etiquette of collegiality, but surely a habit (again according to students) deemed irregular by some teachers. These qualities of independence and a loose definition of his role status are greatly admired by some of Forrister's students, and seem instrumental in gaining their trust and respect.

"Hard-working" is the trait cited most often by Swain teachers and administrators. And a large measure of his success is due to his enormous investment of time and energy in the program. In class he is a blur of movement from student to student for seven class periods a day, and even, during some periods, from classroom to weaving room to darkroom. On closer inspection, the blur becomes a mosaic comprised of individual exchanges between Forrister and students—such as a mini-critique of a choice of subjects, a quick nod of affirmation concerning a color mixture, or a one-on-one demonstration of a new technique. An arts course consists of an untold number of such interactions, each a piece of an emerging pattern. And Forrister's dedication extends well beyond the school grounds and class time. He can be found on weekends escorting a group of students to an art exhibit in Asheville, consulting with an individual student on a photographic project and so on.

The students prefer the word *"caring"* to describe this "hard work." But the latter, it seems to me, is simply a manifestation of the former, just as the perseverance of the early spinners and weavers followed their desire for beautiful coverlets and quilts. That Forrister does indeed care very deeply about his program was exceedingly obvious. One anecdote in particular highlights this quality: In attendance at an award ceremony honoring the Arts program was the mother of a former Swain student who had won a ten thousand dollar scholarship to a prestigious art institute, thanks, she said, to "that man."

"And when we telephoned him to tell him the news, do you know what he did?" she asked.

"He cried."

Forrister himself admits to "getting emotional" whenever a student creates a particularly beautiful work. That emotionality is touching, of course, but it is important mainly insofar as it illuminates that which lies at the heart of the Swain County success story: the simple but intense mission of a single teacher to enhance the lives of his students through art. And it is a cause that achieved fruition not only through the unswerving dedication of that one man, but by his shrewd intelligence as well.

Which brings us to our final commonality between the character of the Appalachian people generally and Don Forrister in particular: namely, a deep-seated *pragmatism.* We saw that pragmatism in the hill folks' ingenious combinations of the useful and the beautiful, the melding of aesthetic qualities into the utensils of everyday living. Forrister's work of art was his program, and his methods for assuring not only its survival, but also its flourishing in terms of its own values and definition of "success," were also pragmatic.

Part of what Forrister did was to make the program famous. This high visibility was achieved through active participation in a wide variety of arts and crafts contests. Of course the students' talents won the awards, and the incentive produced by the recognition was developed in the classroom through the teaching process described above. Bur Forrister also played a leading role in the selection of student work for entrance in competitions, a tactic that often resulted in a legitimation of his expertise. One senior described to me the growth of his respect for Forrister's judgement:

> I would want to enter one of my drawings in a contest, and he would say "Why don't we try this other one"—because he thought it was better—and he would tell me why he liked it more—and I would say "Well, OK"—and . . . when he chose the ones to put in (the contest) I would win (an award), and when I chose which ones, I wouldn't . . . a lot of the time that happened . . . So I figured he must really know what he's doing.

Forrister's primary aim in emphasizing competitions, I am convinced, was to heighten student interest in art, not to increase the visibility of the program. Furthermore, I believe Forrister's assertion that his students' career decisions are of secondary importance to him. Nevertheless a significant side-effect was also spawned by these two measures of success. Both the obvious vocational influence and especially the contest results greatly impressed many parents and the school's administrators. The regional and even national recognition stirred local pride (and, according to Ms. Lance, has been noticed in Raleigh). As a result, Forrister had acquired a little of the aura of a winning football coach. His job certainly seems secure: Mr. Frizell has stated that, even if the vocational funds were slashed, "we would find the money to keep Forrister here."

Such a change in funding sources would probably increase Forrister's autonomy, and a few changes might ensue (such as the inclusion of "non-vocational" art forms like painting). But these should be minimal since Forrister already possesses freedom to pursue his own aspirations under the existing arrangements. The acquisition of much of this freedom seems less a result of forethought than of fortune. This is how it came about: During the 1970's, said Forrister, a regional representative from the State Vocational Education Department would visit his classes to monitor the orientation of his pedagogical methods and choice of curricular content. "For one or two years I wouldn't hear anything and then a new person would take over (in the regional office), and complain about my emphasis, and I would have to concentrate on commercial art, and lead them more into the crafts."

In the last three or four years, however, Forrister says that he has acquired greater latitude in his choice of content and methods, with more emphasis on generating intrinsic interest and less on vocational. What has brought this about? A "reduction in force," a decrease in the staffing of the regional office, that has forced the Vocational Department to rely on a less direct, more quantitative, and less informative program evaluation procedure. I have only Forrister's word for this shift in emphasis but the irony in such an occurrence would be rich indeed. Is there any other example of a budget cut possibly resulting in the enhancement of artistic self-expression in students? I know of none.

Thus have the seeds sown by Forrister sprouted in the cracks of a concrete technocracy. The success of his efforts belie any notion that schools are necessarily the kinds of "total institutions" posited by the radical critics. Indeed, as institutions become more complex and cumbersome, their management and the monitoring of official mandates tend to become more problematical. Corporate hegemony tends to diminish while individual prerogative is enhanced.

So while Forrister's actions may in some respects resemble the kind of "resistance" in educational institutions described by Jean Anyon and others,[22] i.e., an individual agent's direct contestation of the systematic imposition of the technocratic will—a metaphor less antagonistic in tone seems more appropriate, one that suggests an accommodation of aims from a variety of sources. Direct contestation is not necessary in an organizational arrangement whose unwieldiness allows for a peaceful coexistence between formally sanctioned aspirations and those held by individuals charged with conduct of the program.

Note that in the Swain County program official criteria are indeed being met. The development of individual self-expression has not been accomplished at the expense of the mandated vocational outcomes. On the other hand, neither has Forrister allowed the vocational imperatives to overwhelm the curricular decision-making and pedagogical processes—even though compromises (already documented) were sometimes necessary. Even early in the program's history, Forrister certainly never resorted to any methods even vaguely resembling the essentially anaesthetic Cole System of training students. He has shown us that preparing students for an occupation in the arts and crafts does not, today, require an alienating, spiritually exhausting regimen of mindless exercises. Indeed, evidence suggests that the personal rewards flowing from the creative activities often encourage a lasting devotion to the artistic process and therefore an inclination toward an arts or crafts-related career. (And it seems fitting to learn of the potential compatibility of aesthetic and vocational program outcomes from a native of the Southern Highlands where functionality and aesthetic pleasure have traditionally cohabited within the "arts-and-crafts.")

On Effectively Arguing for the Arts: A Hint from Swain County

This demonstration of a successful eclecticism of purpose has, I believe, important implications for the manner in which those of us close to the arts argue for their inclusion in the curriculum. Too often we display (as has, for example, Jacques Barzun)[23] a tendency to dismiss the necessity of justifications less "rudimentary" than those involving self-expression and aesthetic appreciation. The sources of this tendency are surely noble: an acute awareness of the intense satisfaction to be derived from the aesthetic experience, and a desire to enhance the capacity of members of the younger generation for engaging in such experiences. Such an acquisition might even lead (as Harry Broudy has hoped) to "the good life, . . . the kind of life that finds its expressions in the so-called 'good' works of art."[24] I would suggest, however, that it is an over-reliance on the "art-for-art's sake" arguments which has, regardless of their intrinsic validity, partially contributed to the sadly consistent relegation of the arts to the curricular caboose. Despite the "lip service" sometimes paid to the arts, the American public (including legislators and many educators) obviously does not share our devotion to a belief in their intrinsic worth. Perhaps a generally low level of aesthetic literacy prevents a sizable number from appreciating the profundity of the life-enhancing capacities of the arts. Or perhaps not. At any rate, the survival of school arts programs may, especially in an era of economic stringency, require emphasis of rationales more sensitive to the fundamentally pragmatic character of the American people.

How much, for example, would the people of Swain County value a program— even an award-winning program—that served, in their eyes, no "useful" purpose? Even in this region steeped in a tradition of folk art would there be widespread and sustained enthusiasm for a program that educated solely for "worthy leisure time activities" or "aesthetic appreciation"? My hunch is that the American-style pragmatism of these economically distressed people would ultimately deem such a program frivolous and of low priority.

The Swain County example therefore suggests the judicious employment of *additional* arguments, pragmatic ones that present the arts as instrumental in, and indeed as fundamentally essential to, the development of competent individuals capable of functioning in our society. It is beyond the scope of this essay to identify and articulate all such rationales, but we should note that they include others beside the obvious career-education justifications.

One particularly intriguing and, I believe, potentially fruitful argument sees the growth of aesthetic awareness as fundamental to the development of the "basic skills" of reading and writing. As set forth by Elliot Eisner, it goes thusly: There exists a variety of forms of public representation of privately held concepts and images. We need to increase the literacy of students in a variety of these forms by developing their aesthetic awareness and artistic expression, and therefore a more sophisticated perceptual system, one with greater power for the imaginative perception of qualitative relationships among empirical phenomena. This is important, says Eisner, because:

> Information developed out of a highly differentiated perceptual system can then be used as content for a form of representation, often in a form other than that in which the information was initially acquired. For example, consider the writer of literature. To be able to write, the writer must have something to write about. To have something to write about, the writer must be able to "read" the environment in which he lives. He must become aware of qualities of gesture and nuances of voices, he must have subtlety of vision . . . For those who are unable to see, or to hear, or to taste, or to smell, the content of literature will be little more than something that other people enjoy. School programs that neglect developing the child's literacy in forms of representation that sharpen the senses ultimately deprive the student of the very content he needs to use well the skills of reading and writing.[25]

I wish to stress that I am not advocating a total abandonment of those rationales that point to the intrinsic delightfulness of the aesthetic experience, or that emphasize personal growth and self-expression—especially for audiences that seem, to any degree, potentially receptive to such arguments. But the approaches that emphasize the instrumental value of the study of art would seem to hold greater potential for persuading a skeptical and frugal American public (and American educators who should already know better) that the arts are indeed worthy members of the curriculum household.

And, finally, this: regardless of justifications engaged in, and the program's stated objectives, once a program is in place then the successful attainment of the truly fundamental aim of art education, i.e., the intellectual and emotional growth of the individual, will obviously occur only through the hard "work," the dedication, the caring, the talent and the intelligence of those in charge. Don Forrister has exhibited these qualitites in fashioning a program that, while undergirded by a utilitarian rationale, results in the flourishing of that fundamental aesthetic purpose. His program reveals that, while caution is certainly in order, we need not fear the presence of such rationales to the degree that we might have in an earlier era.

The discovery of that truth has been, for me, both instructive and inspirational. Indeed, I will remember that discovery—as I will the artifacts of the pioneers of the Southern Highlands and those of their descendants, the students of Swain County High School—as, itself, a thing of general usefulness and of a simultaneously singular beauty.

References

The preparation of this essay was supported by a grant from the Rockefeller Brothers Fund.

1. Aristotle, "Politics, Book VIII." In *The Basic Works of Aristotle,* Richard McKeon, editor (New York: Random House, 1941), p. 1308.
2. Quoted in Eaton, Allen H. *Handicrafts of the Southern Highlands* (New York: Russell Sage Foundation, 1937), p. 4.
3. Hausman, Jerome J. "The Plastic Arts, History of Art and Design—Three Currents Toward Identifying Content for Art Education." In *Concepts in Art and Education: An Anthology of Current Issues.* George Pappas, editor (Macmillan: London, 1970), p. 14.
4. *Smoky Mountain Tourist News,* Bryson City, North Carolina, May 21, 1982, p. 8.
5. *Ibid.,* p. 8.
6. "County Development Information for Swain County," Center for Improving Mountain Living, Western Carolina University, Cullowhee, North Carolina, August, 1981, p. 4.
7. "Swain Jobless Rate Climbs," *Asheville Citizen,* Asheville, North Carolina, p. 2.
8. Forrister, Donald and McKinney, Gerald, "Art," Arts Program Booklet, Swain County High School, no date, p. 2.
9. *Ibid.,* p. 7.
10. *Ibid.,* p. 7.
11. *Ibid.,* p. 11.

12. Eisner, Elliot W., and Ecker, David W. "Some Historical Developments in Art Education". In *Concepts in Art and Education: An Anthology of Current Issues,* George Pappas, editor. (Macmillan: London, 1970), p. 14.
13. *Ibid.,* p. 14.
14. Cusick, Philip. *Inside High School: The Students' World* (Holt, Rinehart and Winston: New York, 1973), p. 153.
15. Forrister and McKinney, *ibid.,* p. 1.
16. Dykeman, Wilma and Stokely, Jim. *Highland Homeland: The People of the Great Smokies,* Division of Publications, National Park Service, U.S. Department of the Interior, Washington, D.C., 1978, p. 107.
17. Macdonald, Stuart. *The History and Philosophy of Art Education.* (American Elsevier Publishing Company: New York, 1970), p. 188.
18. Greene, Maxine. "Teaching for Aesthetic Experience." In *Toward an Aesthetic Education,* A Report of an Institute sponsored by CEMREL, Inc., Music Educators National Conference, Washington, D.C., 1970, p. 41.
19. Langer, Susanne. *Problems of Art* (Charles Scribners' Sons: New York, 1957), p. 32.
20. Mattil, Edward. *Meaning in Crafts* (Prentice-Hall: Englewood Cliffs, N.J., 1971), p. 3.
21. Forrister and McKinney, *ibid.,* p. 1.
22. See, for example, the following papers presented at the symposium "Resistance in Education," at the American Educational Research Association Annual Meeting, New York, 1982: Anyon, Jean, "Aspects of Resistance by Working Class and Affluent Fifth Grade Girls to Traditional Sex-role Demands"; King, Nancy, "Children's Play as a Form of Resistance in the Classroom"; Miller, Janet, "Resistance of Women Academics to Curricular and Administrative Discrimination in Higher Education."
23. Barzun, Jacques, "Art and Educational Inflation," in *Art in Basic Education,* Occasional Paper 25, Council for Basic Education, Washington, D.C., p. 9.
24. Broudy, Harry S., "Some Duties of an Educational Aesthetics," *Educational Theory,* Vol. 1 (November 1951), p. 192.
25. Eisner, Elliot W., *Cognition and Curriculum: A Basis for Deciding What to Teach* (Longman: New York, 1982), p. 76–77.

Honors:

An Educational Criticism

JAMES MARSHALL

"It may be that many teachers are claiming to have educational goals which are negated by what they in fact do in lessons."
—DOUGLAS BARNES
From Communications to Curriculum

I
Social Studies

Adam tells me that he will probably go to Stanford, and I believe him. Fifteen years old, clear-skinned and wide in the shoulders, he towers above the other high school freshmen, and would no doubt intimidate them, were it not for boyishly shy eyes and a smile that disarms. With honor-roll grades, a niche on the track team, and a by-line on his school paper, The *Aristocrat,* Adam is a model of intelligent self-confidence. "Since sixth grade," he tells me, "my teachers have told me that I'm an excellent writer." Len Nelson, his social studies teacher, agrees. "I want you to sign up for my honors course next year," Nelson tells him after class one day. "I'll drag you in there if you don't." They both laugh. Adam is the kind of student teachers want in their classrooms. He serves as an exemplar to other students ("I'd like to read you an essay that Adam turned in")—but he is popular enough and physical enough not to cloy. Enrolled in the honors track at Englewood High School, Adam shows all the signs of a promising future. Yet there is another side to him which is telling in its ambiguity: "At Englewood," he says, "you have the cream of the crop on one hand and the bottom of the barrel on the other. And that's good because you get a look at all phases of life. (Only) in athletics, though, do you get a good mix of people. (In classes) there's English for the advanced, English intermediate, and English low—you know, the dummies." He smiles that disarming smile.

I will be studying here one of the classes in which Adam is a student. Its full title is Freshman Honors Social Studies, and it is taught by Len Nelson, himself a graduate of Phillips-Exeter, and Stanford—though the image conjured by those names might be misleading. Len grew up on a farm in Iowa. His voice still resonates with a Midwestern twang and he walks with the quick, sharp steps of a farmer who knows his business. As we are striding to class, he remembers, "When I was just getting out of 8th grade, the local Lions Club decided to fund a scholarship to Exeter. I applied, and God, I won. So I went to Exeter and had (James) Moffett for a teacher, and then I went to Stanford." He cuts into the office on an attendance matter, and I have a chance to look around.

Englewood is built around a grassy central courtyard. There is an olympic-sized pool there, and just now the boys' swim team is doing laps under the tutelage of a female coach. A few girls lean over the guardrail to watch. Students are milling about in small groups, flipping the dials on the multicolored lockers, absent of graffitti, that line the walls of the courtyard. The students seem a sitcom version of "nice"—I don't know how else to describe them. The boys' hair is shorter than it would have been five years ago; the girls wear little if any makeup. Most sport well-cut designer jeans or Adidas running shorts, Nike shoes, Izod shirts. There is a small girl with limp blond hair talking on the pay phone just outside the principal's office. She is describing the rock concert she attended the night before. She has to speak loudly for, beginning at eight o'clock, the communications class airs its morning "radio" show: a short collection of soft rock songs played over the school P.A. system. The "bottom of the barrel" types that Adam spoke of are not in evidence. Later I will find that groups of these gather, before school and at lunch, outside the central courtyard near the parking lot, where friends who aren't in school can drive up to visit them.

Len returns and we continue to class. This is his twelfth year as a teacher. The most important recent event in his professional life was his participation, three years ago, in a Bay Area Writing Project (BAWP) summer institute. Since that summer, Len has made large efforts to incorporate a wide variety of writing tasks and writing instruction in his social studies classes. Moreover, during the last two years, he has been serving as an unofficial writing consultant to his district, and through the offices of BAWP, to the bay area at large, giving workshops on the writing process and writing instruction to content-area teachers. These duties keep him busy evenings and also draw him out of his classroom three to five days a month. "My goal," he says, "is to become a part-time across-the-curriculum writing coordinator for the district." Len has received a good deal of local professional attention for his efforts and he is proud of it. He has been granted a sabbatical for next spring—something of a coup for high school teachers in financially strapped districts—in order to develop curricula in content-area writing. He has made a name for himself.

It is because of that name that Len has been given all three freshman honors classes—classes usually reserved for teachers with more education (Len has taken very few courses since leaving Stanford). Being assigned honors classes at Englewood is itself an honor. It means one is intelligent, well-read, able to stay one step ahead of even the brightest student. It means most of all that one is demanding, for one of the purposes of an honors track is to remove the encumbrances that might impede the rapid learning of "hard" material.

Len's classes are demanding. They do move rapidly. Very rapidly.

II
Form and Function: One Episode

At 8:12 we enter Len's classroom. It is windowless, opening as it does onto an interior hallway. The egg-shell white walls carry eight maps, one poster of Libya's Qadaffi, making a fist as a tank rolls across the desert in the background, a white-faced clock with red sweep second hand on the left wall, and a black phone with no dial near the door. At the front of the room are a green-slate chalk board and a brown metal lectern. Len tells me that there is a premium on seating and asks me to take the teacher's desk which faces the students at an angle; he uses a 5-foot wide work table front and center. The students' desks are students' desks, constructed of indeterminate metals and plastics. As the students glide to their seats I can see why Len was concerned about an extra body in the room; there are 37 students in the class and precisely 37 desks, arranged in 7 rows. Adam enters, laughing with a boy at least six inches shorter than he, takes his seat in the fourth row, and smoothly turns to talk to the girl behind him.

Len is writing on the board:

TODAY
↓

PREWRITE------------->WRITE------------->RESPOND------------->REVISE

The 8:15 bell rings.

"OK," he says in a teacher's voice, "I'd like to have your attention." By the time he reaches "attention" every face in the room has turned to him.

The class has been working for six weeks on a unit on Russia, using Hedrick Smith's *The Russians* as a text, supplemented by Len's lectures on Russian history and Marxist economic theory. Early in the unit, several students staged a debate on the merits of market versus controlled economies; since then, class work has consisted of viewing filmstrips, reading chapters in Smith, taking notes, and writing on assigned topics. The current assignment, worth 50 points, is to write a letter.

"Imagine that you meet an American businessman at a party. After several large glasses of Hawaiian Punch, the two of you begin to talk about a subject very dear to you: factories."

The assignment sheet goes on to suggest that the American businessman is quite ignorant of the Russian factory system. The students' job is to write a letter to the businessman, based on what they have learned from Smith, setting him straight.

"As you are describing the Soviet factory system to your friend, do two things. First, write with your friend in mind. Use definitions, analogies, and concrete examples. And second, use each of the following terms in your paper. You may use them in any order you choose."

Following the assignment itself is a list of fourteen terms including "storming," "bottlenecks," and "Russian nature."

Students were given the assignment sheet a week ago. Since then they have, theoretically, taken the time to "prewrite," that is, to generate ideas and an organization for the letter, and to write a draft. Today, as Len's message on the board makes clear, the students are to "respond" to each others' work—a task, Len tells me, they have never taken on before.

Up to this point, Len's methods have been a model of what one tradition of writing literature has been calling for teachers to do. Elbow, Britton and Applebee have stressed the importance of making students aware of the processes they might employ in preparing to write. Nelson's assignment, moreover, calls for students to write—or pretend to write—to someone other than the teacher, an important step away from writing solely to the teacher as examiner. Finally, in the list of words attached to the assignment sheet, Nelson has provided the students with what Bruner and Applebee have called a "scaffold"—a support which allows students to engage in a task—in this case describing the Russian factory system—which might otherwise be too difficult for them.

Yet undergirding the tradition from which Nelson has consciously drawn his methods is a deeper, perhaps more radical belief: that it is primarily through language, oral and written, that one constructs his representation of the world, and that if schooling too narrowly limits the forms which student language may take, the opportunity for students to shape meaning for themselves will be diminished. Douglas Barnes puts it this way: "By formulating knowledge for oneself, one gains access to the principles on which it is based . . . In Esland's phrase, it is the difference between being a 'world-receiver' and a 'world-maker.'"

Are Len's students "world-receivers" or "world-makers?" Consider:

"You have your work cut out for you today. I'm going to pass out some evaluation sheets."

(He gives a batch to the first student in each row).

"You should each take three."

(Pause for the business of handling the papers).

"Now, here's what we're going to do. I suggest you clear your desk of everything except the evaluation sheets and your paper. Write your name in the upper right hand corner. We're going to set this up so that at least two other people have a chance to look at your writing. OK, one of the things you're going to have to do is learn how to be a good responder."

(Here Len reads the response form).

"What do you like best about this paper? Pick the four terms that are used most efficiently in this paper. In each case give the term, then describe what makes the writing effective. Weaknesses. Of the terms that are used pick the four that were least effectively described and developed. Explain why and offer suggestions for improvement."

(He puts the response sheet down).

"Your job is to help the writer re-see the paper. OK, pass your paper to the person behind you. People in the last seat pass your paper to the person at the front of your row."

(The students do so with much shuffling and giggling).

"I'm thinking it will take about fifteen minutes for each. Do a good job so that you can show me and the other person that you are a good responder."
"OK, go."

The room snaps quiet, and for perhaps the first time in their school lives, the students read each other's work with the sanction of the teacher.

Several matters are apparent here. First is the disproportionate ratio of administrative to substantive issues in Len's remarks (eight sentences to two)—this despite the fact that students had not only never evaluated others' papers before, but, I am told later, did not know ahead of time that they were to share papers today. Although Len mentions that they need to become good "responders" he motivates primarily by giving directions rather than by providing a rationale for their efforts. A rationale would take time, and that is precisely what seems absent here. Len wants each student to read and evaluate a minimum of two three-page papers in 30 minutes. To that end, he has organized the students' time for them ("I'm thinking it will take about 15 minutes.") and has structured the form their responses might take ("Find the four terms that are most effectively used"; "pick the four that were used least effectively.")

Why *four*?

The students here are not in control of what they may say, nor of how long they may take to say it. The atmosphere is tense. Len is at his work table, his own body stiff, marking papers, modeling a posture for his students. Once in awhile, one of them will glance furtively at him, then lock his eyes back on the paper.

A boy finishes reading, slumps in his desk, looks at Len for about thirty seconds, surveys the room while twisting his watch, picks up the response form, puts it down, looks back at Len, pulls himself up, hooks fist to chin, and writes. Around the room, his actions are repeated like a syncopated chorus in mime.

When the first fifteen minutes are up, Len tells the students to exchange papers again. This time, there is no pretense of solemnity. One girl leans to another and whispers, "You should see mine. I couldn't even read it." Small pockets of noise in the room's far corners. With three minutes left, Len gets up and puts on his sport coat, signalling that time is about up. The noise level grows. I hear "What did you put?" three times. The boy who twisted his watch asks, "What if you can't finish?" "Try," answers Len, then tells the class to pass all of their papers forward to him. Several students are scrambling to find out what their peers had to say about them, but Len tells them that they will get the response forms back tomorrow or the next day. "I'm going to read them over and give you credit. Then I'll pass them back."

The bell rings, and the students cluster in groups of three and four to travel to their honors English class. Adam tells me later, "It was pretty easy. You just looked for the obvious stuff."

The preceding describes only one hour of the sixteen or seventeen that I spent in Len's classroom, yet it represents in microcosm both the pace and style of teaching that students obtain there. I might have described a class where a substitute teacher (Len was at a workshop) broke the students into groups, distributed large pieces of construction paper and multi-colored pens, and told them to design a spoke diagram on a chapter of *The Russians* that he assigned—all in forty minutes. Or the class in which Len "gave notes" on certain features of Chinese history, attempted to connect those notes to a discussion of some reading the students had done the night before, and read two longish student essays aloud—all in a space of fifty minutes. In the latter, Len became frustrated with the students for not responding to his transitions quickly enough. "C'mon you guys," he scolded, "you're not making connections."

It is the absence of student-made connections that is disconcerting about Len's classroom—doubly disconcerting because with his emphasis on writing, he has ready the means to encourage them. But the class is divided against itself. On the one hand is the progressive teaching tradition from which Len clearly draws—a tradition based on students' active participation in the process of learning and the shaping of knowledge; a tradition which might be manifested in groups working together to create a design, in students writing letters to misguided businessmen, or in students sharing their work with one another. Yet this tradition is co-opted in Len's classroom by another, equally sturdy set of assumptions which holds that educational value resides in measurable progress through a body of material in a specified amount of time. Len and his students are caught in the middle. The students write letters in addition to essays; but both are read and graded by Len. The students share their work, but only within tightly constrained limits. Even their evaluations of each other's writing must be filtered through the teacher before they can receive the praise or blame of their peers. Educational activities here have been so structured, both intellectually and temporally, that it is impossible for students to register a choice or to make a connection between what they know and what they are learning. The theoretical function of the activities in which Len engages his students is to provide an opportunity for such choice and such connection; but the form which these activities take in practice undermines the function, creating a dissonance between what is intended and what is achieved.

III
The Enacted Curriculum

That theoretically sound educational aims are often closed out of classrooms has been and continues to be one of the central dilemmas facing curriculum theorists. In his historical paper, "Determinants of Curriculum Change and Stability," Larry Cuban summarizes the conflict by suggesting that "current ideology and practice are seldom married in the classroom; more often than not, they are legally separated." Yet what I have tried to suggest here is that some innovative teaching ideas can manage their way into the classroom. Once there, however, these ideas lose their character. In evolutionary terms, it appears that new ideas must adapt to the environment of traditional schooling or face extinction.

The evaluation of a classroom here derives from a particular concept of curriculum. I have taken the term "enacted curriculum" from Douglas Barnes, but the perspective it represents goes back to Dewey. It suggests that the real curriculum occurs in time more truly than it exists in space. It is an event enacted at the interface of student, teacher, subject and classroom, and as such is shaped by the purposes and cross-purposes of each. Given this perspective, one can best gauge the value of a curriculum only by watching it happen.

Still, one must place "what happens" in a context that renders it meaningful. The curriculum that was enacted in Len Nelson's classroom must be placed within the perspective of public schooling at large and Englewood High School in particular. Len did not choose to have thirty-seven students in his rollbook nor fifty minute daily periods. More importantly, perhaps, he did not design the system of expectations surrounding honors classes which encourages teachers to move rapidly, to "cover" material, to provide little space for personal exploration. Rather, it is against these constraints that Len has brought his energy and his determination to use writing as an instructional tool. He has not failed, he has been compromised, and his efforts to move away from full-time teaching toward more consultant work perhaps reflects a desire to make clear to himself and others matters which are often clouded in practice.

The forms which curricula take in practice, however, have their greatest impact on the students. While the honors class leaves the "dummies" and the "bottom of the barrel" types well behind them, they may also be leaving behind something of themselves. Adam tells me:

> (When you're not writing for a teacher) you've sort of had the shackles lifted from you. You're freer and you work within your own limits. You can really put your personality down on the paper instead of putting down what they want on the paper.
>
> Your creativity is broken off when you're forced to do something somebody else's way. You figure, all right, I've got to do it this way or I'm going to get an "F" or I'm going to get it wrong because they're grading it according to how they want it.
>
> Maybe its physiological or something, but to me anyway, creativity is a physical thing rather than just in your mind. You can think of creativity like blood or something—something that flows. The supply is cut when you have to say, 'Oh my God, I have to do this now.' It's just cut right there, and then you feel like a robot.

Portrait of a Ceramics Class:

Control and Freedom in a Delicate Balance

LORNA CATFORD

The Story

It is May in a rather more than less wealthy California middle school. Before the buzz of the bell signals the start of Mr. Gebhart's 7th-8th grade ceramics class, life is well under way in this creative sanctum. This work-space crammed with tools of the trade and busy students hums with life, in striking contrast to the dreary grey angularity of the world outside this class room—where identical beige wings flank concrete walkways. A delicate coating of clay dust clings indiscriminately to faded, dog-eared photographs of ceramics, spotted with finger-prints where umpteen students have traced designs in their quest for inspiration, and to the instructor's laminated, hand-illustrated instructions for slab, pinch, coil and modeling projects, pasted on available wall space. Two birds building their nest in the ceiling chirp loudly to be heard above the rock and roll issuing from the classroom's battered radio.

The students pay no attention. As they position themselves at twelve sturdy tables, their industry matches that of the birds. Some have taken their 18″ coil pots from the pottery-crowded counter and are already building their monuments higher, or paddling or glazing them. Some have pulled plastic-wrapped clay shoes in various stages of design from the unkempt student shelves that are trying to hide themselves behind huge, perpetually gaping, lavender doors decorated with enormous silver stars and mud spots. Other students critique pieces on the overcrowded carts by the kilns, where almost dry greenware, awaiting firing, balances precariously by gorgeously glazed bowls, figures, boxes and assorted items. Yet other students are rummaging through the glaze, tools, slip and sponges in the back of the room, finding what they need and using it. At two back tables, seven students laugh and talk, not working.

At first no teacher is visible. Then he can be discerned in his open-necked shirt and clay-streaked pants, bending over one student's project discussing the aesthetic quality of the glaze, then over another's to suggest how to solve the problem of reattaching pieces that fell off in the first firing. Two minutes after the bell has summoned the faithful, Mr. Gebhart stands up. He has already had individual consultation with five students.

"Bo, turn off the radio please, till everyone is working."

A boy from the non-working table silences the music. Most of the students look up for a moment, then resume work. Some approach him with questions concerning evaluation of their work, further directions, or technical or aesthetic problems demanding solution. Mr. Gebhart attends briefly to them, but directs his attention to the back table where a girl is wrapping her scarf around Bo's head, talking.

"Penny, what are you working on?" She shrugs. "Don't just sit there and chat. You've had enough time to get started." Mr. Gebhart turns to somebody else. Penny pulls out a lacy clay shoe and starts smoothing out its high heel.

The radio is turned on. "Leave that off till everyone is working. I'll say when everyone is working." The radio is turned off. Students admonish one another to get to work. Fifteen minutes into the period Mr. Gebhart turns the music on. Another work-day is in progress.

Every two weeks or so Mr. Gebhart introduces a new lesson. He asks the students to gather round, which they do, some perched on the front tables, one on crutches, balanced dangerously between two tables. This lesson involves sculpting a figure, "doing something, not looking like it just died," from a small block of clay. Mr. Gebhart demonstrates the basic cuts and twists which produce a human form, telling students to attend to proportion, not detail. He shows them how to use their bodies to determine arm length. The students seem captivated by the emerging figure. Working quickly, Mr. Gebhart notes that the figure should be posed after its basic form is established, and then brings forth a seated figure, torso twisted, knee raised.

Having given basic directions, Mr. Gebhart shows the students illustrations in *Sports and Games in Art*—Bellows' boxers, Moore's abstractions, Greek wrestlers. He brings the pictures to life: "This one was probably made in clay first like you're doing." "We call this 'abstracted.' Just put in what you think is essential." "Notice how this conveys a feeling of movement." He throws his body forward to walk. "In art we create the same process by throwing the whole body off center."

Pointing to a Giacometti with slender legs, "What's the problem with this one if you were making it out of clay?" ("It wouldn't stand.") "How could you solve that problem?" With no hesitations solutions are offered, "put wire inside and clay around it;" "a platform;" "support."

Mr. Gebhart expands on the students' answers, showing further illustrations and reminding them to think about how they will present their figure. Then he recaps several tips: adapting ideas from existing art pieces, planning before starting, using one's body as a guide, adding details last.

During the fourteen minute lecture, Mr. Gebhart has the students' attention. Barb, chin on hands, has her eyes riveted to him and the book, nodding to herself. Valerie is unobtrusively observing from behind some more assertive students. Even Bo and Penny watch. "Continue with your work," concludes Mr. Gebhart. The students disperse, and the day continues in the usual manner of individual instruction. Seven or eight different types of projects are underway.

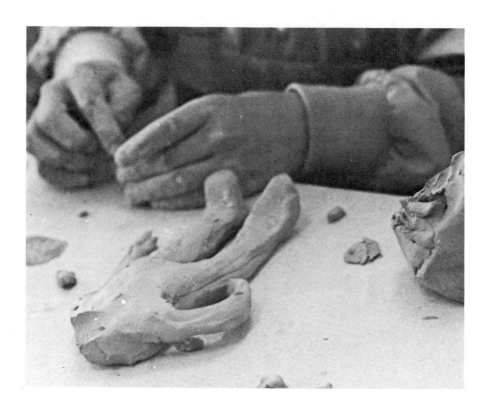

Valerie holds her head down a lot. She has embarked on the new project, the figure in action, but has not progressed far. Its form is still reminiscent of the chunky rectangular slab from which it is fashioned. As Valerie smooths out a shoulder, a crack appears in an ankle. She puts it down and goes to find Mr. Gebhart. Bringing him to her table, she says, "I can't do it." "What can't you do? I see a guy there. You did that." "He doesn't have good shoulders." "What do you mean—not good shoulders?" "They're too big."

Pointing to their bodies, Mr. Gebhart describes the difference between the figure's shoulders and theirs. Valerie watches, nods. Barb, participating in the interchange, manipulates the figure, "It'll go in there. You can cut it off here . . . push it there." Valerie watches, hands clasped, while the others critique the piece and suggest what to do. Valerie comments that she is not sure how to shape it. Mr. Gebhart brings Valerie *Sports in Art,* but instead of looking in it she wrinkles her nose and says, of her figure, "It looks rejected." Mr. Gebhart suggests that she not be afraid to pick it up and view it from various angles. Valerie does this, holding it gingerly.

"Mind if I work on this side a bit?" asks Mr. Gebhart. He describes what he is doing as, in his hands, one leg becomes lifelike. Valerie notices the transformation. Then the crack deepens and the foot falls off. "Oh, don't worry. You can put it on later," remarks Mr. Gebhart nonchalantly. He hands the figure to Valerie, who starts working on it. Mr. Gebhart leaves. He has spent ten minutes with Valerie, more than with any other student at one time. "I think I'll take the feet off for now," she says, much braver, and she does.

Sue approaches Mr. Gebhart with a pot from another class. "Is this glaze bean-pot brown?" When told it is, she asks how the striped effect was achieved, and after telling her and suggesting an alternate method, Mr. Gebhart asks her if she plans this for inside or outside her pot. Sue considers, and replies that if she uses blue and black she will stripe both, but if she uses browns, just the outside. "Well, think about that," says Mr. Gebhart, supporting her decision-making, but not doing it for her.

Later Sue explains what she decided, "Blue, because it's not as serious or gloomy as the brown." She points to two blue pots at the front of the room, on which the glaze had been applied so that the tops are lighter than the bottoms. "I like the light on the top. I'll do blue on the outside and something else inside to make it interesting."

Two students are rough-housing on the other side of the room. One has the other in a bear hold. "O.K., Cool it on the hugs!" Mr. Gebhart raises his voice so they will hear him. With this warning, there are several smiles, and the students get back to work.

Fred, tiny for his age, is the only Japanese student in the class. A timid 7th grader, he is in a special "Core" program for students with problems adjusting to junior high school. For several days it has been sweltering and Fred has worn a huge down parka. He works silently at the outside corner of a front table, perhaps the least frequented area of the room. His tablemate is another quiet boy, engrossed in his work.

Fred bends over his coil pot, patting the dry cracking clay. Mr. Gebhart comes and crouches next to him. "I want you to get a bowl of water and dip your hands in, and put it on your clay as you work, to keep it wet so it doesn't dry out." He straightens up and stands by the table till Fred has fetched the water.

Some time later Valerie's figure has developed a more shapely lean look. The feet have been attached. She leafs through the book for a few minutes and decides on a pose. When she starts bending the figure, cracks appear in the clay, so she asks Mr. Gebhart if he will bend it into position. This time he does not take such an active role in her problem solving. "Don't worry if it cracks," he says. He does not bend it, but shows her how to smooth it over, mentioning that his work cracks too. Valerie nods in acknowledgement of his reassurance.

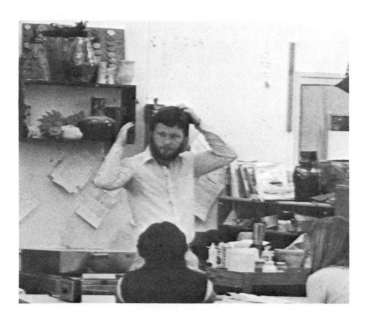

A piece of clay whizzes past Mr. Gebhart's head. "Who's throwing clay?" he asks, looking around the room. No response. He moves to a table of three boys. "Are you throwing clay?" One angelic-looking child slowly shakes his head, and utters a wide-eyed lie, "Oh, no." "Well from the trajectory it looks like its from the direction of this table, remarks the teacher. "If you are, you'll get a written assignment and cleanup duty." There is a murmur of denial from the boys. "I'm not accusing you. I just want to make sure you know the consequences." No more clay is thrown that day.

During the next few days Mr. Gebhart continues his versatile manner of teaching. He scans the room for students needing encouragement, intellectual challenge, or discipline. His manner of interaction seems endless: humor, stern words, touching, doing, watching, inquiring, reflecting on his own work, giving directions.

He gives one other fifteen minute lecture in the ten hours of class during which this story takes place. On this occasion he encourages the students to recall and describe the four basic techniques they have learned and to brainstorm possible applications of these techniques. After a brief lecture on art as problem solving, Mr. Gebhart informs the students that, in the past when he has given problems and steps for solving them, they have not had to create the problems themselves. Explaining that artists, they, and he constantly need to invite challenging problems, he assigns the final project of the semester. The students are to spend a few days browsing through art books, interacting with the environment, allowing an idea to germinate, and then to present a plan for their final project. He acknowledges the value of frustration and negative reactions as containing seeds for problems to be solved. While most students are attentive, the "social group" laugh and talk, not always facing the front of the room. Mr. Gebhart seems to ignore this, and talks to those who are listening. He fields a few questions, then tells the students to take out their work. The hum of music and industry resumes.

Jane, who has been absent for many days, admires Valerie's now smooth and fluid figure. "If I can get the leg back on, it'll be like the picture in a gymnastics magazine," says Valerie, working on the piece. Jane wants to know exactly what the assignment entails. The self same Valerie that was too timid to touch her figure earlier not only describes the project with authority, but reassures Jane that cracks are not a problem, and that removing a limb can make it easier to work on the piece.

Five minutes before the end of class, Mr. Gebhart hovers by the radio, and when a song ends, turns it off. "We interrupt this program to announce cleanup." Groans from some students; hurried last minute modifications; sponges grabbed to wipe tables. At the bell the class empties and the walkway comes to life.

Mr. Gebhart stretches, and begins unloading and restacking the kilns. The birds chirp and fly from nest to open door. The clay dust sparkles in the sunshine.

Analysis

The preceding story is factual. I saw and heard the events and words in it. Where thick description is used, ascription of motives or meaning is based on further observations, interviews and a questionnaire completed by twenty-six students. My observations are shaped by ten years' experience as a therapist, trained to perceive and interpret nuances of human interaction.

Mr. Gebhart is concerned about what he calls the "delicate balance between control and freedom" in his ceramics class. I saw him weaving the two into a rich educative experience in numerous ways, aided by his apparent sensitivity to students' needs. In this section I examine this balance in three areas: classroom management, curriculum and teaching. In each area I try to understand the relationship between control and freedom in terms of the teacher's philosophy, student reactions and educational theory. In the final section I discuss the relationship between Mr. Gebhart's teaching style and his personal style. Lastly I suggest implications for teacher selection and training. The story enables readers to draw conclusions beyond those discussed here.

Classroom Management   While there are many facets to classroom management, the term here refers to discipline. Beth Lyon, the school psychologist, describes Mr. Gebhart's class: "It looks as if everyone is running around being wild, but it takes structure to run a class like that. The kids and teacher know what the structure is, even if from outside it doesn't look like much." It is true that the movement, clutter, dust and noise could suggest the unhappy stereotype of the "free art class." This is belied by the underlying self-direction of the students, and the quality of their aesthetic and intellectual judgments.

Mr. Gebhart realizes that the individualized way in which he runs his class invites students to test the limits of their freedom. However, he insists that developing skill and knowledge in art requires discipline and work, and that "Control is the basis for everything else that goes on in this class."

He is comfortable with the discipline level in his class, which he has come to via the road of hard knocks. He recalls that the students would "walk all over" him when he started teaching, and was attempting authoritarian control. Describing this, he stated, "if you decide *now* they have to clean up their act, you create a battle you can't win." Herman Hesse (1968), in an essay on schooling, calls this sort of battle a "struggle between rule and spirit." After being trained in Cantor and Cantor's "assertive discipline" (a behavioral program with rewards and punishments for rule following or breaking), Mr. Gebhart developed a more effective way to maintain control. Rather than attempting to force compliance, thus ignoring the students' need for self-expression, he reminds them of the rules, respecting their ability to take responsibility for their actions. The exciting thing is that not only does he not have to work so hard, but the students are less disruptive.

In the daily pseudo-battle concerning the radio, the students test Mr. Gebhart, who states the limits, and tells them how they can direct their energy so that they can have the music. Here, as in the clay-throwing incident, Mr. Gebhart attempts to structure the situation so that the rules are not oppressive—thus spirit finds an alternative mode of expression. He encourages an active rather than a passive response in his students—doing work rather than being quiet. Thus he allows a certain type of personal freedom in his social control. While the "social group," as Mr. Gebhart calls them, seem to take advantage of the freedom to talk and move around, they also tend to turn their attention to the task at hand at a few words from the teacher.

One student expressed a sentiment shared by several, that the freedom "makes it so that I don't just do my work to get it over with." Only one student, out of twenty-six answering a questionnaire, feels that Mr. Gebhart "hardly ever" has adequate control over the class, and only three state that they tend to "goof off" more in this class than others.

With minor variations in words and cast, the ritual dance of the forces of control and freedom, of rule and spirit, are enacted five days a week. The choreography is superb. There is a dynamic tension in which it turns out that the forces of freedom do indeed have a good amount of control, and vice versa.

It is clear that while the students appear to challenge the teacher's authority, the rules of the dance are such that the challenge is a token act of self-assertion. Penny's immediate return to work in response to Mr. Gebhart's statement suggests that she has an internal locus of self-control. (A Marxist educator might view this as compliance as the result of the system during the student's previous seven years of schooling. Penny's—and others'—vitality suggests that this is not so.) Examination of the manner in which the teacher exerts control reveals that he is not forceful, but allows the students the freedom to create their own control.

While the challenges happen, the majority of the students can be likened to the Greek Chorus, the actors in the background who call to our attention the "truth" of the situation. Their physical movement in the room and conversation are predominantly task-related (I noted several interchanges daily concerning techniques or aesthetic judgment, and few extraneous conversations), and the emotional color of their expression reflects elation, frustration or pride about their work. In Dewey's (1938) terms, the exernal freedom is a means to intellectual freedom. Most students initiate work before the bell rings, and do not want to stop at cleanup time. I have a sense of time running away because of the students' involvement. As one student put it, "The problem with this class is it's over before you can start."

Most students are involved. Quality work is done. The formal rules of discipline and meta-rules of the dance are known by all. This suggests to me that Mr. Gebhart uses freedom and control effectively in his classroom management. The following words of Walt Whitman (1969) come to mind:

> *Of life immense in passion, pulse and power,*
> *Cheerful, for freest action formed under the laws divine.*

Curriculum   Mr. Gebhart's curriculum involves gaining control of terminology and materials. It consists of knowledge and application of five technical skills—pinch, slab, coil, modeling and glazing. Is this not made clear by the instructions on the wall, and the mountains of student work? As is the case with classroom management, what might seem so at first does not necessarily reflect the extent of what is there.

True, Mr. Gebhart teaches skills according to "a recipe," and students are required to learn these skills. Making a coil pot requires the use of a specific technique, and its size requirement ensures that in completing it the students would be practiced in this. Mr. Gebhart notes the necessity of drill to become proficient, and describes this acquisition of technical control as "freeing, because once you have this, you can go on and do anything." While technical control is necessary, too much "concern with technical skill can interfere with aesthetic expression and appreciation," he comments.

Susanne Langer (1957) describes the difference between a product and a creation. While both involve technical mastery, a creation is an expressive form—its meaning goes beyond the limits of the materials and how they were shaped. Mr. Gebhart's aim is that his students learn to *create*. He states that his curriculum is designed to maximize the problems of creativity, which call on control of material and freedom of aesthetic expression and judgment for their solution.

Mr. Gebhart, therefore, does not just present his students with instructions on how to manipulate material, but includes emphasis on ways of seeing and thinking. The lesson on figure sculpting includes recognition of existing art work, and appreciation of the motion and shape of the students' own bodies to suggest ideas. He encouraged them to plan before working, and to consider how to solve problems that might arise during the conceptualization and construction of their pieces. His creative problem-solving reflects the *creative design* orientation of the Bauhaus. (Eisner, 1972).

Watching him work with Valerie, I saw him attempt to increase her control over her material by explaining what to do and giving her the opportunity to practice. He increased her freedom by presenting an alternate way of viewing broken limbs—as an asset rather than a liability. Over the next few days, I noticed a marked difference in the quality of Valerie's figure, and the self-confidence with which she talked about it.

I saw a relationship here, of greater control yielding greater freedom, and vice versa. This is an example of Dewey's notion of the continuous interchange of intellectual and aesthetic components of an educative experience.

The curriculum also reflects Deweyan philosophy in its sequential organization of subject matter. Students progress from concern with technical skill to increased attention to artistic vision and judgments, both within each lesson and during the semester. Each lesson starts with a lecture-demonstration in which Mr. Gebhart presents "the watch-points, the crucial steps." As students gain control of a technique, say slab, he encourages them to select more complex applications—perhaps a mug first, then a mask with raised, textured and cut out areas, a square box with a fitted lid, a model of their shoe. The final project allows students, after they have gained control of basic skills, the freedom to create and solve an artistic problem (which also gives them an opportunity to show control over all that they have learned).

The comments and actions of a number of students suggested that Mr. Gebhart's curriculum actually affected them. Sue's reasoning concerning her glaze revealed aesthetic judgment and appreciation. When I asked two students if one made a coil pot smaller by using smaller coils, they raised their eyes and shook their heads (as if incredulous at my ignorance) and ably showed me how to score and smooth a coil, supporting and pushing in on the pot. Although there was no consensus on a specific assignment, sixteen students noted that their most creative project involved freedom to make judgments about it: for example, "You had to think about what kind of creature you wanted to make, and what kind of details there'd be on it."

On the questionnaire I administered, a majority of students (over thirteen) said they usually are challenged to use their minds, express themselves freely, are encouraged to make independent decisions, discuss their work with others, put a lot of effort into the course, enjoy it, and find it worthwhile. Only six students indicated that they found the course especially easy, and only three indicated that they were not learning as much here as in other courses.

In contrast, students in several art classes offered by four other teachers in the school district did not show such *consistent* technical control, aesthetic and intellectual thought, or involvement in their work. For example, in one class of twenty-eight students, the seven I questioned told me that the most important thing they had learned was to use their imagination and not to copy, but their work was relatively simple and trite. By comparison, Mr. Gebhart's curriculum weaves a fabric of control and freedom such that the students are doing much more than learning terminology and techniques. His students truly seem to be developing a creative eye.

> . . . esthetic cannot be sharply marked off from intellectual experience since the latter must bear an esthetic stamp to be itself complete.
> JOHN DEWEY [1934]

Teaching   The structure of Mr. Gebhart's teaching strategy is an outgrowth of the curriculum. To help students gain initial control over the material, he introduces lessons with teacher-centered lecture-demonstrations. He is center stage, and the student audience is in his control as they gather round the center table.

Freedom, as it concerns the structure of Mr. Gebhart's methodology, is manifested in the individualized instruction that occurs most of the time (95% of the time I observed). Mr. Gebhart believes that the teacher should "plug in to where the students are at" (Dewey's notion of the experience of the student as the starting point for education), and that "everyone has aesthetic values and the ability to create in varying degrees." Thus his task is to "make contact with each child daily" so that he might know what that student needs, and assist or push him or her towards success, given that particular student's capacities.

Structurally, Mr. Gebhart's methodology consists first of control—giving students technical and cognitive tools in whole-class instruction. Next, freedom to discover how to use these tools is assisted by individual instruction. However, there is another aspect to his methodology, in which there is not such a clear-cut delineation of control and freedom. This aspect is the psychological level, the manner in which he relates to his students.

Mr. Gebhart states, "I'm critical of my students. I expect everyone to participate and reach closure . . . At this age level they don't reach closure. You need to structure the lesson or they won't do it." Hence, within the flexibility of individualized instruction, Mr. Gebhart's role is that of constantly exerting control, pushing students, challenging them to seriously attack the creative problems at hand. Like Dewey, he recognizes that the growth he is trying to develop in his students involves their being able to use intelligence to overcome difficulties. He does not aim to solve his students' problems for them. "Learning involves frustration. If you eliminate frustration, you eliminate learning."

Sometimes Mr. Gebhart extends support and simplifies a problem into small steps, as with Valerie, who had paralyzed herself with anxiety about her piece. Sometimes, as with Sue, a minor suggestion and acknowledgement of her decision making is all that is needed. Several times I observed Mr. Gebhart say firmly, "I want you to . . ." to students who were not progressing, and demand a specific amount or type of work.

He is not a soft teacher, not easy. But he is sensitive. Within Mr. Gebhart's control there is a sense of freedom because he attempts to lead out each student to whom he is or might be. There is not a mold that all the students have to fit. He puts effort into knowing each student's personality, style and needs. This shows in his appropriately differential treatment of the students. Penny could be set to work with a few words. Fred needed to be touched gently; a less aware teacher might simply have told him to put water on his clay, or to remove his parka.

Thus, in terms of the structure and philosophy of his lessons, Mr. Gebhart's methodology can be seen as the relationship of separable elements of control and freedom. In terms of the psychology of his methodology, Mr. Gebhart exerts control to give students the freedom to discover their capacities. This allows them to develop their own manifestation of control. Like Dewey, he wishes to educate his students for ongoing growth, "To get them ready to begin learning on their own. To get them to see how to create their own problems to solve."

> *Come to the edge, he said.*
> *They said: We are afraid.*
> *Come to the edge, he said.*
> *They came.*
> *He pushed them . . . and they flew.*

GUILLAUME APOLLINAIRE (1981)

Reflections

I have presented a glimpse of Mr. Gebhart's ceramics class, and examined the "delicate balance of control and freedom" in his classroom management, curriculum and methodology. It was not appropriate to come up with a simple statement of the way in which Mr. Gebhart weaves these elements together. For one thing, "control" and "freedom" demand slightly different definitions, and are in slightly different relationship in each of the three contexts considered. Also, Mr. Gebhart does not simply look for a middle ground on the continuum between control and freedom. A characteristic of his class is the dynamic interplay of these elements, whether it be in classroom management, curriculum or methodology. The nature of this interplay, as well as Mr. Gebhart's philosophy, give his teaching a strong Deweyan flavor.

Three things remain to be discussed. These are considerations for the improvement of Mr. Gebhart's class, the influence of Mr. Gebhart's personal style on his teaching, and the implications of my observations.

Considerations for Improvement   In the *Analysis* I focus on the strengths of Mr. Gebhart's teaching because I view him as the most effective middle school art teacher in this school district. (I spent about thirty hours in the classes of all five middle school art teachers in the district.) His dynamic interweaving of control and freedom results in students with relatively sophisticated technical and critical skills in ceramics. There are, however, some areas in which consideration for improvement seems to be in order.

The ritualistic pseudo-challenge to authority occupies ten to fifteen minutes of class time daily. This ritual may not be necessary. Perhaps if an aide were used to manage organizational matters, Mr. Gebhart's time could more efficiently be used for teaching.

Individualized instruction necessarily limits time for whole-class lecture, idea sharing, and student critiques of one another's work. Mr. Gebhart has expressed frustration at the resultant loss of momentum and productive competition, and at having to repeat things thirty times. At this age (eleven to fourteen) children are exceptionally critical of their art work (Lowenfeld, 1947). Some (Pasto, 1965; Burt, 1921) have referred to this stage of artistic development as "deterioration" or "repression." Regular aesthetic appraisal sessions might solve some of the problems mentioned in this paragraph.

From my observations I tentatively assumed that the students had considerable freedom in their choice of projects. Yet, in response to the question, "What, if anything, would you change in this class," nine out of twenty-six students stated their desire for more independent choice of work. Perhaps this is a reaction to Mr. Gebhart's insistence that they all learn the basic techniques, indication that there is little choice, or that they have not developed the ability to make that choice.

The students ranked this class virtually equal with Physical Education as the most enjoyable of six school subjects. However, they ranked it sixth in importance and fifth in amount learned. This does not reflect the philosophy Mr. Gebhart attempts to convey in his curriculum. Perhaps these ratings reflect the school system's and community's views. An attempt should be made to alter this attitude. It may be that the students perceive the freedom as indicative of low importance of art. Perhaps expanded work time, homework, or a tidier room would correct this impression. The low ranking of learning may reflect the lack of quantifiable measures of accomplishment in art.

These observations and ideas for change are suggested to improve what is already a comparatively effective class.

Personal Characteristics   In the *Analysis* I examined what Mr. Gebhart does, and its effect in the classroom and on the students. I was struck by how much his personality seemed to shape his classroom management, curriculum and methodology. Five personality characteristics were salient. These are respect for and sensitivity to students, humor, and his tendency to be strong-minded and reflective.

Mr. Gebhart's respect for his students is evident in his tendency to ask them questions and to consider their responses. This is noticeable in his aesthetic criticism and implementation of assertive discipline. This is in contrast to some teachers who, according to the school psychologist, interpret the program as a punishment system. Mr. Gebhart also gives students the freedom to set up displays of student art work in the school. The "hidden curriculum" here is that their thoughts and feelings are of worth, and that they are responsible.

Mr. Gebhart's sensitivity to students has already been mentioned. Small actions, such as his interchange with Fred, eye contact, a hand on a shoulder, or asides to students about their lives show that he is attentive to their emotional as well as educational needs. He has the capacity to enter into a relationship with each student, recognizing that "other" in what, on occasion, seems to approach (in Martin Buber's terms) an I-Thou relationship.

Mr. Gebhart's humor is not that of a stand-up comic. Rather, he has a subtle whimsy with which he defuses potentially tense situations, as in the bear-hug incident. On another occasion, a student responded to an order with: "What are you? A dictator?" Without hesitation, Mr. Gebhart responded, "I'm training to be one. This is the first step." The girl laughed and the problem was solved.

What Mr. Gebhart says goes, whether it is an instruction for attaching an armature or an order to clean off a table. Mr. Gebhart is clearly the authority in his classroom. He has strong opinions, and can be demanding at times. This complements his gentler side, establishing a natural union of freedom and control in his manner.

His reflectiveness facilitates this union. He notes that he constantly evaluates and revises his teaching. For example, he is currently rethinking how he might more efficiently teach technique without losing aesthetic appreciation in another class. His final assignment for the ceramics class was "an experiment" based on a conversation he and I had about creativity. Mr. Gebhart was anxious for feedback from me, and regrets the paucity of inservice training. He is flexible, and concerned with his growth as well as his students'.

Mr. Gebhart's personality colors how he creates his "delicate balance between control and freedom." The quality of his personal interaction with students and his considerable technical skill enable him to be an effective teacher. It is clear that *personal* qualities are an integral part of his effectiveness. What is the implication of this for teacher training?

Implications   The implication is obvious. Theory and technique are only part of the story. Personality characteristics of the teacher are the electricity that brings the parts to life and determines the quality and ultimate effectiveness of teaching.

Obvious though this may be, current selection and training of education students and teachers pays pitifully little attention to personal development. Test scores and statements of purpose get students into schools of education, where they are filled with theory and techniques, and sent out to teach. If they are lucky, inservice training will equip them with more theories and techniques.

It has always struck me as odd that therapists are required to develop personal sensitivity as a tool to help people expand their vistas, while teachers are not. Both are involved in the professional task of educating people, of facilitating others' development. We remember our most influential teachers not primarily by what they did, but by who they were, how they inspired us. It is their qualities as human beings that profoundly affect us.

The idea of considering personal sensitivity as an important quality of the educator, and in the students' education, is not new. In high Athenian culture (around 400 B.C.) the ultimate aim of education was not simply acquisition of knowledge, but development of self-understanding and sensitivity. This concept of *paidea* has become lost. Myopic educators, unaware of important factors that do indeed shape educational experience, give students partial education and wonder at the low correlation between particular techniques and student achievement.

It is time for educators of educators to formally recognize what has been known since Ancient Greece, what is known intuitively by every student, and what is neglected in our present educational system. The skill of a good teacher does not consist of only theory and technique. Sensitivity to self and others, ability to communicate, and to inspire students are essential. If we are to have meaningful education, schools of education and inservice training programs must acknowledge this and radically alter their curriculums to recognize and cultivate teachers' internal educative qualities.

Bibliography

Appolinaire, Guillaume. In Marilyn Ferguson, *The Aquarian Conspiracy*. Los Angeles: J. P. Tarcher, 1981.

Buber, Martin. *I and Thou*. Walter Kaufmann (trans). New York: Charles Scribner's Sons, 1970.

Dewey, John. *Art as Experience*. New York: G. P. Putnam's Sons, 1934.

—————. *Experience and Education*. New York: Macmillan Publishing Company, 1938.

Eisner, Elliot. *Educating Artistic Vision*. New York: Macmillan Publishing Company, 1972.

Hesse, Herman. *Beneath the Wheel*. Michael Roloff (trans). New York: Farrar, Straus and Giroux, 1968.

Langer, Susanne. *Problems of Art*. New York: Charles Scribner's Sons, 1957.

Lowenfeld, Viktor. *The Nature of Creative Activity*. New York: Harcourt, Brace & World, 1947.

An Educational Psychologist Goes to Medical School*

STUART J. COHEN

The case is that of a 38 year-old male, employed as an associate professor in the Department of Internal Medicine at Indiana University School of Medicine. On August 13, 1980, he was admitted to the medical center as a sophomore with no evidence of a prior history of biochemistry, microbiology, gross anatomy, histology or physiology. His chief complaint was the inability to understand how physicians make decisions about patient care when managing chronic illnesses.

A review of symptoms and his previous medical history were unremarkable. Since his insatiable medical curiosity is of recent onset, the recommended treatment is tincture of time. If his symptoms persist, consider obtaining a serum porcelain and a referral to psychiatry.

Today I will share with you my experience as a sophomore medical student. Since the meanings I derived are dependent upon my background and the context in which the events were experienced, I will start by describing my background and my reasons for attending medical school.

I am an educational psychologist and serve as Director of Research in Education for the Department of Medicine. My undergraduate and masters degrees are in experimental psychology and my doctorate is in educational psychology. My science background is limited to having taken a few biology and chemistry courses in college along with neurology and physiological psychology in graduate school. I spent nine years as a faculty member and later Department Chairman of an educational psychology department prior to coming to Indiana four years ago. Among my current responsibilities, I am an associate director for training of a National Diabetes Research and Training Center. In that role, I am involved in the training and evaluation of a variety of health professionals including house staff in internal medicine. My observation of physicians' interactions with their diabetes patients has led me to question how physicians are trained to care for patients with chronic diseases.

* Supported in part by the W. K. Kellogg Foundation

Two years ago I was fortunate in being awarded a W. K. Kellogg National Fellowship. Each of the 40 Kellogg Fellows, representing a variety of disciplines, was given a three-year award including a 25 percent released-time commitment from his or her own institution. One of the goals of my fellowship was to try to understand how physicians make decisions when caring for patients with chronic diseases. Towards that end, I proposed obtaining first-hand experience in the socialization process by which physicians are trained into making clinical decisions. The tolerance of the faculty at the medical school along with the blessings of the Chairman of Medicine afforded me that opportunity of attending medical school as a sophomore student. I chose the sophomore year because it was the introduction to clinical medicine and involved the first contact with patients.

I wanted to examine three major issues. My first concern was how students learned to make decisions about patient care. Included in this area were questions such as how were students socialized in problem identification. Related topics were how they learned to interact with patients and to view preventive and chronic diseases management.

My second major concern focused on the impact of stress on the social and personal development of medical students. How did they cope with the demands of an overwhelming schedule. How did they learn to handle experiences with death, disfigurement and incurable diseases? A third and lower priority issue was evaluating the quality of instruction. I considered evaluating the quality of instruction of lesser concern because I didn't feel that such evaluation required full-time attendance in medical school. Despite my protestations, the director of the sophomore course, with whom I had worked previously, assumed that evaluating instruction was an occupational hazard of an educational psychologist and, therefore, would be a major function of my attendance.

On August 13, I left my office for the five minute walk to the large, turn-of-the-century lecture hall in the Emerson Building. I was clutching a white lined notepad, a copy of the locally produced medical history taking text and *Physical Diagnosis— The History and Examination of the Patient* by Prior and Silberstein (1977). The discomfort in the pit of my stomach increased as I entered a cavernous lecture hall and selected a seat which I hoped would be unobtrusively located in the middle of the left side, a third of the way into the auditorium. The hall began to fill with the 270 students who, despite the mixture of ages, shapes and colors, seemed to be unified by their cut-off jeans and t-shirts. Only the lecturers and I wore neckties. So much for anonymity!

We were welcomed to the sophomore year and told how sophomore medicine was the bridge between the basic sciences and the clinical clerkships. Lectures would be organized by organ systems with emphasis on the pathophysiology of diseases and their clinical manifestations. Since one of the goals of the course was to gain proficiency in obtaining a medical history and performing a physical examination, we were handed a card (See lists p. 326 and p. 327) detailing a history on one side (Outline of the Medical History), and the physical on the other (Outline of the Physical Examination) and told to memorize it. The rest of the orientation lecture was devoted to a review of the syllabus, the procedures for purchasing medical instruments, and a discussion of grades and dress code when serving on the hospital wards.

OUTLINE OF THE MEDICAL HISTORY

I. Identifying Data:
   1. Date history taken
   2. Biographical data (patient's name, age, sex, race, marital status, occupation, hospital record number)
   3. Source and reliability of history

II. CHIEF COMPLAINT: briefly state the patient's primary complaint and indicate the duration

III. PRESENT ILLNESS: listen, ask open ended questions and finally specific questions to develope description of all symtpoms in chronologic order considering:
   1. Onset—date and manner (gradual, sudden)
   2. Characteristics—quality, severity, location, temporal relationships (continuous, intermittent). aggravating and relieving factors, and associated symptoms
   3. Course (continuous, progressive, intermittent)
   4. Effects of therapy

IV. PAST MEDICAL HISTORY:
   1. General health and vigor
   2. Growth, development and childhood diseases
   3. Immunizations
   4. Previous illnesses, injuries and surgical procedures
   5. Allergies and Drug Reactions
   6. Toxins and/or Industrial Exposures
   7. Recent medications

V. REVIEW OF SYSTEMS:
   1. General: change in weight, weakness, fatigue, fever, state of nutrition, heat or cold intolerance
   2. Skin: eruptions, pruritus, color, texture, hair or nail changes, bleeding or bruising tendency
   3. Head: headaches, dizziness, trauma
   4. Eyes: vision, diplopia, pain, inflammation
   5. Ears: hearing, pain, discharge, tinnitus, vertigo
   6. Nose and sinuses: epistaxis, obstruction, discharge, pain
   7. Mouth and throat: dental hygiene, bleeding gums, sore tongue or throat, hoarseness
   8. Neck: pain, stiffness, thyroid or lymph node enlargement
   9. Breasts: pain, masses, discharge
   10. Respiratory: chest pain, cough, sputum, hemoptysis, wheezing, asthma, dyspnea, tuberculosis or exposure, recent chest x-ray
   11. Cardiovascular: substernal pain or distress, exertional or nocturnal dyspnea, orthopnea, edema, palpitations, hypertension, heart murmurs, recent electrocardiogram
   12. Gastrointestinal: appetite, dysphagia, nausea, vomiting, food intolerances, eructation, hematemesis, heartburn, abdominal pain (discomfort, aching, colic), jaundice, character of stools (form, color), melena, constipation, diarrhea, change in bowel habits, hemorrhoids

13. Genitourinary:
    a. Urinary—urgency, frequency, dysuria, hematuria, color of urine, difficulty starting the stream, incontinence, polyuria, nocturia, renal colic, stones or infection, recent urinalysis
    b. Female—menstrual history, post menopausal bleeding, vaginal discharge, contraceptive history, obstetrical history, sexual history
    c. Male—scrotal pain or masses, hernias, genital lesions, discharge, sexual history
14. Back and extremities: joint pain, stiffness, swelling, limitation of motion, varicosities, edema, redness, phlebitis, claudication, cramps, resting pain
15. Neuropsychiatric system: syncope, alterations of consciousness, convulsions, mentation, memory disorders, orientation, tremor, incoordination, paresthesias, weakness, paralyses, affect, thought processes, behavior, degree of anxiety

VI. PERSONAL HISTORY:
    1. Personality patterns or adjustment, behavior during interview
    2. Marital and sexual history
    3. Social and economic status, education, occupation, standard of living, environment
    4. Habits sleep, diet, exercise, drugs, tobacco, alcohol (note recent changes)

VII. FAMILY HISTORY:
    1. Summary of age and state of health or cause of death for immediate family
    2. Family members with similar symptoms and signs
    3. Presence of infections or chronic disease in family members

OUTLINE OF THE PHYSICAL EXAMINATION*

I. Vital Signs: temperature, pulse, respiratory rate, blood pressure, weight, height (orthostatic hypotension).
II. General Appearance: apparent health, developmental status, apparent physiologic age, habitus, nutrition, gross deformities, mental state and behavior, facies, posture.
III. Skin: color, texture, moisture turgor, eruptions, abnormalities of hair and nails (pallor, pigmentaiton, cyanosis, clubbing, edema, spider nevi, petechiae).
IV. Head: symmetry, deformities of cranium, face and scalp (tenderness. bruits).
V. Eyes: visual acuity, visual fields, extraocular movements, conjunctiva, sclera, cornea, pupils including size, shape, equality and reaction, ophthalmoscopic exam including lens, media, disks, retinal vessels and macula, tonometry (pallor, jaundice, proptosis, ptosis).
VI. Ears: hearing acuity, auricles, canals, tympanic membranes (mastoid tenderness, discharge).

---

* Selected abnormalities in parentheses

VII. Nose: nasal mucosa and passages, septum, turbinates, transillumination of sinuses (tenderness over sinuses).

VIII. Mouth and Throat: breath, lips, buccal mucosa, salivary glands, gingiva, teeth, tongue, palate, tonsils, posterior pharynx, voice.

IX. Neck: range of motion, thyroid, trachea, lymph nodes, carotid pulses (venous distention, abnormal arterial and venous pulsations, bruits, tracheal deviation).

X. Lymph Nodes: cervical, supraclavicular, axillary, epitrochlear and inguinal nodes (enlargement, consistency, tenderness and mobility).

XI. Breasts: symmetry (nodules including size, consistency, tenderness, mobility, dimpling, nipple charge and lymph nodes).

XII. Thorax and Lungs: configuration, symmetry, expansion, type of respiration, excursion of diaphragms, fremitus, resonance, breath sounds (retraction, labored breathing, prolonged expiration, cough, sputum, adventitious sounds including rales, wheezes, rhonchi and rubs).

XIII. Cardiovascular System: precordial activity, apical impulse, size, rate, rhythm, heart sounds, abdominal aorta, peripheral arterial pulses including carotid, radial, femoral, posterior tibial and dorsalis pedis pulsations (thrills, murmurs, friction rubs, bruits, central venous distention, abnormal venous pulsations).

XIV. Abdomen: contour, bowel sounds, abdominal wall tone, palpable organs, including liver, spleen, kidney, bladder and uterus, liver span (scars, dilated veins, tenderness, rigidity, masses, distention, ascites, pulsations, bruits).

XV. Back and Extremities: symmetry, range of motion, joints, peripheral arterial pulses, color, temperature, (curvatures of spine, costovertebral angle tenderness, joint deformities, muscle tenderness, edema, ulcers, varicosities).

XVI. Neurologic Exam: cranial nerves, station, gait, coordination sensory and motor systems muscle stretch reflexes (paresthesias, weakness, muscle atrophy, fasiculations. spasticity, abnormal reflexes. tremors).

XVII. Genitalia:
1. Female: external genitalia, vagina, cervix, cytology smear, fundus, adnexae, rectovaginal exam (vaginal discharge, tenderness).
2. Male: penis, scrotal contents (urethral discharge, hernias).

XVIII. Rectum: sphincter tone, prostate, test for occult blood (hemorrhoids, fissures, masses).

XIX. Personality Status: affect, intellectual functions, thought content and processes in motor behavior. Consider patterns of adjustment, ability to handle life crises and behavior during the interview.

SUMMARY AND INTERPRETATION

1. Summary of Important Data
2. Initial Problem List
3. Initial Management Plans (for each problem)
4. Signature and Date of Completion

From that day in August until the fourth of May, 1981, I attended medical school. Although I was officially an auditor, I participated in most of the activities including sitting for a number of exams. Mornings were spent attending lectures. Classes were large since there is only one medical school in the state. A lecture could contain as many as 270 students, although the usual number was much less.

With the exception of one half-day free, afternoons were devoted to either physical diagnosis, specialty physical diagnosis (e.g., ophthalmology), pathology or radiology. Physical diagnosis was usually taught by fellows or junior faculty to groups of four or five students. My preceptor was an endocrinology fellow. We saw patients on the wards of a medical center hospital which served the indigent of Indianapolis and Marion County. Each week we would learn about and often practice on each other some component of the physical exam. We would then go on the wards and, with the aid of the preceptor, examine patients who presented interesting or pertinent findings. Weekly we had to conduct a history and physical on a new patient, and submit the results in writing to our preceptor for evaluation.

The specialty physical diagnosis rotations ranged from activities such as using life-like simulators for learning venepuncture and spinal taps, to conducting a gynecologic examination on paid instructors. The radiology rotation involved learning how to read various x-rays and scans. The radiologist would first describe a particular technique and then break the class of thirty into small groups of five stations where radiographs and a set of questions would be located. Each group attempted to answer the questions which would be reviewed at the end of class. Few students knew one another. This was not surprising considering the size of the medical school class and the fact that many students had spent their first year learning the basic sciences at any one of eight regional campuses located around the state. The first question involved an x-ray of a chest into which a catheter had been inserted. The question asked to name the point of insertion of the catheter and the location of the tip. With no previous instruction in anatomy, I was unwilling to venture a guess. Perhaps, because of my age or the fact that I wore a suit, the eyes of my fellow students all turned to me awaiting my answer. I did not know the correct answer but was sure that it wasn't "into the shoulder and out the chest." I pleaded ignorance but did concur with the suggestion that the catheter was probably inserted into the subclavian vein and the tip was located in the superior vena cava.

I did not attend the pathology lab since I needed at least two afternoons a week to perform many of my regular tasks for which I still had responsibility. Fortunately, my colleagues and secretary assumed many of my chores, so that 80 percent of my weekly effort could be devoted to medical school.

Throughout the year I did not seek to identify my special status, nor did I make an effort to conceal my identity to the other medical students or to instructors. If questions arose, I would explain that I was a special student and, although a faculty member in the Department of Medicine, I was auditing sophomore medicine, since my training was in educational psychology.

In order to more systematically examine my experiences, I usually kept two sets of notes. To the right of the margin, I would record at breakneck speed the information being disseminated. To the left of the margin, I would comment on unusual events or remarks. For example, I noted that it wasn't until the middle of October that any lecturer mentioned the cost of a diagnostic test. I also tallied the sexist remarks made by lecturers. In my sample, sexist remarks were made approximately four times more frequently by surgeons than internists.

Occasionally, I would record students' comments and my own thoughts. An example of the former occurred after a particularly confusing radiology class. One of my classmates lamented that radiology was pushing her to a career in psychiatry. I often recorded my own reaction to exasperating events. When lecturers were attempting to establish their claim in the *Guiness Book of World Records* with new standards for speeded speech and showing slides in microseconds, I would record the appropirate expletive while resisting the urge to leap up on the stage, grab the microphone and yell "STOP."

While my system for observation might appall an ethnographer, it seemed manageable and appropriate for my objectives. I wanted to devote most of my energy toward experiencing life as a medical student. I did not want to consume my time detailing the experiences of myself or others.

On a typical day, I arrived at my office about a half hour before class to review my checklist of tasks for the day and to leave messages asking favors of my secretary and colleagues. I attended lectures from eight until noon. I then returned to my office in three to five minutes, depending on the weather and the status of my running injuries. While eating lunch, I would attempt to complete a diabetes center task before dashing off for my one o'clock rotation. Most of the rotations finished by five and I returned to the office for an hour or so before going home. Evenings were usually spent studying. Ideally, I would try to stay ahead of the next day's assignment. More realistically, I was usually trying to keep from falling further behind. Depending on my state of fatigue, I studied from four to six hours a night. Contributing to my burden was my limited background in the basic sciences. In case anybody questions the necessity of the basic sciences for medical training, let me offer myself as evidence of their merit. The deficits that I faced were overwhelming. I would often sit with an anatomy and a physiology book opened in order to begin to comprehend the medical text assignments. Medical texts like *Harrison's Principles of Internal Medicine* (1980), while difficult for most sophomore students, were impossible for me. Little did I dream that I would do such things as spend an entire weekend trying to teach myself steroid biochemistry, and at the end of Sunday night, realize that I probably knew little more than I did when I began.

As you can sense, my year was challenging and frequently frustrating, but not without its rewards. I hope I am able to convey some of the richness and intensity of my experience. To aid in their interpretation, I will focus upon three major issues that prompted my quest:

1. How are medical students taught to think about patient care?
2. What stresses occur when going to medical school and what, if anything, is done to help students cope with them?
3. What is the quality of instruction in lectures, laboratories and at the bedside? What might be done to remedy deficiencies?

Thinking About Patient Care   Medical students in general, and sophomores in particular, are not taught to think. Sophomores have profound deficits in their medical knowledge. The faculty attempts to remedy this situation by inundating students with information. It was not uncommon for me to record a dozen pages of single-spaced notes during a fifty minute lecture. Knowledge-level questions predominate on examinations. Thus, success in medical school often depends not on your ability to reason, but on your willingness to memorize vast amounts of information. Cramming inordinately large bits of information that are rarely meaningfully organized produces a steep forgetting curve. Therefore, it is not surprising that a month or two after studying a particular area, students could be paralyzed by a remark such as "Cohen, what are the names and functions of the ligaments of the knee?"

The heavy emphasis in lectures and examinations on rote learning coupled with little effort to help students synthesize the material or allow them adequate time to do so is a source of numerous conflicts. The fundamental fact of life facing any sophomore medical student is that you cannot become a competent physician if you are not advanced to your junior year. Consequently, any test, quiz or experience which might jeopardize the chances of becoming a junior medical student is viewed as career-threatening. On the other hand, faculty believe that the goal of medical school is to train people to become competent physicians. Predicated upon this assumption, instructors assume that the more a student is taught about a particular organ or disease—usually the one in which the subspecialist has expertise—the more competent a physician he or she will become. Thus, the goals of the students and those of the faculty are frequently incongruent. Faculty are distressed by questions about "what's going to be covered" on an examination, whereas students are frustrated by lectures which overwhelm them with information. Like most novices, students have difficulty seeing the forest for the trees. Since medical students are bright, they employ a number of survival strategies such as purchasing class notes, relying upon upper-classmen for information about examinations, and cutting classes which they do not feel aid in preparing for tests. Unquestionably, these survival strategies displease faculty and help promote adversarial relationships.

Just as thinking becomes subordinate to memorizing, so too the focus on patient care is transmuted into an emphasis on diseases and physiological measures. "Let's examine the diabetic with a BUN of 70" would not sound like an unusual comment a preceptor would make to students on the wards. What would sound strange would be a statement such as "Let's talk to the man with diabetes whose kidney failure is jeopardizing his career and his family relationships." While it is undeniably important that students learn to diagnose and manage diseases, it is also imperative that they not lose sight of the human context in which their knowledge and skill will be applied.

One of the most important goals of sophomore medicine is to become proficient in obtaining a patient history and performing a physical examination. Many students are uncomfortable about their initial interactions with patients. While they usually take pride in wearing white jackets and carrying a stethoscope, they are often anxious about asking intimate quesitons and fumbling throught a physical, especially with patients who are dying or are in severe pain. If students question why they should obtain a sexual history for a patient who is hospitalized for a fractured leg, they are told that they have to learn to ask these questions so they may as well start now. Students soon discover that they are there not to serve the patients, but rather it is the patients who are there to serve them as teaching material. Even though I understood this problem, I was astounded at how readily I became desensitized to viewing patients as instruments for my own learning. My reaction to performing a physical examination on an obese woman who had had a radical mastectomy of her left breast was not one of revulsion or of pity, but rather one of relief—relief at how easy her cardiac examination would be since I could readily listen to her heart. Thus, even if you are sensitized to the potential influence of your environment, it can still affect you.

Just how profoundly we can be shaped by our environment became evident to me as a result of another experience with a patient. Most sophomore students are given two or more hours to complete a history and physical before they even begin to record and present their findings. Medical residents and faculty attendings take much less time. In fact, the time taken usually decreases as one increases in training. Students are taught to ask open-ended questions and to encourage the patients to talk; yet, these behaviors decrease as physicians advance in training. I now understand why this is so. One day my preceptor for physical diagnosis told us that we were each to perform a history and physical examination on a patient we had not seen before and to write up the results and turn them in within an hour. I was in trouble! My write-ups required at least twenty minutes and usually much longer, since I often had to look up the medical terminology for parts of the anatomy. I would have at most forty minutes for conducting the history and physical. Under the time pressure, I controlled the entire conversation restricting the patient's discussions only to what I considered as the pertinent aspects of the chief complaint. Needless to say, my write-up was incomplete and included numerous abbreviations.

I was astounded by my behavior with that patient. Intensive training in interpersonal communications would not have altered how I behaved. Given the time constraint, I dispensed with small talk, barely retaining a semblance of amenity. I omitted my usual preventive medicine questions about seat-belt usage and my chronic disease questions such as problems in complying with his therapeutic regimen. The focus of my thinking was on the patient's physical signs and symptoms and the physiological reasons for them.

In light of my experience, it is easy to see how medical students learn to think about problems (i.e., diagnoses) in the context of biomedical measures. This same context is then applied for selecting and evaluating the merit of a therapeutic intervention. While biomedical measures are essential, they are not the only criteria for identifying problems and for choosing among alternative therapeutic strategies or solutions.

The focus of sophomore medicine is on the pathophysiology of disease rather than disease management. Discussions about therapy were infrequent, but were always limited to the biomedical consequences of therapy. I once attempted to discuss the importance of psychosocial criteria for evaluating medical therapies. My hematology/oncology small-group section had a lecture on the management of lymphomas. The instructor used five-year survival as a criterion for choosing among therapies. He stated that treatments were equivalent if they did not produce differences in five-year survival. I suggested that "quality of life" measures would aid decision-making. I mentioned research done at the National Cancer Institute which used both survival and quality of life measures such as return to social functioning in deciding between irradiation and amputation in the management of soft tissue sarcomas. The results indicated that the five-year survivals were equivalent. However, the quality of life measures showed considerable differences. When the tumor was located below the knee, those with surgical management suffered greater depression and longer delay in returning to work than those who had radiologic management. The results were quite different when the tumor was located in the thigh. People who had a hemipelvectomy, an obviously disfiguring operation, actually had less depression and earlier return to social function that did those treated by radiation. Evidently, irradiation destroyed sexual function, which people viewed as far more disfiguring than the loss of a limb. I am sad to report that after presenting my argument for the consideration of psychosocial values, my discourse was viewed by both the instructor and many of my peers as a needless diversion. I was probably preventing the coverage of material that would be included on an examination.

In summary, medical students are not taught to think about patient care. They learn to memorize organ systems and disease states.

Stress and Personal Development   As I mentioned previously, one of my major concerns was understanding the stresses experienced by medical students and determining what, if anything, is done to help them cope with them. Two important conflicts seemed inevitable. The first was the conflict between a student's desire to be an autonomous and productive member of society and the enforced dependence of medical school requirements and procedures. The second dilemma arose from the desire for personal growth and the expression of social needs which often conflicted with academic demands.

The majority of sophomore students are in their mid-twenties with most having gone directly from college to medical school. They are preparing for an autonomous career that is greatly respected by our society. What they experience as students is a state of prolonged dependency. There are no electives in the sophomore year. Your life is preplanned and your only choice is the degree of compulsivity for following assignments.

On the wards, you are at the bottom of the totem pole. Everyone else knows more about medicine and hospital procedure than you do. When the staff physician says "Jump," your only thought is "How high." While many senior students, house staff and attending physicians try to help you through the "rites of passage," some house staff and attendants delight in flaunting their medical knowledge and publicly interrogating students. For example, one lecturer used an electric pointer to select students to answer his questions. Although I did not approve of this technique as a motivational strategy, it did serve to demonstrate that my sympathetic nervous system was functioning. I found such public interrogation particularly frustrating. I knew that I could embarrass most inquisitors with quesitons about diabetic microangiopathy that they would be unable to answer. However, retribution was unthinkable. Learning to cope with prolonged dependency was a necessary survival skill and one that seemed to decrease with age.

The time and energy required for becoming a physician are enormous and have impact upon personal development and social relationships. Spending eight hours in class and having four to six hours of reading each night leaves little time for social activity. Academic demands strain existing relationships and retard the development of new ones. Prototypical of this conflict was the request by students to cancel one of the daily neurology quizzes in order to watch Indiana in the finals of the National Collegiate Athletic Association basketball game. The quiz was retained with the response "Physicians have to make difficult decisions."

While most students struggle to become physicians, little is done to help them in the coping process. They are never asked to explore their feelings about expe-

riences such as seeing a cadaver, caring for a dying patient, examining a quadri-
plegic or seeing children with severe congenital anomalies. Although counseling
services are available for those experiencing adjustment problems, the stigma
attached to seeking help precludes countless others who are wrestling with doubts
about their career decision and themselves.

Social maturity and an interest in health policies that would affect their lives and
those of their patients were uncommon among the medical students. Admittedly,
most twenty-three-year-olds are neither worldly nor politically aware. Yet, I was
surprised at the embarrassed giggling and boorish behavior of some of these future
physicians. I had the opportunity of examining the final grades for sophomore
medicine. I looked up the results of the handful of students who I thought characterized my ideal of a physician as being caring, thoughtful, sagacious and socially
mature. I also examined the scores of those who, because of their immaturity or
lack of perspective, I had difficulty envisioning as physicians. Not surprisingly, there
was little relationship between my evaluations and their grades. In sum, the message
seems to be that the medical school takes some responsibility for a student's intellectual growth but that personal growth is a student's own responsibility.

Quality of Instruction   It had been eleven years since I completed my doctoral
studies. In the interim, I attended lectures and workshops at professional meetings
and at grand rounds in medicine. Nevertheless, being thrust again into the role of
a student took considerable readjustment. My survival as a sophomore was, in large
part, dependent on the quality of instruction I received. In evaluating that instruction I will focus first on what was taught and then on how it was taught.

As I mentioned previously, the emphasis was on the pathophysiology of disease.
Little is said about therapy and even less said about psychosocial factors such as
stress. While there are studies which indicate that stress can elevate both blood
pressure (Shapiro et al., 1977) and blood glucose (Hauser and Pollets, 1979), nontraditional issues were ignored or downplayed. During a break after a lecture on
asthma, I asked the pulmonary professor if stress could be a precipitating factor in
an asthmatic attack. His response implied that my question was equivalent to an
inquiry about the moon's being made of green cheese.

Another content area virtually ignored was preventive medicine. Little attention
was given to either the risk factors for diseases or their prevention. Even in the
discussions of chronic disease, in which the prevention of complications from the
disease is the ideal, the management of complications received equal if not greater
emphasis than did their prevention. When presenting our history and physical
exams, I was the only student who ever inquired if the patient wore a seat belt.
Trauma, much of which is caused by automobile accidents, is the major cause of
death for people under the age of forty. Therefore, inquiring about seat belt usage
assesses a major risk factor. Similarly, I was the only person to ask patients with
chronic diseases about problems encountered in trying to comply with their medical
regimens. Since many patients misunderstand their regimens and/or believe that
the benefits of adherence do not outweigh the barriers, I would ask patients what
medicine they took, for what purpose, how frequently, what mnemonic they used
to remember to take their medication, and whether they thought the medicine was
helping them. Needless to say, I was the only sophomore medical student to ask
patients these questions. While preventive medicine and patient compliance are real

health issues, they were overlooked in the training of physicians at our medical school.

Perhaps the most persistent and pervasive issue for sophomore medicine was information overload. Students were inundated with material during lectures. They had lengthy and difficult reading assignments, and precious little time for synthesizing the material. While the gap between a sophomore medical student and a competent physician is great, it cannot be closed appreciably in just one year. The failure to remember this fact is a source of frustration for both faculty and students.

Most of the sections of the sophomore course were organized by organ systems. They were taught by subspecialists who were so far advanced in their level of expertise that they forget what it was like to be a novice. We know from the work of deGroot (1965) and Chase and Simon (1973) that experts and novices do not share the same world-view. Experts may keep in mind fewer pieces of information than novices because experts are able to sort through, analyze and rule out what is irrelevant. Unfortunately, novices don't see the big picture which would allow them to be more efficient as well as accurate. This inefficiency is clearly seen when a medical student takes two hours to do a history and physical, which a competent physician could do better in much less time.

Since sophomore medical students do not think like competent physicians or even like residents or senior medical students (Mazzuca and Cohen, 1981), their current level of development needs to be considered more carefully in the design and implementation of the curriculum. As an aid to this process, a feedback system for instructors and course directors needs to be developed. While there are hundreds of student evaluation systems extant, the one I am proposing is intended to reduce some of the information overload by highlighting "fat" in the curriculum. A sample of sophomore students and a sample of the generalist faculty should evaluate every examination question (i.e., de facto objectives) by responding to the following two questions: First, does this question ask something that is important for a practicing physician to know? Second, does this question ask something that is important for a sophomore medical student to know? A response of "yes" to the first and "no" to the second question can identify information which may be deferred to a later stage of training.

In the remainder of my time I would like to focus on the "how" of instruction and examine the three basic instructional settings: lectures, skill laboratories and bedside instruction. In all three areas the quality of the instruction varied from superlative to abominable, depending on the section leader and the instructors. On the whole the instruction was as good if not better than the instruction I had as a graduate student taking courses in departments of psychology and of education. Much of quality of the sophomore course was due to dedicated section heads and the conscientiousness of the course director. Certainly, there were weaknesses. While my discussion will be devoted to what can be done to remedy deficiencies, I don't wish to leave the impression that all was not well.

The lectures and sections which received the highest praise from the students were well-organized within and across lectures and, without spoon-feeding, geared material appropriately for sophomores. Those lectures and sections which caused the most complaints were those in which the lectures were poorly organized and contained too much information. Often an excessive number of slides were used, including many which were overly detailed. In addition, coordination among lecturers was lacking. Illustrative of the worst was one excruciating pathology lecture. The first forty-five minutes were spent in elaborate descriptions without visuals. In the last five minutes, the lecturer flashed about twenty slides to illustrate everything previously described.

Lecturers need to focus on the three or four of the most important points and to organize their material so that these points are highlighted and integrated. Educational psychologists and other medical educators can help in this effort. There were occasions in which I was almost willing to establish arbitrary rules for the number of slides that could be shown per hour or the maximum amount of information that could be put on a slide. However, I trust that the advice of an educational consultant would suffice to arrange the details in each particular setting.

Related to the problem of information overload is the dilemma students face in trying to synthesize and apply what they learn. One technique ideally suited to facilitate synthesis is the use of patient vignettes or small case simulations of patient problems. These devices take advantage of literature on adult learning which suggests that adults learn the most and retain best when learning about problems that they actually face or will face. As most basic science professors will attest, medical students are more highly motivated when the information about which they are learning is related to patients. Appropriately designed patient management problems with feedback can help students draw upon their knowledge to select, analyze and evaluate information (Elstein et al., 1978). In essence, it helps them begin to think like clinicians and not become repositories of clinical information, devoid of the context in which it will be applied.

Some of the principles that apply for improving lectures also apply for the teaching of psychomotor skills such as conducting a physical or reading a CAT scan. Again, the quality of instruction varied dramatically. The best skill instruction had the following components. First, a framework was given for the skills being taught. Second, the appropriate behavior was demonstrated either live or by an audiovisual model. Third, students practiced the skill, and lastly, they were given feedback on their practice. Unfortunately, these conditions were not always met. For examples, the ophthalmology instruction consisted primarily of lectures about opthalmology with numerous slides of retinopathy and little opportunity for practicing fundoscopic examinations. You may not be too surprised to know that when I first practiced using an ophthalmoscope on a family member, I mangaged to hold it incorrectly and blinded myself. Fortunately, that did not happen at the bedside.

Patient simulators can be invaluable for learning motor skills. Most medical schools have some patient simulators such as Ginny for the gynecologic exam, or Resusci-Anni for learning cardio-pulmonary resuscitation. These devices can enhance diagnostic acumen and minimize awkwardness when working with patients.

There are a number of excellent audio-visual aids available for learning how to perform a physical examination. The videocassettes produced by Dr. Barbara Bates at Rochester are very helpful in learning the components of the physical examination and how to orchestrate them. My only criticism of such models is that the patients are healthy models, examined under ideal conditions. For example, in one of Dr. Bates' tapes, the cardiac examination was conducted on a normal weight man. My first cardiac exam was performed on an obese lady. In turning her on her left side, as is done on the film in order to hear mitral sounds more clearly, her right breast whipped across her chest, knocking my stethoscope off her body. Such mishaps are never illustrated by the audio-visual models.

A common problem students have in skill acquisition is smoothly coordinating separately learned skills. One helpful technique for facilitating fluid performance is covert rehearsal. I taught my peers to rehearse mentally their physical examination prior to performing them. A potential disadvantage of covert rehearsal is the possiblity of becoming locked into a routine. I usually did the cardiac exam after completing the pulmonary exam and before assessing the abdomen. One day I had just begun the cardiac exam and was listening very carefully for a low grade murmur, when I heard a loud thump, ka-thump, thump, ka-thump. No, it was not a grade six murmur. Postural drainage of the lungs was initiated on a patient in the next bed. Obviously, I needed to proceed with something which didn't require the use of a stethoscope.

The most effective of the special diagnostic skills labs was given by the Department of Obstetrics and Gynecology. Performing a pelvic examination can be anxiety-provoking for many medical students. After a week of lectures, reading, films and frank discussions about obstetrics and gynecology, students in groups of four attended the special diagnosis instruction. We again reviewed the films of breast and pelvic examinations with an instructor present to answer any questions. The instructor explained that with her guidance we would conduct an exam on women who were trained to help medical students perform a thorough pelvic exam without hurting or embarrassing a patient. The patient-instructors praised appropriate performance and helped students improve deficiencies. This unit of instruction was universally acclaimed.

The last type of instruction takes place at the bedside. Since medicine is an apprenticeship system, bedside learning can be very valuable. At the same time, bedside instruction can be difficult for patients. Our physical diagnosis preceptor was able to ensure the dignity of the patient while at the same time making bedside instruction worthwhile. Our preceptor would ask a patient the following, "I have some young doctors with me who would like to have the opportunity of listening to your heart if you are feeling up to it." In this way the patient was not compelled to comply, and recognized that he or she would be contributing to the education of inexperienced physicians. Some preceptors showed little respect for the rights or the feelings of patients by holding discussion, replete with medical terminology, in front of the patient. All too often, I watched patients become anxious during these discussions. Since bedside teaching serves as an important model of patient care, it is imperative that preceptors respect patients' feelings.

Bedside instruction also demonstrated the influence of expectations on perception. Our preceptor would ask us to examine a particular system, and then compare our findings with his. I was amazed at the number of times I would, having missed a murmur or other physical finding the first time, notice it upon reexamination. It appears that the more you know about medicine, the more you expect a certain constellation of findings. These expectations help sharpen detection. Thus, while the patient may afford the same information to an expert and a novice, the latter is less likely to ascertain it.

In summary, both the content and process of instruction can be improved. Information overload may be reduced if test questions are evaluated in terms of their relevance for sophomore medical students and for practicing physicians. Skill learning can be improved if students are given an adequte context, models, practice and feedback. Bedside instruction provides the opportunity for modeling thorough, thoughtful and humane patient care which will be imprinted upon fledgling physicians.

Postscript I would like to make a final point about my own "rites of passage." Although I had been on the faculty of my medical school for two and a half years, it was only after my year as a medical student that I was encouraged by the faculty to round with them when they saw patients. Also, for the first time, I was asked to discuss the medical curriculum at the meeting of the Executive Committee of the Department of Medicine. In addition, I was invited by the Dean to serve on the School of Medicine Education Committee. While these events could be coincidental, attending medical school may have been the precipitating factor.

References

Chase, W. G., Simon, H. A. Perception in chess. *Cognitive Psychology, 4,* 55–81, 1973.

de Groot, A. D. *Thought and choice in chess.* The Hague: Mouton, 1965.

Elstein, A. S., Shulman, L. S., Sprafka, S. A. *Medical problem solving: An analysis of clinical reasoning.* Cambridge, Harvard University Press, 1978.

Hauser, S. T., Pollets, D. Psychological aspects of diabetes mellitus: A critical review. *Diabetes Care 2(2),* 227–232, 1979.

Isselbacher, K. J., Adams, R. D., Braunwald, E. (Eds.). *Harrison's Principles of Internal Medicine.* New York: McGraw Hill, 1980.

Mazzuca, S. A., Cohen, S. J., Clark, C. M., Jr. Assessing clinical knowledge across five years of medical training. *Journal of Medical Education, 56,* 83–90, 1981.

Prior, J. A., Silberstein, J. S. *Physical diagnosis: The history and examination of the patient.* St. Louis: The C. V. Mosby Company, 1977.

Shapiro, A. P., Schwartz, G. E., Ferguson, D. C. E. Behavioral methods in the treatment of hypertension: A review of their clinical status. *Annals of Internal Medicine, 86,* 626–636, 1977.

13

A Criticism of an
Educational Criticism

"Believing, with Max Weber, that man is an animal suspended in webs of significance, he himself has spun, I take culture to be those webs, and the analysis of it to be therefore not an experimental science in search of law but an interpretative one in search of meaning."

CLIFFORD GEERTZ

The preceding chapter presented five examples of educational criticism. Each of the criticisms was undertaken by an individual who was interested in finding out about some aspect of the educational world. In Barone's case, it was an art program that had been cited as outstanding. What was it that made this program excellent? What dynamics were involved? In Porro's case, it was an effort to understand the qualities of educational life for a low-achieving sophomore student. What was the school experience like for the student? How did he cope with the demands his teachers made upon him? In Catford's case, it was an effort to understand how a middle school art teacher functioned in the classroom. What was it that he taught? How did he engage middle school students in art? What was the quality of his classroom? In Marshall's case, the classroom was devoted to the teaching of the social studies at the high school level. And for Cohen the object of study was the second year of medical school as seen through the eyes of an educational psychologist attempting to understand how medical education proceeded for students a year into the program.

The Features of Meta-Criticism

This chapter is intended to examine one of those educational criticisms; to do what might be called a *meta criticism,* a criticism of criticism. How does the author proceed? What is the nature of the language that is used? What metaphors and categories are provided in the piece? What insights does it yield? How does the author support her conclusions? How does the reader "verify" what he or she has read? These and other questions can be asked of an educational criticism. Which particular questions are appropriate to raise will, of course, depend upon the kind of criticism that has been written. In the field of literature there are schools of criticism: structuralism, Marxist criticism, the Chicago school of criticism, formalist criticism, as well as others. In educational inquiry, literary writing in general and educational criticism in particular are neither old enough nor sufficiently well-developed to have such schools. In any case, my own interests are not in the development of schools of critics or criticism, but in the creation of material that will help educators improve the quality of educational life for students and teachers. Educational criticism is a general approach to that end. Thus the aim of this chapter is understand how one such critic went about her task.

Before going into Porro's criticism, the piece that will be used for this critique, there are a few observations worth making about all of the criticisms found in the previous chapter. First, each critic has his or her own style of writing. In each criticism a sense of the author's voice comes through. Unlike many of the conventional research articles published in educational research journals where format is standardized—consisting of the problem, subjects, method, findings, discussion, and implications—or schema for writing are prescribed, and unlike the attempts to neutralize the writer behind the words one reads, educational critics exploit their own sensibilities and their own unique perceptions. They invoke their own voices to give life to their writing. Each educational criticism has its own signature. What one seeks in educational criticism is not fealty to a common format for voiceless writing, but quite the opposite. One hopes that the refined vision and skilled writing that marks the competent educational critic will be exploited in order to share with the reader that fact that a person, not an impersonal machine, wrote that criticism.

It is often claimed that such an approach to research or evaluation is ineluctably subjective and therefore undependable. I wonder how one can ever have objectivity without a subject who perceives and interprets the meaning of the object of attention. Furthermore, the efforts to eliminate through convention the subjectivities that must inevitably enter into any interpretation of reality seem to be less candid than an upfront recognition that a human being is providing his or her best effort to describe, interpret, and to appraise some aspect of the world in which he or she lives.

The credibility of the observations, whether written or verbal, will be a function of the coherence they possess and the extent to which the observations are helpful in illuminating the situations they seek to describe.

The statement that credibility can be a function of applying the observations of an educational critic to situations like, but not identical to, those described by the critic is intended to convey the notion that the believability of a set of observations is influenced by the congruence between what a critic has to say and what one remembers about situations relevant to those the critic has described. Our memory is replete with images of school practice. These images are data for "verifying" the critics' observations. Hence, when a critic observes that "schools have few soft surfaces," we can check out this observation by reflecting on our past. The images of the past, even though they contain many features of classrooms and schools, might still leave us unaware of this particular quality of classrooms and schools until critics' observations bring them to consciousness. In short, through the criticism we, in a sense, learn what we already "knew" but were not aware of.

A second feature or characteristic of the criticisms in the previous chapter is that all were created without the use of a formalized observation schedule. None of the critics who visited the classroom came armed with a standardized check-off form upon which frequencies were recorded. What each critic did bring to the class or school was an immensely more complex set of categories and criteria, schema and frameworks, sensibilities and interests. These, however, were already in the critics' cortex. They approached the task of observation with a highly differentiated network that enabled them to "capture" and interpret what they had experienced. The task was not only one of picking up cues—or perhaps more aptly, clues—but also of construing patterns that ultimately made for a coherent view of the situation they studied.

The achievement of such coherence and the formation of such patterns hardly ever occurs independent of writing or speaking. It is virtually impossible to carry the kind of intellectual load that these criticisms represent as fully formed bodies of meaning outside of their inscription in words or images of one kind or another. The act of expression is not simply a means for conveying what is already formed; it is also a means for shaping thought and for editing it once expressed. The act of writing and speaking is, I am saying, a necessary means for construing the patterns we might dimly perceive in the situations we observe. In each of the foregoing criticisms a creative construction of the situation observed occurred. What we read is no mere recording of events, no chronology of facts, no photographic replica of a scene. It is a human construction.

A third feature of the foregoing criticisms is that each displays a different way of organizing the writing. Several individuals in the field of education have urged me to provide a standard format for writing (as well as for observing) classrooms. I have resisted. I do not wish to circumscribe the ways in which critics go about their work. There is but one ultimate criterion for appraising a critic's work: Does it shed light on the situation it describes, interprets, and evaluates? *How* a critic chooses to achieve that end is, in principle, an open issue. In Porro's case poetry is used, with three views of schooling conceptualized, and telling quotations from the major actors of the drama inserted into the body of the text. Catford uses photographs, Barone a literary style of writing, and so forth.

There are, to be sure, complexities engendered when such openness in approach is not only permitted but encouraged. Different forms of reporting (*reporting* is much too passive a word) need to be read using somewhat different kinds of skills. The demands upon the reader are likely to be more diverse and at times more complex where personal style is given an opportunity to flourish. Yet, that price is one I believe worth paying if it helps us free ourselves from a standardized and often homogenized approach to the study of educational practice. In the foregoing criticisms each writer made his or her own thumbprint quite visible. Let's look at how one critic did this.

Playing the School System—A Meta-Criticism

"Playing the School System: The Low Achiever's Game." Consider first the title. Porro creates through this title a foretaste of the message that the piece as a whole is designed to convey. The metaphor is that schooling is a game, that there are players who play the game, and that there are differences in the way in which different classes of students engage in that game. In this case the focus in on the low achiever.

What she has done in the title is not only to create an image of schooling as an "unreal" type of sport, but by implication she reveals that the rules are different for students who achieve differently within the school.

What immediately follows the game metaphor is a very serious verse. What comes to the reader after the game-playing metaphor has been read is a statement about the meaning of adolescence, about the relationship of adolescence to death, about spending one's life waiting to be in another place and in another space. The verse is enigmatic; it provides a tone that creates a sense of intrigue and suspense. The title with its game-playing metaphor is polar to the couplet that follows it.

In the first paragraph of the criticism Porro provides some facts and creates some credibility. She tells us that this criticism was part of her graduate study at Stanford University; she informs us what the general aim of her work was; she conveys to us the fact that she is not a newcomer to schools, having worked for nine years as an elementary school teacher. She creates a sense of trust by her candor in explaining that despite her nine years of classroom experience the public high school was "new territory" for her. This candid acknowledgement of the newness of the setting reassures us that we are dealing with neither a cocky professor nor a self-assured graduate student intent on telling us how American schools should be run. The tone is one of appropriate modesty.

Paragraph 2 takes us immediately into the setting. We are introduced to the low-achieving student Porro is to shadow. What she does not yet say, but might have said, is that her task was to attend school with Bob for a full two-week period: five full days, a week's break and then another five-day period, and that Bob had volunteered to be shadowed. This information, had it been included, would have filled out for the reader the procedures used in her work.

Porro's first paragraph not only takes us into the scene without preamble, but she also tells us something about the sense of affiliation that these low-achieving students have, and about the camaraderie they share. She comments about these and then supports her observations by using a direct quotation from one of the students. The quotation adds credibility to her initial impression.

The third paragraph introduces a paradox. The school labels these students low achieving, apparently expecting that their days in school are numbered—*terminal students,* they are called. But Porro points out that while these students' academic achievement is low, they are remarkably higher achievers in meeting their own goals. Their own goals, "to get through high school by doing the least amount of academic work necessary to pass their courses", are attained with skill and intelligence.

In the third paragraph, not only is the paradox of contrasting views of achievement noted, but Porro also creates a picture of Bob. She describes his appearance, his comportment, and reveals an obvious admiration for him. We get the sense—perhaps too early—that Porro's view of Bob is a sympathetic one. We also get the sense—perhaps too strong—that Porro is not altogether sympathetic with the system that Bob has so skillfully learned to play.

As the reader comes to the first subhead of Porro's educational criticism, the reader is provided a focus. Porro's criticism will attend to educational life outside of the classroom before moving into the classroom. Her first sentence, "High school is played in two main areas—outside on the patios and lawns, and inside the classrooms," divides the world of schooling neatly for us. First, we will find out about life on the lawns and patios, then we will proceed into the classrooms.

What comes through in Paragraph 5 is impressive categorization of the ways in which students decide which classes to cut. Porro's presentation of these options conveys to us several things. First, they indicate that the students who are regarded as low achievers are sufficiently analytic to consider complex alternatives; they are not really "dumb," despite the implicit labels the school seems to assign to them. Second, we are impressed that Porro has sufficient rapport to be able to secure such a candid response from adolescents asked such a direct question. Candor and the array of options they provide give the reader a sense that what he or she is reading is not shallow but that it is displaying an important aspect of schooling for a significant group of high school students. The boxed inserts that Porro includes throughtout the piece encapsulate observations that support the message that the body of the criticism is designed to convey.

In Paragraph 6, the section on the outside game is concluded with a message about the irrationality, from the student's perspective, of the school's rules about suspension. "It's stupid to kick you out of school when you do something wrong. We don't want to be here anyway . . ." Their logic seems impeccable. To support their observation, Porro shows us how Bob was able to convert suspension into a socially and financially productive experience. Such observations have credibility and give the reader pause: Is there a better way to think about how schools might handle "behavior problems"?

The overall message of the criticism thus far is to point up the paradox that exists between the students' needs and aims and those of the school. We are shown how the low-achieving students cope with expectations to which they do not subscribe. It points out the sophistication of their reasoning—at least with respect to their own goals—and how bureaucratized rules can, upon inspection, appear less than fully rational.

In doing this, Porro has also authenticated her observation by sharing with us intimacies that the students shared with her. We consequently get the sense that we are learning things that are not self-evident. Porro thus seems to be a credible observer and writer. But so far we have not entered the classroom.

Paragraph 7 brings us inside the school. We now move into the insider's game.

In Paragraphs 7, 8, and 9, Porro gives us factual information regarding the number and duration of classes teachers teach (seven periods of 45 minutes each) and conveys the sense of impersonality that generally pervades these classes. Evidence is provided: "A map of Vietnam, a poster of San Francisco, and a picture of a girl dancing." We get the feeling that the environment is shaped by a collection of ad hoc choices regarding room-decoration.

In contrast to this impersonality, the students provide the color and vitality that makes a place a school. What one grasps through Porro's seemingly casual observation is the camaraderie and informality, the spirit of sharing that the students create.

The urgency of getting through the school day is conveyed in Paragraph 10 by the direct quotation of students asking how much time is left. Porro creates a view of school from the perspective of the student. She uses direct quotations to do so.

Now it is clear that her view of the students' view of schooling is, in the last analysis, *her* perception of the students' views. Perception is selective, and Porro has chosen. Yet, the criticism that she has written is replete with quotations, observations of subtle but significant events (the sharing of lollipops, candy bars, etc.) that creates credibility. We get the sense that what she describes has occurred and what she concludes is supported by the situations as they unfold. Her conclusions are structurally corroborated even though one might argue that another educational critic might have focused on other phenomena. That may very well be the case, but even if it were, it would not diminish the quality of what Porro has written.

In Paragraph 12, the subhead "Pretend School" moves the reader into the classroom. This subhead, like the title of the educational criticism itself, embodies some of the major points Porro wishes to make. *Pretending* is a form of play, and playing is what Porro has told us a part of schooling is about.

The primary message of Paragraphs 12, 13, 14, and 15 is one that adumbrates one of the major conclusions of the study: There is between teacher and student a tacit agreement to help each other to get through the school day without severely imposing on each other's comfort. In developing this idea, Porro does not, for example, cast Mr. Arnold in the guise of a "bad guy" and the student as the "good guy." Mr. Arnold, she tells us, *is* a good story-teller; he *is* entertaining. He seems to understand what students will be receptive to and what "they'll turn off to."

Yet, he does not seem to challenge the low-achieving student with whom he works. He takes their status as a given, almost as a natural condition. Even though we might be sympathetic to him and to his needs as a teacher, we cannot help wondering whether his accommodating attitude is contributing to their underachieving status. Is this an example of a self-fulfilling prophecy? His readiness to accommodate to the students' apparent lackadaisical attitude might be one of the factors that contributes to the situation with which he must deal.

In Paragraph 19 we move into Bob's general science class. The same syndrome found in Mr. Arnold's mythology class continues. Mr. Cleary, Bob's general science teacher, does not expect much from the low-achieving student, and these students do not violate his expectations. He expects little and they provide little.

What happens here, however, from the standpoint of educational criticism is fortuitous. A visiting scholar who happens to be a professor of Science Education visits Mr. Cleary's class, observing and talking with Porro about his observations. What is significant here is that not only are the teacher's expectations low, but that Mr. Cleary pays inadequate attention to the substantive aspect of the biological content that he is attempting to teach. He focuses upon marginal material, and engages in excursions into anecdotes but does not infuse these excursions with material designed to illuminate the central scientific points that are really important. In a word, the teacher consumes the students' time with diversion *from,* rather than *into* the scientific substance of biology.

At this point it is necessary to comment about the ability to critique curriculum content in the context of instruction. It is not likely that Porro, who for nine years was an elementary school teacher, would have been able to appreciate what Dr. Pinot was able to see. He is a specialist in science education. She is not. His knowledge of biology and science education allows him to observe and appreciate what others who do not have expertise are unlikely to see. Educational critics who do not possess subject-matter expertise are not in a good position to appraise or even to recognize the content being taught (or not being taught) in a given field. To be able to critique competently the substantive aspects of biology, one needs biological expertise. To be able to appraise the quality of an art course, one needs expertise in art, and so forth.

Yet, not to have such expertise *does not* mean that no useful criticism can be developed. Porro's own critique of secondary school classes, a level of practice in schooling with which she is unfamiliar as a teacher and a subject matter that she does not know as an expert, did not prohibit her from making extremely interesting analyses of what she was able to see. As I have already indicated, we should expect that different critics will see somewhat different situations in any complex array of occurrences. Dr. Pinot might very well have missed what Porro did not.

In Paragraphs 21 and 22 we learn why, from Mr. Cleary's point of view, he proceeds the way he does in his teaching. Mr. Cleary believes that his students' major problem is one of low self-esteem, and he wants to help the students improve the way in which they regard themselves. Mr. Cleary has good intentions. Yet, he seems unable to recognize that positive self-esteem is also related to the reality of human performance; one is not likely to feel positive about one's self if one continually fails at the tasks one undertakes. Mr. Cleary's science teaching is not likely to help students deal effectively with scientific ideas.

In Paragraphs 24, 25, and 26 we are introduced to another of Bob's teachers, Ms. Morton. Here we find, as is true of the other examples of *pretend* school, a continuation of low expectations and small intellectual stimulation. Health instruction is supplied through the use of films.

Films can be an extremely useful vehicle for stimulating thinking and generating interesting discussion and debate. A film can act as a catalyst to help teachers reach ambitious educational goals. But in Bob's Health class we get the sense that films are used to provide a kind of babysitting service.

Films, videotapes, and slides were used in over half of the Health classes Porro attended. The level of use might give us some concern, but what is really troublesome is the way in which they are used. No discussion, debate, or analyses follow their use. Instead, lectures are given, worksheets are completed. In spite of the fact that the teenage consumption of alcohol is a problem of national scope and that is certainly present at Claremont High, no attention is paid to it in Health.

As one reads about these "pretend classes," something like a somnambulistic episode seems to be present: sleepwalkers pass each other in the night, but never touch each other either intellectually or emotionally. There is compliance with routine. The class goes through the motions of educational activity but is not really engaged in an educational process. What one begins to appreciate is that one is observing a kind of machine that works; relatively few problems are created, and those that are, are handled through routine procedures. No one in the descriptions and analyses we have read thus far comes off as having an evil intent or a malicious motive.

High Standards Classrooms signals a shift in category. When we come upon it, we wonder what it means. We don't wonder for long, because in Paragraph 27 Porro tells us that the high standards classroom refers to those in which teachers base their curriculum and instruction on what they believe students *should* be able to do, especially if these pupils are to succeed in college. Claremont High is a school in a community that has high expectations for its students. Many of its students go on to attend highly selective colleges and universities. Hence, preparation for such colleges and universities is an important educational priority within the community.

How does Bob fare in the high standards classroom in which he is enrolled? Not well—but not disastrously either. Although Bob received a negative evaluation on the midterm, he received a B on the Abnormal Psychology unit afterward. Porro's message: Bob has developed a keen understanding of what he must do to get through with a minimum of effort.

Porro's comments on the high standards classroom are focused more upon the general character of curriculum and instruction than on Bob's particular reaction to this particular classroom. What we might infer is that Mr. Kelly, the teacher of the class, treats the class according to his image of what a college course would demand. Mr. Kelly's classes are largely lectures, and lectures delivered slowly enough for students to copy the material delivered verbatim. They are expected to take notes. They are expected to pass the test in order to pass the course. They are expected to perform in a manner consistent with college student behavior. What does Porro make of this? Why is this not "real school," her title of the section that follows? Probably because even though the teachers have high standards, the students were, apparently—we are not really told and the situation is not clearly described—not genuinely engaged in this course. They are complying with the teacher's expectations because Mr. Kelly is hard to out-fox; he "knows how kids are these days." Even, it seems, in classrooms with high achieving students, something significantly less than "real" education can occur. It is clear here, also, that Porro has a particular image of what counts as real education and that she uses this image to evaluate what she has seen.

It is sometimes suggested that educational critics should state their edu-cational values at the outset. The purpose behind such recommendations is to inform the reader of educational criticism what values the critic holds so that the reader can understand how a classroom or school was inter-preted and appraised by that critic. Although I have no objection to such an approach to writing, there are certain difficulties that it creates. First, how many of us can state our educational philosophies in a paragraph or two, or even in a few pages? Can we lay out in writing as a preamble to a piece of educational criticism a statement of what we believe? Will such a statement be so general that it will be difficult to use to anticipate how we would regard particular events and practices? Second, are not the varieties of educational excellence multiple, and is it not likely that no one state-ment of philosophy will do justice to all that we might value? I take a leaf from the fine arts. I value different painters and different styles and paint-ings for different reasons. I like the paintings of de Chirico because of the surrealistic mood he creates through the juxtaposition of objects one nor-mally would not expect to see together—giant artichokes and clocks, trains, and sleeping figures. I find his use of color offbeat, yet well-related to the scenes he paints. Yet I like Monet for very different reasons: his color is scintillating. It vibrates with life and creates an atmospheric quality that is opposite to what de Chirico creates. I like the work of Barnett New-man for still other reasons. Is there a single philosophy of art that could be used to enable others to predict that I prefer the work of Mark Rothko to that of Morris Louis, and that I am less enthusiastic about the work of Paul Jenkins? I doubt it.

We learn of Porro's educational values *through* her educational criti-cism. Her philosophic preamble, as it were, is embedded in the statements she makes about Bob, Mr. Kelly, Mr. Arnold, and the other teachers and places she comments upon. I believe that in "real life" it is precisely in this way we come to learn about someone's values. We do not ask for a pream-ble, a manifesto, a statement "up front"; and even if we were to get one of these, it would be used only to see if the actual behavior of the individual were consistent with what he or she told us. It is in the ongoing course of human activity that the operational values an individual or institution pos-sesses are expressed.

Yet, after having said that, I should repeat what I said earlier: I have no objection to someone who wishes to put up front a statement of his or her educational values. What I do object to is the requirement or expectation that those values be so stated.

Paragraph 31 brings us to the third type of class that Porro has identified as operating within Claremont High—"real school." She tells us what she means by "real school," but her use of a phrase "a fair amount of time" is not particluarly helpful. In real classes teachers gear their instruction to the academic level at which their students are actually at; they use a mode of instruction that is tutorial or personal in character; and they provide activities for students that require them to be active rather than passive receivers of lectures delivered by the teacher. These characteristics are provided by Porro up front; they define the categories of classes about which she will write and are helpful to us as we read on.

Porro then attempts to differentiate between what it is that makes for real school as contrasted with pretend schoool. In this she is identifying characteristics on the basis of her observations and using those characteristics to create categories. These categories could then, in turn, be used to determine if other schools have similar types of classes. Do such classes exist at the middle and elementary school levels? What are the effects of such classes on students? Do students of different abilites react differently to such classes? And so forth. The formulation of concepts—images that differentiate one type of object or situation from another—are the necessary conditions for theory development. The categories that Porro formulates for Claremont High could have an important use in the study of classes in other schools.

What, in addition to the features that have already been described, accounts for "real school"? For Ms. Golden's math class it is that she sets clear expectations for students: they know what is expected. But Porro is quick to point out that high expectations are not enough. Another factor, and perhaps a crucial one, is that Ms. Golden cares about the students with whom she works. Porro makes this clear in her description of how Ms. Golden talks to students, but lest there be any doubt, she quotes Bob as saying in response to why he produces for Ms. Golden, "because she deserves it." What Porro does is to support her interpretation and conclusion with direct quotations from students. She quotes their casual comments and gives examples to back up what she has said. All such devices help increase the credibility of her criticism. In addition, she is analytic about her observations: "I realize that she [Ms. Golden] treated them individually and related to them on two different levels—as their teacher and as their friend." She then proceeds to give the reader some examples filled with quotations to illustrate that distinction.

Woodworking II is the second class, according to Porro, that is an example of "real school." (I wonder if two out of six classes of real school is about average for high school classes.) Here the feature that makes for real school is the active engagement of students in the work to be done. Wood-working, like auto shop and similar courses, does often require a level of active physical participation that is absent from many academic classes. Also contributing to the real-school character of Woodworking II is the respect students have for Mr. Teicher: "He's a real good teacher. He knows what he's doing." "He can fix anything. And he jokes around a lot." The image we get is of a teacher who is in control, competent enough to have an informal relationship with his students and able to demonstrate his skills to students. He thus gains their respect.

For my taste, this segment of Porro's criticism is thin. The entire class is treated in two paragraphs, and even though the description of this class is only a part of a larger body of work, it would have been helpful to have found out more about how this class functions, what students are learning and why. Classes such as woodworking, auto shop, cooking, and even the fine arts are often regarded as frills, as courses with no intellectual challenge. Yet these classes might be among the most "real," the most *educationally* meaningful in which the student is enrolled.

Paragraph 40 brings us to the final section of Porro's educational criticism. Here she devotes her attention to the question "What does it mean?" Porro's talk here is one of further interpretation and evaluation. What does she have to say?

In this section she distills observations that were made only partially in the previous material. Bob, though not working, is winning the game he is playing—he is passing his courses and in doing so is not exceptional. Although the school is running smoothly, much of what goes on is not particularly educational for students. There are some significant educational experiences provided by some teachers in some classes, but these, according to Porro, are due to the exceptional quality of the teachers as people, not because of the structure of the school. In the end, it seems, Porro focuses upon the particularity of individual teachers to account for the quality of what occurs at Claremont High.

I wonder if such an interpretation is a bit too glib. Does it not underestimate the potential influence of the educational leadership in the school? Cannot the principal and department heads, the community, and the other teachers have a significant role to play in moving the school from one place on an educational continuum to another? Is Porro not inadvertently assigning too much responsibility to the individual teacher and, by implication, suggesting that educational leadership can account for too little? Or am I perhaps expecting too much from context and leadership? I don't think so. If we can *only* rely upon the talents, sensibilities, and commitments of individual teachers, the quality of education will be determined largely at the point of selection. Who chooses to go into teaching as a career, and who schools of education permit to enter the profession, will be the crucial decision points. Clearly, those decision points are important. The optimization of whatever it is that a faculty possesses in the way of talent, sensibility, and commitment is what educational leadership is about. Porro says precious little about this aspect of Claremont High.

Porro explains Bob's behavior on the basis of his inadequate academic skills, the paucity of really effective teachers he encounters at Claremont, and that for him school is boring. She speculates that being able to choose is something that is very important to Bob and that school is compulsory— Bob has not chosen and he "doesn't like to be told what to do, so he rebels in any way he can." Yet he does work for Ms. Golden and for Mr. Teicher. He is willing to work in classes where the teacher cares, where they have clear expectations, and where they are skilled. The ability to choose as an explanation for Bob's behavior goes only so far.

Near the end of her criticism in Paragraphs 46 and 47, Porro speculates further that Bob's actions may be modeled after the game that she believes to be ubiquitous among adults he observes. "It is quite possible," Porro observes, "that Bob is mimicking the approach to life we unconsciously teach through our actions. How do we play the game?" Here she is commenting not simply about Bob's behavior but upon our culture. She then proceeds to relate our preoccupation with making the grade, with success, and—perhaps most of all—putting off real life today for a brighter day tomorrow—to the kind of game that Bob has learned to play so well. Her comments begin to develop a more general theme, a theme that runs deeper than the analysis of the high school experience. One senses in this section of the criticism a focus on the meaning of life. We are reminded of the verse with which Porro opened the piece:

> *So much of adolescence is an ill-defined dying,*
> *an intolerable waiting*
> *a longing for another place and time,*
> *another condition.*

We have returned, it seems, to the place from which we began. She provides both a description of the state of affairs and an interpretation. Through Becker's excerpt from *The Denial of Death,* she urges us to pursue a meaningful life.

Porro concludes her educational criticism on a note of optimism. There are times during the school day when Bob rises to the occasion of real school. What is needed is to go beyond the warm friendly relations between student and teacher, which are so generally a part of life at Claremont, to something that is genuinely educational. While Porro has shed significant light upon the experience of schooling for Bob and his peers, she does not say much about how the construction of such an environment can occur. But having a better fix on the problem is, after all, one of the important steps toward the achievement of such an end.

The Uses of Educational Criticism

The importance of attending to the processes of schooling as a basis for understanding what needs change is made clear by the foregoing educational criticism. Most efforts to evaluate schooling focus upon the students' level of performance. Tests are administered to students—often having little relevance to what they had been taught—then performance is noted, and a mean derived from individual scores and recommendations is made, often for improving test performance. The National Commission on Educational Excellence recommends a longer school year and more time in the classroom. Is more time in the classroom appropriate for Bob and his peers? Why—it escapes my logic—if schools are huge mediocrities for students, should the situation for them be educationally better if they spend more time there? Some critics of schooling in America recommend more discipline and more homework, harder courses and more clearcut expectations. Only the latter of these appears to have any relationship to performance and satisfaction with school in Bob's case.

Part of the reason why such nostrums are suggested is that they are comparatively easy to administer and to monitor. It is easy to find out if the school district is requiring its students to be in school 215 days in contrast to, say, 180. It is not so easy to determine if it is helping to improve the teaching practices of its professional staff. The kind of problems that exist for the students at Claremont High will not be resolved by requiring more homework, more time in school, or higher standards. Such prescriptions are much too superficial and much too simplistic. What needs significant change, and what is excellent in schools, can be known best when an observer is able to see the way in which schooling unfolds. It requires the connoisseurship to see what is significant but subtle, to appreciate the muted cues, the achievements that do not shout from the quarterdeck, the hidden lessons that are being taught. Porro's own sensitivity and, I am sure, her nine years of experience as a teacher enabled her to hear the melodies of the classroom played in the lower registers of experience. Her writing skills and her conceptual ability made it possible for her to share those observations with us.

Can we generalize from what she has to say? Not in a formal sense. Claremont is not a random selection. Her observations were not random. There is no statistical measure of the reliability either of her observations or her interpretations. Yet we can learn in at least two ways about things that can help us in the future. First, we can use what she has disclosed to reflect on our own experience. To what extent does what she has written square with what we already know? Second, we can, if we are able, go to Claremont High and see for ourselves if what she has said is occurring. For the vast majority of readers, this is an undertaking that will not be possible. What is possible? There are other schools like Claremont High.

Do they also display the features Porro has described? What her educational criticism provides is a guide to the perception of schools that we can have access to in our own locale. She provides a guide for making our own perception more perceptive and efficient. What is generalized from the study are anticipatory schemata for the perception of other situations. This method and these consequences are the stuff of ordinary life. It is how, in fact, we most characteristically go about dealing with the world. All we are doing here is refining such processes, bringing them to consciousness, and using them to understand and improve the processes of schooling.

14

A "Final" Word

I'd rather learn from one bird how to sing than teach ten thousand stars how not to dance

E. E. CUMMINGS

give sketchy outline

On the preceding pages I have tried to adumbrate views of education and to identify some of the problems and issues that pervade educational planning and evaluation. In many respects, the ideas I have expressed fly in the face of those that now dominate our thinking about education and evaluation. For this I make no apology. So many of the assumptions that we have used have, in my view, been inappropriate for the problems with which teachers and others concerned with planning school programs must deal. Rather than to continue to pursue, virtually exclusively, goals and methods that have borne so little in relation to the effort, it has seemed to me useful to try to broaden the base from which educational inquiry can be undertaken. One aim of this book is to help establish that base and to contribute to its legitimation by indicating how qualitative forms of educational inquiry might be undertaken. In this final chapter, I would like to identify and discuss some of the major ideas found in the pages of this book that have given direction to my thinking.

The metaphors and images of schooling and teaching that we acquire have profound consequences for our educational values and for our views of how schooling should occur.

All of us, through the process of acculturation and professional socialization, acquire a language and a set of images that define our views of education and schooling. These images do not enter our cortex announcing their priorities. They do not herald a position or proclaim a set of virtues. Rather, they are a part of the atmosphere. When we talk about learners rather than children, competencies rather than understanding, behavior rather than experience, entry skills rather than development, instruction rather than teaching, responses rather than action, we make salient certain images: our language promotes a view, a way of looking at things, as well as a content to be observed. This language, I am arguing, derives from a set of images, of what schools should be, of how children should be taught, and of how the consequences of schooling should be identified. Language serves to reinforce and legitimize those images. Because differences between, say, terms such as *instruction* and *teaching* are subtle, we often use a new word without recognizing that the new word is capable of creating a new world.

The process of professional socialization is particularly influential in this regard. When prospective teachers and graduate students are trained (educated?), they are in a vulnerable position. Their careers are at stake. The selection of reading lists used in courses, the student's dependency on his or her professor's positive regard, the language that pervades the culture of the professional school or department, the need to use the right jargon on essays and exams: all of these factors create a powerful culture for socialization into the profession. The images are easily instilled: it is an overstatement to say that the student's professional life depends on it, but not much of an overstatement. Doing well means at least in part being able to use—indeed, to believe in—the images, concepts, and language of the culture within which one works as a student.

In arguing the importance of images and metaphors in shaping our conception of schooling and teaching, I am not suggesting that we would be better off imageless. All of us need some conception of education, schooling, teaching, and the student's role in order to deal with the professional world, just as we need some conception of honesty, truth, virtue, and affection to deal with our world in general. Images are the bedrock upon which we build our theoretical palaces. They are indispensable. What I do argue is that the critical analysis of these images is seldom undertaken, and because they enter our minds unannounced we are in a poor position to treat them with the kind of scrutiny they deserve. What so often happens is that when our views are challenged by those holding different ones, instead of examining our own we tend to attack theirs, thereby avoiding the critical examination of what we believe by investing our energies in demolishing other views. The moral here is not to rid ourselves but rather to recognize what these structures are. This will help us guard against the unwitting internalization of subtle but powerful concepts that pervade the pages of professional journals in education, public debate about schooling, and other forms of persuasion and socialization.

The dominant image of schooling in America has been the factory and the dom-

inant image of teaching and learning the assembly line. These images underestimate the complexities of teaching and neglect the differences between education and training.

Tolerance for ambiguity is not a national characteristic. We are a nation of happy endings. In the preceding pages, I have argued that both image and language play a crucial role in shaping our conception of schooling and that the images and the language that they yield are necessary for conceptualization to occur. Imageless thought is empty.

At the same time, the images we hold—whether of education, society, democracy, or the good life—deserve analysis and critical appraisal. All images are not created equal. The images of schooling, teaching, and learning often reflect a factory view of schooling and an assembly-line conception of teaching and learning. Consider, for example, our interest in control, in the productivity of schooling, in the creation of measurable products, in the specification of criteria against which products can be judged, in the supervision of the teaching force, in the growing breach between labor (teachers) and management (administrator), in the talk about quality assurance and quality control, in contract learning, in payment by results, in performance contracting, in the hiring of probationary teachers on the one hand and superintendents on the other. What happens is that such terms become ubiquitous, their conceptual implications are taken for granted, they become a part of our way of educational life without the benefit of critical analysis. The consequences of such concepts and the images they imply are, in my view, devastating. They breed the illusion of a level of precision in practice that is likely to be achieved only by reducing education to training. The assembly-line mentality that was so persuasively described by Callahan in his study of the scientific management movement in education between 1913 and 1930 is still with us. Such an image of education requires that schools be organized to prescribe, control, and predict the consequences of their actions, that those consequences be immediate and empirically manifest, and that they be measurable. In such a school, the exploitation of the adventitious, the cultivation of surprise, and the use of ingenuity are regarded as "noise." They disturb routine and require that formula be replaced with judgment. For, as everybody "knows," judgment is not to be trusted.

There are several motives for the use of industrial metaphors in educational discourse. First, the use of such metaphors implies technical acumen on the part of the user. It affords educationists with a technical language that suggests systematization and rationality. When one is working in complex organizations that do not lend themselves well to systematic control and long-range planning or prediction, the illusion of control and prediction can be secured by using language from domains where control and prediction are possible. Eventually, the use of such language changes the aims of the enterprise. Aims that do not lend themselves to the precision or criteria that the users of such language value are deemphasized. If none of the old aims will do, new ones are created. The curriculum specialist's position gets converted to that of a program manager. The education of school administrators increasingly takes place in the business school. Education becomes converted from a process into a commodity, something one gets and then sells.

For the lay public, the use of industrial metaphors is reassuring. Schooling is, after all, serious business. It is not surprising that business procedures should be regarded as more effective than discussions about mind, culture, wisdom, imagination, sensibility, and the like. Such terms and the images they convey have no business in an enterprise concerned with the really serious business of getting ahead in the world.

Rationality has been conceived of as scientific in nature, and cognition has been reduced to knowing in words; as a result, alternative views of knowledge and mind have been omitted in the preparation of teachers, administrators, and educational researchers.

The use of industrial metaphors in educational discourse is itself reflected in the ways that both lay people and professional educators conceive of human rationality. This conception is one that is scientific in nature. By *scientific* here I mean scientific in the context of verification rather than scientific in the context of discovery . *To know* has come to mean to be able to state some form of proposition and to be able to verify the truth of that proposition through scientific criteria.

Consider, for example, the term *cognition*. Cognition to a great many educators is contrasted with affect: cognition refers to thinking and thinking means linguistically mediated thought. Hence, unless one can utter in discursive terms what one believes one knows, one does not know. Given such a view of thought and rationality, human performance and experience that take form in nondiscursive modes of conception and expression are regarded as nonrational, somehow less a function of human intelligence and clearly having little to do with knowing or understanding.

This is perhaps nowhere better exemplified than in the use of the Scholastic Aptitude Test and the Graduate Record Examination, both of which focus on the use of discursive language and mathematical reasoning. Each of these areas depends on the student's ability to apply rules to the tasks that constitute the tests. The intelligence needed to create poetry, music, or visual art simply does not count.

This view of human rationality is not only reflected on those widely used tests; it is also reflected in elementary and secondary curricula. At the elementary and secondary levels, the primacy of scientific rationality is evidenced in the subject areas that are given priority, in the forms of human performance regarded as most important, in the amount of time devoted to particular fields of study, and in the requirements for graduation from secondary schools. Approximately 90 per cent of all high school districts require some work in the sciences as a condition for graduation. Only about 10 per cent require any work in the arts in order to graduate.

This view of human rationality permeates programs in teacher education, school administration, and educational research as well. Part of the impact results from an overt emphasis on the importance of systematic planning, on the use of operationally defined goals, and on the need for scientifically valid methods and criteria for determining educational effectiveness. The tacit ideal is that of the hard sciences, the methods used in the laboratory, and criteria that can be quantified and hence made "objective." The other part is due to the absence of other views of mind, knowledge, and intelligence, views that have a long and distinguished intellectual history but virtually are never considered in the curricular conversation.

I speak here of the views that argue the importance of tacit forms of knowing, of nondiscursive knowledge, of the expressive power of qualitative symbols, and those of Dewey as expressed in *Art As Experience,* one of his books that goes unread by American educators. When one view of mind, knowledge, and intelligence dominates, a self-fulfilling prophecy emerges. School programs emphasize certain modes of expression and certain subject matter fields. Educational evaluation uses modes of assessment consistent with the assumptions in fields that are emphasized, and "the most able" students are then rewarded by criteria that do not afford equal opportunity to students whose aptitudes reside in areas that are neither attended to in school programs nor adequately assessed. We legitimize our own view of what counts without serious consideration of alternative or complementary views.

The model of natural sciences on which much educational research is based is probably inappropriate for most of the problems and aims of teaching, learning, and curriculum development.

One might be more sanguine about the promise of conventional forms of educational research if past efforts had been more productive in guiding practice. The fact of the matter is that there is precious little practice in education that is data-based. When research does guide practice it is often because the values embedded in the research are consistent with the values of the practitioner. In such cases, the practitioner uses the research to legitimize what he or she already believes.

Some argue, of course, that the reason practitioners do not base their practices on research is because they do not read it. Although it is true that most teachers and school administrators do not read educational research, one can only wonder about the relationship between the effort and the return. There is little in research that can be used to guide practice; for example, the descriptions of the methods used in experimental research are minimal, dependent measures almost always underestimate the range of outcomes with which teachers are concerned, and one is almost always forced to violate the limits of scientific generalization in applying research findings to one's own teaching circumstance. Even those who do experimental educational research in teaching seldom use the results of such research to influence their own teaching.

If research conclusions as they are now presented in the pages of educational research journals do little more than advance the careers of educational researchers, what function do they have in guiding practice at the elementary and secondary levels? Educational research provides not so much conclusions or recipes for practice as it does analytical models for thinking about practice. I believe the models that are most readily used are those that are consistent with the educational views one already holds. Rogerians are seldom converted to a Skinnerian world on the basis of data.

In emphasizing the impracticality of conventional forms of educational research, I may have risked overstating the case. There are *some* educational practices that are based on research findings—computer-assisted instruction, behavior modification techniques, the Distar Reading Program, are examples—but compared to the world of educational practice, research-guided practices are rare. When they do occur, it is because they are highly focused and control-oriented. When it comes to educational aims that focus on the cultivation of productive idiosyncrasy, the development of imaginative thought, the acquisition of the skills of critical thinking, the invention of new modes of expression, educational research has not been notably productive. The character of the context has imposed itself too prominently. The contingencies are too salient when people are allowed to exercise free will. In such contexts, rules cannot replace judgment; procedures cannot be substituted for intelligence. The natural science model may not after all prove to be the most helpful means for improving the quality of educational practice or for understanding what occurs in human affairs. Our most difficult task might reside in determining when in our concerns and aspiration such a model of inquiry is appropriate and when other forms of inquiry are more felicitous.

The canons of behavioral science have too often determined what shall be studied and what shall be regarded as important in education.

The point here is straightforward. When an enterprise tacitly or explicitly establishes certain criteria for respectable intellectual work, problems are defined that can be treated by the methods that can meet those criteria. In educational research, this has meant that problems that do not lend themselves to methods regarded as empirically rigorous are neglected or, even worse, dismissed as pseudoproblems or inherently meaningless ones. The paradigm case of such occurrences is in doctoral programs, in which students are expected to do some types of inquiry but not others, with the true experiment being the most rigorous ideal. Students who see other lights, who wish to march to other drummers, are often subtly persuaded that they will be seriously out of step, that nonscientific modes of inquiry (with the exception of analytic philosophy and history) are not really acceptable ways to do a doctoral dissertation. Furthermore, there is precious little offered in the way of courses on nonscientific research methods that would prepare students for such inquiry. In professional schools of education, research is defined by methods taught in courses on statistics and research design—which almost always means quantitatively oriented inquiry.

When one adds to this the fact that research journals—access to which determines many young assistant professors' chances for promotion—define research in the ways that research methods courses conceive of research, the significance of method in circumscribing the problems into which one can inquire is magnified even further.

The influence of canonized research methods does not stop here. Not only do such methods define what is amenable to study, they also often result in naive and misleading conclusions about teaching and learning in school. That this should occur is ironic, because scientific research procedures are intended to yield objective, unbiased, factual conclusions. Consider, for example, research on class size. According to a great many research studies, class size has no bearing on what students learn. But when one looks to the indices of learning that were used in such studies, it turns out that learning is defined as achievement measured on standardized achievement tests. No attention is devoted to what children learn that tests don't measure.

What happens is that our view of learning is shaped by what we can measure, because what we can measure defines what we regard as learning. Because what is not measured is not considered, the conclusions we draw from what we do measure may seriously bias our perception and understanding. The bias in this respect is not a function of the logic of the inquiry but rather a function of what the criteria used in the inquiry exclude. We come to regard the ear of the elephant, if not as the whole, as its most critical feature.

The procedures and criteria used to evaluate students, teachers, and school administrators have profound effects on the content and form of schooling.

By and large, tests and testing procedures are not developed to influence the content and form of schooling. The major commonly held reason for their use is to determine how well students and teachers are doing in their respective roles. One uses tests to find out if students are learning, if teachers are effective, if school administrators are providing adequate leadership and guidance. Tests are used for these purposes, but their ancillary consequences are even more important. Because test performance is used as an index of educational quality, being able to do well on tests becomes a critical concern for students and teachers alike. As this concern grows, educational programs become increasingly focused on those content areas and forms of teaching that are related to test performance. The curricula of the school and the priorities that both students and teachers come to hold are influenced by what they think will influence test performance. Because tests test what psychometricians can measure, the canons of measurement indirectly influence what is taught in schools and what priorities will be established among those fields that are taught. Consider again the Scholastic Aptitude Test. This test is given to approximately two million students each year. It has two major parts: one verbal and the other mathematical. Scoring well on this test is important for admission to many colleges and universities. Students who want to score well believe—whether true or not—that the more courses they take in mathematics the more likely they will receive high scores on the mathematical section of the SAT. Thus, students often feel compelled to forgo courses in which they may have a genuine interest in favor of courses in mathematics that may improve their chances for admission to the college of their choice.

The influence of testing on school curricula is also felt at the lower levels of schooling, at the kindergarten and primary levels, where the quality of education is judged in terms of student reading scores and at the intermediate level where tests in mathematics and language arts become the public criteria of educational quality as test scores find their way onto the pages of local newspapers. Few teachers can withstand the almost certain public pressure for high scores on district- and state-mandated tests, even if the teachers wanted to pursue educational values that those tests did not assess. The social significance of the means used to measure student performance through testing is profound. I do not believe that major changes can be made in the content and aims of educational practice in schools without significantly broadening the criteria and methods used to assess educational effectiveness. The formalized rites of passage provided by tests are likely to constrain any effort to put into practice a really broad view of human development, despite our aspirations to the contrary.

Operationalism and Measurement have focused so heavily on behavior that the quality of the student's experience has been generally ignored or seriously neglected.

The employment of empirical procedures that lend themselves to operational definitions, defintions that can be measured, has been one of the tenets of the social sciences. In education this has meant that overt behavior is to be the primary referent for determining the success or failure of a new teaching method, curriculum, or form of school organization. The measured variable referenced in what students do is critical for achieving objective description. The quantified variable can provide a score to the third or the fourth decimal place. Scores have attractive features; they can be added, subtracted, averaged, multiplied, and divided. They can be subjected to sophisticated forms of statistical analysis on the most up-to-date modern computers. Statistical conclusions can be derived that provide a compelling illusion of precision and objectivity, a value-free image of pristine description, untouched by personal judgment, bias, or human failing. Furthermore, the tests that often yield such data are prepackaged, almost hermetically sealed, before the students open them, and they are identical for all students taking the test. It is almost as if we did not want to touch or get to know the student; the aim is to remain distant, dispassionate, aloof, unbiased.

This attitude, often erroneously regarded as a mark of scientific objectivity, leads us away from understanding the quality of life the student is experiencing. Because our focus is on behavior, our aim is to shape that behavior and our success is achieved when that behavior is displayed. But what of the student's experience? How does he feel about what he is doing? Is what she is learning becoming a part of her world view? Are the major lessons he is learning those that are being taught? To answer these questions, we must of course look beyond behavior. We must make inferences from behavior about experience. We must seek an empathetic understanding of the kind of lives children lead in school. But this means that we must make judgments, that we must attend to what is not easily standardized, and that we must get to know students as people. These are not relationships to which operationalism and quantification lend themselves. And when we add to this our penchant for efficient forms of standardization, all in the name of impartiality, we risk seriously misreading what students are learning in school. Beethoven's Fourth Symphony is not, after all, the incidence of d minor occurring in its four movements. It is not even the notes taken in their entirety on the score. Beethoven's Fourth Symphony is first and last music, sound, and experience. Rank forms of reductionism miss the point, and I fear that in our efforts to be "objective" and operational we too often miss the most telling points of school experience. Our penchant for standardization hampers our ability to perceive what is truly unique about students, and our preoccupation with measured behavior distracts us from appreciating and understanding what students experience in school and what they genuinely learn after all the test taking has been completed.

In urging that attention be devoted to the quality of life students experience in school, I am not suggesting that attention to performance be neglected. There has been in some schools at some periods in our educational history so much romantic attention to the students' feelings that the development of various forms of competence was seriously neglected. The neglect of competence and the failure to foster it appropriately can be a major source of emotional difficulty for children. Yet, our focus today is not in that direction. Our infatuation with performance objectives, criterion-referenced testing, competency-based education, and the so-called basics lends itself to standardization, operationalism, and behaviorism as the virtually exclusive concern of schooling. Such a focus is, I believe far too narrow and not in the best interests of students, teachers, or the society within which students live. Empathy, playfulness, surprise, ingenuity, curiosity, and individuality must count for something in schools that aim to contribute to a social democracy.

The history of the curriculum field has been dominated by the aspiration to technologize schooling and to reduce the need for artistry in teaching.

Except for notable exceptions during the progressive era and during the free school period of the 1960s, the pervasive orientation among curriculum theorists and school administrators has been an effort to develop a scientifically based technology of curriculum and teaching. This aspiration was first articulated during the scientific management movement I have already alluded to. But it also was central in the writing of those who attempted to ground educational practice in scientifically based knowledge derived from educational research. The optimum aim of such inquiry was to yield laws that would do for educational practitioners what the work of Boyle, Einstein, and Bohr did for physical scientists. It was aimed at eliminating the chancy and undependable, and replacing them with rule, procedure, and method. What is the best method for teaching reading? What is the best method for instruction in mathematics? What is the optimal ratio of students to teacher in the classroom? How can we formulate aims that are so clear that anyone who can see can determine whether they have been achieved? How can we study the community to discover what our educational needs really are?

In the curriculum field, per se, this orientation culminated in the aspiration to develop teacherproof curriculum materials. Nothing was to be left to chance. The intelligence of the teacher was not something one trusted. Ideally, the teacher was to serve as a handmaiden to the materials that were produced by a set of methods that approximated those used in the manufacture of cars, washing machines, and television sets. If such procedures worked so well in these industries, why would they not work in schools, particularly in the design of curriculum and in the process of teaching? Examine our metaphors: they are right out of the computer sciences and the assembly line. Somehow, if curriculum planning could be systematized and teaching appropriately monitored, the complexities of large schools and school systems might be managed more efficiently. The whole affair would be simplified, everyone concerned would know just where we want to go and how to get there: nothing would be left to chance.

For teaching, the tack has been the same: what we need is precision teaching; we must diagnose and prescribe; we must above all individualize instruction. Never mind that these concepts have seldom been analyzed, they possess an aura of conceptual rigor. Particularly when the pressure is on, the vicissitudes of art and artistry can hardly be tolerated.

What is ironic is that most administrators, I believe, would regard most of what they do as resting on judgment rather than rule, as more a matter of art than a matter of science. Getting a feel for an organization, developing a sense of where your support rests, looking for openings in which you can move, bringing coherence and spirit to the central staff, keeping your finger on the pulse of the community, enjoying the playing of school politics: these are some of the features that dramatize the lives of school administrators. Indeed, they are crucial for survival.

The same holds for teachers; at its best, theirs is largely an artistic act. This is not to say that neither teachers nor administrators can use concepts grounded in scientifically based research. It is to say that concepts and generalizations must always be interpreted and that judgments that exceed the information provided by the generalizations must always be made if they are to be used in classrooms. Yet, despite practitioner's recognition of the arts of the eclectic, to use Schwab's phrase, those arts seldom get examined in the research literature. Indeed, they are often regarded with derision, something to be excised rather than cultivated, appreciated, or emulated. If scientific research on teaching provided more to practitioners than it does at present, its potential might appear more promising and the assumptions on which it is based more robust. This is not the case. Perhaps it is time that other assumptions about teaching and curriculum planning be entertained, not as a substitute perhaps, but surely as a complement to what we have been doing over the last seventy-five years.

Knowing, like teaching, requires the organism to be active and to construct meaningful patterns out of experience. At base, such patterns are artistic constructions, a means through which the human creates a conception of reality.

Man, Aristotle once observed, by nature seeks to know. To construct a meaningful world requires that we conceptualize patterns of the environment, recognize the rule that are both tacit and explicit in our social life, feel sufficiently free to play and to take risks so that conceptual invention can occur. The creation of these patterns means in part the construction of structures that hang together, that are coherent, that express both order and interest and enable us to make sense of the world. This sense-making is, I believe, an artistic act. We function as the architects of our own enlightenment; we build our own conceptual edifices and we want them to be beautiful as well as serviceable.

How telling that in our vernacular we talk about a *sense* of justice, making *sense* of things, having a *sense* for what is fitting and proper. Pattern is an inescapable quality of the organization of thought. Logic in action preceded logic as rule. The former made the latter possible, not vice versa. But patterning is not limited to propositions, it is a part of practical action and of activities aimed at the creation of art, per se. For schooling, or more properly for a theory of education, the notion that the human organism is stimulus-seeking and pattern-forming is crucial. What it implies is that all forms of learning, and some more than others, are at best creative acts.

The organism must always act, even to make simple distinctions among sensory qualities. For the more complex forms of conception, more complex distinctions and patterns are necessary. But to make such patterns well requires an environment supportive of exploratory thought that encourages children to entertain ideas in a spirit of tentativeness. It is an environment that recognizes the desirability for children to have opportunities to create and play with patterns that enable them to appreciate the structure of ideas and to enjoy the process through which those structures are formed. In short, the aesthetic of both process and form must become a consciously sought virtue in schooling if schooling is to be converted from an academic experience into an intellectual one.

Teaching that is not hamstrung by rule-governed routine also requires the creation of patterns of thought by a teacher orchestrating an educational environment. Such a mode of thought is of course not required when teaching is like working on an assembly line. But to move teaching in such a direction is to deny students the opportunities to see creative intelligence at work. The classroom should be what it is trying to foster.

Practical judgment based on ineffable forms of understanding should not be regarded as irrational. It might reflect the highest forms of human rationality.

Universities have a tendency to make those who have high degrees of practical knowledge feel uncomfortable if they cannot provide reasons for action. In the academy, knowing how is nowhere near as honorable as knowing why. To know means, whether one can act appropriately or not, to be able to state in words what one knows.

Yet the tasks of teaching are far more demanding than discursive knowledge can explain. Indeed, if our activities as teachers and school administrators needed to be justified in relation to data-based, scientifically validated knowledge, most of educational practice would come to a standstill. We know, as Polanyi has pointed out, more than we can say.

The foregoing remarks should not be taken as a prolegomenon for mindless teaching or for curriculum development unenlightened by theory. In any case, neither is possible: mind requires conception to operate just as conception requires mind to exist. What the foregoing remarks do emphasize is that the process of knowing often uses qualities that are ineffable, that these qualities exist in both profusion and interaction, and that they must be "read" quickly and acted on swiftly if the information they yield is to be educationally useful. One example of how such knowledge is used is found in the activities of the standup comedian. To be sure, a comedian is not necessarily a teacher and a teacher is not necessarily a comedian, but an examination of the overlap between the two will be instructive.

For the standup comedian to function effectively, he must be able to "read" the qualities emanating from an audience. These qualities change as he proceeds with this act. The tone of the laughter, the tempo of his

own words, the timing from line to line: all of these must be grasped immediately. Indeed, it is almost as though acting becomes second nature; no
time to formulate hypotheses, no time to consult and compare theory, no
time to seek substantiating evidence or data, and certainly no time to
administer tests to determine the level of interest. Out of the flux of interacting the comedian must blend his own; a line one second late falls flat.
And the configurations change. Automaticity and reflectivity must go hand
in hand. The act must reach a crescendo and finally, when the audience
has nearly had enough, be brought to closure.

The exercise of intelligence involved in such action is apparent in a Bob
Hope, Carol Burnett, Joan Rivers, or Richard Pryor, yet no comedian
could give a theoretical account of why what he or she does "works." We
appreciate the comedians skill, we recognize their artistry, but we do not
expect from them psychological explanations that account for their
effectiveness.

Because such explanations are not forthcoming, should we regard such
activity as irrational or arational? Should we regard it as outside the realm
of intelligence? I think not. What we are seeing when we see artists work—
on the stage, in the studio, in the concert hall, and in a classroom—is not
the absence of rationality and intelligence but the ultimate manifestations
of its realization. Such individuals work with the creation and organization
of qualities, the actor with the qualities of speech and gesture, the musician
with those of sound, the painter with color, line, and form, and the teacher
with words, timing, and the creation of educational environments. What
all of these artists have in common is the aspiration to confer a unique,
personal order on the materials with which they work. And most work in
contexts that are in a state of continual flux. No recipe will do. No routine
will be adequate, even if routines must be acquired as a *part* of one's repertoire. The point here is that much of what we know and the basis for
much of our actions rest on inexpressible forms of consciousness that recognize the feel of things and sense the qualities that lead to closure and
consummation. When we see such abilities displayed in public, whether on
the stage or in the classroom, we should give them their due. The achievement of art is not, after all, a menial accomplishment.

*The process of curriculum development, like the process of doing quantitative
empirical educational research, appears much neater and much more predictable
in textbook versions of curriculum development and research than it is in practice.*

Philosophers of science characteristically distinguish in their writing
between the context of discovery and the context of verification. In the
context of verification, the rules of inference and logic are applied to
determine the veracity and consistency of statements about the world. The
context of discovery, however, is another matter. How ideas are generated,
how insights are formed, and how fresh conceptions emerge into consciousness are not now adequately understood. And so, too, in writing

about curriculum development and in reporting the results of empirical quantitative research, the illusion is created that the "rational" procedures outlined for describing curricula are the ways, in fact, that curricula are, can be, or ought to be created. It is not that the vicissitudes of curriculum development are denied; it is simply that they go unmentioned. As a result, the novice may get the impression that curriculum development typically proceeds or ought to proceed with the neatness with which it is described in textbooks. This is misleading on several counts. First, it gives the inexperienced reader an oversimplified image of a process. Second, such descriptions tacitly imply that if one does not proceed along the lines suggested in the textbook, something is wrong. One isn't doing one's job well. Third, such presentations make curriculum development seem essentially like a technical task. Once the objectives are formulated, the task is simply to follow a set of steps to achieve them. Such an image fails to help students of education know how messy program planning really is and how much flexibility, ingenuity, and tolerance for ambiguity are needed to do it well. But perhaps most importantly, such a rendering of what is a complex, fluid process serves to sustain a limited conception of rationality and tends to underestimate the qualities of playfulness, humor, and artistry needed to do really excellent work in the curriculum field. It is important for students of education to understand that what is finally published is a sanitized version of the reality that preceded it, a reality that in many ways is often far more interesting than its written description.

The aspiration to create teacherproof materials rests on a mistake. Teachers need materials that stimulate their ingenuity rather than materials to which they are to be subservient.

There is a temptation in the development of curriculum materials to try to create materials that will replace the need for teachers to exercise judgment. The aim is to design materials that are so robust that they can withstand even the most incompetent teaching. The reason for this aspiration is clear: if such materials can be created, then one can control the educational process from a distance; one can build an error-free program. Having done this, one need not rely on the frailities of human judgment; decision on the part of the teacher can be minimized. Routine can replace reason.

Such an aspiration operates, of course, in the creation of the assembly line. The ultimate manifestation of such an orientation to development is to have the worker become an extension of the machine he or she uses. Personal identity and idiosyncratic thought are replaced by something more impersonal and more predictable.

Because some curriculum developers want the materials they develop to be effective, they seek to make them as errorless as possible. All one needs to do is to follow the directions right on the package. The aspiration to construct such teacherproof materials is, in Illich's terms, the aspiration to create anticonvivial tools, tools that eventually define and determine what a person should do. Although the assembly line is a paradigm case of an anticonvivial tool, such tools abound in cultures with high technology. In the long run, such tools restrict rather than expand choice.

Convivial tools—the telephone, for example—expand one's options, can be used without extensive training, do not restrict what messages one can convey, and do not impose time constraints on their use. Convivial curriculum materials can have similar characteristics. They can provide a structure within which a teacher can operate, but they still can provide options; indeed, they can stimulate ingenuity.

Although different teachers may require different amounts of detail in the curriculum materials they use, the ultimate aim of such materials is to minimize the teacher's dependency on them, to offer to the teacher materials that will foster a sense of competence both in pedagogical matters and in the content to which pedagogy is directed. In short, one function of well-designed curriculum materials is to free the teacher to teach, with ingenuity, flexibility, and confidence.

Now such an aspiration, such a conception of teaching and the materials that teachers use, seems to some to be a utopian dream. Teachers, some say, do not as a group have the intelligence to use such materials, most do not want to change or learn, and the creation of such materials requires a level of sophistication that teachers do not possess. And on and on.

I believe that most people want to make their lives more interesting and that we seek events, ideas, and materials that help us achieve a more interesting life. The view that teachers are largely dullards is, in my opinion, false. It is simplistic and leads to a control-oriented conception of curriculum and an assembly-line view of the tasks of teaching. And even on the assembly line the results fall far short of their goals.

The creation of curriculum materials cannot be separated from our conceptions of what teaching is and what the teacher's role is to be. If the teacher is to be a functionary in a system that is standardized, a system that is intended to yield common outcomes for all students, then the aim of standardized materials in form, content, and use is consistent. Although there may be some educational services that lend themselves to such a view, its pervasive use diminishes the very qualities that educational programs, as distinct from training programs, can foster.

Differences among both educators and lay people regarding particular educational issues and practices are often based on more fundamental, deep-seated differences regarding the functions and aims of schooling.

Differences of opinion about the virtues of particular educational practices are often the hubs of intense educational controversy. Should students be placed in tracks according to achievement? Should children be given letter grades in elementary school? Should curriculum content include controversial issues? Should common minimum standards exist for students at each grade level? Should elementary schools assign homework to students regularly? Should teachers be encouraged to take children on field trips? These are some of the questions for which a great deal of disagreement exists. Yet the differences among lay people and educators alike with respect to these questions are not limited to the particular questions posed. If one digs a bit deeper, one finds far more fundamental differences in the ways in which the contesting parties conceive of the school's function—indeed, in how they conceive of education itself.

The existence of disagreement about educational practices should not be conceived of as a liability. It would be a serious liability indeed if a subject so important as education were not a matter of concern and dispute. The resolution of these views, even a temporary one, can be treated on two levels: through accommodation and compromise and through encouraging the contending parties to penetrate more deeply into the values that animate the controversy. It is here that the school administrator has a truly educational function to perform. That function is one of helping community members understand the implications of their educational values, to appreciate the alternatives, and to anticipate the second- and third-order consequences of the practices they are considering. Clearly, at some point in the debate, a state of readiness exists; the community or a portion of it is interested in an educational issue. Before positions get crystallized, before the prospect of a public reversal of a position makes it impossible for positions to be altered, the school administrator can help initiate the kind of dialogue that might educationally enlighten a community about an educational policy.

The major orientations to education that underlie disputed policies in schooling have been identified in Chapter 4. Although these views do not exhaust the possible positions groups might take, the five views described provide a framework through which the value base underlying the symptomatic issues might be identified and discussed.

The factors that influence schooling may have their source far from the school or school district.

Because schools are social institutions—that is, institutions created by the society for the achievement of socially defined purposes—they are influenced by the forces that pervade that society. Some of these forces operate in close proximity to the school: the availability of excellent teachers; the support, both moral and financial, that the professional staff enjoys from the community the school serves; and the quality of the physical resources with which teachers and students work are a few examples. But other factors also shape the direction and priority of the school, and some of these are subtle. The development of a pill to control conception, for example, has had an enormous influence on what schools will offer students in the way of school programs. The influence is not direct, but it is extremely potent nevertheless, because with fewer children in school, there is less money made available to schools by the state. With less money, school boards must cut back on expenditures. Because most of the money a school district expends goes into salaries, when funds are cut salaries must be cut, and this means the loss of programs.

I use the birth control pill as one example of an important source of influence on schooling, an influence that is several times removed from schooling itself, yet has had significant consequences.

Other influences such as national testing programs, college admission criteria, and federal funding made available for some fields but not others also have important effects on the climate within which schools operate. This climate makes it possible for certain priorities to emerge and for certain groups to exercise influence. Sputniks I and II put the capstone on a growing sentiment during the first half of the 1950s that American public schools were too soft. With Sputnik, those holding this view had the leverage they needed to drive home the message and to have it supported by increasing amounts of federal funding for curriculum development and teacher training in mathematics and the sciences. Thus, what occurred halfway around the globe influenced what happened in our educational backyard in the United States.

What such examples illustrate is that educational practices and educational priorities are not the sole consequence of the aspirations of either educators or those in the communities that educators serve. Schools are a part of a large cultural ecosystem. They respond to that system in ways that are not always obvious. If those interested in educational change are to be successful, aspects of that system—though they be far removed from the school—may need to be altered. In sum, the alteration of constraints and other forms of influence at several levels removed from the school may be the most effective way to change what goes on in schools. A direct attack on an immediate school problem might not be the most effective way of dealing with the problem.

To identify these distant contraints calls for a holistic, ecological view of schooling. One must be in a position to see the system as one whose boundaries extend beyond the contours of the school district. Furthermore, one must have the conceptual ability to identify and analyze the relevant forces. Politics, the so-called architectonic science, is one potentially useful frame of reference for such an analysis. But whether the framework is that of political science, sociology, social psychology, economics, or cultural anthropology, analytic skills are not sufficient. One must know what is educationally significant in order to give direction to analysis, and one must be able to exercise the arts of political action if analysis is to lead to more than an academic understanding of a state of affairs; the point of analysis is to lead to the creation of the conditions that will allow the educational process to thrive.

The arena of school practice and the arena of education in institutions of higher education are so far removed from each other as to function in almost total independence.

The study of education in institutions of higher education and the world of educational practice as it occurs in the public schools exist in a state of benign neglect. Aside from teacher training, it is rare that schools and school districts look to universities as resources for improving the quality of what they do. Similarly, it is relatively rare that scholars and researchers in education regard the operations of the school as a primary concern. For those doing educational research as it is typically conceived, schools are places where one can secure the data one needs. As often as not, the results of such research are not fed back to the schools that provided the place where the data were collected. Whether the research that is done has any utility to practitioners is a secondary or tertiary consideration. What matters most is that what is published impresses the group that the scholar or researcher believes important.

Now it might be argued that in doing research or other forms of scholarship that impress other scholars or researchers the interests of the school are being served. I don't believe that such an argument holds. The central issue in gaining a reputation, whether for an individual professor or for a school or department of education, is to have material published that increasingly approximates the publications in the mother disciplines. The more educational philosophy is indistinguishable from philosophy in general, the more educational psychology cannot be distinguished from "pure" psychology, the more educational sociology reads like the articles published by sociologists, the more respectable they become. Indeed, in some institutions of higher education this orientation is pushed so far that when new faculty appointments are being considered in philosophy of education, educational psychology, or educational sociology, only those trained in the "pure" branches of those fields are considered. (It makes one wonder why if those most competent to teach philosophy of education, educational sociology, and educational psychology are trained in the pure departments, there should be a need for doctoral programs in these fields in schools of education.)

The reasons for the breach between the public schools and the departments and schools of education in universities are several. First, the reward structure for university professors is seldom, at least in prestigious universities, found in providing services to the public schools. One does not consult elementary or secondary school teachers to find out about the usefulness of a professor's work when it comes time to consider the professor for promotion. What does count is published material, more often than not in journals that educational practitioners do not read.

Second, engagement with problems of educational practice in the schools is time-consuming and theoretically messy. To spend one's time in the field is to have less time to spend doing work that is methodologically neat. There are few nontenured professors who are willing to risk the chance of promotion by too heavy an involvement with problems significant to teachers and school administrators.

Third, the aptitudes, attitudes, interests, and skills of professors of education are often unsuited to problems of school practice. Many professors teaching in schools and departments of education have had no experience as practitioners in the public schools, have little interest in the problems practitioners face, and regard their work in universities as theoretical or basic, that is, without immediate application. They often express a hope and some an expectation that what they do will ultimately have practical utility, but recognize that for the present this is not the case. Their skills and expertise are, in fact, in an area independent of schooling. For some, too close an association with the public schools and public school practices is a professional liability, because it may imply to others that they are more practical than theoretical in their work.

Educational slogans serve to replace educational thought and enable school practitioners to avoid dealing with the persistent problems of practice.

The problems that beset schooling are not due to the behavior of any single group. I have already argued that, by and large, those working in universities tend to have marginal interest in the improvement of educational practice, per se. Similarly, educational practitioners, particularly those serving in administrative positions, have a tendency to avoid the tough educational problems by grasping the slogans that parade through the field of education year after year. Consider, for example, the back-to-basics movement. Throughout the United States, communities (or vocal segments thereof) are urging a return to "basics." School leaders are all too willing to oblige. Because the mass media proclaim that schools are slipping in their effectiveness, that test scores are dropping, that bonehead English is oversubscribed in colleges and universities, the time appears ripe to return to the basics. But what are the basics anyway? Are they the same for all students? If they are the skills of reading, writing, and arithmetic—the three R's—does it matter at all *what* is read or written? Does imagination count in writing? Does any book or magazine article count equally in demonstrating the ability to read? At what level does competency in mathematics exceed what is basic? Alas, such questions seldom get asked. Instead, slogans replace analyses, and school practitioners too often lead the race toward an ideal that has not had the barest form of analysis or critical scrutiny.

This example is not an isolated case; *individualization* is another one. What counts as a form of individualization? Does individualization refer to the rate at which students move toward the achievement of common objectives? Does it require that goals be differentiated, as well? Does individualization refer to the differentiation of teaching methods for different students, to the differentiation of the response modes that students can use to demonstrate what they have learned, to the forms of presentation by which they encounter new concepts? If one looks at the field, one finds hardly a soul who is against individualization, but when one presses for a clarification of what the term means, too often a superficial understanding of the term's possibilities is revealed.

Similar conditions exist with respect to terms such as *open education, flexible scheduling, peer tutoring, learning by discovery, the inquiry method,* and the like. The virtues of such slogans for the practitioners—particularly for those in administrative positions—is that they provide a public image of up-to-date educational practice. In addition, they confer on the educational practitioner who uses them in the presence of lay people an aura of technical sophistication. Such a consequence of technical language is not unusual: medicine is another prime example of an area where language is so used. And technical language has, of course, its virtues; properly used, it increases precision in discourse. But in education, such language is all too often pseudotechnical; it covers up or substitutes for the kind of rigorous thought that educational problems require.

The school is the basic unit of educational excellence.

By and large the most "natural" unit in schooling is the school. The school both physically and psychologically defines the environment of teachers and students. It is the school that establishes the structure within which teachers and students must function and that establishes a territory distinct from the rest of life. The school possesses a physical character that no other aspect of education can achieve: a school district is too large and a classroom is an integrated part of the physical structure of the school. The school stands out as an entity; it is something that secures allegiance and provides students with an identity.

But beyond the physical characteristics of the school and their impact on our perception, the school defines a set of social parameters, as well. The structure of classrooms, the rules, time schedules, and the psychological climate create the milieu within which the purposes of schooling are realized.

For the school to function as an organization, some modus vivendi must be established, some balance must be secured among the forces that animate it. As in a living organism, the parts exist in a transactional state, and changes in one part must be compatible with the rest of the structure or the changes must be so potent as to change the rest of the organizational structure. If the structure of the school as a whole is resistant to change, as is true of many schools, then it is likely that the change agent will itself be changed rather than the school.

Consider, for example, the life style of beginning teachers. Beginning teachers often enter the school with strong aspirations acquired during their professional training or on their own. Most new teachers soon realize that their aspirations must be significantly changed to fit the school. For some teachers, the compromise is such a difficult ethical problem that they choose to leave teaching rather than alter their core educational values. After a few years of teaching, those who choose to remain adapt to the institutional press and eliminate the sharp corners of professional idiosyncrasy. They become a well-rounded lot, a more homogeneous and adaptive group that does what it must to survive.

Because the press of the institution is so significant, the problem of bringing about change within classrooms cannot be isolated from the school's constraints on and incentives for change. In this regard, the principal of the school is of central importance. In general, the principal sets the tone for the school and provides the formal positive and negative sanctions, even when a well-regulated evaluation system is not in force. His or her expectations for punctuality, record-keeping, student performance levels, educational priorities, and the like are communicated in both formal and informal ways. Other factors, including timetables, the allocation of fiscal resources, and the allocation of space, further define both what counts in school and what is possible. Given these conditions, attention to the macrostructure of the school becomes crucial for those interested in raising the quality of the educational experience for students. It is difficult for a teacher to sustain a mode of teaching or to achieve educational aims that are contradicted daily by the culture in which he or she works. Such a teacher must almost always adapt to or leave the school; only in rare cases can a teacher alter the macrostructure. So what I am arguing is that the professional lifestyle of the teacher is significantly shaped by the characteristics and structure of the living organism we call a school. In a rational model of schooling, the form of the school organizationally as well as physically follows the function it is intended to perform. In the real world, it is more often the case that the function of the school is defined by the forms we create to manage it.

The current emphasis in schools on verbal and mathematical reasoning seriously biases our conception of human intelligence and significantly impedes the development of socially valuable interests and aptitudes.

The coin of the realm in schooling is words and numbers, so much so as to constitute a form of educational inequity for students whose aptitudes are in realms other than verbal or mathematical. Consider the impact of testing on the educational mobility of students. Virtually all achievement tests given to students in elementary and secondary schools by school districts or state education agencies assess verbal or mathematical performance. Students whose aptitudes are verbal or mathematical or who have opportunities out of school to learn in these areas of human performance are advantaged. The game being played, as it were, is consistent with their backgrounds or capacities.

But what of those students whose aptitudes lie outside of these realms: the dancer, the poet, the painter, the filmmaker, the composer? As things now stand, their aptitudes never enter the equation for calculating intellectual ability. To clarify this problem, consider what would happen if current practice were reversed. Instead of verbal and mathematical criteria, suppose that a student were admitted to college on the basis of the quality of his or her drawings, musical performance, dance, or films. Suppose that written skills did not count, nor did mathematical skills. How equitable would that be?

This is not a plea to substitute nonverbal and nonmathematical forms of performance for the forms now used but rather to broaden both the curricular options and criteria that affect students' lives.

A part of the reason such skills are now emphasized, I believe, is that they lend themselves to forms of testing that appear objective. For example, Educational Testing Service, which once tested the writing skills of students by having them write compositions and having readers judge their quality, has now devised a "writing test" in which students respond to multiple-choice questions that can be machine-scored. Because the multiple-choice test correlates highly with the scores assigned by judges to written compositions, the latter is an efficient way to learn about the former. Yet one cannot help but wonder what readers were attending to when they were judging compositions that were actually written: insight, imagination, sensitive use of language, ability to use metaphor, inventiveness, significance of the substance of the topic?

We see once again that our technique defines our ends; rather than being servant, it becomes master. What we can efficiently do that meets one model of objectivity sets the ceiling on what we believe we ought to do. This goes so far as to determine who is gifted. In California, for example, students who have a measured IQ of 130 or more are classified as "mentally gifted minors" and the school is entitled to additional state funds. What about the artistically gifted minor?

The cost of such a parochial view of the human mind is borne not only by the students who must experience the inequity of denied opportunity but also by the society that may never reap the benefits that such children could provide to the culture at large. The time for changing this situation is long past.

What often goes unnoticed by both secondary school faculty and those working in colleges and universities is the impact of testing on the curriculum of both institutions. This impact is essentially a conservative one. Because universities use high school test scores to predict success in college and because those scores are derived primarily from performances on written and mathematical tasks, the predictive ability of the scores increases as the tasks in college increasingly approximate the skills tested. The same holds true for high school grades. If one seeks to make good predictions, one can do this by designing programs and using criteria that share common assumptions and require similar skills. Either the secondary school program must approximate that of the university, or the university program that of the secondary school. Given the aspiration to predict, a conservative circle emerges. The greater the competition for admission to universities, the more conservative the secondary school program becomes for those who seek such admission.

When one adds to this the fact that many university admission committees discount grades in art, music, theater, and other creative forms in calculating grade-point average, the liability to the student who wants to take secondary school courses related to his or her interests—if those interests are in the arts—is quite clear.

The school must be a growth environment for the teacher if it is to be an optimal growth environment for the student.

Very little attention has been devoted in educational planning to the impact the school has on the professional staff who work there year after year. Somehow we expect the central problem in planning educational programs to be that of designing an environment or a set of learning opportunities that will foster the growth of the student, almost independent of the effects those conditions may have on teachers and school administrators. I want to suggest that neglecting the needs of the professional staff of schools is one of the surest ways to decrease the quality of the educational service provided to students. Teachers, like everybody else, somehow adapt to or change the environment in which they function. When change is not possible, adaptation occurs. For many teachers and school administrators, such adaptation has resulted in the development of routine repertoires and stock responses that they have learned to use to cope with the demands made on them. Rather than having an environment that stimulates, they function in an environment that affords them few new challenges. They want to do well in the eyes of their students, and many have developed the kinds of routines that will enable this to occur. But life in the fullest sense is that lived outside of school; it is reserved for weekends, vacation periods, and sabbaticals. Growth occurs outside rather than inside the place where teachers spend most of their waking hours.

For many teachers, especially midcareer teachers, this has begun to pose a problem of the first order. Opportunities for professional advancement are not as plentiful as they used to be, because of the decline in school enrollment. Because of budget cuts, sabbatical leaves are more difficult to secure. The public's desire to judge the school's quality by the measured performance of students exacerbates these pressures. For many teachers unionization has been one way of coping with these problems, but increases in pay will never adequately compensate for an inadequate professional life space. What will it require of school programs to provide the conditions for teachers and school administrators to have time for reflection, for experimentation, for adequate planning, for consultation with new colleagues? Would the achievement level of students decrease if teachers were given three or four hours each week to meet for purposes of educational planning or individualized work?

The specific forms that such planning might take may differ from school to school, but the need to work in an environment that allows—indeed puts a premium on—the teachers' and administrators' professional growth will not.

One of the things I have learned in talking to school administrators is that a great many of them moved into school administration to escape the constraints and the routine of the classroom. What they were seeking was not so much power or money but a more interesting professional life, a wider field in which to play. The creation of an expanded professional life space, the development of an environment that is educational for teachers and administrators as well as students, is, I believe, one of the most seriously neglected needs in education.

Incrementalism is a useful way to change schools if one has a sense of the place of the increment in a larger pattern or strategy for change.

Virtually every student of education has the aspiration to change schools, that is, to bring about improvements in the ways in which schools function. Yet it has been observed by students of change and by those who are old enough or interested enough to have a long view that, although change in schooling occurs, it often occurs in spite of our efforts to bring it about. Schools change—and they have changed significantly in structure and form over the last fifty years—because of developments in the society more than because of the efforts of educators to bring them about. This should not be surprising. The form and function of schooling are closely related to the values and expectations of the society. People expect the schools to support the values they hold. Significant deviation from those values is seldom tolerated.

For some students of education, the situation called for a radical or revolutionary approach to schooling. They believed that, somehow, enlightened pupils and the enlightened adults in the community could radically alter the character of American schooling. If this could not be done within the existing system, then new schools—free schools—would be established to serve as an alternative.

The animation of the late 1960s has all but dissipated, and free schools are largely dead. Even in their prime they touched less than 1 per cent of the students in American schools. If revolution within the schools is not a viable means of bringing about improved forms of schooling, then what is? Two answers seem to me to be possible. One is that educators can have no significant impact on the character of schooling and therefore must always follow rather than lead the aims of the polity. The other is that schools can change on a guided, incremental basis through the efforts of those in the field of education. The former view severely constrains the aspirations of those who attempt to conceptualize and develop better educational programs. If one regards change in the schools as a result of the forces of history, the prospects for professional educational leadership are dim. To be sure, those forces occur and are potent, yet history also indicates that there have been schools that have had the kind of leadership and community support to rise above these so-called irresistible forces. Furthermore, in an incremental process educators can develop the kind of coalition with other educators and lay groups to support the forms of educational practice that they value. This process is at base a political one, but it can, and I would argue should, be based on an educationally enlightened constituency. This means, of course, that the leadership of the school or school district must regard its clients to be not only the pupils who attend the schools, but also the community that supports them. This kind of leadership must tread a narrow line between the desire to impose a perspective—which is likely to fail—and the desire simply to serve the prevailing perspective. School administrators and teachers, theoretically at least, are by virtue of their training better prepared to contribute to the dialogue about both the means and ends of schooling.

I realize that many—perhaps even most—teachers and school administrators do not have such skills and understandings at present, but it is the principle I am arguing for, not the status quo. I would like schools to be better than they are. I believe that educators should lead the dialogue about schooling, and I believe that enlightened dialogue can contribute to the creation of improved educational practice. Such an aim need not require a revolution. It can be achieved through a gradual process that incrementally seeks the approximation of an educational ideal.

Schools teach both more and less than educators realize.

In Chapter 5, I pointed out that each school offers children three curricula: the explicit curriculum that is public and advertised, the implicit curriculum that teaches because of the kind of culture that a school is, and the null curriculum, those voids in educational programs that withhold from students ideas and skills that they might otherwise use. The utilities distinguishing among these types of curricula are several. First, it allows one to raise questions about what children are learning that would never be identified if one were to focus only on the intended goals of the explicit curriculum. We tend in the planning of school programs to act as though what schools explicitly teach constitutes the whole of what students learn. Yet what schools teach by virtue of their structure, their expectations, their timetables, and their rules might in fact have a much greater impact on what students learn.

Second, by distinguishing among these three types of curricula we are in a position to evaluate the consequences of each. A school might offer an exhilarating course on critical thought about social problems and yet might, in its general culture, be promulgating a type of intellectual dependency that contradicts the values and skills the course attempts to foster. Consider, for example, the use of student hall guards in secondary schools. In some schools, such guards are on duty at every intersection in the building. Monitoring these halls guards are teachers, one assigned to each floor or section of the school. Monitoring these teachers is a vice-principal who from time to time makes rounds to be sure that the teachers are on duty; the teachers in turn monitor the hall guards, who in turn ask each student who walks through the halls after classes have begun to see his or her hall pass. What we have is a hierarchical system, all in the service of control. One might wonder what such a system teaches students who are enrolled in courses dealing with critical thought about social problems.

Third, these distinctions remind curriculum planners to look beyond what is now traditionally offered in school programs in order to identify areas of human understanding that have been neglected. A great deal is offered to students in school that is not a function of choice but rather a function of tradition. Much of what we teach, we teach because it has always been taught. The concept of the null curriculum reminds curriculum planners to ask about what has been neglected. For example, which forms of knowing have been omitted and what is their significance? What are the potential consequences of curricular neglect? I am not suggesting that the program of the school can teach everything or that it can be all things to all people. I am suggesting that content inclusion–content exclusion decisions are among the most important decisions curriculum planners can make. These decisions, as far as possible, should be made with appropriate consideration to what one rejects as well as to what one accepts for inclusion in school programs. What we don't teach might be just as important as what we do.

The complexities and significant qualities of educational life can be made vivid through a method used to describe, interpret, and evaluate other cultural forms. This method is one of criticism; in education it can be regarded as educational criticism.

One of the central focuses of this book concerns the influence that testing has on the ways in which we conceive of the effectiveness of schooling, curricular content, and educational aims. Since the turn of the century, testing has rested on fundamental beliefs about how we come to know; our use of testing as means of educational evaluation is itself rooted in the epistemology of science. Knowledge about educational practice and its consequences is to be derived by applying methods of social science to the study of education. The more closely those methods approximate those used in the laboratory, the more positive we can be about their conclusions.

Although I do not advocate abandoning scientific methods to study educational phenomena, I have argued in this book that those methods in no way exhaust the means through which educational phenomena can be studied. This book has attempted to provide not an alternative but rather an invitation to the pursuit of a complementary approach. The approach that my students and I have been using at Stanford University is called educational criticism. It depends on the observation and appreciation of the events or materials that constitute educational life. The object of such attention is to perceive those qualities that are educationally significant.

The appreciation of such phenomena requires, I have argued, the application of educational connoisseurship. But connoisseurship is a private event, and, to be made public, some externalization of what one appreciates must occur. It is there that criticism operates. The aim of criticism is to reeducate one's perception of the phenomena to which one attends. Criticism is a written or spoken statement about something. Educational criticism is about educationally important matters. Because criticism is in large measure—although not exclusively—an artistic creation (the critic must render the qualities he has perceived in a form capable of eliciting, in part, an empathetic understanding), the skills the critic needs are significantly artistic in character. The critic needs to perceive what is subtle and complex, must appreciate the connotative meaning as well as the denotative meaning of events, and must be able to make those meanings vivid through the language he or she uses to communicate. The major aim of such activity is not primarily to discover laws but rather to illuminate, to provide those concerned with education with the kind of understanding that will enhance their own teaching or professional deliberations. In this sense, educational criticism leads to a more complex and particularistic view of an educational situation. It aims not at the reduction of complexities but at their illumination in order that the factors and qualities that make situations unique as well as general can be understood. With such understanding I believe that both educators and lay people are more likely to be able to exercise intelligence about the matters of concern to them.

That such an approach to educational evaluation has not been salient in the literature is obvious to anyone familiar with it. Our conception of research, our conception of knowledge, and our conception of evidence have derived from other premises. The time has come, I believe, to look to other views, not as a rejection of the old ones, but for the promise that a fresh perspective can provide. Educational criticism represents one place on which to stand.

Index

C

D

E